PSYCHOLOGY OF RELIGION

HEIJE FABER

Psychology of Religion

✿

1565

SCM PRESS LTD

Translated by Margaret Kohl from the Dutch
Cirkelen om een geheim,
first published 1972 by Boom Pers,
Meppel, Nederland

334 01354 2
First British Edition 1976
published by SCM Press Ltd,
56 Bloomsbury Street, London
© SCM Press Ltd 1976

Printed in Great Britain by
Western Printing Services Ltd, Bristol

Contents

Contents

Preface

A preface to the two parts of this book seems indicated. Both sections deal with the same theme – religion in the light of psycho-analysis – but they deal with it in different though mutually complementary ways. In the first part we shall primarily be looking at the subject from the historical aspect, whereas in the second we shall mainly be considering it systematically.

In considering the way in which to treat the subject, I have been largely influenced by two factors. First, it is impossible for theology to put off a discussion with psycho-analysis about religion any longer. In spite of considerable resistance, during the last decades psycho-analysis has grown into one of the most important movements in our civilization and – in spite of all the doubts and opposition to which it is exposed – it is going to continue to exert a permanent influence on our cultural life in the years ahead as well. There is no doubt that the view which many people have about the phenomenon of religion in our time has taken its stamp primarily from psycho-analysis. In spite of this, theology has not succeeded in arriving at a real 'encounter' with this important counterpart, if we except a few, still unsystematic attempts. Secondly, I should like to try to fill up the existing gaps to some extent, because I believe that, in spite of the wide antitheses existing between the two fields, it is possible for theology to see psycho-analysis at certain points even as a partner. I am thinking here not so much of the practical co-operation between psychotherapists and clergy which already exists, and exists to an increasing degree, in many countries. I am thinking principally of the possibility that psycho-analysis can help to shed light on a whole series of problems with which religion confronts us in the twentieth century. I see psycho-analysis particularly as offering new opportunities for the psychology of religion; and I have tried to show this in the second part of the book particularly ('Religion in the Light of Modern Psychoanalytical Theory').

I am aware that psycho-analysis as a scientific theory has been challenged in recent years by the supporters of certain theories of learning. We ought to try to penetrate more deeply into the mystery of religion with the help of these theories too. But I am confining myself deliberately to psycho-analysis, even though it seems to be evident – as will be brought out in the present book – that its theories are in need of revision at various points.

At the same time, no one should approach the present study with extravagant expectations. I know very well that what I am presenting to the reader are hypotheses rather than established results. For me, psychology is still a young science, which is trying on the one hand, through a constant recollection of its scientific claim, to produce results which are as irrefutable as possible; but which on the other hand is still at the stage of having to determine the direction and methods of its investigations by means of a sound definition of the problems. In his excellent book *Methodologie*, Professor A. D. de Groot has introduced into the scientific discussion the 'forum', this as it were representing the group of readers for whom we are primarily writing. But in its processes of thought this forum is also the host of scholars and interested people who think and investigate with the individual scholar. Is it not then the obvious course, in view of the incompleteness of our scientific investigations, for us to offer for consideration, not only more or less established results, but occasionally new hypotheses for examination as well (with the appropriate explanations), in the hope that they will lead to discussion and a closer investigation? And there is yet another factor. At the moment radical changes are taking place in the religious domain, changes which confront responsible people with great problems, so that investigations in this sphere inevitably take on the character of 'action research'; consequently the hypotheses formed in the course of such investigations can only be provisional.

The first, more historical section of this book was completed some years ago, and I have merely introduced a few minor corrections or additions. I finished the second part in the summer of 1971. For me it represents the fruits of a long process which now finds a provisional completion, developing as it has out of lectures and discussions which I have held with various groups over the years. As I have already said, the book does not claim to be anything definitive, but I hope that it is at a sufficiently advanced stage for me to submit it to interested readers.

Preface

In closing I should like to express my thanks to Dr T. Govaart-Halkes, Professor P. C. Kuiper, the psychiatrist N. Treurniet and Dr W. Zijlstra for the often outstanding help which they have given me in my work on the book in past years.

HEIJE FABER

PART ONE

Depth Psychologists on the Subject of Religion:
A Contribution to a Discussion

I

Introduction

It is with some hesitation that I lay this study before the public. In the years in which I have been concerned as a theologian with different spheres of pastoral psychology, psycho-analysis has come to assume an increasingly important place in my mental horizon; and because of this I have entered more and more into discussion with psycho-analysts. In the course of these contacts, one difficulty, whether expressed or not, became increasingly perceptible: neither side knew what he was dealing with in the other. This was partially due to the statements made by psycho-analysts about religion in the past. On the basis of these largely practical considerations, I felt the need to study the views which analysts have held about religion in the past and hold at the present day. The results of my investigations can be found in this first part of the book. My aim was to form a clear picture of the opinions of the most important researchers and writers, and in this way to gain some insight into the most important problems standing between psycho-analysis and theology – the problems that ought to be the primary theme of a closer discussion between representatives of the two disciplines.

In spite of these limited aims, I am publishing the result in book form because, with the increasing thought that is being devoted to the structure and practice of pastoral care, contacts between theologians and psychiatrists – and above all between theologians and psycho-analysts – are on the increase, and it is my hope that a study such as this one may be able to make some contribution to the discussion between the two groups.

This section does not of course contain a minute investigation of all the detailed statements made by psycho-analysts about religion. My concern is a history of the problems rather than a history of the persons. Nor shall I enter into the difficulties with which psycho-analysis confronts theology. I shall indicate what these difficulties are rather than look for an answer to them, because I am convinced that it is only through co-operation, that is to say through a genuine dialogue, that a permanent clarification of the problems can be achieved. I see this study, therefore, – let me repeat once more – as being above all a contribution to an active discussion, which will, I hope, serve the interests of both parties with increasing success in the coming years.

I can say confidently right away that there are three things in particular which we can learn from the investigation, and which will provide a useful stimulus to the discussion. First, a change seems to be taking place in the attitude of analysts to religion. Second, in the course of the years we shall have to deal with a whole series of important problems which deserve a closer investigation. Third, the trend as well as the actual themes of the coming discussion are clearly emerging, even now.

I may perhaps make a few other preliminary remarks at this juncture. First of all, the title of Part One contains the term depth psychology, whereas here I have only talked about psycho-analysis. This is not chance. The partner whom I principally have in mind for the discussion I have mentioned is psycho-analysis, and especially Freud and his school. But these provided the starting point for a whole series of research workers and trends, completely inconceivable without Freud, yet at so far a remove from him (because their conceptions are so different in kind) that we should cause confusion if we were simply, without more ado, to apply the term psycho-analysis to them. For this reason I have used the term 'depth psychology' in the heading of Part One, which also deals with psychologists whose work does not belong to the Freudian school. None the less, the true analysts stand at the centre of my concern, first because they exert the greatest influence, but secondly because they are often by nature the most consistent and fundamental.

This book is written by a theologian, or to be more precise, by a theologian who is concerned professionally with religion and with pastoral psychology. The coming to terms with developments in the field of psycho-analysis has a twofold significance for the theologian. As a pastor I am often faced with the question of what actual view to take of psycho-analysis, and sometimes also how to regard the psycho-analyst as a therapist. (I am thinking for example of the problem of passing on a member of my congregation to a psychiatrist.) Among theologians there is often a kind of fear, as well as lack of knowledge; the theologian gets 'cold feet'. Investigation could probably eliminate both ignorance and fear. On the other hand, through its theories psycho-analysis has become an important factor in our modern civilization, and one that theology must not ignore. Without analysis much modern 'unbelief' remains incomprehensible. Under this aspect too it is important for theology to be well informed about developments in psycho-analysis.

To put it in very general terms, it is necessary for the theologian to learn to distinguish more clearly than is generally the case between analysis as a therapeutic method (which rests on an objective and empirical investigation of the patient) and the theories which are and have been upheld by analysts; the latter reveal themselves as more evanescent than is often assumed.

In this connection it strikes me that a closer definition of the individual terms which are used throughout the present book could help to define the limits of our investigation more clearly.

Psychiatry can best be defined as the medical science which is concerned with the sickness of the psychical life. It has existed for centuries and has been primarily occupied with the classical syndromes or clinical pictures, with psychoses and psychopathies. At first psychiatry was practised in institutions. Its particular characteristic was that it was confined to theoretical clarification, having very few possibilities for therapy at its disposal. This has altered radically in recent years through the discovery of different forms of chemotherapy, as well as through surgical developments. A book such as Peter Hayes' *New Horizons in Psychiatry* can convey an idea of all this even to the layman.

Accordingly, the *psychiatrist* was originally the physician of people suffering from psychical afflictions. But his field has been extended in recent decades through the development of psycho-analysis. He is now able to treat patients with particular psychical illnesses.

For *psycho-analysis* has made us familiar with a quite different kind of illness – the neurosis. This develops through repression and hence demands a different kind of therapy.

This different kind of therapy is generally called *psychotherapy*. Its task is to heal the neurotic by means of a personal contact between doctor and patient, a contact which takes a particular form. At the beginning, psychotherapy was a therapy without drugs; and in Freud we therefore find psychotherapy and psychiatry set in antithesis to one another. This antithesis has, however, gradually been overcome, even if not yet everywhere. Today, as we have seen, the psychiatrist frequently uses psychotherapeutic methods, and is trained in these as well; while on the other hand psychotherapists also work with so-called tranquillizers as therapeutic aids. In a book for general practitioners, Weijel even calls these one of the most important aids in the psychotherapy which is to be employed by the general practitioner.

Another definition of psychotherapy beside this one is gradually growing up. In this sense everyone – whether doctor or not – who systematically helps someone else in his conflicts with the aid of psychical methods is carrying on psychotherapy. Rogers' 'counselling' method, which is sometimes also termed clinical psychology, is a good example. The relationship of this kind of psychotherapy to the original medical one is not yet quite clear.

Let us pause for a moment at the main object of our investigation, *psycho-analysis*. It may be useful to point out here that Freud himself, who saw the birth of psycho-analysis, talked on a number of occasions about the nature and development of this scientific discipline. In order to give us a clearer insight into the purpose of our investigation, let us look at three particular facets which are of decisive importance for a proper understanding.

Psycho-analysis is a particular method of psychotherapy and that is its primary importance. As we have already said, its aim is to create a situation with a particular structure. Within this situation, an attempt is made to heal the neurosis through the interpretation of certain symptoms which has the effect of lifting repressed experiences into the consciousness. In an analytical treatment of neurotic patients the religious sphere is frequently touched on, and touched on in the most varied ways: as a power which produces fear, as a father fixation, as a means of revolt against one of the patient's parents, etc. These forms are lifted into the consciousness and are discussed. At the beginning, then, psychotherapy only has to do with religion as a factor in the neurosis. But psychotherapy does not therefore have to be anti-religious. In the choosing of a psychotherapist, consequently, it is in principle of no importance whether he is religious or not. Psychotherapy is, from a religious point of view, neutral. It is true that I can imagine that in actual practice difficulties could arise here on occasion, as they can in every important relationship in our lives; but that would not affect the principle that religion only appears within the framework of the therapy to the degree in which it is related to the neurosis. The analysis as such does not always have to bring in the patient's religion, but sometimes that very analysis can uncover a healthy religious life.

Secondly, the importance of psycho-analysis is that it represents a unified complex of theories. A theory always tries to find an explanation for a series of phenomena. In this way it is like a hypothesis, which after sufficient examination is accepted as a theory, though with the limitation that it is in constant danger of being replaced by another, better theory after a certain time. It has therefore a provisional character and is at the evolutionary stage. Here it is a not unimportant factor whether knowledge of the phenomena on which the theory is based has meanwhile increased, and whether through the progress of science in general (i.e., through an alteration in the whole scientific climate) the same material is now to be seen under a new aspect, so that new hypotheses and (after sufficient testing) new theories have to be set up.

Since Freud's time, work on analytical theory has gone on unremittingly in this way. The structure he set up certainly stands firmly enough, but it is permanently surrounded by scaffolding. We shall see that an important development has taken place in the formation of analytical theory about the phenomenon of religion especially, and that some new hypotheses have been set up. We shall be looking at these in Part Two of the book.

It might also be noted that, under the influence of the criticism levelled against the scientific tenability of psycho-analytical theories, thinking is going on in psycho-analytical circles about the validity of the hypotheses and theories in question. In his penetrating article 'Psychoanalyse en wetenschap' (Psychoanalysis and Science), published in *Hollands Maandblad* in March 1972, W. F. van Leewen distinguishes between what he calls A hypotheses (i.e., explanations in terms of psychological motives and meanings, which have been tested) and B hypotheses (explanations in terms of causal mechanisms or the processes of a hypothetical 'psychic' machinery, Freud's 'metapsychology', which are not testable and which Freud himself did not view as being indispensable). P. C. Kuiper emphatically subscribes to this deduction in his study *Psychoanalysis: actueel of verouderd?* (Psychoanalysis: Topical or out of date?), which appeared in 1972 (see also pp. 244ff. below).

A further point about psycho-analysis which is significant is the striking solidarity among the analysts. I believe that an analysis of the psycho-analyst himself would show that with analysts we are really dealing with a kind of family or community. In this group Freud is an unmistakable father figure, to whom his sons feel bound in a particular way. The institution of the 'training analysis', as well as the resistance met with in the early stages, have contributed to the development of this group consciousness. Freud's reputation and identification with him thus play an important part in this group and here every secession was and is experienced with quite particular emotion.

It is important to note in this context that Freud himself was a person of outstanding integrity and of unusually high quality as a scientist, as well as having made the important discoveries and developed the main lines of the theory.

The initial result of this situation was that the authority of Freud's writings and views was very great indeed within his own circle, whereas outside it they met with considerable resistance. Because of this isolation a real discussion with other schools and groups only developed gradually, and for the same reason there has been no discussion between psychoanalysis and theology to this day. But in view of the growing numbers of contacts between representatives of the two disciplines which can be observed in different countries, especially since the war, we can, I think, expect this discussion to come about in the near future.

The First Period

2

Sigmund Freud and his School

Freud can justly be called the father of psycho-analysis, not only because he created it, but also because he dominates this scientific field like a kind of 'father figure'. Emotional relationships between him and his pupils, as well as among his pupils themselves, have always played a large part. Jung stands beside him as his real 'second', although his influence seems to have diminished compared with Freud's. At first he seemed to be the crown prince, who was to take over the leadership at the appropriate moment; but then he went his own way. We shall be dealing with the relations between Freud and Jung at a later point. Adler originally seemed to be the third in the triumvirate, but he has now clearly receded into the background.

Freud must be seen in the first place as the great discoverer. It was he who, in the course of his neurological studies, discovered a whole sphere which had till then been unknown. At the same time he is the movement's great theorist. The most important theoretical conceptions in psycho-analytical theory were worked out by Freud, and even though we know that it is possible to strike out new paths in this field, to develop new concepts and to make corrections, it is quite clear that all this takes place on the foundations laid by Freud. At the same time it must be said that some of Freud's views are seemingly being pushed into the background. His theory about the death wish is not so frequently discussed; and we shall see that his view of religion is no longer accepted so much as a matter of course either.

Freud lived from 1856 until 1939. He spent almost his whole life in Vienna, only living in London for the last two years, after the *Anschluss* between Austria and Germany. He came from a good middle-class, somewhat undevout Jewish family. Freud knew what hard work meant. He was guided by strict moral principles and, as a scientist, had an especial gift for empirical investigation. Originally he was a neurologist. Throughout his life he suffered from much misunderstanding and opposition. He had difficulties even with his own pupils. In contrast to this, he enjoyed a particularly happy family life. His daughter Anna is a well known psycho-analyst.

Freud's influence can be traced throughout Western Europe (though it perhaps lags somewhat behind in France and Germany) and is equally strong in the United States and Japan. For theologians, his relationship to the Swiss pastor Oskar Pfister is of particular interest. Pfister was friendly with Freud throughout his life and some of their correspondence was published a few years ago. In spite of his completely different view of religion, Pfister considered himself Freud's disciple. We shall return to Pfister and his views in the course of this chapter.

Before we go more closely into Freud's ideas about religion, let us look briefly at his most important concepts, because we shall be better able to understand his view of religion within this wider framwork. Here we shall be drawing primarily on what he has to say in his *Introductory Lectures on Psycho-analysis* (*Complete Works*, Vols. XV–XVI).

One of the pillars of Freud's system is his thesis about the contrast between our conscious and our unconscious life; this is clearly revealed in our 'everyday mistakes' (the errors we make, the things we forget, our slips of the tongue, and so forth), as well as in our dreams and our neurotic symptoms. Basically we have to do here with an antithesis between the ego, which attempts to adapt itself to the realities of life, and what he calls the id, the sum total of our drives and instincts – i.e., everything which is determined by the pleasure principle.

Freud's interest is directed primarily towards the nature and the history of the tension-laden relationship between ego and id, as well as towards the question of what impulses are at work in us, and the form in which they reveal themselves. As far as the first point is concerned, he maintains the thesis that there is a dividing line between the conscious and the unconscious which is hard to cross. This line is watched over by a censor (a conscience, a superego) who sees that no unwanted content from the unconscious flows into the consciousness. In his investigation of the urges or drives, Freud uses the concept of the libido. The libido manifests itself primarily in sexuality, but this is later ever more obviously joined by aggression. Human sexuality is a fundamental feature of the life of man; it is not present in a uniform way at any given moment, but develops gradually in a person's life and has its own experiences in each of them. Thus, starting from a person's birth, Freud distinguishes between oral, anal, phallic and genital phases.

Tension between the conscious and the unconscious arises through repression, a factor which plays an essential role in Freud's ideas. One might even say that the neurosis is really the tension. For a neurosis comes into being when things which have been suppressed in the unconscious make themselves felt in a pathological way. Certain things belong to the clinical picture of neurosis: the trauma, the thing that has been wounded and hence repressed; the regression, the retreat to already experienced phases; and the fixation, the incomplete detachment from earlier phases.

Psychotherapy tries together with the patient to illuminate and so to solve the neurotic complications. One might even say that psychotherapy attempts to release the healthy forces present in the patient so that he is once more able to lead a normal life. In considering the sphere of the normal, Freud's stress lies primarily on a healthy sexuality, as well as on work. The liberation of the healthful forces also leads to a sublimation of what is instinctual and belongs to the drives – though in saying this we are introducing something into the discussion which has always remained somewhat schematic in psychotherapy.

What place, we must now ask, did religion have for Freud in the whole complex? He conceives of it in somewhat simple terms: in religion the adult person preserves for himself a piece of infantile, libidinous life. Religion is not rooted in a healthy, mature understanding of reality; it is an illusion, a neurotic symptom.

Freud expressed his views about religion and the church in a number of different publications. It is not my intention to sum up all his statements on the subject; instead I propose to discuss the books in which he was primarily concerned with religion, in order to bring out the basic outline of his viewpoint as clearly as possible.

His first full-scale book on religion, which appeared in 1913, is *Totem and Taboo*, and it is not improbable that it may have been prompted by differences of opinion with Jung. Jung's work aimed increasingly clearly at discovering more about neuroses with the help of mythological material. In *Totem and Taboo* Freud takes the reverse method. He tries to illuminate the religion of primitive peoples with the help of what he knows about neuroses. He considers that Jung's work is mystical and open to criticism.

Totem and Taboo (*Complete Works*, Vol. XIII) consists of four sections. The first is concerned with the fact that among primitive tribes prohibitions of incest play a particular role: the intense horror of incest suggests that seduction was thought highly possible. The second part is devoted to the taboos laid on people and things. One must not have any contact at all with anything that is taboo. These things are evidently imbued with a particular power. Here Freud points to parallels with compulsive-obsessional neurotics, who are also afraid of touching particular objects. There is in general an evident correspondence with obsessional neurotic phenomena. In primitive peoples we meet with strongly ambivalent feelings – towards slain enemies, for instance, or towards kings, or towards the dead. Apparently unconscious aggressive tendencies can only be repressed with difficulty. Here is one point of contact with neurosis. Repression is also the word used when what is repressed is more sexual in character. In the third section the phenomenon of magic comes to the fore. For Freud magic is a man's heightened belief in the power of his thoughts, or rather in the power of his wishes. He establishes that this primitive view is present in the fantasies of neurotics and children as well.

The fourth section, which deals with totemism, is the core of the whole book. Here Freud reveals the associations which are basic to his view of religion. In his opinion the astonishing veneration of the totem animal, and the customs associated with it, must not be viewed in isolation from the taboos mentioned above, which consciously go back to sexual relations between members of the same totem-tribe. As explanation of the complicated practices of totemism, Freud adduces the Oedipus complex, which was one of his own discoveries. The totem animal, he says, is none other than the father and the tribe, the clan, the family. Here he goes back to the hypothesis developed by Darwin that at the beginning of man's evolution he lived together with his fellows in a primal horde. The father had exerted the exclusive power of disposal over the horde's women, so the sons had killed him out of envy. This frightful secret, and all the sense of guilt which it involves, stands behind totemism. The sexual taboo with regard to the women belonging to the same totem tribe is to be traced back to the sense of guilt: because they have murdered their father, his sons are not free towards their father's women. The totem feast at which the totem animal is ceremoniously eaten is really a repetition of the father's murder, and hence involves both grief and joy. The history of religion begins on the basis of this event and these ritual customs. The totem animal later becomes the god; but the relationship to God has been stamped throughout the centuries by the secret of the father's murder.

According to Freud, therefore, the sense of guilt belongs to the very nature of religion, but this sense of guilt is based on a highly concrete event. In Freud's view, the traces of these beginnings and this development can be followed down to Christian times. The reconciliation on the cross and the ritual of the Last Supper must, according to him, be traced back to the basic ideas of totemism.

These conjectures show that Freud assumed that the infantile pattern is a fact that has to be assumed in every religion. One clear component in the relationship to the earthly father is a feeling of guilt deriving from the fact that the boy is incorporated in the relationship between father and mother in a particular way. And according to Freud it is merely this infantile pattern which is present in man's relationship to God as well.

Of course such a view of religion is not built up entirely on fantasy. Freud has clear evidence in view, based on reality – for example the obvious parallels between neurotic symptoms and religious practices. The ceremonial of the compulsive-obsessional neurotic displays unmistakable agreement with that of certain religious fanatics, for example in their purificatory ceremonies. Moreover, no observer of primitive religion can ignore, any more than Freud did, the strongly libidinous and obviously sexually coloured elements which are to be found there. The appropriate symbols and customs show this unequivocally. Here the parallels to what psychotherapy has found out about neurotics cannot be denied either. So the pressing question is: what explanation can there be for all this?

One of the most interesting aspects of the Freudian view of religion, as this is expounded in the book we are considering, is the discovery that the sense of guilt is a central phenomenon in religion. The many opponents of religion never arrived at this notion in the course of centuries. They pointed to quite different basic features. There is no doubt at all that this is one of the many points at which the discussion between theology and depth psychology deserves our full attention.

It must be said that theology for the most part entirely failed to take any notice of *Totem and Taboo*. There was no question of a discussion of Freud's ideas, and there are hardly any signs of such a discussion even in research into the history of religion, or in books on the psychology of religion. As a rule we are told that in the particular field he is dealing with here Freud was obviously no expert, so that his hypotheses (for example his theory about the primal horde) seem highly unlikely, and that it would be better to get on with things as usual.

We shall see, however, that this provides no solution to the problem with which Freud confronts us: the relationship between religion and neurosis. And even without the dubious historical explanation of the sense of guilt in religion (by way of the hypothesis of the primal horde) we cannot eliminate the problem of whether the sense of guilt towards God, which places man in existential insecurity, is not connected with the primordial human relationship to the father figure, which plays so large a part in the years of human insecurity, especially childhood. Is it conceivable that the Oedipus complex, whose existence can be ascertained in almost all psychotherapy and which influences the child's vulnerable life down to its very roots, gives its impress to the pattern with which a man later faces every authority he meets in life? In my own opinion there is something artificial about Freud's hypothesis, and I would not myself therefore be prepared to answer with a simple affirmative; but for that very reason there is all the more need for a closer enquiry into the problem of guilt. Such an enquiry would bring to light and explain both the parallels and the differences between neurosis and religion at this point. If we theologians want to differentiate between a neurotic and a genuine sense of guilt (and this could well be the result of our present study) then we must enter into the problem as Freud defines it in a more adequate way than we have done hitherto. For the moment we shall leave it at that; but of course we shall be returning to this point in the course of our discussion.

The second book in which Freud deals expressly with the problems of religion appeared in 1927, and bears the familiar title *The Future of an Illusion* (*Complete Works*, Vol. XXI). If I am right, this book has, strangely enough, given the theologians considerably more concern (and is also more frequently quoted in theological publications) than *Totem and Taboo*. The question is whether this book met with greater opposition than the first one because it traces religion back to highly primitive feelings. This is not impossible.

In *The Future of an Illusion* Freud is not concerned with religion's origins, as he is in *Totem and Taboo*, but with its nature and its future. He starts from the problem of civilization or culture. He later showed his interest in this aspect of human life in *Civilization and its Discontents* (*Complete Works*, Vol. XXI), where he maintains that there is a tension in human life between the demands of culture on the one hand and man's instinctual nature on the other. Man cannot become enthusiastic about culture because it rests on compulsion and 'instinctual renunciation'. In

The Future of an Illusion he writes that culture, if it is to prevail, demands an inner assent to commandments. It therefore needs morality, which represents this inner assent. After that, if it is to maintain itself, culture requires a narcissistic satisfaction of the human drives in ideals and in the arts. Freud therefore maintains that a culture without ideals and art is not viable at all – not so much because these things represent what might be called the meaning of culture, but because in this way man can to a certain degree give rein to the egoistical desires which he cannot satisfy through direct fulfilment. And finally, a culture, if it is to endure, demands certain illusions, dreams of wish fulfilment, so to speak. Religion has a function to fulfil here. It creates a necessary illusion. It is important to realize that in this way Freud finds a *functional* access to religion; he assigns it a particular task. This is an essential aspect of his interpretation. He then asks: in what does the value of religious ideas consist? Here too we are touching on an important element in Freud's view of religion. It is quite conceivable that someone who takes a functional view of religion should be interested in love, service and a striving for righteousness – i.e., in certain aspects of religion which could be termed valuable from the point of view of their usefulness to society. There are many people who, although they reject Christianity as a faith, are none the less convinced of its value for our civilization. Freud ignores all this. For him the value of religion for man consists solely in the (dubious) importance which religious *ideas* have for him. He starts here from the notion that life on earth is a burden. Man is the continual victim of natural disasters and of a destiny over which he has no control. On earth he is a helpless being and because of his helplessness he is in need of a father, God. We are familiar with the saying *primus facit deos timor* (fear creates the gods); belief in God therefore springs from fear. Freud maintains that the idea of God develops and is maintained through remembrance of the situation of childhood years. God protects man against the perils of nature, the perils of destiny and the perils of society. We see, therefore, that although Freud brings up new arguments, which go beyond what he has to say in *Totem and Taboo*, he still clearly remains stationary within the basic outline of what he says there: the origin must be looked for in the feelings of the infantile situation which dominates man. It is a phenomenon belonging to the years of childhood which persists into maturity.

Freud points out that there is no proof of the teachings of religion. In spite of this, doubt of these teachings was severely punished in earlier times. Freud sees this fact as suspect. It suggests that people were not prepared to grant to others what they were not – out of fear – prepared to grant to themselves, namely doubt of the truth of what religion teaches. It is obviously for Freud no recommendation that doctrines which (as he says) claim to solve the riddle of the universe and have the task of reconciling man to suffering, cannot be proved.

The opinion about the essence of religion which Freud seems to support here is important. In his view religion has to solve the riddle of the universe and to reconcile man to suffering. In other words he sees religion entirely in the framework of the conception which he has of life: it is marked by the tension between the pleasure principle and the reality principle. Man would prefer to follow his desires, but reality forbids him to do so; consequently he has to learn to accept it. For Freud, accordingly, religion is merely the – unreal – attempt to come to terms with the problem of reality. By means of religion man tries to solve the riddle of reality and to reconcile himself to it, in its aspect of suffering. According to Freud this attempt is unsuccessful, for religion is an illusion, a wish fulfilment. It might perhaps be said that religion *could* under certain circumstances be true, but in the form in which it actually appears, it is fed by wishes which carry no power of conviction; for they are the wishes of a helpless child who is incapable of coming to terms with reality.

But for us, Freud says, science is the only way of arriving at knowledge of reality; and there is therefore no other way of solving the riddle of the universe and reconciling man to suffering. Moreover religion is for him a *dangerous* illusion. We can see from the world around us how dishonest and intolerant it makes people. Culture – as we have already said – has a certain interest in the existence of religion, but it would be better for it to abandon its religious ties. It is not a good thing for man to live with the notion that only God is strong and good, whereas man is weak and sinful.

Moreover mankind must grow out of religion. It is a neurosis deriving from man's youth. It is really a compulsive-obsessional neurosis developing out of the Oedipus complex (here Freud picks up ideas which he developed in *Totem and Taboo*). Religion must be seen through rationally and will then lose its power over the human mind. In my opinion we come up against a weak point in Freud's argumentation here, and it is one which he had already dealt with at an earlier stage. In an article written in 1907 he discusses obsessional-neurotic acts and religious practices, terming religion an obsessional neurosis in which aggressive impulses were warded off. In his book about Moses he expounds in detail the view that the obsessional-neurotic character of certain religious phenomena is only to be explained by the suppression of a historical event (the father's murder) and through inheritance. Here I should like to put the following question. Is there such a thing as a collective obsessional neurosis? If the answer is yes, then is religion one? Is not Freud viewing this situation in too simple a way? Are not certain elements of the obsessional neurosis missing in religion – for example the compulsive character at many points? (I am thinking of the congregational experience of a liturgy, and the way in which the obsessional neurotic is tied to his ceremonial.)

Freud then goes on to maintain the view that a child would never arrive at the idea of God by himself – an assertion which, to my mind, will not quite stand up to examination in this wholesale form, in view of what we know about the development of the child's psychic life.

Freud therefore pleads for reality, intellect and science. Science is not an illusion. He follows up his argument with a kind of creed. He believes in science; science gives us something to hold on to; it gives us power over reality and makes it possible for us to organize our lives. In spite of a certain superficiality which becomes evident here, we cannot deny the sincerity of his creed.

Freud gives a good survey of his view of religion in his *New Introductory Lectures on Psychoanalysis*. There he writes (*Complete Works*, Vol. XXII, p. 168):

> In summary, therefore, the judgment of science on the religious *Weltanschauung* is this. While the different religions wrangle with one another as to which of them is in possession of the truth, our view is that the question of the truth of religious beliefs may be left altogether on one side. Religion is an attempt to master the sensory world in which we are situated by means of the wishful world which we have developed within us as a result of biological and psychological necessities. But religion cannot achieve this. Its doctrines bear the imprint of the times in which they arose, the ignorant times of the childhood of humanity. Its consolations deserve no trust. Experience teaches us that the world is no nursery. The ethical demands on which religion seeks to lay stress need, rather, to be given another basis; for they are indispensable to human society and it is dangerous to link obedience to them with religious faith. If we attempt to assign the place of religion in the evolution of mankind, it appears not as a permanent acquisition but as a counterpart to the neurosis which individual civilized men have to go through in their passage from childhood to maturity.

Here a number of comments might be made. In the first place, Freud's exposition is illuminating – it is even touched with genius. Nor must we fail to recognize that the type of religion which he is apparently thinking of really does exist. It is the same type which Feuerbach and Marx subject to critical scrutiny and which many psycho-analysts meet in the lives of their patients even today. For me, his critical analysis is hence criticism of particular facets of the religious life, which – and we have to recognize this – really exist and which even have far more influence, probably, than we realize. At the same time, his observations are not applicable to all types of religion. Freud went intensively into the study of religious history, but he did not take the oriental religions into account at all. The stress on the father figure which is so significant for Freud's view of neurosis, and is also so typical of his view of religion, is, for example, quite unknown in the religions of the east. Here Freud is obviously influenced by his Jewish background, in which the father figure plays a central part, both in family life and in religion. We must therefore ask whether Freud's judgment – a judgment which he makes on the basis of his knowledge of the life of the human psyche – really covers religion in its totality, or whether it does not merely apply to certain aspects of religion which were familiar to him, more or less by chance.

Secondly, Freud himself never struggled with the question of religious truth. From the very beginning it was as an agnostic that he was concerned with the problems of religion. His observations do not rest on empirical investigation; we are not dealing with the study of concrete cases, nor do we have the impression that he has arrived at his theories in the course of his dealings with his patients. His statements are rather the applications of already existing convictions in a sphere for which he shows much interest, on account of his past and his background, but which is not really congenial to him. It was therefore not difficult for Freud to declare that religion could certainly be correct in its hypothesis about the existence of a God, but that it could also very well be explained without this hypothesis; on the contrary, to say this seemed to him more or less a matter of course. This is the point of view which his pupil Ernest Jones has always maintained as well and it is the position which Jung also takes up, fundamentally speaking (though he carries it through less consistently), when he remarks that as a psychologist he can talk about religion as a psychical phenomenon, but this does not mean that he is making any statement about the reality of God's existence.

Thirdly, the question must be raised whether Freud's own youthful experiences could provide an explanation.

This question has of course been frequently asked – for example in connection with a Catholic nursemaid who looked after little Sigmund until he was two and a half years old, who may have influenced him, and who was suddenly dismissed for dishonesty. It is a factor which Jones questions in his biography of Freud – in my view rightly. Here the lines of continuity cannot be reconstructed so simply. The suggestion has also been made that Freud was influenced by secret death wishes, which he is supposed to have had after the early death of his little brother. I would myself doubt whether a clear connecting line can be traced here.

In my own view we must primarily draw on the secularized milieu of Freud's Jewish parents for an explanation. Freud came to know the Bible well (in his case it was the Old Testament). On the other hand he developed into a modern man who took his impress from science and felt the need to emphasize clearly his aloofness from the traditional and institutionalized forms of religion, whereas in his researches he reveals how greatly he is interested in the subject.

This remarkable trait has led Gregory Zilboorg, in his brief essay *Freud and Religion* (1958), to find a new formula for an old dispute. He notes quite rightly that Freud seems to have had a more than theoretical interest in the questions of (his) religion. Moses evidently always fascinated him. Very early on, he contemplated Michelangelo's statue of Moses with admiration. In 1914 he wrote an essay about it, but as early as 1901 he was asking how Michelangelo saw Moses. Jones askes whether Moses represented the father image, or whether Freud identified himself with him. Freud's last book (to which we shall be returning later) again deals with Moses. In addition it might be added that throughout his whole life Freud wrestled with the problem of death, a problem which it is probably permissible to call an essentially religious one. Zilboorg sees in Freud's statements about religion a certain need to defend himself. He was apparently more uncertain than he himself wanted to admit. The picture of religion which he draws is not free of the necessity to turn religion into a caricature. The emphasis with which he turns against the tradition in which he grew up is also noticeable; he passed over the great religions of the East. And curiously enough he never quotes the sayings of any of the great men of faith.

Perhaps one might say that in many conscious 'atheists' there is an unconscious tie with what they so consciously reject, even though I do not feel the necessity to call Freud a 'potential believer' as Zilboorg does. In my opinion there is a 'potential believer' hidden in everyone, as I hope to indicate in the present book. But in my view it is going too far if we defend Freud, of all people, against himself; for this is rather what it looks like.

The fact that the notion of an 'unconscious tie' is not completely without foundation seems to me to emerge above all from the prejudice which we can discover in Freud (and in other analysts as well) with regard to religious ritual. Experience teaches that people who turn their backs on the synagogue or the Catholic church often feel a bond with the ritual for a very long time. Probably deeper underlying factors also play a part in the background in such a bond – we might think here of the nurse-maid's influence, or Freud's relationship to his dead brother; I would also add the relationship to his father, which played a decisive role in Freud's subconscious, though with our meagre knowledge of Freud's auto-analysis we cannot say anything definite about this.

In the fourth place, Freud is also an exponent of the spirit of his age in his views. The idealism of the Enlightenment, which sought to lead man out of the darkness of the primitive centuries into a period where he could breathe freely in the light of reason (or rather in the light of the intellect) exerted a deep influence on the nineteenth century, and on the twentieth century as well. The one-sided scientific, positivistic explanation of reality also resulted in negative reactions to theology and philosophy. The outcome was, among other things, that in anthropology the attempt was made to explain the life of man through instinctive or economic factors. Feuerbach, Marx and Freud all belong mentally to the same climate of opinion. It must be clear by now that in this a more or less open anti-clericalism played a part.

Fifthly, nothing of the one-sidedness or the fanaticism which were typical of certain 'representatives of the Enlightenment' is to be found in Freud's life. He could be tolerant and could avoid wholesale judgments. His friendship with the Swiss pastor Pfister, to which we owe a fine correspondence (published in English as *Psycho-analysis and Faith*), is proof of this. In order to give an impression of Freud as a person I should like to quote a letter which he wrote on 4 October 1909:

Dear Man of God,
    A letter from you is one of the best possible things that could be waiting for one on one's return. But do not believe that I believe everything or even a large part of the delightful things that you say to me and about me – i.e., I believe them of you, but not of me. I do not deny that it does me good to hear that sort of thing, but after a while I recall my own self-knowledge and become a good deal more modest. What remains behind is the belief that you honestly mean what you say, and the pleasure given by your kind and enthusiastic nature. What I should like would be to win over more such people as yourself, Jung (one must not continue, 'and others of the same sort'), but there are not very many.

What Pfister wrote to Freud's wife after his death is also undoubtedly important for a complete picture of Freud as a person:

> On examining your husband's letters it was with both grief and pleasure that I was once again reminded of how infinitely much his family meant to him. I vividly remember his introducing me to you, his three fine sons, the vital Sophie, and the little mother of the lizards on April 25, 1909. I, who grew up fatherless and suffered for a life-time under a soft, one-sided bringing up, was dazzled by the beauty of that family life, which in spite of the almost super-human greatness of the father of the house and his deep seriousness, breathed freedom and cheerfulness, thanks to his love and sparkling humour. In your house one felt as in a sunny spring garden, heard the gay song of larks and blackbirds, saw bright flower-beds, and had a premonition of the rich blessing of summer. To the visitor it was immediately evident that a large part of that blessing was to be attributed to you, and that you, with your gentle, kindly nature, kept putting fresh weapons into your husband's hands in the fierce battle of life. The more human beings struck him as trash (he used that expression once in his letters), the more the 'grim divine pair Ananke and Logos' (that is his own phrase too) forced him into their grim service, the more need he had of you, and without you even the giant that he was would have been unable to achieve the tremendous task on behalf of good-for-nothing humanity that his life-work represents. His letters show that his friends also meant much to him, and the fact that I had the privilege of counting among his closest friends cheered me in the sad business of paying him tribute.

That Freud was capable of discriminating in his thinking emerges from a letter to Pfister dated 9 February 1909. He writes that the therapist has the disadvantage that his patients have often been ill for a long time, or that they have very little vitality at their disposal.

> In your case they are young persons faced with conflicts of recent date, who are personally drawn towards you and are ready for sublimation, and ... sublimation in its most comfortable form, namely the religious ... You are in the fortunate position of being able to lead them to God and bringing about what in this one respect was the happy state of earlier times when religious faith stifled the neuroses.

In the same letter he says about the relationship of analysis to religion:

> In itself psycho-analysis is neither religious nor non-religious, but an impartial tool which both priest and layman can use in the service of the sufferer.

When he and Pfister were involved in a detailed correspondence about Freud's book *The Future of an Illusion*, Freud wrote (26 November 1927):

> Let us be quite clear on the point that the views expressed in my book form no part of analytic theory. They are my personal views ... If I drew

on analysis for certain arguments – in reality only one argument – that need deter no-one from using the non-partisan method of analysis for arguing the opposite view.

This brings us to an important question. What influence have Freud's ideas at that time had on other psycho-analysts?

Analysts have been influenced by them in two ways. It is possible either, on the basis of the facts discovered by Freud, to adhere to analytical methods and at the same time to remain religious, even in the positive sense, or else to pursue the path taken by Freud, trying to examine particular religious phenomena more closely and to explain them.

Pfister is a famous example of the first method. He expresses it in a letter of 24 November 1927:

> You know that neither my attitude to you nor my pleasure in psycho-analysis is in the slightest degree diminished by your rejection of religion. I have always emphasised that psycho-analysis is the most fruitful part of psychology, but is not the whole of the science of the mind, and still less a philosophy of life and the world. You are certainly of the same view.

We have already seen that Freud reacted positively to the last remark.

Pfister therefore used analytical methods, not only as a lay therapist but also in his pastoral work. In a letter of 2 February 1929 he says: 'In innumerable cases I have done nothing but this negative work, without ever mentioning a word about religion. The Good Samaritan also preached no sermons . . .' On the other hand, as a pastor he does much more than this. 'Your marvellous life's work and your goodness and gentleness . . . lead me to the deepest springs of life . . . I with my feeble powers can only fit your brilliant analytical discoveries and healing powers into that gap. Do you really wish to exclude from analytical work a "priesthood" understood in this sense?' To this letter Freud replies that he sees no need to exclude the priest from analytical work, but that he himself views the nature of religion as lying in the pious illusions of providence and a moral world order which are in conflict with reason.

Although knowing nothing of Pfister's practical work, I see certain problems at this point. Analytical therapy is something different from pastoral care and we should have liked to know from Pfister how he was able to combine the two in his pastoral work. In recent years especially, we have become ever more clearly convinced of the value of a correct definition of the clergy's role, and the problems which are bound up with the picture that is made of the clergy's work and the pattern of expectation that is applied to it. I would willingly agree with Pfister in his positive evaluation of psycho-analysis, particularly as pastor. But none the less we ought to adhere to the fact that therapy and pastoral care are two different dimensions, even if they encroach on one another.

Perhaps it is worth while pausing briefly to see how Pfister reacted in 1928 to Freud's book *The Future of an Illusion* when it came out in *Imago*, the well-known periodical for psycho-analysis. With Freud's knowledge and indeed his agreement, he himself published in *Imago* an article called 'The Illusion of a Future'. First of all he expresses his enormous respect for Freud as enquirer and psychotherapist. He praises his seriousness in the search for truth and his concern for the suffering. He admits that psycho-analysis is right in pointing to many dubious points about religion. But he rejects Freud's criticism of religion *per se*. He then directs his attention to Freud's theses, first describing them briefly and then developing his counter-theses:

(*a*) In religion (above all in primitive religion) there are many compulsive-obsessional phenomena. In the higher religions, and in Christianity especially, it is precisely the obsessional character that has been abolished.

(*b*) In religion there are elements of wish fulfilment. Theology is concerned to get beyond these. Moreover life after death does not play nearly so large a part for the believer as Freud assumes.

(*c*) Religion is 'the enemy of thought'. Here Freud is wrong.

(*d*) Religion is a kind of police for enforcing detachment from the needs of the drives – the detachment that is demanded by civilization. On the contrary, religion liberates immense potentialities; Christianity must actually be termed 'realistic'.

Pfister then goes on to discuss Freud's estimation of science, and writes:

(*a*) Freud is a kind of devotee of science; his god is the Logos.

(*b*) With this he himself represents a particular scientific trend.

(*c*) Freud does not see the metaphysical problems; he himself lives from a kind of illusion.

(*d*) Science only covers a limited area of life. It cannot confer values and is thus not decisive in the way that Freud thinks. Pfister points here to art, morality, etc.

In closing Pfister expresses his own views about the religious situation. He believes in a harmonious combination between faith and science, in a religion which permits itself to be purged by science. Christianity takes its bearings from reality. In Freud he sees a comrade on the road to brotherly love and the diminution of suffering. In this respect he is an example to many church-going Christians.

As a whole, therefore, this is an article which presents a factual answer to Freud's assertions and touches on the most important points, even though, in retrospect, we shall probably feel the need to go into matters more deeply here and there.

Pfister was not content to 'place' Freud in this way. In a number of publications he investigated and illuminated religious phenomena – of a more or less pathological kind – with the help of psychoanalytical methods and hypotheses. An obvious example is his study *Die Frömmigkeit des Grafen von Zinzendorf* ('The Piety of Count Zinzendorf'), which he wrote in 1910 and in which he shows how the sexuality which Zinzendorf repressed in his youth later appeared in all kinds of sexually coloured pronouncements and feelings. This emerges clearly from his Christology and from his pastoral advice. With the publication of his large-scale book *Christianity and Fear* Pfister made available a great part of the knowledge and experience he had acquired in this field in the course of a long life. Two trends of thought become apparent. In the first of them Pfister is concerned – along Freud's lines – with various fear-provoking aspects of Christianity (both normal and abnormal ones). In this connection he discusses the New Testament, Roman Catholicism, the Reformation (Luther and Calvin), as well as various post-Reformation trends. The following quotation (p. 502) shows vividly how he looks at things:

> Our historical study has shown that Christianity in various periods has tended to create fear and to injure health. It has created fear through fear fantasies and by imposing restraints upon the impulses. The commonest types of fear have been those connected with the conscience or guilt; these Freud admits to be medically normal: Christianity has been a source of piety but it has also been a cause of individual and collective neuroses. When these fears are repelled hysterical symptoms and depressive and in certain circumstances manic excitements may occur in individuals or in entire Christian communities, together with other symptoms of disease which are bound to cause the gravest misgivings to any Christian, provided he still possesses a normal conscience.

In his second line of approach Pfister's point is that love deprives fear of its power (p. 506):

> The Christian treatment of fear must conform to the fundamental commandment given by Jesus. From the Christian standpoint the first principle is that fear must not necessarily be eradicated in all circumstances, but that it must be dealt with in such a way as to cause the minimum injury to, and if possible even to foster, the individual's love of God, man and self. It may be found that the complete prevention or eradication of fear is most advantageous for Christian love . . . .

In Pfister's view this can and must be done, partly by means of psychotherapy and partly through pastoral work.

In Pfister we have someone deeply experienced, both pastorally and in psychotherapy, who also discusses the theoretical aspects of psychoanalysis, and who did much to disseminate it, especially among teachers. (I am thinking here of his book *Psychoanalytic Method*, which appeared in 1913 and went into several editions.) But perhaps in the present discussion between psycho-analysis and theology we are in need of a more acute and deeper power of reflection than Pfister displays.

We have already mentioned a second possible line of approach, which was taken up by Freud's pupils: to investigate along his own lines where and in what way particular religious phenomena are rooted in man's libidinous stratum.

We may look at two examples: Ernest Jones and Theodor Reik. But first of all we must consider another book of Freud's. In his previous investigations he forgoes detail, although the general and particular point of view is considered in *Totem and Taboo*. Here he is concerned with a concrete datum in the realm of religion – with the genesis of the Jewish religion in the figure of Moses. This book is a good example of how, through the methods made available by psycho-analysis, one can try to illuminate particular religious phenomena. Appearing in 1939, it was the last of Freud's works to be published. Its English title is *Moses and Monotheism* (*Complete Works*, Vol. XXIII). The book consists of three parts, parts I and II already having appeared in *Imago* in 1937. Part III was completed in England (where friends had enabled Freud to take refuge after the *Anschluss* between Austria and Germany); it was then published together with the other parts. The book contains two prefaces. In the first, written while he was still in Vienna, Freud writes that he did not want to publish the book. In the second, written in London, he explains that he has now decided to publish, in spite of some reservations, since the external circumstances which had hitherto prevented him had now changed. Freud's words suggest uncertainty, not only about external factors, but also about his own identification (if one may so term it) with this child of his mind:

> The inner difficulties were not to be changed by the different political system and the new domicile. Now as then I am uneasy when confronted with my own work; I miss the consciousness of unity and intimacy that should exist between the author and his work.

Did Freud, as a Jew, perhaps feel himself more strongly involved with the figure of Moses than he was in the general observations about religion with which he had occupied himself up to that point?

The book deals with Moses and monotheism – i.e., with two highly central and historically related religious phenomena, which he views from the psycho-analytical viewpoint.

Part One is headed 'Moses, an Egyptian'. Freud says that truth must triumph, though it is only with a heavy heart that he can deprive the Jewish nation of the greatest of its sons. In this way he really already answers the question asked above. In support of his thesis that Moses was an Egyptian, not a Jew, he adduces the following arguments. First, he has an Egyptian name – the Egyptian word Moses means child. We are familiar with it in compounds such as Thut-moses and Ramses (really Ramoses). Secondly, the story of Moses in the bulrushes is one of the familiar birth myths told about a hero. Rank made a particular study of these, and Freud points to the myths about Sargon, Cyrus and Romulus, which treat the theme of the prince who is exposed in a basket which is floated on the water and who is then brought up by peasants. In Moses' case the story has been altered for national reasons. It is a pity that Freud did not pursue the question of whether there may not be a difference between these myths and the story passed down to us by the Old Testament. There seems to me to be a problem at this point.

Freud begins Part Two by saying that he has misgivings about following the path which he has entered upon in Part One; but he is going to pursue it none the less, even though he does not feel quite sure of his ground.

In this section, however, Freud does not say everything that is on his mind; he keeps back the most important thing of all. His starting point here too is the hypothesis of Part One, from which he concludes that Moses was an adherent of Akhenaten (Ikhnaton), a monotheist whose ultimate aim was to preserve his monotheistic religion from decline, and who passed it on to the Jews who were living in Egypt at the time. This is undoubtedly an ingenious theory, but Freud does not enter into any of the important questions which arise from it, such as whether Egyptian and Jewish monotheism were so closely related that such a transference was conceivable. Again, he does not comment at all on the problem of whether and how religions can be passed on. Modern research into the history of religion no longer sees things as uncomplicatedly as formerly, and the matter is certainly not as simple as outsiders think. Freud argues as follows:

(*a*) Neither Egyptian nor Jewish monotheism was interested in a life after death – whereas in general Egyptian religion was particularly concerned with the problem of the afterlife.

(*b*) Circumcision was originally an Egyptian custom.

(*c*) The dating of the exodus of the Jews from Egypt, as well as the date of Akhenaten's appearance on the scene, would support his hypothesis. Freud searches for a foundation for his hypothesis in the sources which the Old Testament puts at our disposal, but also in legends containing perhaps only a grain of historical truth. In these legends we hear about an ambitious man named Moses, who wanted to be Pharaoh himself, as well as about successful campaigns led by an Egyptian general. The Old Testament, on the other hand, describes Moses as being quick tempered and hasty. In Freud's opinion, we could undoubtedly have to do here with historical traits of character, and he even connects Moses with certain features in the ancient picture of the God Yahweh, which, he supposes, came into existence through projection. He even asks whether the Old Testament statement that Moses 'was slow of tongue' might not be connected with his Egyptian origin.

From this point onwards Freud follows the historian Eduard Meyer, who supports the view that the Jews adopted Yahweh worship in Kadesh, on their journey into the promised land, and that the Moses described there differs considerably from the Egyptian Moses. Then a number of bold hypotheses follow. First, what happened in Kadesh was due to a fusion between the Jews coming from Egypt with other related tribes under the influence of the Midianites, who were Yahweh worshippers. Moreover the Levites formed Moses' Egyptian escort. But, secondly, this Moses was already dead; here Freud takes over a theory of Sellin's, who believed that he had discovered a reminiscence of the murder of Moses in the book of Hosea. Freud knows how open to attack these hypotheses are, but he believes that he can adduce quite strong arguments in their favour. This was at least a way of explaining the antitheses between what we know as the Yahwist (J) and the Elohist (E) traditions in the earliest sources. The text has been manipulated, but that is understandable, since of course Egypt and Kadesh had to be repressed.

With this Freud arrives at his familiar theme: in religion emotions of all kinds play a part, emotions which often have to be repressed. Behind the history of the text of the sacred stories about the exodus and about Moses, stands the murder of the real liberator, Moses the Egyptian – a traumatic event, which left deep traces in the emotional life which had to be 'forgotten'. In this connection he points to the great influence which the Levites knew how to exercise, as well as to the preaching of the prophets, which he views as a victory of the original, enlightened Mosaic mono-theism over the volcano god Yahweh. For Freud this is a sign that the 'repression' was not complete.

In Part Three one might say that Freud gives the result of a more deeply penetrating psycho-analysis of these emotions and repressions, and here he also picks up the ideas he had developed earlier in *Totem and Taboo*.

Yahweh, he claims, was originally a volcano god belonging to the desert, but in the course of the years he took on the character of the god of Akhenaten (whose attitude was ethical, universal and anti-ceremonial – we have already pointed to the role of the prophets). Historically we might say much about this, but it is of the greatest interest to see how a man like Freud conceives of the rise of monotheism.

After the death of Moses, who conferred monotheism on the Jews, there was, according to Freud, a kind of 'latency period' in which the tradition nevertheless remained alive. In this way we would have obvious parallels to a neurosis: the trauma is 'repeated' (there is 'fixation to the trauma') but it is at the same time also 'repressed'. Freud therefore goes back here to *Totem and Taboo*, in which the murder of the father is especially stressed. In monotheism we would, according to him, also have to do with the father, towards whom man feels guilty (in both the Old and the New Testaments). Why have the Jews clung so closely to this monotheism? Only because they had murdered Moses, who was for them a father substitute. Here Freud wants to demonstrate how psycho-analytical viewpoints can be applied to concrete religious phenomena; but at the same time his exposition is somewhat speculative in its one-sidedness. Later analysts – I am thinking of Erikson and his book *Young Man Luther*, which we shall be discussing later – are much more cautious.

Freud also sees that a viewpoint of this kind provides one reason for antisemitism. The Jews did not want to admit that they had murdered Jesus Christ (who was also a father substitute); but the Christians were ready to recognize Jewish guilt.

One important problem which Freud deals with in detail in this con-text is the transition from the psychology of the individual to the psy-chology of the group. He believes that here there are no differences in principle; the masses too would preserve an impression from the past through traces of unconscious memories. Here he comes very close to Jung's theories about the collective unconscious. Biologically, however, the transmission of acquired characteristics has not been proved. Freud and Jung have unmistakably pointed to remarkable phenomena, but up

28

to now they have failed to convince me. Are there no other possible explanations? Does not Freud see certain phenomena in Israel's history in a completely distorted way – quite apart from the shaky historical foundation? I am thinking of his theory about the suppression of the murder of Moses, for example, or his view of the role played by the Levites, or what he says about the preaching of the prophets.

His assertion that libidinous elements played a part in religious life seems to me correct – we theologians often close our eyes to this fact – but is he not going too far when he stresses the ritual element in religious life so much and declares it to be a phenomenon belonging to obsessional neurosis and derived from the libido? If ever a discussion was necessary between two fields of knowledge, then it is between theology and psychoanalysis on themes like this. One feels that Freud is expressing his views about religion from too great a distance and that he is not involved in a real discussion with the believer and with theology.

Freud, then, sees Moses as the 'great man' who, as a father figure, was of essential significance for the people. Because of him the rise of the prophets becomes comprehensible; they continue his efforts on behalf of monotheism and what Freud calls Jewish spirituality. This spirituality is for him a result of the prohibition of images; it is marked in his opinion by a readiness for detachment from the drives (and this increases the prophet's self-confidence), as well as by the marked emphasis on morality. But here there is no doubt that Freud is biased and speculative. Now, however, he goes a big step further. Pointing to *Totem and Taboo*, he sees in Moses the old primitive totemism revive once more – that suppressed tradition which runs through all 'religious' life and which crops up again in, for example, the Christian doctrine of original sin.

This study of Freud's is a fine example of the application of psychoanalytical views to religious phenomena. It shows us what psycho-analysis has in mind, the approach it takes, and the arguments it uses. At the same time, as a theologian I am bound to say that the study contains many weaknesses, some of which I have already mentioned. For that reason it is all the more necessary for us to arrive at a discussion about books of this kind with students of the history of religion, so that through joint reflection we can clarify, on the one hand, the limits of the light which can be thrown by psycho-analysis on historical facts such as these; and on the other, can establish the contribution which we can none the less expect psycho-analysis to make to the better understanding of religion as a historical phenomenon.

. . .

In order to give as clear a picture as possible (even if it is an incomplete one) of how psycho-analysts have tried to view phenomena belonging to the history of religion, let me set beside Freud's study of Moses Ernest Jones' *Essays in Applied Psycho-Analysis*. Jones was one of Freud's closest associates, and the author of the biography *Sigmund Freud, Life and Work*, which is well worth reading. The *Essays* are in two parts, the second dealing with 'Folklore, Anthropology and Religion'. The conjunction of these three terms shows clearly what Jones thinks religion is – namely, a phenomenon belonging to mankind's childlike and primitive phase which is the object of anthropological research and which – we can probably say – continues to exist among us in the form of folklore and religion. We then discover how in these essays the author constantly traces connecting lines from folklore to religion and vice versa. The second volume of Jones' *Essays* comprises fourteen studies, seven of them dealing with purely religious themes.

Because of his Jewish origin, Freud was particularly interested in subjects connected with the Jewish faith, like monotheism, the father figure, the problem of guilt and forgiveness, ritual regulations, etc. Jones, on the other hand, displays an interest primarily in particular aspects of Christianity. His starting point is the same as that of his teacher: 'The religious life represents a dramatization on a cosmic plane of the emotions, fears and longings which arose in the child's relation to his parents' (II, p. 195). He primarily aims to prove this in the case of Christianity. In the course of this proceeding, he does not say whether there is a God or not, any more than Freud does. Like Freud, he maintains the view that the existence of God is not necessary to explain the phenomenon of religion.

The book contains a number of exemplary investigations which are undoubtedly deserving of a short discussion. Jones knows a great deal about the subjects he deals with and he tries to defend his theses with considerable ingenuity. I am thinking, for example, of his essay 'The Significance of Christmas', in which he shows that Christmas is made up of a combination of many pagan motifs, which Christianity has filled with a new spirit. 'Psychologically it represents the ideal of resolving all family discord in a happy reunion, and to this it owes its perennial attraction' (p. 223). This is understandable if we remember that 'the ultimate significance of all religions is the attempted solution on a cosmic stage of the loves and hatreds that take their source in the complicated relations of children and parents' (p. 224). Jones presents a wealth of historical material, but for the taste of the religious person (he is the typical scientific outsider) he puts it together in a rationalistic way.

Jones' essay on 'The Madonna's Conception through the Ear' ought certainly to be mentioned as well. Here Jones starts from the idea that the sources of artistic achievement, as well as the springs of religious actions, lie in the unconscious; but the sources for artistic inspiration are more psycho-sexual in kind, whereas the impulses for religious acts, interests and rites derive from a second group of infantile interests, namely incestuous fantasies. Here we are apparently to think of Freud's *Totem and Taboo*. Both art and religion, however, ultimately go back to a single root. Consequently in later phases of development lines of connection are continually to be traced between the two spheres.

Jones goes on to demonstrate this from the legend about the Virgin's conception through the ear, which has played quite an important part in the traditions of the Catholic church, as we can see both from the visual arts and from a whole series of literary documents. Jones cites numerous examples. He shows that the legend is deeply rooted in unconscious fantasies. It displays, for example, connections with primitive ideas – which are often still slumbering in the unconscious – about the fertilizing activity of the breath. These notions themselves were connected with childish anal fantasies. The dove and the lily in the pictures of the Annunciation are sexual symbols; the dove is a phallic symbol and the lily is the embodiment of innocence. In these legends the ear represents the sexual organ of conception. Jones produces evidence for this, drawing many examples from early art as well as from the texts of ancient legends. Fantasies of this kind, for their part, proceed out of a deeper and repressed stratum of unconscious psychic life, the Oedipus complex. Anyone who reads them from the point of view of the analyst, who can fall back on knowledge acquired in the treatment of individual patients, will establish that here man has arrived at a kind of compromise in his ambivalent attitude towards the father whom he wants to castrate and whose power he at the same time wants to possess. For Jones this compromise, with its remarkable fantasies, is a regression from the difficulties of the incest barrier on to a lower level. Referring to the problems which emerge, he goes on to point to primitive rites discovered by ethnologists.

A further example of the way in which Jones works is the concluding article in his book, 'A Psycho-Analytic Study of the Holy Ghost Concept', which he expressly links up with *Totem and Taboo*. Here he expresses his hope that a study of the parallels may strengthen Freud's thesis that the religious story represents the unending attempt to overcome the Oedipus complex and to find real peace through reconciliation with the father. He refers here to the essay about the Virgin mentioned above. It is noticeable that the mother figure is not found in the Trinity; it has apparently been replaced by the Holy Spirit. Jones then comes to the conclusion that 'the replacement of the Mother-Goddess by the Holy Ghost is a manifestation of the desirability of renouncing incestuous and parricidal wishes and replacing them by a stronger attachment to the Father' (p. 367). We cannot discuss Jones' argument in detail here; but a great part of it again consists of pointers to primitive myths and the related childish fantasies which we find in the psycho-analysis of neurotic patients. Here again the problem of the Oedipus complex crops up in the background. Jones remarks at this point – entirely along Freud's lines – that 'Christianity constitutes in large part both a veiled regression to the primitive totemistic system and at the same time a refinement of this' (p. 369). But the fact that, despite the replacement of the mother-figure in the Trinity by the Holy Ghost, the worship of Mary, the Virgin Mother, has won for itself a distinct place, shows that not even the tensions bound up with this problem have been totally resolved in Christianity.

This brief recapitulation of Jones' ideas cannot unfortunately do justice to the ingenious way in which he attempts to explain striking religious phenomena on the grounds of unconscious dynamisms, such as we find among primitive peoples and in childish fantasies. It has become clear to me that theology must concern itself far more with these theories than it has done hitherto. Setting aside for the moment a scientific discussion about the theory itself, and confining myself to a number of fundamental questions arising from a consideration of the theme, my personal reactions to an essay like this are as follows:

(*a*) The development of the themes is obviously too rationalistic, if we set it beside what religion means to the believer himself. We ask whether the enquirer is really investigating religion as such here, or whether he is not rather concerned with a few remarkable phenomena in the religious sphere, which probably require a deeper study.

(*b*) We must ask whether it is permissible to understand religion as a compendium of symbols or rites, independent of the personal experience of the believer. Psycho-analysis is literally the study of the life of the human psyche, but here particular theories taken from research into the individual psyche are applied to certain aspects of religion without the intermediary psyche of the believer.

Naturally (*a*) and (*b*) are not independent of one another. I am convinced that later analysts, like Fromm and Erikson, who investigate religious *people* and not religion *per se*, have picked a better approach. This line of thought concentrates on particular aspects without knowing how essential they are.

Another publication which gives a good picture of how religion was studied and evaluated in the Freudian school during the early period (and of course Freud still has followers who continue to treat religious phenomena in this way), is Theodor Reik's book *Ritual*, for which Freud wrote a preface. Reik starts from the idea that religion and neurosis represent basically identical processes, as the believer's ritual and the obsessive-compulsive actions of the neurotic prove. He merely terms neurosis a 'distortion'. Both neurosis and religion are trying to solve the same problems. This view does not differ in essentials from Freud's.

Reik takes as example the 'couvade' – a custom practised by primitive peoples, according to which at the birth of a child the man takes over the woman's role, puts himself to bed, is attended as if he were giving birth, etc. Reik believes that the 'couvade' developed out of the attempt to ward off latent aggression towards the woman. He shares the view taken by most analysts that the emotional life of primitive people, like the emotional life of the child, is characterized by a strong ambivalence and so by distinct defence mechanisms. Primitive man certainly loves his wife, but he also harbours aggressive feelings towards her, which he tries to ward off by means of the 'couvade', in which he identifies himself with her. A special form of couvade is the 'dietary couvade' in which the man, in his role as the woman in childbed, is not allowed to eat certain food. Reik traces this back to the assumption that in the newborn child the man experiences the returning and threatening father. The totem animal which he is not allowed to eat now represents the father, a theory with which we are already familiar from Freud's *Totem and Taboo*. In this connection Reik also reminds us of the custom, known from various primitive tribes, of sacrificing the eldest son to the deity; he traces this back to the need to be reconciled with the father out of fear of reprisals. In particular religious phenomena, therefore, different motives can operate simultaneously. We could also deduce the same thing from Jones' investigations.

In our present book, which is concerned with the views held among depth psychologists about religion, we have drawn on the published work of Jones and Reik because they are a clear example of how in the early period people belonging to the closest circle of Freud's followers tried to explain religious phenomena along the master's own lines. Religion and neurosis are by nature identical and thus religious phenomena can be explained in the same way as neurotic symptoms; they have no autonomy of their own. I believe that it has become clear – and the analysts have opened our eyes to much that was concealed before – that connecting lines really do run from religion to neurosis and vice versa. Neurotic elements can be shown in the religion of adults. Among primitive people – as in children – the libidinous and the religious are not clearly differentiated, nor is the relation between the two clear. Here we have two possibilities, which have now become evident to us and which we cannot overlook. Of course there are still other possibilities, but we have not yet in my opinion reached the stage of having to accept that there is in principle no difference between religion and libidinous experience – a thesis which is no longer supported in every case by later Freudians, as we shall see in the following chapters, where we shall be citing various examples.

From the side of theology and the Christian churches, reactions to the statements made about religion by Freud and his followers were in general negative. Men like Pfister, and in England R. S. Lee, the vicar of St Mary's, Oxford, during the 'fifties, were exceptions. Only a small group recognized the importance of psycho-analysis and was prepared to concern itself seriously with psycho-analytical work. One consequence among others was that at the beginning many analytical practitioners were non-religious or anti-religious in attitude. But gradually more and more attempts were made to arrive at a more positive relationship. Analysis is still not completely accepted by theology and the church, but the reaction is no longer a merely negative one – positive opinions are voiced as well.

In this context let me draw attention to the following facts. First, it is becoming increasingly clear that people are feeling the need to understand more about Freud and his school; and there is no lack of appropriate information in this field. Secondly, there is a growing readiness in the most widely varying spheres (including that of psychiatry) to see and accept Freud's work in its true significance. Third, even if one does not accept Freud's view of religion as a general thesis, it is recognized that he was an acute observer of certain aspects of the actual life of religious people. Fourth, it is recognized that certain viewpoints belonging to psycho-analytical psychotherapy can be usefully transposed into pastoral work. Fifth, Freud's ideas about religion are taken seriously even if they have to be rejected in their unqualified form. I am thinking of his discovery of libidinous and aggressive elements in religion, which sheds a particular light on religious development, both in the individual and from the angle of the history of religion. I am also thinking of a concept like projection, the truth of which is increasingly the subject of investigation by theologians.

If I see the situation rightly, we must come to an understanding with Freudian anthropology, among other things, if we are to enter into a fruitful discussion. Is it a picture of man which has been methodologically pared down to the framework of the therapeutic situation? Or is it a view of man that can also claim validity outside the borders of therapy? I have the impression that, for one thing, the picture of man implicit in the therapy is not sufficiently thought through; and that on the other hand the question of the limitations of this view and its points of contact with the anthropology of other disciplines has hardly been raised at all up to now. For therapeutic use this view of man seems to be well suited – with certain limitations. For a wider context it is probably too narrow and too one-sided.

3

Carl Gustav Jung and his Circle

Since the publication of Jung's autobiography, *Memories, Dreams, Reflections*, we know that Jung's life makes an essential contribution to a better understanding of his work; and in this he differs from Freud. Freud is a representative of the modern generation of research workers belonging to the scientific school in its widest sense – men and women who introduce their own subjectivity as little as possible into the objectivity of their work. Jung is a romantic: not only the choice of his subject of research – the way in which he investigates it as well, bears the impress of his own subjectivity.

Jung lived from 1875 to 1961. His autobiography is for the most part a reproduction of conversations with his pupil Aniela Jaffé and it is one of the most interesting publications in the field of psychology. Its title is an appropriate one. What is important about it is not so much the treasure-trove of biographical reminiscences – that is not even particularly extensive; it is the gradual transition to the author's conversation with his own self, which follows the account of his youth. The reminiscences about other people gradually take up less and less space, while dreams and reflections increasingly move into the foreground.

The external facts which are of importance for an understanding of Jung's work are quickly told. He was the son of a Swiss pastor and spent most of his childhood in various villages near Basle, where he went to grammar school. As a small boy he is supposed to have been sensitive, and in adolescence he was troubled by severe religious problems, especially in connection with his father's pastorate and his 'rationalism', for which Jung came to have an aversion. He hesitated for a long time about which profession to take up. In his autobiography he writes about his interest in science, as well as his inclination towards philosophy. He finally decided for medicine, studied in Basle and specialized in psychiatry in Zürich, where he settled down permanently. Here he came into contact with Freud's work, later getting to know him personally. He was drawn to Freud, and particularly to the psychological perspectives he developed in psychiatry. It was along Freud's lines that Jung himself carried on the diagnostic studies in association for which he became known. In 1914 he left the university in order to devote himself entirely to private practice and to his scientific investigations, which grew into a considerable body of work in the course of the years. The relationship to Freud was a very close one at the beginning (they visited the United States together in 1909), but in 1913 there was an irremediable breach between them which was to be of crucial importance for the development of psycho-analysis, and which we shall discuss in detail later (pp. 55ff.). Jung's work was directed primarily to the structure and the activity of the unconscious, where he devoted great attention to the recording of dreams and to a subsequent study of the different phenomena belonging to the 'collective' unconscious – mythology, gnosis, kabbala and alchemy. Particular theological and exegetical problems also interested him, as we can see from his books *Psychological Types* and *Answer to Job* (*Collected Works*, Vol. 11). Jung was married and had several children. He travelled several times to America, Africa and Asia. He was a man of tremendous industry, a trait in which we can perhaps trace something of the Swiss peasant element.

Jung is a psychologist who captivates us by his immense intuitive gifts. At the beginning he was enthralled by his empirical researches in the usual sense of the word, but later he increasingly ceased to adopt the attitude of the scientifically trained psychologist.

One remarkable aspect of Jung's life is his relationship to Freud. What really happened between them cannot be totally explained, but there are a number of striking facts.

The first is the difference in style of their scientific work. Freud is an empiricist and a scientist, with an obviously positivist strain. Jung, on the other hand, is much more speculative and romantic. The picture of man in Freud and Jung also reveals differences. The Freudian picture has a strong biological colouring. Jung's is less one-sided and all-inclusive, but it is not so sharply drawn either. One factor in the breach between the two was apparently that Freud feared that analysis as a science would be 'debased'; he makes Jung's 'mysticism' a reproach, and he finally arrived at a radical rejection of him. Nor did he make any later attempt to see the significance of Jung's contribution in a more discriminating way. Jung, on the other hand, always tried to do this with Freud's work.

Secondly, there were tensions in the personal relationship of the two men. Jung was for Freud the 'crown prince' whom he consequently regarded with ambivalent feelings. The 'attacks' which Freud had on a few occasions – fainting fits which greatly affected him – were undoubtedly connected with a certain 'fear' which he felt towards Jung. In his reminiscences of Freud, Binswanger reports certain remarks which show his ambivalent attitude. Jung complains that although as a teacher Freud allowed his pupils a great deal of liberty, yet he demanded a certain conformity which Jung himself was unable to give.

Like Freud, Jung influenced the whole world. But today it seems as if his influence is less than Freud's. It is only in Switzerland that he still has considerable weight. We notice with interest that both in his work, and in the activities of the institute named after him in his native country, no deep antithesis arose between psycho-analysis and theology as it did elsewhere, although his book *Answer to Job* (to which we shall return later) has caused unrest among Swiss theologians. Because of his positive attitude to religion, Jung has always found disciples even among theologians. I am thinking of the late Hans Schär of Berne University, for example, who wrote about psychotherapy and pastoral care along Jung's lines.

We are bound to say, however, that the more carefully theologians followed up Jung's ideas about religion, and the more discriminating the the reflections on his work, the more a certain change took place in an evaluation which was, at the beginning, often too wholesale. The book *Analytische psychologie en godsdienst* ('Analytical Psychology and Religion') by R. Hostie is clear evidence of this. In theological circles Jung's statements about religion were at first sometimes played off against Freud and his psycho-analysis, but later there came to be an awareness that his support also has its drawbacks. In the framework of Jung's system psychotherapy is a help in man's coming to selfhood – in what Jung terms individuation. For him, as we shall later see in more detail, this individuation is essentially a religious process. We know that in 1932 Jung, talking to a group of Protestant clergy, made the following assertion, which must be interpreted in the context of what we have just said: 'Among all my patients who are middle-aged or more – that is to say, who are over 35 – there is not a single one whose ultimate problem is not one of religious attitude.' In this process different religious symbols play an important part in the unconscious. On closer consideration, religion (the question about the existence of God, for example, which Jung, like Jones, excludes as a psychologist) is detached from the question of its truth and becomes a more or less useful factor in the process of acquiring selfhood. Indeed it becomes a kind of gnosis. The basic ideas of Jung's system can be quite broadly indicated. Like Freud, he takes his stand on the psycho-analytical foundation. That is to say, there is a tension in man between the conscious and the unconscious life of the psyche. Where this tension leads to a neurosis, healing can only be expected if a successful attempt is made to lift the unconscious into the consciousness. Freud would say: to let the 'id' become 'ego'. Jung works out further a number of points which are still in the background in Freud, and so his conclusions run parallel to Freud's and often also contradict him.

In their therapeutic work both Freud and Jung assume as their starting point that man has an inherent power to regain health. Medically the expression is the *vis medicatrix naturae* – the healing power of nature. When, for instance, Freud and his pupils make a sufficient capacity for integration the basic condition for beginning an analysis, this is a reference to the *vis medicatrix*. Jung says that the ego, the soul – his definitions are not so exact as Freud's – strives to become a self. He calls this the process of individuation. Here dreams are an important auxiliary. For Jung dreams are more than the products of repressed desires; they are in his opinion often prospective and reveal in veiled form a truth not as yet discovered but already guessed at. In dreams the unconscious ego speaks, expressing itself in symbols. It is the nature of the symbol both to unveil and to veil a truth that is not as yet clear. Now, symbols often derive not only from the individual unconscious but also from the collective unconscious – the sum of the primordial experiences of mankind, which are expressed in these symbols as well as in what he called archetypes ('ideas' which have become images and which speak to men, like God, heaven, hell, the dragon, etc.).

We saw in our discussion of Freud's book on Moses that Freud too was familiar with the notion that mankind's great experiences are preserved in the unconscious. In mythology as well as in the artist's creations we are dealing with expressions of the collective unconscious – Hamlet, for instance, might be called an 'incorporation' of the Oedipus complex.

Freud and Jung differ from one another in that Freud sees the process of healing (i.e., Jung's individuation) as being above all a clarification of the person's ties with his parents, which have not yet been properly settled, whereas for Jung it is more a process that continues throughout the whole of life. Jung takes his stand here on a series of observations which we do not find in Freud and which are important for our knowledge of man. I am thinking of the contrasting terms introvert and extrovert, or feeling and thinking, or sensation and intuition, as well as animus and anima. Although these concepts are not always precisely defined, and Jung uses them intuitively, in his hands they none the less seem to be of practical use. In this way, for example, he arrives at important discoveries about the position of woman in Europe and about what he calls the 'dominance change' (or shift of interests) round about the age of forty.

There is no doubt that Jung made an important contribution to research, even though his work has to be more clearly integrated into the whole of analytical science through a confrontation with the study of the first years of life, as well as with transference – the great Freudian contribution. Storr attempts this in his little book *The Integrity of the Personality*. On the other hand the quality and limitations of Jung's work also call for an immanent critical investigation; I am thinking here of the study by Hans Trüb, one of Jung's pupils, *Heilung aus der Begegnung* (Healing through Encounter).

Having given this short outline of Jung and his work, we will now attempt to discuss his numerous and widely differing individual statements about religion. They deal both with religion *per se* and with particular religious phenomena, such as the contrast between Catholic and Protestant, the figure of the Virgin Mary, Job's dispute with God, mythology, etc. It is impossible to give a complete picture of all the statements about religion which we can extract from Jung's work. Hostie's book *Jung und die Religion* (1954) is a good introduction, as well as a fundamental discussion of the problems with which Jung deals; but since Jung's autobiography (which illuminates much that Jung has to say about religion) had not then been published, Hostie's introduction is not a complete one.

In our present chapter we shall try to analyse some of Jung's main writings, so as to convey as accurate a picture as possible of his views about religion.

Let us turn our attention first and primarily to the Terry Lectures, which he gave at Yale University in 1937 and which were printed under the title *Psychology and Religion*. The German edition (translated in the *Collected Works*, Vol. 11) is somewhat fuller than the text of the lectures. The book has three chapters. The first deals with 'The Autonomy of the Unconscious Mind'. Here Jung shows that as a psychologist he is an empiricist; he feels himself to be an onlooker, not one who is making metaphysical or philosophical observations. Within the framework of his investigations, particular ideas are for him only psychologically true. His attitude is therefore no different from that of the scientist.

His view of religion derives from Rudolf Otto. In his book *The Idea of the Holy* Otto analyses religious experience on Schleiermacher's lines, terming it 'the feeling of the numinous' (the experience of the divine as a fascinating and awesome mystery). Jung talks about a particular attitude of the soul, namely 'careful consideration and observation', an attitude which is rooted in the experience of the numinous. Following Schleiermacher, he goes on to say that the different denominations and creeds are 'codified and dogmatized' forms of this experience. Here, in my opinion, he has decided in favour of a particular definition of religion which will be rejected as false by many people. It is of course correct that the psychologist proceeds independently of the question of truth, leaving the discussion and solution of that problem to the theologian; but Jung would in my opinion have done better if he had not made his definition of religion dependent on a view of religion current at the moment, but had instead taken his theological bearings as comprehensively as possible. Otto certainly points to a particular aspect of religion in his book, but his definition is not an exhaustive one. We shall see later that Jung's decision was not taken by chance. In deciding for Otto's definition, he was deciding for a view of religion which linked up with his own religious attitude and which was contrary to a view which he had rejected from his youth – that of his father. But we have a right to expect a more objective attitude from a psychologist.

Jung goes on to say that he is a physician who treats neuroses. In saying this he means that he is familiar with the complexes which have an effect on the consciousness. But the human consciousness, he says, is not simply a purely individual affair. It is influenced by forces which come from the collective unconscious. Among primitive peoples the consciousness is weak and must defend itself against the dangers of the unconscious with the help of various rites. Here Jung is expressing a favourite idea – that the Christian church (and especially the Catholic church) exerts a protective function between these influences and man. Here we have to think of Freud's view about rites. Freud saw them as obsessive neurotic phenomena, which he simply and without more ado viewed as negative. Perhaps one might say that the 'enlightened' Freud wanted to shed light on the obscurity of the unconscious, whereas for Jung the romantic this obscurity is an unavoidable part of our life, and one with which we have to try to live. It is the shadow which we have to accept, without its casting us into fear. From this point of view it is understandable that Jung has a series of weighty objections to Protestantism. It takes away from man the protection which rites give him and

delivers him up to the disruptive and schismatic influence of an individual revelation. In Jung's work as a whole there is evidence of an appreciation of Protestantism – for its stress on the personal conscience, for example; but in the comments we have just mentioned he wanted to express what seemed to him particularly important.

Jung now asks: how do we acquire information about the content of the unconscious? His answer is staggeringly simple: through dreams. For Jung as well as for Freud, the interpretation of dreams is the royal road to the unconscious. Dreams are the reflection of unconscious psychic processes. Jung takes a different view of dreams from Freud. Freud sees the dream as a façade, behind which something is deliberately hiding. For Jung it is a normal, natural happening, which one must take for what it is: the dream interprets itself. If I see the matter rightly, the difference between Freud and Jung here is not as fundamental as Jung – and Freud too – maintains. The dream with its symbols is both concealment and revelation. Freud stresses the aspect of concealment; for him the dream is a – disguised – wish fulfilment. But in discussing the dream with the patient he starts from the assumption that the dream also wants to 'say' something. Jung on the other hand stresses the aspect of revelation. He sees in the dream an attempt from the side of the unconscious to 'say' something in a disguised way, something which the person needs in the process of individuation but which has not as yet penetrated to his consciousness. But Jung does not go into the question of why this 'saying' only takes place in a symbolic way. Does not something like 'censorship', as Freud would say, play a part here too? Very probably there are also dreams in which emphasis lies more on concealment. Cases are known from psychotherapeutic practice in which patients dream the dreams which fit into their therapist's system.

Jung establishes that in dreams we have to do with remarkable phenomena. In their dreams, for example, men often have the experience of meeting a female figure, which represents the 'anima', the other side of their personality. In women the reverse takes place. This is reminiscent of the notion of the co-existence of male and female in a single person. We can think of ancient myths or Hermetic philosophy. These figures are an embodiment of the unconscious and consequently often have an 'irritating' character in the dream. According to Jung, dreams often establish the psychic state of a patient. They often crop up in series and are then the 'visible links in a chain of unconscious events' (p. 33). Here Jung's views about the process of individuation obviously play a considerable part.

Chapter II of the Terry Lectures deals with 'Dogma and Natural Symbols'. The starting point is Jung's conception of the relationship between the consciousness and the unconscious in man. According to him, our – intellectual – consciousness is something like a skyscraper, whose ground floor covers our whole past. The unconscious, however, is more than merely a storehouse. It has intelligence and is active and purposeful. Here too we must not forget Jung's fundamental idea that man's growing into consciousness is a process of individuation. The ego is only partly conscious; it is unconscious as well. It therefore embraces more than merely our intellectual, conscious ego.

In Jung's opinion most of our Western intellectuals are what he calls fragmentary personalities. He developed highly emphatic ideas about the problems of our Western civilization. There are people who exist largely as fragmentary personalities – people who often employ substitutes in place of what is genuine. Here he is alluding to religion, when it takes the form of a denominational allegiance which replaces direct religious experience, and indeed protects people against that experience. For Jung, as we have already seen, dogma and rites have a certain 'hygienic' value. For him dogma is a dream, a reflection of the spontaneous and autonomous activity of the objective psyche, the unconscious. Protestantism has lost many of the protective possibilities of the Catholic church, including its images and rites, and has therefore helped to create modern man, who has lost his defences. Protestantism is therefore bound up with a considerable risk, although Jung also recognizes that it contains great potentialities. Thus through the loss of the church's protection, as well as through his own personal conscience, the Protestant has lost 'the unique spiritual chance of immediate religious experience'.

Jung then once more turns his attention to dreams. In his opinion they also contain much collective material, fixed themes, for example – what he calls archetypes – a concept which plays a considerable part in Jung. In this context he discusses the number four, which often occurs in dreams and which he thinks also had a great importance in fixed forms (the so-called quaternity) in Christian iconography and in mystical speculation, but above all in gnostic philosophy and in the Middle Ages. We meet it in connection with the circle, the ring, which is a symbol of divine unity but whose unity embraces a fourfold division. Plato already developed ideas of this kind. Contemporary people who come across this symbol in dreams declare that it symbolizes themselves or something in them – as it were the creative primordial ground, God himself. For Jung the quaternity is a symbol of 'the God within'. His perceptions are for him a proof of the existence of an archetypal image of God. As a psychologist he is not prepared to go beyond this. He does not believe that the existence of God can be proved on the basis of this statement. But the fact that this arechetype crops up so frequently is for him a pointer towards a natural theology, a *theologia naturalis*. We should do well not to forget this. For Jung's autobiography seems to suggest that natural theology has for him a greater meaning than he would like us to suppose here. His own religion, which is closely bound up with natural theology, already emerges at this point.

Jung now finds it extremely interesting that the symbol for the unconscious is the quaternity, whereas the main Christian symbol is the Trinity. Here we feel the contrast between Christian theology and Jung's natural theology. He does not believe that the Trinity is sufficient, because it does not absorb the principle of evil within itself but allows the devil a life of his own. Here the voice of nature is heard. It is a voice which the church is probably bound to reject, since it distrusts everything that has to do with the unconscious, with the occult, with the ancient interpretation of dreams and with alchemy. All this seems suspect to the church and is accordingly rejected. On the basis of ancient speculations, Jung declares that the Trinity is rationalistic and male, whereas the unconscious is the fourth element which puts both the female and evil into the foreground as essential. This brings us to the centre of Jung's 'system', which theological circles did not apparently always see in its totality and its whole consistency at the beginning. Jung himself (who ended this chapter with the remark that 'it needs no particular effort of imagination to guess the far-reaching spiritual consequence of such a development') was apparently more alive to this in 1913. In his opinion the presence and the activity of the unconscious reveal deep contradictions in the roots of our human existence and our faith. Since – on the lines of analytical therapy – he was able to see his exclusive goal simply and solely as the integration of the contents of the unconscious in the person's total life, he was bound to arrive at a viewpoint which he and his pupils termed 'life with the shadow' – in religion as well. It is obvious that this was bound to bring him up against the same great difficulties of principle with traditional theology that Freud had.

The last chapter (III) of his book treats the 'History and Psychology of a Natural Symbol'. Here Jung goes further into the dreams and their symbols that played a part in the treatment of one of his patients (who had already been mentioned in another passage in the book). This patient had a vision of a double, vertical and horizontal, ring, with various characteristics which, among other things, constantly point to the number four. This vision is reminiscent of the Buddhist Mandalas, which we know as circles with four points or four towers, and which are also symbols of unity. They also remind us of mediaeval pictures containing the Trinity and the Virgin. The meaning of this vision, with its feeling of sublime harmony, is for Jung nothing less than the union of the soul with God. He apparently means the union of the soul with its own divine ground, with itself, in the deepest meaning of the word, since for Jung this is the nature of the individuation process. His natural theology is the religious overtone in this process and hence in his therapeutic work.

These quaternial ideas about the Trinity, which are missing in the actual dogma, are for Jung far more than the products of human reason.

> I have always taken the view that they belong to the type of revelation to which Koepgen has recently given the name of 'Gnosis' (not to be confused with Gnosticism). Revelation is an 'unveiling' of the depths of the human soul first and foremost, a 'laying bare'; hence it is an essentially psychological event, though this does not, of course, tell us what *else* it might be. That lies outside the province of science (p. 74).

The important thing therefore is an opening up of the depths of the human soul, a becoming conscious of the unconscious. This means that what we are dealing with really is something psychological. We carry the shadow with us and it has to be integrated.

> Everyone carries a shadow ... We carry our past with us, to wit, the primitive and inferior man with his desires and emotions, and it is only by a considerable effort that we can detach ourselves from this burden. If it comes to a neurosis, we have invariably to deal with a considerably intensified shadow. And if such a case wants to be cured it is necessary to find a way in which man's conscious personality and his shadow can live together (pp. 76f.).

There must be a reconciliation between the antitheses. 'The shadow is merely somewhat inferior, primitive, unadapted, and awkward' and the educated person tries to repress these things.

> Such problems are never solved by legislation or tricks. They are only solved by a general change of attitude. And the change does not begin with propaganda and mass meetings or with violence. It begins with a change in individuals (p. 79).

Here Jung points once more to the significance of the mandala. The mandala is a uniting symbol, that is to say it is an expression of reconciliation. But what is it that is reconciled? Here we again touch the heart of Jung's theory. Man is not reconciled with God, as he was in the past, but with himself, an important aspect in the development of the religious consciousness. Now we do not find God outside ourselves so much as within us. The development of the human consciousness demands a withdrawal of all attainable projections, and thus according to Jung no doctrine of God, in the sense of a non-psychological existence, can be maintained any longer. If religion is primarily the consciousness of the numinous, God is then in reality virtually the strongest psychical position. And from that the next step leads logically to the proposition: the integration of man now seems to take the place of God. We can see with this that Jung's agnostic attitude towards the existence of God is not merely linked with his reservations as a psychologist; it is also connected with an increasingly clear natural theology, which is inherent in the core of his psychological work. Religion is in the theological sense 'the consciousness of the numinous' but psychologically it is 'a relationship to oneself' and in both systems of co-ordinates also 'a relationship to the archetype God who is present in the unconscious'.

Psychotherapy is hence for Jung in its very nature a support of the religious growth of consciousness and as such it is also a religious and theological – really a priestly – occupation. We should remember that we are not dealing here with a special 'hobby' of Jung's but that in this way he is linking on to a tradition that is still alive in the medical world, in which the practice of healing was originally the work of priests and where calculating the mysterious forces in the healing power of nature, and wrestling with death, was a religious matter. For us theologians Jung's theories, especially those of his later years, often seem strange, but they are rooted in convictions that are frequently maintained and quite normal. In analogy to these ideas, Jung then goes on to give his views about the life of Christ. He thinks that believing Christians will find it difficult to follow his train of thought. But indeed he can expect nothing else. They are the *beati possidentes* – the happy possessors – and his discussion, which starts from an archetypal Christ, will probably seem to them absurd. But, says Jung, I am addressing myself to the many for whom the light is obscured, the people for whom the mystery has disappeared and for whom God is dead. Most of them could no longer get back, and Jung even doubts whether the way back is always the best course. He is apparently thinking here of the change in human consciousness which we mentioned above.

> To gain an understanding of religious matters, probably all that is left to us today is the psychological approach. That is why I take these thoughtforms that have become historically fixed, try to melt them down again and pour them into moulds of immediate experience (p. 89).

This no doubt means simply that all theological statements are seen and understood from the standpoint of natural theology. Christ himself is the type of the dying and risen god.

Jung then leads us again to the heart of his theory when he writes (p. 96):

> It is clear that, in the modern mandala, man – the deep ground, as it were, of the self – is not a substitute but a symbol for the deity.

These symbolizations are not chance ones, he says; they can be rediscovered in history. Jung spent a considerable part of his life looking for historical parallels for dream symbols. He has shown their existence not only in the history of religion but also in gnosis, and especially in alchemy, which was one of its manifestations. We can of course hardly go into the detailed chain of evidence he produces; but in order to sum up his views briefly, and above all to demonstrate his relationship to the church and to theology, let me quote a short passage from the close of the book (p. 105):

> We must confess in all humility that religious experience is *extra ecclesiam*, subjective, and liable to boundless error. Yet, if the spiritual adventure of our time is the exposure of human consciousness to the undefined and indefinable, there would seem to be good reasons for thinking that even the Boundless is pervaded by psychic laws, which no man invented, but of which he has 'gnosis' in the symbolism of Christian dogma.

Let us try to sum up as far as we have gone.

1. In order to understand Jung properly it is important for us to remind ourselves continually that the starting point for his reflections is provided by his work as a psychiatrist. In the course of psychotherapeutic work he established that the healing of a neurotic patient consists of a process of individuation. Because in this process the person is confronted with the numinous content of his unconscious, which strives towards illumination out of primitive darkness, the process is essentially a religious one. The symbols in which the unconscious manifests itself in dreams play an important part here. They are symbols which we meet elsewhere as well in the history of human thought and religion, and which apparently derive from a collective unconscious. Jung calls the illumination which we try to win from symbols 'gnosis' and I would say that like him we can talk about a natural theology (or perhaps a natural religion) when we are dealing with the religion which he has in mind here.

2. This idea about religion and its symbols has a number of points of

contact with Christian theology and the practice of the churches. We can think of the following:

(*a*) Within the framework offered by his special standpoint, Jung shows a particular awareness of the relationship between religion and dogma. Dogma is secondary in kind, although it has great importance for the individual person, since it protects him against the dangers emanating from his own unconscious.

(*b*) What Jung has to say about the concept of God is important for a proper understanding of his standpoint. He does not attack the convictions of people who have a transcendent concept of God. But the 'consciousness' of modern man differs from the consciousness of earlier generations and he can only rediscover God through the archetype God in his own unconscious – that is to say, he can only find him, in a certain sense, 'immanently'. Starting off from this picture of God, he must and can make certain corrections to particular dogmas, for example to the dogma of the Trinity, which is derived from an intellectual consciousness.

(*c*) Within the framework of his view of the unconscious, Jung also has a certain insight into the history of religion. Like Freud, he sees primitive religious phenomena as being expressions of the unconscious – an unconscious which he, more clearly than Freud, terms a collective unconscious. Both Freud and Jung are convinced that the primitive conciousness is less exposed to repression and that because of this it reveals the ambivalence of our inner life more clearly. Jung differs essentially from Freud in that he does not think that the problems connected with the Oedipus complex are the origin of religious belief. Because of this view, faith for Freud is something that has to be overcome. According to Jung, on the other hand, faith has to be renewed. It must be filtered out of its dogmatic and intellectual forms and must be remoulded into a new kind of 'Gnosis', or natural theology.

Perhaps I may make a brief comment at this point. It is a remarkable fact that neither Jung nor Freud (who are both, after all, convinced of the formative value of the very first ties for a person's development and who also connect religious faith with these ties) never tested the growth of the religious consciousness in actual cases. They looked for parallels in the history of religion, but never really subjected their view of the problems of faith to proofs based on the analysis of particular patients. This is a remarkable difference compared with psycho-analysis in its later developments. Subsequently, psycho-analysis became less generally concerned with faith and the structure of faith *per se* than with showing the complications involved in the growth of human belief in particular cases. Erikson's book *Young Man Luther*, which we shall be looking at later, is an eloquent example.

(*d*) Jung opens our eyes to the difference between male and female influences in man's life and hence in his religious life as well; and this is of importance for theology. Jung sees the influences of a mother religion in Catholicism; Calvinism could without any doubt be called a father religion; whereas a mother element is dominant in the primitive religions as well as in his own natural theology. We must undoubtedly devote more attention to this phenomenon in the psychology of religion. In recent years – I am again thinking of Erikson's book, which is particularly important in the framework of our investigation – it has moved into the foreground once more.

3. We now come to the final point in our provisional summing up. Jung certainly calls himself an empirical psychologist, which means a psychologist who is objective and religiously neutral; but he himself lives from a particular type of religion, and this applies to his psychological work as well. We have pointed out that psychotherapy has a religious component for Jung, and this is a view which he shares with many therapists. We can sum up the particular character of this religion by saying that man must and may trust himself to the liberating aid of the symbols which spring from the unconscious. It is in this, in this aid, that God reveals himself. We can easily understand that a particular view of man's conduct, as well as of different religions and theological conceptions and ideas, is inherent in a religion of this kind.

We have already touched on this train of thought but we shall now develop it in more detail through an analysis, first of Jung's autobiography, and then of his disputed study of the Old Testament book of Job, *Answer to Job*, which gives us perhaps the deepest insight into his 'gnostic' world of ideas and emotions.

1. *Memories, Dreams, Reflections*, the autobiography published in 1962, contains, as we have already said, a series of conversations between Jung and his colleague Aniela Jaffé which took place in the last years of his life. We also find in it some passages written by himself, the most important of them being his account of his youth and the chapter headed 'Late Thoughts', which contains his religious theories. The book is indispensable for a proper understanding of Jung's view of religion, and especially for its role in his own life. I myself would say that it is one of the most interesting human documents published in recent years. No one ought to pass this book by who wants to understand the attitude,

especially towards the church and Christianity, of a large number of modern intellectuals, including those who may well take a different road from Jung in religious matters.

The book is mainly an attempt to trace Jung's inner development. It builds up the picture of that development by way of all kinds of more or less theological reflections, especially in the field of religion. It really primarily discloses to us Jung's 'inner life', concentrating on the world of his religious ideas, which he himself called a form of existence that fitted his life, a way of life as necessary to him as eating and drinking. What he meant becomes comprehensible in the light of some other statements in the book: 'My life is a story of the self-realisation of the unconscious', or in other words, 'the myth of my life', i.e., 'What we are to our inward vision, and what man appears to be *sub specie aeternatis*' (p. 17).

It is a fascinating book, in which we really do come to know Jung in his inner self and above all Jung the philosopher, a man with an entirely individual view of life and a faith of his own.

The most important biographical facts about Jung have already been mentioned. What interests us here is mainly what he has to say about religion, and his own beliefs in particular.

In the prologue, which he wrote himself, he says (pp. 17f.):

> Like every other being I am a splinter of the infinite deity ... Life has always seemed to me like a plant that lives on its rhizome. Its true life is invisible, hidden in the rhizome. The part that appears above ground lasts only a single summer. Then it withers away – an ephemeral apparition. When we think of the unending growth and decay of life and civilizations, we cannot escape the impression of absolute nullity. Yet I have never lost a sense of something that lives and endures underneath the eternal flux. What we see is the blossom, which passes. The rhizome remains.

With this view of things – that every being is a splinter of the infinite deity – Jung belongs to a quite definite philosophical and religious tradition which has played a considerable role in the background of our Western culture. From the religious aspect, we may think of the religious humanism which took clear shape in the philosophy of Plato, Spinoza, Hegel and Jaspers. It is – again from the religious point of view – related to the Hindu view which we find in important Eastern thinkers of ancient and modern times. Radhakrishnan's philosophy is a well-known example. The central problem of all humanism, whether it is philosophical or religious, is individuation.

In this tradition, reflection about the background of his ideas played an important part in Jung. He is not an acute thinker; he is rather a man of sometimes vague and often romantic intuitions. It is understandable that he is inclined to link his theory of the collective unconscious with his consciousness of being a new shoot on old wood. There is undoubtedly a danger that the psychological theory and the philosophical and religious concepts may merge into one another, and I should guess that he did not always know how to avoid it.

2. Furthermore, it ought to be pointed out that from a very early stage Jung was already putting a negative valuation on everything to do with the church. For example, we read about a Jesuit who inspired him with terror when he was a child; about stories of Jesus which made Jung distrust him; about the oppressive effect of church-going and religious teaching; and about the trouble he had as a child to find a positive relationship to his father, who was a pastor. What he says at the very beginning of his book about his relationship to his parents is very striking. His mother was away from home for a long time because of illness:

> I was deeply troubled by my mother's being away. From then on, I always felt mistrustful when the word 'love' was spoken. The feeling I associated with 'woman' was for a long time innate unreliability. 'Father', on the other hand, meant reliability and – powerlessness. That is the handicap I started off with. Later, these early impressions were revised: I have trusted men friends and been disappointed by them, and I have trusted women and was not disappointed (p. 23).

Throughout the whole book we feel how the duality that comes out here put its stamp on his religious ideas. His father was a pastor, and Jung's incapacity to identify himself with him (an incapacity which emerges again and again) obviously influenced his relationship to Christianity and to the church. He never saw his way to finding a positive relationship to them, although he could respect them from a certain distance. On the other hand, in spite of the mistrust he mentions, he was continually drawn by women. Unlike Freud, who was surrounded practically entirely by male colleagues, Jung had several women among his own pupils. He felt the problems of the modern woman much more keenly than those of the man. In his books he does not plead for truly masculine ideals, but rather for ideals which belong to the woman's sphere. His judgment of Mariolatry is a highly positive one. And in the primitive realm of the unconscious, where Freud (against the background of a 'paternal' cultural ideal) again and again found Oedipal problems, Jung continually discovered feminine elements. For him the collective unconscious was, emotionally speaking, a womb pregnant with images.

Duality already plays a part in one of the first dreams which Jung had as a boy of about four, a dream which was to occupy his mind all his life. It was a dream about a terrifying phallus called Man-eater. Jung writes (p. 28):

> At all events, the phallus of this dream seems to be a subterranean God 'not to be named', and such it remained throughout my youth, reappearing whenever anyone spoke too emphatically about Lord Jesus. Lord Jesus never became quite real for me, never quite acceptable, never quite lovable, for again and again I would think of his underground counterpart, a frightful revelation which had been accorded me without my seeking it.

Analysts belonging to the Freudian school will perhaps ask whether this dream does not point to other conflicts than the ones Jung thought he saw in it. This could be used to show the relativity of Jung's theories. But that is a problem between the two analytical schools, about which we will therefore withhold judgment. We are far more concerned with the results of the dream in Jung's own life and especially with its effects on his religion. There are two striking things about the last quotation: first, the mention of a God in the unconscious who forces himself on the dreamer in a terrifying way; and secondly that this God is experienced as a counterpart to Jesus, to whom Jung was never able to find a real relationship. Another quotation (p. 30) shows how fundamental this duality was for Jung:

> Through this childhood dream I was initiated into the secrets of the earth. What happened then was a kind of burial in the earth, and many years were to pass before I came out again. Today I know that it happened in order to bring the greatest possible amount of light into the darkness. It was an initiation into the realm of darkness. My intellectual life had its unconscious beginnings at that time.

In other words, through this dream Jung remained fixed on the darkness in the unconscious, but he came to realize that this was necessary in order that he should later be able to explain the secrets of the unconscious and to begin his own process of individuation out of that unconscious.

3. Finally, we must point to the fact that the pages in which Jung describes his early years show that we are dealing with a vulnerable boy, growing up under the weight of his own difficult secrets. He tells of the blackened figure of a little 'manikin', which he carved himself and secreted in the attic, and which had an immense significance for him. Later, in his ethnological studies, he came across parallels to this figure among primitive peoples. He could also remember that when he was young he had had the indefinite feeling of relationship with a 'stone' in

connection with this figure, and that in a mysterious way it represented his 'ego'.

From the time when he was eleven years old, he writes (p. 43), he was interested in the idea of God, 'while it became increasingly impossible for me to adopt a positive attitude to Lord Jesus'. This God, as he conceived of him, did not fit into the usual ideas of the church. He was a 'mystery' and, according to Jung, 'A certain analogy with my secret in the attic began to dawn on me'. The notable thing is that this secret in the attic was the blackened figure which we have already mentioned and which he already felt was connected with his own ego. So here we have the duality once more.

4. This duality in Jung's life demands our especial attention and it emerges with increasing clarity in Jung's own consciousness. Two different personalities develop simultaneously. There is the extrovert, who lives in and reckons with everyday reality, a person who is aware of his duties; and there is the introvert, who 'flees' from reality into fainting fits, which seem to be epilectic in character, a man acutely aware of the wonders of nature, who feels himself to be an 'old man', and who at the age of twelve had what he thought was a terrible dream which was apparently connected with the split in his inner life. In this dream (and he experienced it as an appalling secret) God was destroying the cathedral – Basle's famous church – with his excrement. A number of fundamental associations were bound up with this dream. Jung was now obviously divided from his father. He was obedient and felt this as a certain liberation and as grace; but at the same time God was something terrible. His dream made him feel inferior, but he found comfort in the idea that in the Bible the outcasts are the ones who are chosen. Against this background we can understand why Jung writes (p. 58): 'My entire youth can be understood in terms of this secret. It induced in me an almost unendurable loneliness...' He lives with the terrible darkness through which he also becomes a special person who experiences things that other people do not know. So he is again and again overcome by doubt about what his father says; and the church and everything to do with it becomes an increasing torment.

5. We can discover the same duality in his relationship to his parents. This is naturally of importance for the analyst. Jung was apparently conscious that the reason for the duality in his life is to be sought for here; but he never said anything about it in more detail, nor did he, for example, associate it with Oedipal difficulties. He points to the contrast, but does not enter into it. He says that his mother had an 'animal' warmth,

but was also made up of two personalities. The one he experienced as innocuous and human, whereas the other seemed to him uncanny and often gave him anxiety dreams in the night; for it was the embodiment of the archaic, the non-rational in nature, of a deeper understanding which for Jung was apparently associated with the unconscious. With his father, unlike his mother, he had no emotional contact. He found his teaching boring. Indeed his father disappointed him greatly by simply passing over the problems connected with the concept of God in his lessons. At his first communion after his confirmation, which was celebrated by his father, the boy found that the whole thing meant nothing to him, and he was filled with guilt as a result. He even got to the point of feeling sorry for his father.

6. It is understandable that at puberty a boy like this should be deeply concerned with the problems involved in the concept of God. In the official theology of the church he came across subjects which were a closed book to him. He rejected the idea of conceiving God as a 'personality', in analogy to himself; the riddles to be found in the world could not be reconciled with the love of God which was supposed to be expressed in creation. He asked where the devil and evil came from, and felt a bond with Goethe, who took the devil seriously, and with Schopenhauer, who saw suffering as an essential factor in creation, although neither of them satisfied him completely. He felt that he was becoming depressive and discovered that really all burning questions – like his primordial mystery – had to do, not with normal life, but with the divine world about which it was better to be silent. Thus he became increasingly silent, while he was unable to overcome the duality in himself.

7. It now becomes evident that dreams played an increasingly important role for Jung whenever he had to make weighty decisions. His resolve to become a doctor was based on dreams. But the effects went even deeper. A dream (he describes it on pp. 107f. of the autobiography) virtually altered his whole attitude to life. The dualism was not overcome as a result, but he grasped that he had to live in and with the reality of his conscious ego. This meant more or less that he felt himself to be a part of his unconscious ego, yet without the chance of identifying himself with it. Here Jung was actually taking an important step in the process of individuation. It is a step which also shows how deeply both his view of man and his psychology are rooted in his own life and in his own psychical development.

8. We also find that the duality which had always been present in the background of Jung's life now made itself felt in a particular way in the

reality of his studies, as he prepared for his profession. Jung reports that his relationship to his father became increasingly difficult and that his aloofness from the church and theology took on ever clearer form in his life. During his first year at the university his father died, without there having been any reconciliation between them. Jung now devoted himself a great deal to philosophy, and read Hartmann and Nietzsche. But both were for him too remote from empiricism. At this period he discovered, through the duality in Nietzsche's life, that to talk incautiously about this Other, 'this thing not to be named' (p. 123), can only lead to trouble. We must remain within the bounds of facts. It was against this background that he arrived at his decision to become a psychiatrist. In psychiatry he could unite his inclination towards the empirical with his leanings towards the 'Other'.

> Here alone the two currents of my interest could flow together and in a united stream dig their own bed. Here was the empirical field common to biological and spiritual facts, which I had everywhere sought and nowhere found. Here at last was the place where the collision of nature and spirit became a reality (p. 130).

9. We now come to an important point in Jung's life, which also has a particular significance for our investigation: his friendship with Freud and his later breach with him. From 1900 onwards, Jung was psychiatric assistant at the 'Burghölzli' in Zürich. There he came across Freud's work, which interested him because here the manifestations with which the psychiatrist is concerned are also seen from the angle of the psyche, not merely from the standpoint of the biological organism. The two men discovered one another because they both saw a psychic significance in pathological manifestations. 'At this point,' writes Jung (p. 35), 'Freud became vitally important to me, especially because of his fundamental researches into the psychology of hysteria and of dreams ... Freud introduced psychology into psychiatry ...'

In 1909, led by this interest in the psychic significance of pathological manifestations, Jung began to interpret and study as mythology the symbolism he found in his patients. He also acquired an insight into the significance of so-called parapsychological phenomena, discovering, for example, the synchronism in the (collective) unconscious. He 'felt' the psychological situation of a patient who committed suicide somewhere else. The interest in phenomena which play a great part in his later work thus appeared at a very early stage and was in line with the way in which he had tackled his work from the beginning.

From 1907 onwards he was in personal touch with Freud, who was also interested in Jung's publications. Jung defended Freud's basic position, but reports that he did not directly agree with him in his view that sexual trauma was the sole reason for repression and consequently for neurosis.

This divergence made an essential difference to their personal relationship. We can see from Jung's account (p. 173) that there were evidently unconscious tensions. Freud said about his own theory of sexuality: 'That is the most essential thing of all. You see, we must make a dogma of it, an unshakable bulwark.' 'He said that to me', Jung goes on, 'with great emotion, in the tone of a father saying, "And promise this one thing, my dear son: that you will go to church every Sunday."' One can understand what effect this had on Jung, with his rebellion against the father figure, dogma and the church. 'This was the thing that struck at the heart of our friendship.'

It appears that Freud was afraid of 'occultism' – of everything that philosophy, religion and parapsychology had learnt to say about the psyche; and it was this that was for Jung the really important thing. He even interpreted this as meaning that Freud obviously felt himself to be threatened by an eruption of unconscious religious factors. Or, to put it another way, the point at issue was again a father figure who seemed to be powerless. It came to the point – in Jung's interpretation – when Freud again fainted and, after Jung had carried him outside, 'In his weakness he looked at me as if I were his father' (p. 180). For Jung Freud quite obviously toppled off his pedestal at this point. This becomes even clearer when Jung a little later tells how, in a conversation about the interpretation of dreams, Freud refused to communicate particular details from his personal life, giving as his reason, 'I cannot risk my authority.' 'At that moment', Jung writes (p. 182), 'he lost it altogether.... Freud was placing personal authority above truth.'

Quite apart from the question of what really happened – and we shall probably never be able to establish that objectively – and apart too from the question of how Freud felt all this (Jones goes into that in detail in his biography) it must have become clear that Jung, with his difficult relationship to the father figure, was bound to react emotionally to these events. He himself says: 'Freud . . . meant to me a superior personality, upon whom I projected the father.'

According to Jung, it was the problem of interpreting incest in the history of religion that led to an open breach. He had been confronted with this problem in his study of sacrifice. For Freud the Oedipus complex, and with it the problem of incest, belonged to the heart of the whole neurosis problem, and hence to problems of religion as well. We must see this against the background of the Jewish and patriarchal pattern of his own civilization and family. But on p. 191 Jung writes (and here we must also remember his resistance to the paternal principle and his fascination by what was maternal and womanly – a fascination incidentally not unconnected with the Oedipus complex, in the Freudian view!):

> To me, incest signified a personal complication only in the rarest cases. Usually incest has a highly religious aspect, for which reason the incest theme plays a decisive part in almost all cosmogonies and in numerous myths.

This, therefore, if we see the matter rightly, is the point at which Freud and Jung also diverge in their view of religion. Freud continues to underline the paternal aspect in religion as well as elsewhere, and Jung stresses what is maternal. For Freud the unconscious, infantile religious elements have to be freed from their oppression, so that they can emerge into the rational consciousness, having been recognized as infantile. For Jung, on the other hand, the (collective) unconscious religious elements have to be brought into the light so that they can be incorporated into the conscious life and so that the one-sided rational element can be remoulded into something much richer and deeper. Freud took up an increasingly aloof and suspicious attitude to the unconscious, and consequently to religion as well. Jung, on the other hand, allowed himself to be increasingly absorbed by it; but at the same time we need only think of his relationship to the different churches and their representatives to see that he was eagerly searching for a new form of religion which was nothing other than the revivification of an ancient one, a religion which for him belonged within the framework of the collective unconscious. Freud thought that all this was merely 'mysticism', a word which on his lips could only have a highly derogatory meaning.

It is obvious that this fundamentally divergent approach was bound to crystallize out in a different relationship to dreams and to historical religious material. We have already indicated this. For Jung the dream is not the veiled wish fulfilment on which Freud and others laid such stress. It is not a façade. It is a part of nature, something that has to do with the collective unconscious and whose efficacy is connected with the archetypes which are present in that unconscious. We said earlier that at long range the basic views of the two men about dreams do not diverge as widely as they themselves thought; but in practice the long-range view led to great difficulties, particularly where their opinions about religious manifestations were concerned. Freud did not take so positive an attitude to the collective unconscious as Jung who, because of his doctrine of the archetypes, brought a strong and positive receptivity towards the motley mythological and gnostic material with which history presented him.

Jung forged far ahead along these lines. In his book he tells how he also acquired an increasing interest in all possible 'parareligious' phenomena, including alchemy. This went so far that he not only became full of unrest himself, but that he experienced all kinds of ghost-like manifestations in his own house: figures in white, bells that began to ring of their own accord, a ghostly choir in the rooms. It was only his scientific insight that enabled him to preserve a certain detachment from all this. But it is clear that in this sphere Jung was undoubtedly the diametrical opposite of Freud, whose suspicions must have been not entirely without foundation. At this period Jung felt that he was being forced to go through the processes of the unconscious himself – that is to say, he himself had to follow the path of individuation. Formally speaking, this was of course quite in conformity with Freud's autoanalysis, but the whole thing took a different course with Jung. He drew mandalas, for by means of these drawings he had to make his dreams a path leading to his own self; he did not arrive at his goal solely by way of the scientific approach.

This process lasted until about 1920. Jung himself (p. 225) writes about this period:

> The years when I was pursuing my inner images were the most important in my life – in them everything essential was decided. It all began then; the later details are only supplements and clarifications of the material that burst forth from the unconscious, and at first swamped me. It was the *prima materia* for a lifetime's work.

10. In this 'lifetime's work' – and here we come to the point which of course interests us most as theologians – the question at issue was always the problem of a philosophy of life, a *Weltanschauung*, as well as the confrontation of psychology with the problems of religion.

> It is only natural that I should constantly have revolved in my mind the question of the relationship of the symbolism of the unconscious to Christianity as well as to other religions (p. 236).

We have already discussed Jung's 1937 Terry Lectures in some detail and in this connection we cast a glance at the broad lines of his theory. In his autobiography we find the background to these theories in the processes of his own personal growth; and at the same time we see the links between this process and his other interests. As far as Christianity in its actual historical form is concerned, as well as the figure of Christ that stands at its centre, we can now understand what Jung means when he writes (p. 238) that 'the collective mentality of his time – one might also say: the archetype which was already constellated, the primordial image of the Anthropos – was condensed in him, an almost unknown Jewish prophet'. Religions in their concrete forms are crystallizations of the archetypes present in the collective unconscious.

We feel how close these ideas of Jung's are to the realities of his personal life when we absorb the impressions of his many journeys which he works into his book. These journeys in other continents were for him a confrontation with the living remains of the collective unconscious. Thus in North Africa he felt himself to be a European stamped by a rationalistic culture, who was threatened by the primitive unconscious that met him there. Among the Pueblo Indians he arrived at the gloomy certainty that knowledge does not make us richer, but alienates us more and more from the mystic world in which we were once at home. In Kenya and Uganda he was deeply impressed by 'the stillness of the eternal beginning' of creation; but at the same time he felt that for him the primitive meant danger. Deep within his soul there was a longing for consciousness. In India he avoided contact with 'holy men', feeling that he had to live from his own inner life and must not 'borrow'. He gained an impression of the way in which the psychological nature of evil was seen and integrated in the East. We have already mentioned how important this idea was for Jung. In Buddha he recognized the embodiment of the self, as he did in Christ. In Ravenna he was confronted with his anima and he almost drowned in the unconscious; but, he says in his book (p. 317), 'The integration of the unconscious contents made an essential contribution to the completion of my personality.' We can then well understand that when he was taking a ticket to Rome he fainted, out of fear that he might not be able to stand the whole thing. He never saw Rome.

We know that Freud was also afraid to go to Rome; but in his case it was because he did not want to anticipate his father, who had not yet been there (the Oedipus conflict!). So his journey to Rome was put off until he was an old man.

11. Finally let us turn to Jung's own ideas in the field of religion, and to the content of his own faith. He wrote about these things in the final section of his book. Here, in a special chapter, he discusses the problem of life after death. In his view we *know* practically nothing about it. It is true that we receive hints from the unknown, which we remould into

'myths'; and according to these myths there are such things as super-natural perceptions and supernatural possibilities. 'Consider synchronistic phenomena, premonitions and dreams that come true' (p. 333). A little further on he writes:

> True, the unconscious knows more than the consciousness does; but it is knowledge of a special sort . . . we are dependent for our myth of life after death upon the meagre hints of dreams and similar spontaneous revelations from the unconscious. As I have already said, we cannot attribute to these allusions the value of knowledge, let alone proof (pp. 343, 347).

According to Jung the process of individuation goes further. Here he is dependent on the indications which he gathers from dreams and the like. He admittedly finds the 'myth' of reincarnation and Karma alien, as he tells us; and this is in line with what we indicated above, namely that he did not want to 'borrow' from Indian wisdom but had to draw on his own inner life. This brings him to the problem which stands at the centre of this kind of religious interpretation, namely individuation. At the beginning of his book, as we have seen, Jung tells how he was split off from the eternal godhead, 'a splinter of the infinite deity'. It is of course part of the content of the individuation process that he should realize this in his own life.

> The decisive question for man is: Is he related to something infinite or not? That is the telling question of his life . . . In such awareness, we experience ourselves concurrently as limited and eternal, as both the one and the other. . . . As far as we can discern, the sole purpose of human existence is to kindle a light in the darkness of mere being. It may even be assumed that just as the unconscious affects us, so the increase in our consciousness affects the unconscious (pp. 356–8).

Or, to put it another way, we are a part of the divine life which strives out of the unconscious towards awareness. In accord with its strongest tendency, natural theology develops into theosophy, into a knowledge of the wisdom of God, into thinking about God in ourselves. With his often tentative thinking about the ultimate questions, Jung belongs to a very important tradition in human history. I would almost say that he stands on the battleground of the two great protagonists in the field of religion, Christianity and humanism, theology and (religious) philosophy.

It is not by chance that some of the great questions cast up by these contrasting ideas are continually discussed in 'Late Thoughts', the last chapter in the book, which was written by Jung himself. Here he is above all concerned with the problem of evil. Christian dogma's notion of a process of metamorphosis in the deity must, he considered, be thought through further. As a psychologist – and, I might add, as the adherent of a certain type of religion – he sees this as the becoming visible of the ground of the psyche. From this point 'the myth of the necessary in-carnation of God – the essence of the Christian message – can then be understood as man's creative confrontation with the opposites and their synthesis in the self, the wholeness of his personality' (p. 370). Jung mentions Nicholas of Cusa and Boehme in this connection, but there are undoubtedly ideas in his book which are related to Hegel. A further theme is the nature of religion, which we have already discussed above. 'Naive' faith talks about a God outside ourselves, but the thinking person knows that what is really in question is the relationship of man to 'the ground of his psyche', to himself: Jung goes on (p. 386):

> What the ego wills is subject in the highest degree to the interference, in ways of which the ego is usually unaware, of the autonomy and numinosity of archetypal processes. Practical consideration of these processes is the essence of religion, in so far as religion can be approached from a psychological point of view.

Finally (p. 387) he comes to talk about love – eros as the highest and deepest that a man can say about life and God. Remarkably enough, he does not use the word agape here. With great modesty ('Being a part, man cannot grasp the whole') and at the same time with a clear conscious-ness of the greatness of man, he writes impressively, entirely along the lines of the great thinkers of both West (Plato, Spinoza and Hegel) and East: 'We are in the deepest sense the victims and the instruments of cosmogonic "love".'

We have therefore been able to establish that there was a growing cleft in Jung's psychological work between two trends in his thinking. On the one hand we have the 'paternal' trend, with its church and theology, and on the other the 'maternal' trend, with its natural theology or, better, its theosophy. It is understandable that a man like Jung, with his passion for investigation and above all his desire to venture into the obscure depths of life in the course of that investigation, felt the need to think through the lines of this theosophy to the end in order to search out 'even the deep things of God' (I Cor. 2.10). He did this in a book which, as we can easily understand today, created a considerable furore when it appeared in 1952, his *Answer to Job* (*Collected Works*, Vol. 11). Let us look briefly at this book, in order to gain as complete a picture as possible of Jung's contribution to the discussion between depth psychology and theology.

Answer to Job is not easy reading. It is sometimes difficult to understand. It must be seen against the background of the alchemy and gnosis which Jung incorporated into his studies. Really, this is in my opinion a piece of theosophy which can best be compared with Hegel's work – or at least with the problems Hegel raises – although compared with Hegel it makes a somewhat dilettante impression and (because of Jung's use of material from the unconscious) a somewhat arbitrary one.

I would be inclined to set this book beside Freud's book about Moses. It seems as if at the end of their lives both psychologists felt the need to render an account of their relationship to the heart of things, or perhaps we should rather say, to the phenomenon which was for them a central one – the Bible. It is not improbable that for them the Bible was not merely one of the great books of Western civilization but was also and pre-eminently a book which, because of the figure which was for them central, forced them to consider the value and the truth of their life's work. It is no exaggeration to say that in their work both Freud and Jung hesitated to identify themselves with the traditions of their 'fathers'. Because of this Freud was constantly concerned with his relationship to Christianity. The two books we have mentioned are final reflections, as it were, about the great problem of their life and work – one might call them a final reckoning. How can we, with what we have discovered, give Moses and Christ (the book on Job is really about Christ) a place in our system? How can we 'explain' them, so to speak, thereby justifying our lives to our fathers? This is for both writers the keynote of their thinking. On the pages of his autobiography in which Jung is considering the mental growth of *Answer to Job*, he mentions his father more than once.

Jung reveals that he was led to this subject by dreams. These dreams make it plain that Jung understood the problem that was really at issue better than his father. It is the problem of suffering. Job in his suffering is for Jung a prefiguration of Christ and he traces the suffering back to the tragic contradiction in God.

In the preface to the book he terms his work an analysis of images which point to an X (the godhead). These images, in the meaning which Jung ascribes to them, are expressions of the soul. The primary concern is therefore with psychic phenomena, but also with the X, which is identical with the image but also transcends it. For Jung the significance of the book of Job is that it leads to a discussion within God himself. 'Job is no more than the outward occasion for an inward process of dialectic in God' (p. 378). In God's answer to Job, he expresses doubts of his own almighty power – justifiable doubts, because 'Yahweh had let himself be bamboozled by Satan!' (p. 379). Through Job, therefore, God becomes restless. For God cannot avoid his dark side, his unconscious, and project it on to Job. (In this context we remember the notion of the God who is coming into being, the idea hinted at in the closing section of the autobiography.) Jung puts it even more strongly: 'He has seen God's face and the unconscious split in his nature' (p. 396). We must confine ourselves to the broad line of the argument and we cannot therefore go into the extensive material which Jung draws upon to support his remarkable 'gnostic' interpretation. Jung sees belief in the pre-existent Sophia of the last centuries before Christ as being the approach of a great change. 'God desires to regenerate himself in the mystery of the heavenly nuptials . . . and to become man. . . . The real reason for God's becoming man is to be sought in his encounter with Job' (p. 397). The Virgin Mary, as 'the bride of God', is an incarnation of Sophia. Anyone who reads the Old Testament carefully, Jung says, continually discovers the tendency within God himself to become man. We really have to do with stages in the process of coming to awareness. This sentence and what follows clearly shows Jung's relationship to Hegel. 'It was only quite late that we realized (or rather, are beginning to realize) that God is Reality itself and therefore – last but not least – man. This realization is a millennial process' (p. 402). Christ is thus the answer to the encounter with Job which is necessary within the divine development. Moreover there is something particular about his death. 'The sacrificial death was a fate chosen by Yahweh as a reparation for the wrong done to Job on the one hand, and on the other as a fillip to the spiritual and moral development of man' (p. 410). This incarnation also takes place in the people who are called by the Holy Spirit to be the children of God. Christ is therefore the central point in the drama of God and creation. The book goes on to give Jung's views about the different New Testament writers and writings, as well as his opinion of later authors such as Eckhart and Boehme. For him it is an essential fact that there is a dialectic inherent in God: he must be loved but he must also be feared. This, according to Jung, lays a responsibility on man, especially contemporary man, with his atomic bomb and his chemical weapons; for it is in man that the solution of the antinomy has to take place. Man may no longer remain blind and unconscious. At the end Jung once more formulates the book's fundamental thesis: that the human process of individuation is essentially a divine one. We have already said above that this idea shows the point at which in Jung the therapist and Jung the believer are united.

Jung had many pupils, and some of them carried on his investigations in the field of religion. As an example of his school's methods here, we may take Erich Neumann's book *Dieptepsychologie en de ontwikkeling der religie* ('Depth psychology and the development of religion'). It shows that Jung's pupils followed their master's example in somewhat slavish fashion. (We noticed the same thing about Freud and his closest disciples. But from chapter 5 onwards we shall see that a new group began to emerge which carried on Freud's work in a critical and independent way, in the religious field as well as elsewhere. We shall not, however, be dealing with any of Jung's pupils in these chapters.) Neumann was a psychiatrist working in Tel Aviv. In a series called 'Movement round the Centre' he tried to develop a depth psychology of culture, and the book we have just mentioned is the first part of this series. (Earlier Neumann had already treated an ethical theme in *Depth Psychology and a New Ethic*.) His thesis is that the development of religion is really the development of man's becoming man. Man grows out of the unconscious into a situation in which he stands in close contact with that unconscious. It is a process of growth which began with the cave-men and continues down to our own times.

The headings of the three main chapters are significant. The first is 'The Psychological Significance of the Rite'. A few quotations may serve to show how close the author is to Jung. 'The ego which is active during the rite unites with the self which directs the cultic act;' or according to Hegel, the cult is 'really the eternal process in which the subject identifies itself with its essence'. This is a quotation which Neumann interprets as follows: 'Through close adherence to ritual rules the archetype is also held fast, and the danger is only averted because the archetype is admitted in the framework of a fixed form.' In the rite, therefore, there is an identification of the ego and the self – an idea which is in a way reminiscent of Hegel and is yet numinously charged. We find these ideas equally clearly in Jung as well.

The second chapter is headed 'The Mystical World and the Individual'. The subject here is solely the growth of the person into a conscious ego, as well as the importance that contact to the archetypes has in this context.

In the third chapter, 'Mystical Man', Neumann tries to show that man can arrive at selfhood through various stages of mysticism.

The book follows Jung's lines entirely, and really offers little that is new compared with Jung. The problem of individuation is the central one for Neumann too, and the ideas he develops about it are completely analogous to Jung's. Jung however shows more originality and daring in his publications.

4

Transition: a Provisional Survey

In chapters 5, 6 and 7 of this part of the book I shall try to show that, in
considering depth psychology's view of religion, we must distinguish
between two different periods.

The first came to an end with the death of the two great masters Freud
and Jung; in a certain sense the second already began while they were
still alive. As a whole series of their pupils went on developing psycho-
analytical work on the foundations laid by the two pioneers, they were
working in a changed cultural climate and had to do with different prob-
lems and different perspectives in the field of religion, which in turn led
them to different ideas in their work. At the moment we are in the middle
of the second period. It is a period of upheaval and of slowly growing self-
consideration.

In order to understand the particular character of this second period
better, let us list and discuss some important characteristics of the first
period, with which we are still concerned at the moment.

The first thing that has become obvious in this book is the fact already
mentioned that both the masters of psycho-analysis and their pupils
tended to try to come to terms with religion quite independently of
religious people – which sometimes meant, independently of the patients
they were treating. Freud always talks about 'religion' as a general
concept, and when he is dealing with particular religious phenomena (as
he is in *Totem and Taboo*) he confines himself to primitive peoples, who
were the centre of interest in his own time but who were not then – as
they were later – the object of an empirical research carried on *in situ*
and as extensively as possible. In his study of Moses, too, we do not come
across a single believing present-day Jew; instead Freud is dealing with
very risky hypotheses which are hardly open to the test of reality. Further-
more, on the basis of these hypotheses he is influenced so one-sidedly

by biology that he does not include any other possible explanations at all for the manifestations he deals with in his exposition. We find the same characteristics in the publications of Jones and Reik. There too their assertions are hardly tested at all against experience with their own patients; they continually work with material which belongs to the distant past and has become very remote from us; and the light which they throw on this material is drawn purely from psycho-analysis, in a very one-sided way. Pfister is really the only member of this group who goes to work empirically and critically.

As far as Jung is concerned, he does continually introduce living patients into his writings, but he does not do so in order to interpret their statements as cautiously and critically as possible, with the aim of finding the clue to their religious development and the problems involved in it. For him their dreams are rather the starting point or springboard for highly speculative and often only superficially tested theories. Consequently it is not surprising that a discussion between analysts and theologians about the theories developed during this period has not been very productive up to now. Not only was it difficult for theologians to take seriously the often bizarre-sounding statements made on the analytical side, but the way in which these assertions were arrived at seemed to them so arbitrary and so one-sided that – backed by the traditions of a century-old scholarship – they felt relieved of the necessity of investigating them at all.

I have in mind three factors which could, I think, contribute to a better understanding of this situation. And we must take these factors into account when we are considering the possibility of a discussion.

1. Freud and Jung lived at a period of general views and assertions in the cultural sphere. The nineteenth century, with its idealistic tendency, was imbued with the impulse to discuss general concepts in the form of philosophical proofs or semi-literary or semi-scientific treatises. People liked to talk about culture, romanticism, citizenship, and so forth. In this respect, therefore, Freud and Jung are clearly children of their time. There was no empirical research into particular manifestations in the field of religion and culture, as is the case today in sociology or cultural anthropology. It was a purely philosophical, literary or theological discussion that was in progress.

2. Not only the period but their own science in its youthful form easily led to a disregard of its proper limitations, as well as to the formulation of general statements. At the beginning of the scientific era, its practitioners felt themselves to be 'prophets', and they experimented

with their theories in contexts which were far removed from their direct spheres of research; and now the analysts did the same. The intoxication of the great adventure of a budding science played a big part here.

3. Freud, Jung and their first pupils were either brought up outside the church, or they had their own inner difficulties with the faith of their 'fathers'. They did not therefore know the participation which is essential for successful empirical research into human phenomena. This does not mean that only researchers with a positive attitude to religion or the church have the right to work in this field; but it does mean that a certain measure of sympathetic thinking and feeling is essential if one wants to achieve truly empirical research. Both detachment and attachment are necessary. At the beginning all that really happened was that questions were put to the theologians from a distance – questions which, because they did not spring from real participation, soon degenerated into reproaches and hence stood in the way of a discussion. The greatest readiness for participation can be sensed in Jung, but we have seen that in his case there were too many hindrances in the way for a true understanding to be arrived at, so that contact with the theologians was bound to lead to disappointment, as he was painfully forced to discover over his study of Job.

Another striking thing about this first period is the convincing way in which psycho-analysis is able to depict the important part played by the unconscious life of the soul in the build-up of the religious life. This, primarily, is the great hypothesis which psycho-analysis offers to theology as a subject for reflection; and it must be said that psycho-analysis itself – even at this period – presented impressive material for the confirmation of this hypothesis. Consequently our discussion will not have to concentrate on the hypothesis itself so much as on the limits of its applicability. Let me list a few points which can count as being already established.

1. It is above all a person's relationship to both parents which plays a decisive part in the unconscious psychic life. Neither Freud nor Jung conveys a clear picture of how this is reflected in the religious development of people in our own time. In Freud, however, it is at least clear that because of the material he is working with he is continually impressed by the relationship to the father figure; whereas Jung, according to his autobiography, experienced his own religious problems particularly in the light of his relationship to his mother. This is the point where a closer empirical investigation is most urgently needed.

2. In Freud, the investigation of religion comes to a head in two

problems: on the one hand feelings of guilt towards the father (the Oedipus complex) and on the other hand a feeling of security in being with him. Both these aspects continue to exist in religion as infantile problems unless they have been healthily resolved by the beginning of maturity. Indeed for Freud religion is a piece of collective immaturity.

3. Pfister points to another problem which can be associated with religion, namely the repressed sexuality which can become noticeable from time to time in the religious field and which really uses religion (its ideas, precepts and so forth) as a form of release. Generally speaking we can say that today theologians are prepared to see this as a real problem.

4. An important question which psycho-analysts asked the theologians in the first period was: how are we to view the religious life of primitive man? For them primitive man was extremely ambivalent, because his consciousness was not yet 'developed' and the unconscious life thus lay directly below the surface of the conscious one. In both Freud and Jung, therefore, interest in the myths and rites of primitive man plays a great part. In their view primitive man is neurotic in a 'healthy' way, so that we can continually link up his (religious) life with the symptoms which can be observed in neurotics. Even dogma can be seen under this aspect.

There are two things to be said here. First, at this period the student of the history of religions was not, and could not really be, familiar with these questions at all, whereas today we are bound to say that there undoubtedly really is a problem here. The question is whether cultural anthropologists (who view religion in the context of their cultural problems), see this problem in such a way that they provide the theologian with clearer connecting links. I believe that this is the case, even though the problem has not for them the fundamental and far-reaching effects that it had for Freud. There is no doubt that this is a problem deserving closer investigation. Furthermore, in the second period this problem apparently no longer stands in the foreground at all. It has simply been passed over; and this seems to me a pity.

5. Jung drew express attention to the impulse towards self-realization which is present in man and which determines his spiritual development. It is no exaggeration to say that it is with this impulse that man proves that he is a religious being, a *homo religiosus*. This urge is the 'driving power', as it were, of an inborn natural theology. We have pointed out that in this respect Jung is part of an important tradition of philosophical and religious thinking. Two things leap to the eye here. First of all we

gain the impression in Jung that religion is connected with the maternal ground of human life. We have already pointed out that this deserves closer investigation. And secondly, we discover in Jung that it is not easy to determine the relationship between 'natural' religion and a 'concrete' religion, which man meets in the form of some particular tradition (Christianity, for instance) and which in Jung is stamped by 'paternal' features. We come up against the same phenomenon here that we have just pointed to in paragraph 1 above. I shall be going a little deeper into the concept of natural religion at the end of this provisional survey, with a view to the following chapters, in which we shall come across the same problems.

6. The last questions which we have to ask ourselves with reference to this first period is: how far is the believer able to recognize himself in the picture which many analysts draw of him? He will probably be inclined to reject this picture, yet he must not avoid the question of whether there are not many believers who give occasion for a view of religion of this kind. This ought undoubtedly to be explicable through a closer contact with depth psychologists; and it connects up with the question of how these degenerations of religion are possible and how they are to be explained. Moreover we must not avoid the fundamental question: how far is every religion not, in part or in whole, the defence mechanism of particular human conflicts? Every depth psychologist, with his knowledge of the life of the human psyche, is bound to ask himself this question. It has become one of the main questions of our modern civilization. The theologian must recognize that the question is a justifiable one, and he must consequently be prepared for a genuine discussion with the psychologist. In such a discussion it is of course important how far the psychologist has, for the mind of the believer, an adequate picture of the nature of religion – and an adequate picture of *his* religion in particular.

Here it becomes clear yet again that the essential condition for a genuine conversation between the two disciplines is the analysis of concrete material drawn from the lives of contemporary people. And in this respect especially we shall be taking an important step forward in the second period. It will emerge there that when we come to the second generation we have to do with a different kind of analyst. The disciples have different interests from their masters. Moreover they are working in a different climate of opinion, for the two world wars have, after all, decisively influenced our views about civilization, about the human condition, and about faith and the church. This is true to some extent even in America, where the reaction against the churches and against belief which is so evident in Europe is, in general, far less noticeable.

Having come to the end of provisional survey, we shall now, as I have already indicated, go somewhat deeper into the concept of 'natural religion', or 'natural theology', and the problems which are inherent in it. We have already mentioned this concept several times, but a certain clarification is essential.

In my view we must distinguish between two types of religion in our Western civilization.

1. There is one type which we have to call 'natural religion' because it is a datum given *ab initio* with man *per se*: he arrives *by nature* at a positive relationship to the wholeness of life and the world in which he finds himself; and he wants to prove this, not only in what he does but also in what he says. In being *homo* at all, he is also *homo religiosus*.

This relationship is not wholly and simply a positive one. Man's place in the total pattern is bound up with all kinds of fears, feelings of guilt, uncertainties and doubts. Man must, so to speak, continually discover the path to the heart of his 'relationship', in order to find and maintain his place in the 'inexhaustible cohesion of life', to take a phrase used by my teacher Dr H. T. de Graaf, when he was trying to bring out the nature of religion.

The world of religion therefore contains rites, prayers, formularies, theories, etc., which are all in their own way an attempt to help man to find the path to the central core. Natural religion is to be found among primitive peoples, in higher religions such as Hinduism, and in various kinds of philosophical systems.

We know from psychological research (into which we shall be going more closely later) that a person's relationship to his parents (and especially to his mother) plays a great part in the development of this religion. It is built up on the foundation of a 'basic trust' proceeding from the person's relationship to his mother.

2. The other type of religion is the kind known to theological circles as revelatory religion. We find it in the Bible, in both the Old and the New Testament. Here man does not merely 'know' God by nature; he also has a relationship to him based on 'encounters' or 'revelations'. The I–Thou relationship, which Buber analysed so closely, combined with a personal image of God, is an essential feature of this kind of religion. Here man is the one who is called by God and addressed by him. One characteristic of this type of religion seems to me to be the fact that it

works with imagery, and often also with projections taken from the relationship to the father. We have already said that Freud maintained that religion *per se* could be explained by the problematical relationship to the father figure. For him feelings of guilt belong to the very nature of religion; and he believed that this whole nature, with everything it includes in the way of usages and dogmas, can be traced back to the problems of the Oedipus complex.

In our Western civilization both types of religion exist side by side. There is a 'philosophical faith' (Jaspers) and a Christian dogma. But the two influence and interpenetrate one another in the most varied way. One might almost say that the history of Christian theology is the history of the attempts made in every period to render a new account of the relationship between the two trends.

Both types can also be found, at least potentially, in the personal life of the individual as well. The second type develops round about the age of six or seven, on the foundation of basic trust, but influences stemming from the first type naturally make themselves felt in the background. We still know very little about the ramifications of this influence, but we are already in a position to set up a number of working hypotheses about it. I myself have made a modest beginning here with my 'sketch of a normal religious development', which is to be found in the appendix to my book *Problemen rond het ziekbed*.

For the philosophical and theological aspects of the relationship between the two types, perhaps I may refer readers to my study *Het christelijk humanisme van Dr H. T. de Graaf*; for this relationship plays an important part in Dr de Graaf's work.

The Second Period

5

Rümke on Belief and Unbelief

In 1939 H. C. Rümke (then Professor of Psychiatry at the University of Utrecht) published a book which was later translated as *The Psychology of Unbelief. Character and Temperament in relation to Unbelief.* This book (which appeared in a series called 'The Psychology of Unbelief') gave a new accent to depth psychology in its bearings on religion. Rümke is not a psycho-analyst in the strict sense of the word, but in his work he quite obviously employs the basic psycho-analytical viewpoints, and his thinking is a constant critical coming to terms with analysis. This is a reason for us to examine and discuss the ideas which he develops as a contribution to the development of depth psychology's view of religion.

The problem with which Rümke deals is the unbelief which, as we know, exists parallel to belief. How can it be explained? Is it a question of human disposition, so that one person reaches belief on the basis of the characteristics he has inherited, whereas another arrives at unbelief because of different inherited characteristics? Or are belief and unbelief connected with the individual's life history, with his character – that is to say with the 'upper genetic structure' which develops out of deeplying experiences deriving from early childhood and later not absorbed, or only partly so?

We can say that for Freud belief is a disturbance of human development, a sticking fast, as it were, in immature patterns of feeling and behaviour. Belief, therefore, is the revelation of a still infantile character. That is the working hypothesis from which he starts and which he maintains is confirmed by research. Rümke raises the question whether we cannot start from another hypothesis, namely that it is unbelief, not belief, which is an interruption to development – in other words, that unbelief is caused by certain disturbances on the road to maturity. We must understand what Rümke means by this. He does not mean that there is not such a thing as immature, still infantile belief; belief of this kind can undoubtedly be demonstrated. Only – this is not belief in the true sense of the word.

Rümke's working hypothesis is: there is a *homo religiosus*. Religion is part of the normal structure of human life. But during the years when he is coming to maturity man can be led astray by a great variety of hindrances to his development, and he can thus fall victim to unbelief. Often it is a question of disturbances which take place in the unconscious (and here Rümke is moving within the framework of depth psychology); these can only be deprived of their power when they are lifted into the consciousness. Hence for Rümke, within the limits of this problem, unbelief is not (or perhaps it would be better to say, not as a rule) a matter of the understanding, which would be open to discussion; it is something in which man is led by unconscious motives – in spite of rational arguments, which then have the effect of rationalizations. The aim of Rümke's investigations is to prove the existence of a number of unconscious motivations which he believes he has discovered. He thinks that his hypothesis explains the phenomenon of belief and unbelief better than Freud's, and he stresses here with some emphasis that there can be no question of a particular prejudice or bias. Of course prejudice exists in the strict sense of the word, but that applies equally to the contrary view.

From the side of depth psychology (for I really believe that this is the field in which Rümke is working) the most important step forward here is that the discussion about religion is moving expressly in the framework of scientific research and the building up and testing of hypotheses. Emphasis no longer lies on observations about civilization and the role which religion plays there, as is tacitly the case with Freud. These observations are certainly based on analytical research work, but they cannot be tested against specific cases. Rümke really wants to bring out the fact that a discussion about religion is a discussion about actual people, and has to be tested against the lives of these people. For anyone who is particularly alive to alterations in the climate of opinion, which are reflected in changing views, it will be clear that this essay of Rümke's heralds a revolution.

Now the way in which Rümke defines belief is of course important, and so is the way in which he arrives at his definition – namely through his own experience. This would not matter if he then went on to enquire whether his experience agrees with the experience of other people whom he thinks are believers. Unfortunately he does not do this. The result is that the book has a very one-sided point of departure, i.e., the author's own beliefs; or, to put it another way, the book is based on a certain theological view, and it is by no means certain whether it is a view that corresponds to the reality of other types of belief – indeed, as a theologian, I would doubt whether it does. Convinced though we are about the great importance of this study for the development of the idea of religion among depth psychologists, its fundamental weakness cannot be overlooked. And, as we shall see, this weakness takes its revenge on the writer. Rümke writes (p. ix):

> If we define 'belief' as something we consider true, something we are in agreement with regardless of being unable to supply a sufficiency of intellectual reasons for it, we may immediately conclude that there are no people who do not believe. The whole of life is based on a trustful belief.

Man, he says, allows himself to be led by his instincts or his intuition. He is then also able (p. x) to agree with Monakow 'when he speaks of a "religious instinct", though I would prefer "intuition" because of its religious rather than its biological sense'.

In my opinion we are here moving, theologically speaking, in the sphere of 'natural religion', i.e., in the realm of the faith which belongs to man by reason of his disposition or his nature. I even have the impression that what Rümke is talking about is the 'basic trust' which is so frequently mentioned in present-day psycho-analysis and which man has to retain from his very first contacts with his mother. It would be in accord with this that, according to Rümke, a truly unbelieving attitude can only be a pathological condition. There is undoubtedly such a thing as natural religion. We are familiar with it, for example, in the philosophical and theological form it takes in Karl Jaspers; and in his book *The Perennial Scope of Philosophy* Jaspers expresses this faith in what is, in many respects, a fascinating way. But we also see clearly from Jaspers that natural religion does not cover all kinds of religious belief. He himself devoted a detailed study to this problem in *Philosophical Faith and Revelation*. The belief that rests on 'revelation', which is not therefore given *ab initio* with our human existence but which lives from 'special' contacts with the divine mystery (and this is the belief which is characteristic of the Christian faith in its various nuances), is not covered by the definition which Rümke chooses as the starting point for his book. He himself apparently senses that there are difficulties here, for he writes (p. ix):

> Many may find I have given too little attention to unbelief in relation to specifically defined Christian doctrines. I can only explain that by the fact that my research into this form of religious experience has not yet sufficiently progressed to be worth recounting.

Let us now pursue the main lines of Rümke's further arguments, going directly into a number of points which are important in the context of our investigation.

After discussing his starting point – his working hypothesis that 'unbelief is an interruption in development' – Rümke throws a quick glance at the place of faith in the child's life. He distinguishes different stages, such as non-separation, anthropomorphic explanation, the animistic-magic phase, the intellectual-rationalistic phases, etc. It strikes me that he does not bring out the continuity of these childish stages with adult religion. But the continuity must not be overlooked, particularly if one is trying to trace disturbances in development; it is an important factor. It is true that in his book Rümke makes various statements about the points where disturbances can arise, and the reason for them (for example a wrong kind of bond with the father); but in my opinion this is all very insufficient. If I see the matter rightly, the insufficiency is connected with the fact that in his presentation of belief the author does not make a proper picture of the connection between 'basic trust' and the attacks on that basic trust which the child has to absorb in the various stages he describes; nor does he take account of the influences to which the child is exposed during the formation of its 'basic trust'. I am thinking in the first case about the whole problem of 'emancipation' (emancipating oneself from the parent figures), which plays such an important part in modern psycho-analysis and which Winnicott, for example, connects with his theories about 'transitional objects'. And in the second case I am thinking of the talk about God, heaven, etc., which is part of religious education. We know very little as yet about what goes on in the child's psyche, and it is clear that a great deal of research needs to be done here.

Rümke distinguishes between religion and belief, but there is a transition from religion to belief and especially from immature to mature belief – a transition which takes place in various stages. Here too we find that although Rümke recognizes the difference between two kinds of belief, he hardly goes into the difference at all. He certainly says that he sees two ways which lead to a true experience of belief, the way of direct religious experience, and the way via 'the shapes behind the words'; and this distinction is also linked with the difference between religion and belief in revelation. But here too Rümke by-passes the problems that become evident. The point is undoubtedly a correct one, but in considering the first approach we ought to ask whether there really are experiences of the kind he visualizes, without any images or 'shapes'. Of course these images will fade, but the nature, the spirit, the secret, the totality (De Graaf) or the comprehensive (Jaspers) in these experiences are more than mere concepts; they serve to preserve the experience by means of their 'pictorial' character. It is not by chance that Jaspers gives the 'ciphers' such an important place in his thinking.

And on the other hand, what words does Rümke really mean? Obviously, it would seem, the Christian words God, heaven, etc. There really is a phase in a child's life in which 'shapes' emerge behind these words, shapes through which the words come alive, as it were. But the problem that crops up here is: how are we to conceive of the child's growing up with 'basic trust', its growing out of that trust, and its trust in God. Rümke comes up against this problem through the way in which he proceeds.

Rümke's basic idea, therefore, is that the life of man displays a development. According to his further hypothesis, man has to go through seven stages in the course of this development. But he can always be hindered from healthy growth by various disturbances, and of course he can stand still at some particular stage. One difficulty in Rümke's exposition at this point is that he interprets this development genetically, but without going so far as to localize the developmental stages as well. Consequently the whole thing makes a somewhat confused impression and is doubtless open to dispute at various points. It becomes evident, however, that in his view every stage of religion or belief is matched by a corresponding stage of lack of religion or unbelief. We will now look briefly at his account of the seven stages, adding a few clarifying or critical observations at the same time.

At the first stage man feels himself 'meaningfully linked up with the whole of being' (p. 1). In Rümke's opinion this pegs out the foundations on which belief rests, with its initially still undeveloped but later more differentiated forms. This experience does not consciously emerge until puberty, according to Rümke. In fact what he means by this formulation is a 'personally acquired religious feeling', the existence of which can only be very cautiously deduced in the small child. We have to enquire, however, whether this more or less mature experience is not connected genetically with some experience – perhaps an unconscious one – in early childhood. We saw that in the 'primitive belief' of the child Rümke saw among other things an animistic-magic as well as a – later – intellectual-rationalistic phase, which he does not, however, connect with later developments. The question is whether these phases do not represent the development of basic trust, to which we also drew attention above, and whether we should not interpret this first step as being in continuity with that. Does this not also give Monakow's religious 'instinct', to which Rümke refers – the intuition 'which is directed towards relations with the whole' – a clearer and more acceptable place in man's entire development?

Rümke points to one important aspect of this experience: it presupposes the possibility of seeing things through the medium of symbols; something in the external world becomes a 'symbol', that is to say, an expression of a 'meaning' which is not capable of adequate logical formulation. 'Contemplation of nature is very often the first and strongest incitement to this religious experience' (p. 4). There are, however, people to whom 'it is not given . . . to see these symbols', who are denied an experience of this kind and who will hence have difficulty with this kind of primary belief.

It is certainly true that the symbol plays an important part in 'natural religion'. We have already drawn attention to Jasper's 'cyphers'. Rümke himself reminds us of what Jung has to say about the concept of symbol, and since the publication of his autobiography we know how deeply this was bound up with his thinking in terms of 'natural religion'. But we are faced with the question, what significance can we attach to this symbolic knowledge that we are meaningfully incorporated in the whole? What meaning does it have? Here the great thinkers – we can think of Plato, Spinoza, Hegel and Jaspers, but also of a theologian like H. T. de Graaf, or a devout Hindu – point to *love*. In love the secret of the whole is revealed and in love man identifies himself with that secret. We remember Spinoza's *amor intellectualis Dei*. Would it not seem obvious to look here for continuity with the 'basic trust' which comes into being in the earliest contacts between mother and child? Continuity, not in the sense that natural religion is nothing more than the prolongation of the infantile, libidinous stage, but in the sense that this trust is the precondition for a personal experience of the *amor intellectualis* we have mentioned.

Rümke makes clear what he means by his working hypothesis at the end of the chapter (and with this we shall conclude our discussion of the first stage). He asks (p. 6) 'which psychological factors may prevent the happening of the experience' and may accordingly promote 'unbelief'? The disturbances for which we have evidence can in part be rooted in the person's temperament; and in part they can be the result of neurotic complications. Here Rümke names blindness to symbols (which we have already mentioned) as well as undue stress on the intellect, and the suppression of particular feelings. In our present book we are more concerned with the broad lines of Rümke's argument than with the details of its development, so we shall not take up the finer points.

At the second stage 'the whole of being is felt as the primary cause of all being'. The tendencies which began to emerge at the first stage are developed further and the possibility of 'rest and support' in the whole now appears more clearly; but at this stage the person can be hindered by the atrophy of this conception.

At the third stage 'the primary cause is realized as the cause of my being'. A *personal* relationship begins to make itself felt, and many people feel an aversion to the dependence which is inherent in that relationship. Now doubt begins as well. For Rümke doubt has a positive meaning and it must not therefore be suppressed. This is followed by the fourth stage: 'The primary cause is God.' Here, according to Rümke (p. 19), we arrive at a personal I–Thou relationship of belief. 'From this moment onward the word "belief" gets the full meaning given to it by century-long tradition.' I doubt whether Rümke is correct in saying this. In the 'century-long tradition' the word God stands for 'the God who addresses man'. Rümke arrives at the word God because, on the basis of our own, personal human nature, 'it is difficult to realize this primary form of living, this real being human, as otherwise than personal'. Here, in his opinion, two paths coalesce, the path of direct experience and the path of 'the shapes behind the words'. But we have already pointed out that his second path is really the path of religious instruction in the 'century-long tradition', i.e., in 'belief in revelation'. There is no doubt at all that the religiosity of many people does consist of the union of the two elements which Rümke describes. But we must note that it is a matter of two elements which are really mutually exclusive. It is even the question whether for Rümke the necessity for the rational element exists. In the spiritual climate of natural religion, the personal element is generally felt to be a limitation, an anthropomorphism, which one is probably forced to use in the language of belief but which it would be better to replace by 'supra-personal predicates'. Here, as we said earlier, we come up against one of the central problems of theology and of personal devotion. There is no doubt that both types of religion exist and that they can even exert an influence on a person simultaneously. We can also observe that not only theology but every individual as well tries more or less consciously to come to terms with the relationship of the two, whether it be by means of a synthesis (Rümke's solution here, for example) or whether it be through an antithesis – the path taken in the dialectical theology of Karl Barth and his school. What we meet in

Rümke can perhaps best be viewed as a proof that our thinking about God, which is stamped by a century-old, living tradition, shows a tendency to settle down in the forms created by the religion which is part of our human nature.

In referring to this stage, Rümke points to the problems which are psychologically imposed with the Christian education of the child's early years. He believes (p. 21) that

> religious education between the age of seven and the beginning of puberty can only have some value if teaching is done by means of words . . . The words remain with them all through life, in the course of which they become laden with meaning.

It will be permissible to presuppose here that for Rümke puberty is of decisive importance. I have the distinct impression that the course of this development is somewhat more complicated than what Rümke describes. We have already indicated that there is continuity with the years of childhood; and Rümke underestimates this. If I see the matter rightly, about the age of eight 'basic trust' becomes separated from the parents, and the child experiences the whole of 'life' or 'the world' (together with the problems of trust and mistrust) more consciously. Here the figure of the Creator, the providing Father, already emerges from behind the word God, which the child knows from his contact with his parents.

We do not want to enter into too much detail so I will only mention that obstacles can arise at this stage too. Rümke mentions lack of intelligence as well as insufficient independence.

He goes on (p. 25) to characterize the succeeding, fifth stage as follows: 'The urge is felt for obedience to God, the primary cause, and responsibility for guilt towards him. God demands complete surrender.' At this stage, therefore, the Other apparently becomes related to the Other who confronts man. Rümke sees this as 'the difference between a metaphysical and a religiously delineated picture of the world'.

In a relationship of this kind it then also becomes possible to talk about guilt and feelings of guilt. According to Freud, Rümke says, feelings of guilt play an essential role in religion. Religion is a residue of infantile life, in that guilt with regard to the father's demands goes on acting. We have already described this in our discussion of Freud.

Rümke counterposes that the religion of many people is certainly fed by infantile desires but that 'an infantile pseudo-belief, based on innate emotion and a sharp imagination, is something totally different from a mature belief' (p. 28).

Rümke points to a series of obstacles at this stage which are partly understandable in the light of what has been said. First of all they are obstacles which arise from the fact that 'the God-image was hidden by the father-image and its related imagery' (p. 34). We will not follow the author into all the intricacies of his somewhat detailed account here. We will simply mention the possibility that excessive narcissism may be an obstacle which makes it hard for a person to surrender himself entirely to God. Excessive individualism is allied to this. It prevents us from integrating ourselves or from recognizing our guilt. Finally there is also the obstacle of fear; here Rümke particularly stresses fear of passivity, which really does hinder the potentialities of religion, although we can occasionally also see it as a flight into a 'pseudo-belief'.

In this chapter the author as it were lays bare the fundamental pattern of his 'belief'; and it is remarkable that he should so strongly underline surrender as an essential element. It is no exaggeration to imagine that his own type of (natural) religion is recognizable here. Surrender is in line with 'basic trust'. And the fact that Rümke expresses himself with such remarkable vagueness about the problems of guilt and feelings of guilt is connected with this. Basically, he makes no clear distinction between the two things. But in the other type of belief – revelatory religion, or the dialogistic I–Thou relationship – it is not a question of feelings of guilt; it is a matter of objective guilt, which can be forgiven and expiated. Rümke does not discuss this element of belief at all.

He calls the sixth stage 'the approach to an attitude of surrender. The demand is considered urgent, but gives no clear sense of direction.' He thinks that the state of belief of people who are believers in principle, but who can make relatively little of their belief, is a common one. It would seem to be a kind of lukewarmness, but this is not always the case. One does not get any further, but feels unsatisfied. Various factors could play a part here: feebleness of intuition, a certain weakness of character, lack of religious observance, ignorance (which often conceals something like hate), doubt arising from the problem of suffering in the world, unwillingness to be duped (e.g., Nietzsche and many modern intellectuals) and the lack of readiness to enter into any compromise.

At the final stage 'demand and surrender become fundamental rules of life'. It is a demand that only a few can meet. Here the greatest impediment is human sensuality. Basically, in this formulation Rümke is postulating an ideal of holiness in the context of his type of religion. Man here meets the demands of openness, humility and poverty. And 'the last important step forward towards total surrender is also thwarted by our earthly links', above all by wife and children.

Perhaps I may make a few observations here.

1. I hope that it has become clear that in Rümke's book we are dealing with a particular view of belief. Rümke understands by religion the type which theology defines as 'natural religion'. It is a form of religion which does actually exist and there are undoubtedly many people who will recognize themselves in this book, or who will perhaps rediscover a particular facet of their faith in it. But the great concepts which – because they rest on the foundations of biblical faith – are the central concepts in the Christian churches and in the Christian tradition are missing: concepts like forgiveness, redemption, reconciliation, thanksgiving, etc., are not to be found; and indeed the book in general contains little Christian 'vocabulary'. I am thinking of 'the kingdom of God', for example, or solidarity, or community, or church, and so on. In this book as in his other publications, Rümke shows how close he is to the thinking of Jaspers, who can certainly be termed one of the greatest representatives of natural religion in modern times. But this does not mean that there are not Christian elements in Rümke as well. At the climaxes of his account there are pointers to Christ, to the Bible, and to the great figures of church history. This type of belief has a meaning for him as well. In any discussion with depth psychology the greatest attention should be paid to this point about the relationship between the two types of belief which play so important a part in our modern world and which can never be found without any relationship at all to one another. We therefore discover that even for Rümke, anxious though he is to do justice to the particular character of religion, the psychology of our time still has far too little insight into the special character of the traditional Christian faith, in which the I–Thou relationship, for example, is an essential aspect.

2. As we have already mentioned, Rümke's division into stages leaves us uncertain whether the division coincides with a genetic developmental sequence, and if so where. Consequently much in his account remains unclear, psychologically speaking. If a discussion between theology and depth psychology is to bring results, then depth psychology must be able to tell us what it can contribute, in the present state of our knowledge, to what we know about the genetic development of religion.

3. The importance of Rümke's study, therefore, does not seem to me to lie so much in what he can offer in the way of content. Its significance is rather that he develops his working hypothesis (unbelief is an interruption to development) in the field of religious psychology, proving its

applicability through his account. He shows that in the framework of depth psychology there is another empirical way of access to the phenomenon of religion which is both possible and fruitful. His book heralds a revolution; a new beginning has been made.

6

Erich Fromm

Erich Fromm is the author of a number of books in which psycho-analytical points of view are applied to different spheres of our culture; but he cannot be called a psycho-analyst in the strict sense of the word. There is no doubt that he is a follower of Freud, but he does not belong to the inner circle – indeed he is a kind of dissenter. In *Sigmund Freud's Mission* (a book which does not seem to me to be particularly successful), he has even spoken his mind pretty critically about his master. But he has followed up certain aspects of Freud's work more than most of the people who are closer to Freud in other ways. Fromm is particularly interested in the political and spiritual problems of the modern world and he likes to write about them in the 'prophetic spirit' which we also come across in Freud himself; but he is more than a preacher. The field in which he moves ranges from modern democracy (and also National Socialism) to marriage and love, morality and religion. His books are characterized by the same strongly humanistic view of man which we can also find in the background of Freud's work. But Freud did not use that view as a kind of creed. Indeed he often hid behind all kinds of theories which outwardly did not appear particularly humanistic at all.

Because of his humanistic view of man, Fromm also arrives at different notions about religion from Freud. The book in which he is exclusively concerned with the basic problems of religion appeared in 1950 with the title *Psychoanalysis and Religion*, whereas *The Dogma of Christ* is the title essay of a collection he published in 1963. We shall look in some detail at the first of these books especially.

Its first chapter is headed 'The Problem'. In it Fromm maintains the idea that man is by nature a defenceless being who is unable to help himself simply by the aid of reason, as the Enlightenment wrongly supposed. In this situation the psycho-analyst can be viewed as a 'physician of the soul', a function performed by the priests in ancient Egypt and by the philosophers among the Greeks. 'As a physician of the soul he is concerned with the very same problems as philosophy and theology: the soul of man and its cure' (p. 15). For Fromm psychoanalysis and religion are not irreconcilable opposites, as they are with Freud; but they are not an 'identity of interests' either, as many people naively assume. The direction in which his thoughts are moving emerges from the chapter's closing passage:

> The psychoanalyst is in a position to study the human reality behind religion as well as behind non-religious symbol systems. He finds that the question is not whether man returns to religion and believes in God but whether he lives love and thinks truth. If he does so the symbol systems he uses are of secondary importance. If he does not they are of no importance.

After what we have already discussed above, we do not need to point expressly to the fact that these words bring out the problem of the relationship between natural religion, basic trust (here formulated as 'to live love and to think truth') and the specific historical religions (which Fromm calls religious symbol systems). Fromm formulates the problem in a way which is familiar in philosophy as well. We are forcibly reminded of Hegel, but we shall see that the principle just cited does not afford Fromm adequate insight into the reality of specific religions, and above all the biblical type of revelatory religion. At the same time, by pleading for a natural religion (or rather a humanistic one) in the context of depth-psychology's thinking about religion, Fromm undoubtedly takes an important step forward compared with Freud.

In Chapter II Fromm first of all deals with the positions taken up by Freud and Jung. Freud saw religion as a danger for man in his helplessness. Man depends on infantile illusions and does not dare to think critically about faulty attitudes. But Fromm points out clearly how we ought to view the matter. Freud's criticism of religion is connected with his declared ideals about brotherly love, truth and freedom. Or, to put it another way, Fromm sees a 'religious' core in Freud which (as we already noted from another angle) goes back to the Jewish tradition which is coming alive in an unorthodox way.

In contrast, Fromm rejects Jung's ideals about religion entirely. 'Jung reduces religion to a psychological phenomenon and at the same time elevates the unconscious to a religious phenomenon' (pp. 27f.). This blunt sentence is probably incontrovertible, after all that we have said about Jung. In addition Fromm criticizes Jung's standpoint because he stuck fast in a relativism which 'though on the surface more friendly to religion than Freud's, is in its spirit fundamentally opposed to religions like Judaism, Christianity, and Buddhism' (p. 23).

Chapter III is the most detailed of all and it also gives us a good insight into Fromm's point of view. It is entitled 'An Analysis of some Types of Religious Experience'. Like Rümke, Fromm here tries with the help of living material to develop the main points of view which determine his judgment about religion.

For Fromm, again along Rümke's lines, religion is a phenomenon which is deeply rooted in man: indeed it belongs to the nature of man *per se*. Its function is to help man to find unity in living. Man 'has to strive for the experience of unity and oneness in all spheres of his being. Devotion to an aim, or an idea, or a power transcending man such as God, is an expression of this need for completeness in the process of living.'

There are many types of religion. The criterion which Fromm applies to them is their respective contributions to man's development. 'The question is not *religion or not* but *which kind of religion*, whether it is one furthering man's development, the unfolding of his specifically human powers, or one paralysing them' (p. 34). He therefore supports a humanistic type of religion and rejects all others, indeed he attacks them. Equally, in the political sphere he rejects National Socialism and supports a *humanistic* policy. For him – and this is the significant thing – the very core of humanism as an attitude to life is religious, even though that core is manifested more clearly in the form of human idealism. To practise politics can therefore in his eyes become religion, through the way in which it is done. This is the point of view from which he judges the different types of religion which have been passed down historically. As a psycho-analyst he maintains a new and important point of view in this context. His thesis is: anyone who studies neurosis discovers that he is employed in the study of religion. 'We can interpret *neurosis as a private form of religion*, more specifically, as a regression to primitive forms of religion.' There is a whole series of these primitive neurotic forms in our Western society: father or mother fixations, compulsive neurosis, totemism (Fascism), the cult of cleanliness, etc. There is a considerable difference between these religions and true religion. These types give man a feeling of isolation, whereas the genuine great religions had the function of preserving man from a regression of this kind. But here we must differentiate. Not every religion of our time fulfils this function equally well. Measured against the criterion we have just named, certain types fall below the level; they have not in Fromm's opinion escaped neurotic influence.

86

He demonstrates this from the distinction between authoritarian and humanistic religion, which is for him particularly important. In his eyes Calvinism is an example of the first type. Fromm shares the negative judgment of many psycho-analysts about Calvinism, but he forgets the need to distinguish between the unmistakable fact that Calvinism plays on certain neurotic needs on man's part, and the fact that there are demonstrably mature Calvinists where there can be no question of a neurotic religious life.

In the authoritative type of religion man sees himself as small over against an almighty God. Fromm quotes Calvin in this context, for whom humility is 'unfeigned submission of a mind overwhelmed with a weighty sense of its own misery and poverty'. There is no fundamental difference between this and Fascism, which can be called an authoritarian secular religion.

Humanistic religion turns on the experience of oneness with the All, on truth, love and self-realization. The centre of humanistic religion is man and his strength. We meet it in early Buddhism, in Taoism, in Isaiah, Jesus, Socrates and Spinoza.

It is evident that Fromm knows too little about revelatory religion as a type and too little about the Protestantism of the Reformers, among whom he thinks he can only discover a stress on the 'powerlessness' of man. His own humanistic religion, to which he refers in the passage just mentioned, is related to Jaspers' philosophical faith, to which we have already referred at several points.

We cannot reproduce Fromm's evidence in all its details. We will simply briefly mention that he believes that he can show the existence of the two trends he has indicated in both the Old Testament and Christianity from the very beginning. In this connection he points especially to the mystical thinking which he holds to be one of 'the most potent expressions' of humanistic religion in Christian and Jewish history. For the theologian, however, he clearly presents things in too simple a light.

What Fromm has to say as a psycho-analyst about the two types is of course important. Authoritarian religion is in his view masochistic. Man projects everything good in himself on to God, thus becoming alienated from himself. This is not chance; it is connected with the structure of the society in which man lives. Fromm had already developed these ideas earlier, in his percipient essay on 'The Dogma of Christ', to which we shall be returning in a moment. For the analyst, theological systems are rationalizations, in the case of authoritarian religion, fear of standing alone: 'Man by origin is a herd animal . . . Inasmuch as we are sheep, there is no greater threat to our existence than to lose this contact with the herd and to be isolated' (p. 65). That is why we instinctively follow the leader. But in addition we are men who long for freedom and independence. There are 'religious doctrines' which set freedom and human development in the centre by revealing their striving for love, truth and justice. We have already said where Fromm thinks these are to be found.

Against this background Fromm goes on to give an account of the psycho-analyst's work as a 'physician of the soul' (ch. IV). The goal of psycho-analysis is not so much to meet the demands of social adjustment as to help in man's self-realization. We can leave the question open whether to oppose the two things in this way is not somewhat of an exaggeration, and point to the fact that this 'cure of the soul' has for Fromm a religious function, even if it often leads to a criticism of theistic dogma. He terms it a help to the patient in reaching a (humanistic) religious attitude to life. Rümke has expressed similar ideas too at different times. Psycho-analysis strives towards truth and towards freedom (above all from neurotically incestuous ties with other people, but also with the tribe, the state and the party; freedom, that is to say, from the pattern of life which Freud designates with the Oedipus complex). According to Fromm, the transition from incest to freedom is to be found in all the great religions. In this connection he points first to Buddhism and to Jewish prophecy. The tragedy of these religions in his opinion is that they fall back when they turn into mass organizations. Here I may remark that Fromm is apparently no exception to the phenomenon that many modern intellectuals (and often analysts too) turn away from the church but have a certain vague preference for Buddhism.

What Fromm considers to be a special mark of psycho-analysis in this context is that it tries to help the patient to achieve, or to achieve once more, his capacity for living; the capacity, that is to say, not only to be loved but also to love 'productively' himself. Humanistic religion also knows a personal sense of sin and guilt. Here Fromm rejects the notions of authoritarian religion, which rest on the fear of punishment. 'Sin is not primarily sin against God but sin against ourselves . . . The reaction to awareness of guilt is not self-hate but an active stimulation to do better' (pp. 93f.). In the context of the particular type of religion which we have termed in this book 'natural' religion, this view is clearly a tenable one; but it seems equally clear to me that it does not do justice to the nature of the sense of sin and guilt in 'dialogistic' or 'revelatory' religion. Fromm himself demonstates how difficult it is, apparently, for the psycho-analyst to judge this type fairly.

He then expounds the idea that the aim of analysis is the discovery of an attitude to life which one can view as being a moral attitude, as being prayer in religion. To the typical religious sphere he assigns 'the wondering, the marvelling', the consciousness of an 'ultimate concern' (Paul Tillich), as well as an experience of 'oneness', elements which ought not to be lacking in a good psychotherapy.

The final chapter deals with the subject, 'Is Psychoanalysis a Threat to Religion?' and is therefore concerned exclusively with the relationship between the two. As we might expect, Fromm answers the question in the negative. In a certain sense the opposite is true, psycho-analysis can contribute much to the realization of a religious attitude to life, in the sense which he has given to it in previous chapters. At the same time we must distinguish between certain things. First, if we assert that the important thing in religion is 'feeling and devotion . . . a concern with man's soul and the unfolding of his powers of love and reason' (p. 104), then it is not science that is a danger to religion; it is what Fromm characteristically calls the 'marketing orientation'. He means the 'selling oneself' which has to hide an inner emptiness. Secondly, when religion relinquishes its claim to be a 'quasi-science' and confines itself to its own real domain, namely the development of a true attitude to life, no science can endanger it. Thirdly, from the analytical side objections to the ritual aspect of religion have often been raised, and rightly so; but we must not forget that ritual which fulfils the deepest needs of man can also be rational, as well as a meaningful symbolic action. Fourthly, the symbolic language discovered by psycho-analysis leads to 'a new appreciation of the profound and significant wisdom expressed by religion in symbolic language' (p. 118).

If we can talk at all about a threat to religion through psycho-analysis, we have to ask – a threat to which aspect of religion? Fromm is not thinking about the symbol God at this point. The struggle about the existence or non-existence of God 'blocks the understanding of the religious problem as a human problem'. The conflict is not between theism and atheism but between humanistic religion and idolatry; and what counts as being Christian faith is often pure idolatry. It is not chance that the Old Testament has such an undefined concept of God. 'We can unite in firm negation of idolatry and find perhaps more of a common faith in this negation than in any affirmative statements about God. Certainly we shall find more of humility and of brotherly love' (p. 124.)

What is striking about Fromm's book is the genuine attention which he devotes to the problem, as well as his great factual knowledge. He does not talk in generalizations but tries to analyse different aspects of the religious life in specific terms. He also has a clear and responsible understanding of the type of religion which he holds to be acceptable and which he himself, as analyst, would like to arrive at with his patients. He knows it as a research worker not only from the outside, as it were, but also from the inside. We can say more or less the same about Rümke. He too, as he himself says, wrote his book for the most part on the basis of self-observation. But the same thing is true of Fromm that was true of Rümke: he has no understanding of the other kind of religion, which is as much at home in the West as his 'humanistic' type. He has no appreciation of the traditional Christianity of the churches, the type we call revelatory religion or dialogistic faith. We must even say that his factual knowledge is insufficient when he says that he thinks he can find his own type of religion in various kinds of faith, and declares everything that does not agree with it to be idolatry. We must not overlook the fact that the way in which Fromm attempts to make the differences between religions understandable is not quite unknown in the philosophy of religion (the discipline which is concerned with these problems). Present-day philosophy of religion, however, is concerned more with the differentiation between types of religion which in its opinion cannot be so easily explained by a 'natural religion', with all its positive or negative variations. In essentials Fromm and his views still belong to the nineteenth century and thus to the setting of the Enlightenment.

He makes some important observations about the religious situation in America. I am thinking of what he says about the 'marketing orientation' for example: with his psycho-analysis Fromm stands at the centre of present-day reality. Again, with his view of the religious and political idolatry of the last decades, he is an analyst who has opened our eyes to the subconscious background of various political manifestations of our own time (and this is true of his other books as well). Finally, one should point out that Fromm's work, like Freud's, must also be seen against the background of his Jewish descent. In him there comes alive something of the Old Testament biblical humanism which was not only important for the past of our Western civilization, but which we must hope will also make a contribution to its future.

Fromm's essay on 'The Dogma of Christ' also has its particular importance. Published in 1930, in German, it then became the pièce de résistance of a collection published in English in 1963, to which it gave its title. The book also contained a number of other articles which were not so narrowly restricted to the psychology of religion, but dealt with more generally 'cultural' subjects.

In this essay, which is written in style of Jones and Reik, Fromm gives a brilliant analysis, on the lines of the old school, of the development of 'the dogma of Christ', that is, the doctrine of Christ, his 'natures' and his relationship to God, as these were held in the first Christian centuries. He puts the (unconscious) social factors which influenced this development in the foreground, believing that the theological changes which the doctrine underwent in these centuries reflect the social problems which marked the life of the first Christians at that period. I am struck in this essay by the aggressiveness which Fromm shows towards the father element in religion; we meet the same thing in Freud. The thesis – this term seems to me more suitable here than the word hypothesis – from which Fromm starts is that theological development is a result of unconscious processes within the group. On p. 11 he says plainly what he means by this. He starts from the existence of two classes in every society, the rulers and the ruled. Social stability rests not so much on external measures as on the unconscious infantile ties which bind the second group to the first.

> This psychic situation becomes established through a great many significant and complicated measures taken by the ruling class, whose function it is to maintain and strengthen in the masses their infantile psychic dependence and to impose itself on their unconscious as a father figure. One of the principal means of achieving this purpose is religion. It has the task of preventing any psychic independence on the part of the masses, of intimidating them intellectually, of bringing them into the socially necessary infantile docility toward the rulers. At the same time it has another essential function: it offers the masses a certain measure of satisfaction that makes life sufficiently tolerable for them to prevent them from attempting to change their position from that of obedient son to that of rebellious son.

In his analysis of the development of Christian dogma Fromm develops this thesis with considerable acuteness. He terms the first period the period of the 'adoptionist' theory:

> In the early community of enthusiasts, Jesus was . . . a man exalted after His death into a God who would soon return in order to execute judgment, to make happy those who suffer, and to punish the rulers . . . They could identify with Him because He was a suffering human like themselves.

For the community of Christians was a suffering and oppressed group in the oriental society of those days. Moreover, oppressed as they were, they were characterized by hate and by death-wishes, 'consciously against the ruling class, unconsciously against God the Father'. The reconciliation which was necessary also came into being through Jesus, through his death on the cross. Fromm therefore obviously sees early Christianity as a revolutionary movement, and he tries to find the clue to its unconscious motivation. He offers as it were the psychological background for the picture which the Marxist Kautsky had of Christianity – that of a proletarian revolutionary movement (*Ursprung des Christentums*, 1908). It is obvious that this formulation of the problem is a biased one and yet the hypothesis about the influence of social factors and unconscious group processes on the function and message of the church in society deserves a closer investigation. We may ask, for example, whether the Reformation and the fifteenth century does not provide important material for this hypothesis; and it is undoubtedly a question which cannot simply be dismissed with a negative answer. There is no doubt that the link between 'throne and altar' (between the secular power and the church) existed in a great variety of forms.

During the second period, that of the development of the Nicene doctrine about the Son of God who descends from heaven, Christianity became the religion of the state. That is to say, other unconscious longings now awoke in Christians as a group, and so produced changes in dogma. Gone were the ideas of a better future and the revolutionary attitude that went with them. But 'if it was hopeless to overthrow the father, then the better psychic escape was to submit to him, to love him, and to receive love from him' (p. 49). As is often the case in personal life, the abandonment of aggressive feelings towards the father meant that the aggression was turned against the self. Men often reproached themselves and felt guilty. They also tried to atone for sin by self-castration, in order so to win God's love. The church became the institution that communicated salvation, and believers became her children.

Thus a kind of infantilism grew up – an infantilism not of rebellion but of submission. This also changed the picture of God. 'The strong powerful father has become the sheltering and protecting mother', while where Christ was concerned, 'the once rebellious, then suffering and passive son has become the small child' (p. 52). Behind the dogma therefore stands a very definite worship of Christ, influenced by the social situation. Fromm believes that he can prove further stages in this development, stages which vary in kind. But we shall leave the matter there, having given an account of his main ideas. What he means must be clear enough: he traces religious development (in so far as it can be deduced from dogma) to collective, unconscious factors. In this book he entirely ignores the possibility of seeing religion as in itself a legitimate expression of human life, though he considers this in his later book *Psychology and Religion* (which we discussed above). He still maintains Freud's standpoint, according to which development to maturity (i.e., the growth of a realistic attitude to life) withdraws the foundation that nourishes religion. We are bound to see, however, with even a superficial knowledge of the reality of the church's life, that the social aspects related to psychology which were mentioned by Fromm do exist. There is no doubt that in its community forms religion is a part of community reality, and as such is mixed up with various collective, unconscious group processes. A closer empirical investigation of this amalgamation in different situations seems to me an important task for the social psychology of religion. Fromm has investigated the early centuries of Christianity in this light, though his investigation is too one-sided. But research of this kind would probably help us to a better understanding of some of the resistance offered to the church and to Christianity in the course of the centuries.

7

Erik H. Erikson on Luther

The aim of the present book is to trace the development which has taken place in psycho-analysts' ideas about religion, and hence in their attitude towards religion itself. In this context *Young Man Luther* (1958), the study of the young Luther by Freud's pupil Erikson, who later emigrated from Europe to the United States, is one of the most important books of recent years.

I am bearing in mind here that the psychology of religion has still not made a great deal of progress. It is at a disadvantage, because its subject of research does not make sense to everyone, and it does not yet have at its disposal a methodology which is accepted as a matter of course. Consequently hardly any important publications about the psychology of religion have appeared in recent decades; nor is it possible to talk about a systematic investigation of this field, though the work of Pruyser, Fortmann, Sunden and Vergote may be mentioned. One of the reasons for this situation is probably to be sought in the fact that psychology is still a new science in general and one which has not as yet really arrived at the point of investigating the religious sphere. The psychology of religion shares this fate with the psychology of the moral life, for example, or that of creativity or of the artist's life, etc. Because of various factors – often social ones – psychology has developed along particular lines. We know a great deal about the emotions through psycho-analysis, which has tried to find a solution for an increasingly urgent social problem. We also know a considerable amount about certain aspects of the learning process and, related to it, the intelligence – influenced, in this case, by problems connected with teaching, which is taking on increasing importance in our society. But psychology has not been nearly so intensively concerned with an investigation of the will. In very general terms, it may be said that the psychology of the 'spiritual life', in the real sense of the word, is still in its infancy.

The importance of Erikson's book about Luther is that here a psycho-analyst takes an important religious personality in the years of his individual development and, with the help of the theoretical conceptions and methods of his science, makes him the object of a systematic and thorough investigation. Moreover, he does this without having any particular prejudices about religion, which is not unimportant in our context. It is not only fascinating to see what conclusions and reflections such an investigator reaches; it is also a hopeful sign. Even though we shall see in the course of our account that various objections can be lodged against the book, these do not prevent us from seeing it as a very important step forwards. We consider it to be a contribution which opens up new perspectives in the field of the psychology of religion.

Erikson studied in Vienna, partly during Freud's lifetime. He knew Freud personally, but was not taught by him in the direct sense. His book *Insight and Responsibility* includes among other things an essay on Freud which is well worth reading. Erikson originally began as a children's analyst, as his comprehensive enquiry *Childhood and Society* shows. Written in America, this book was built up on the basis of his own studies and researches. If I see the matter rightly, we can trace the same development in Erikson as in Charlotte Bühler. She too began as a child psychologist, became interested in puberty, and went on to make a name for herself with a study about the course of human life, both as a whole and in its most important phases. Erikson's book on Luther is a piece of basic research into adolescence and is an expression of the author's interest in life in its entirety.

Erikson is concerned with the development of Freudian psycho-analysis in the two spheres in which this is taking place. In the first place he wants to help to open up new fields – group analysis and group therapy, cultural anthropology, research into emotional developments in early childhood, and research into puberty and adolescence. In most of these fields he has developed important viewpoints, while also contributing to critical thinking about certain basic conceptions developed by Freud.

I have already mentioned some of his books – his collection of essays *Insight and Responsibility*, and *Childhood and Society*, which he calls 'the study of the ego's roots in social organization' and which must be seen against the background of his researches into cultural anthropology. In addition to a large number of articles published in periodicals, books by him which ought to be mentioned include *Identity and the Life-Cycle* and *Identity. Youth and Crisis*, a collection of essays centring on the theme of identity as an element in the progress of human life. *Youth: Change and Challenge*, written by Erikson and others, is devoted to the same theme in the context of adolescence. He treats the problems of contemporary youth, growing up in a variety of milieus. His most recent book is a study of Ghandi, *Ghandi's Truth: On the Origins of Militant Nonviolence.*

In the preface to his study of Luther, Erikson talks about the book as follows: 'This study of Martin Luther as a young man was planned as a chapter in a book on emotional crises in late adolescence and early adulthood. But Luther proved too bulky a man to be merely a chapter.' These sentences give a good impression of the book's intention, as well as of the way in which Erikson approaches his theme. As the title suggests, the book is concerned with Luther's early life, that is to say with the years he spent as a monk – the period in which he on the one hand acquired detachment from his childhood (particularly from home and parents) and on the other hand prepared himself for his later work. For Erikson the analyst, however, Luther is not a 'case' or a 'patient', who is to be used to demonstrate something. This of course plays a part as well, but the whole book is imbued with interest in the 'mystery' of this mighty personality in itself, and is full of respect for him.

For Erikson adolescence is the time in which the young person attains his identity. Accordingly in his study he tries to find out how Luther in his years in the monastery attained his identity, that is to say, how he became the Protestant Reformer in a Roman Catholic country. Erikson asks whether psycho-analysis is capable of finding a clue here to particular connecting links, which remain obscure if the question is differently posed – in the questions asked by theology, for example. He tries – as in a normal analysis – to interpret particular phenomena, i.e., to interpret them in the framework of unconscious associations or, still more precisely, to make them comprehensible in the light of Luther's relationship to his parents. We must grasp what this means for Erikson. It is not his intention to explain religious phenomena 'entirely' in this way, in the sense that they are 'explained away' as infantile, with the help of Freud's working hypothesis. These phenomena also belong within the contexts of mental history and autonomous religion, and these exert their influence as well. Even in Freud we find the idea that a mental and spiritual phenomenon can be determined in various different ways. It is Erikson's aim to use his hypotheses and his knowledge to bring light to bear on the multiplicity of mysterious connecting links, and then to weigh up the relative importance of the various factors.

Such an analysis of a historical figure is obviously bound by certain limitations. The facts which the researcher has at his disposal are few and cannot, as is the case in a normal psycho-analysis, be supplemented by associative material supplied by the person in question. Nor is it possible to test against the person himself whether and how far the given interpretation is correct. The whole thing therefore has a speculative character. Yet I would not hesitate to call the attempt a successful one. Erikson proceeds cautiously. He has entered fully into Luther and his time and has a great capacity for sympathy at his disposal. In addition he has studied Luther and his ecclesiastical and theological context intensively. Erikson possesses great psycho-analytic experience and knowledge, and does not try to prove too much.

I have *one* objection to put forward, however, which is of decisive importance, particularly in the context of our present study. In my opinion Erikson is a considerable stage further in understanding the religious life of the soul than Rümke and Fromm, and as such he holds an important place in the development of psycho-analysis in this field; and yet we have to add a question mark, even with him, when it is a matter of ultimate interpretation. He has a very definite idea of what religion is, but in my view this idea does not agree with the facts. Consequently, in spite of his great open-mindedness towards Luther, he goes astray on quite essential points in his interpretation. We shall return to this in detail.

The question with which we are concerned here is the place which Erikson's book on Luther takes in the psycho-analytical 'revolution'. This question is for me of the greatest interest. In order to arrive at a better understanding of the book, let us consider some of its most striking aspects.

1. As we have already said, Erikson makes no attempt to explain Luther's religious development 'completely', on the basis of non-religious, libidinous factors. One of his working hypotheses is that Luther found fulfilment through his religious struggles, that is to say, he arrived at a clearer consciousness of his identity, just as others (or so we must assume) find fulfilment in their art or in their work. Religion is therefore for Erikson an aspect of human life which is to be accepted – even though this is for the moment only within the framework of a working hypothesis.

2. A further important point about Erikson's book is that – unlike Fromm – he does not use a discriminating typology. He works much less schematically than Fromm and concerns himself with his subject

far more extensively, being an empirical and open-minded scientist who understands both how to look and how to listen.

3. Erikson takes religion – provisionally – as being what it claims to be: an autonomous sphere of life, which he of course investigates psycho-analytically. That is to say, he connects it up with other data, but he does this without prejudice, showing neither preference nor resistance.

4. Unlike most analysts who are concerned with the religious sphere, Erikson is characterized by his excellent knowledge of the facts. He has immersed himself to an impressive degree in Luther's life and work, in the most important books written about him, and in ecclesiastical and cultural history, in so far as this had a bearing on his investigation.

5. A further characteristic of the book is the author's personality. He is not only in every respect a distinguished expert; he is also a wise man. His book contains a series of brilliant and profound ideas which could count as aphorisms. I am thinking, for instance, of what he says about divorce (p. 141), when he is explaining why it is so difficult to gather important information about Luther's monastic years, either from himself or from other people:

> Whatever ends in divorce . . . loses all retrospective clarity, because a divorce breaks the *Gestalt* of one love into the *Gestalten* of two hates. After divorce the vow 'until death us do part' must be explained as a commitment made on wrong premises. Every item which once spelled love must now be pronounced hate. It is impossible to say how good or how bad either partner really was; one can only say that they were bad for each other. And then the lawyers take over and railroad the whole matter into controversies neither of the partners had ever thought of.

What he has to say about the structure of the analytical 'teaching analysis' as a parallel to the monastic life is equally apt (pp. 146ff.). And one could quote other examples.

6. In my opinion Erikson's book opens up the possibility of attacking the problem of whether psycho-analysis really sees religion correctly in a new way, and in a way which will be much juster towards the reality. With Freud and Fromm no genuine conversation is really possible. They stand at too far a remove from religion as a human, historical reality. Even with a writer like Rümke, such a conversation would not be easy, at least not on the basis of his book. Erikson stands much closer to these things. I hope to come back to this in more detail later.

Erikson is concerned with the young Luther, that is to say with the Luther of the years in which he is struggling for his own identity. He was one of the men who are late in growing up, because they find it difficult to acquire clarity about themselves, their role, their task, their place and their destiny. In his book Erikson concentrates on Luther's monastic years. The section about his childhood and the one on his later life are merely prelude and epilogue. We shall first of all give a brief account of the book's contents and will then spend somewhat longer on some of the viewpoints and problems which are important for our investigation.

According to Erikson (ch. I), Luther's greatness lies in his struggles and his suffering, until he found healing, which often means 'a cause', something for which he could fight. Luther passed through a severe crisis of personal identity, which can only be understood in the context of the cultural and political crises of his time. Erikson is concerned to show how in Luther's struggle the outward sources of tradition mingle with the inner sources of this particular individual and create something new – a new person, and with him a new generation and a new age. Erikson wants to discover how far psycho-analysis can help him to shed psychological light on particular phenomena in Luther's life. Since he is concerned with Luther as a religious person, the picture that he draws of religion is of course of considerable importance. On p. 19 he writes that religion 'translates into significant words, images, and codes the exceeding darkness which surrounds man's existence, and the light which pervades it beyond all desert or comprehension'. We shall come back to the significance of this definition at the end, and first merely establish that religion illuminates and determines man's place in the whole by means of words and images. I should like to put it as follows: for Erikson, man as man is 'religious' in the mystery of his existence, but this potential religion is realized in different specific religions.

The book's focus, however, is, in Erikson's words, ideological. Young people need an ideology for their sense of identity, that is to say, an unconscious tendency which underlies religious, scientific and political thinking, binding together facts and ideas in such a way that a 'world image' (a *Weltanschauung?*) comes into being which supports the collective and the individual sense of identity – the consciousness, one might say, that 'this is what I am and this is where I stand'. In Luther's time religion was the source of the ideology through which one could find identity. This, it seems to me, crystallizes the question behind the book. The concept of ideology, to which Erikson gives such central importance, is hard to define, as seems to emerge from his formulations; and although a connection with religion can be established, this connection and the mutual relationship of the two cannot be expressed any more clearly. Nor does Erikson do so. Through this double lack of clarity, the book's point of departure takes on a certain cloudiness, and this then becomes noticeable in other sections as well. Perhaps the following clue can help to make this cloudiness comprehensible. For it is connected with the question which Erikson asks. Erikson came across Luther in the course of a comprehensive investigation of the basic elements of adolescence. One of these basic elements is the seeking and finding of identity. Erikson therefore asks: how did this seeking and finding of identity take place in Luther? He established that here it is particularly important to have an ideology. (We have only to think of National Socialism, for example.) But Luther's ideology was obviously to be found in the religious field, not the political one. Consequently in the study of Luther's identity crisis, religion appears as the source of ideology. Luther himself was not conscious of this search. He was struggling with God; for him his crisis was a crisis of belief. It may undoubtedly be the case that a young man may use his religious search, unconsciously, in order to arrive at identity and that hence the psycho-analyst may also be able to interpret part of his struggle in this way; but we must not in my opinion overlook the fact that we are dealing with part of a real religious struggle for illumination and truth, and that the two elements are inextricably, and indeed indistinguishably, involved in one another. I sometimes have the impression that Erikson was not able to compress his extensive material into the narrow bounds of his question, and that he starts from the assumption that here several factors are simultaneously at work and that his question can only shed light on certain facets. In this case not only Luther but the book itself would have got beyond him, that is to say would have grown beyond the questions he asks. Nor, it seems to me, does the concept of ideology play the all-dominating role in the other sections of the book that the first chapter would seem to suggest.

This may suffice to show that a number of fundamental and methodological questions arise against the background of this study which are certainly deserving of greater attention. The theologians and the psycho-analysts need to come more closely to grips with each other in discussing the role of religion in the crisis of adolescence.

In Chapter II the starting point for Erikson's investigation of the course of Luther's development is a particular event in the reformer's life which took place in 1507. The precise date is unknown, but at this time, according to the report of one of his fellow-monks, he had a kind of fit in the choir of the monastery at Erfurt. As the story of the healing of the deaf and dumb man in Mark's gospel was read, Luther is said to have cried out: 'I am *not*!' Erikson believes that he can see this 'fit' as the symptom of a serious identity crisis. But before he explains what he means by this, he pegs out the framework of his investigation, bringing his own views to expression in his judgment of this particular event. Thus he cannot agree with the Protestant theologian Scheel, who sees it as 'a catastrophe brought about by God's grace', any more than he agrees with the Catholic theologian Denifle, who rejects a religious intervention of this kind but presupposes the existence of an unstable character in Luther and 'the play of conscious or unconscious self-delusion', even though he thinks that the hypothesis of a spiritual core in Martin's reaction to the passage read demands closer consideration. Erikson cannot adhere to the Danish psychiatrist Reiter's view either; he thought that he could see repeated 'indications of erratic upsets in his nervous system'; whereas the psycho-analyst Preserved Smith – probably because of insufficient training in this field – takes his bearings too exclusively from supposed sexual difficulties (masturbation problems, etc.). Erikson recognizes an 'intrinsic ambivalence' in the 'fit' which on closer observation proves to be the mark of Luther's whole crisis during these years. He stood at the parting of the ways: obedience either to his father or to his monk's vows. But in this way he was also faced with a decision between neurosis (illness) and religious creativity.

Erikson then returns to the notion of ideology, which he here calls a *'Weltanschauung'*, a world view, which in extreme cases is associated with 'a militant system with uniformed members and uniform goals'.

Here too he does not imbue the concept with a precise content, but merely indicates that he is dealing with 'what young people in their teens and early twenties look for in religion and in other dogmatic systems'. In our own words, this would mean that in his monastery Luther *consciously* sought for something different, but also that these factors would certainly have played a role in the *unconscious*. In my view, Erikson does not differentiate enough here, but what he adds is important. The need both for devotion and for rejection which is associated with every identity crisis is revealed in and through ideology. This was evidently so in Luther's case, and the same thing was obviously true among the young people claimed by National Socialism. In addition Erikson points to the important factor, that society is inclined to allow a young man a moratorium in his identity crisis – a certain time limit in which he has time and opportunity to grow up, without what he does being taken too seriously. In Luther's time the cloister was a moratorium of this kind, and Luther apparently viewed it as such.

Finally we must mention yet another striking factor about the 'fit' which, in view of Luther's later life, must have played a great part in his struggle for identity. In my view it is one of Erikson's greatest services that he brings the function of this factor into such clear relief in his study. The words 'I am *not*!', with which Luther repudiated the boy's dumbness, played a significant part in his 'fit'. In Luther's whole life speech, the voice and the word had enormous importance. On the one hand he was the great speaker and preacher, and on the other he was the man who knew himself to be bound to God's Word. 'The eventual liberation of Luther's voice made him creative.' Only then did he find his identity. We shall come back to this point in the course of our account. In this chapter Erikson is concerned, as it were, to unfold the structure of his book, the framework within which he thinks he is going to be dealing with us. He knows that he has to do with a young man who is forced to go through a religious struggle. But as an analyst his initial interest is the way in which this man finds identity in his struggle. He therefore wants on the one hand to show evidence of religious uncertainty and religious search, and on the other to indicate the lines of a mental and spiritual growth. For us as theologians, two questions are of essential importance here in the context of our investigations: First, how does the author see the mutual interweaving of these two different entities? How does he think that they influence one another, i.e., how can religious uncertainty hinder the growth to maturity, or stimulate it? And conversely, how can the will to growth and the help which Luther experienced in this connection (the figure of von Staupitz is important here) be a contribution to finding a path out of the religious uncertainty? And, secondly, what is the analyst's view of religion here? Is it really an infantile survival on the path to maturity, or does it represent an autonomous sphere of life? If the analyst holds the latter view, does he hold the same view about the nature and the difference of the religious life as the theologian, or perhaps as particular theologians? Or to put it another way, in how far can his view of religion be described as theological, and how far is it open to theological criticism and discussion? These are questions which we cannot answer at this point but which we shall bear in mind for our final summing up.

Let us first continue with our survey of the book's content, and come to Chapter III, entitled 'Obedience – to Whom?' Here the problem of obedience really centres on Luther's ties with his past, and above all with his parents. The path to identity is also a road to independence, that is to say, it is a process in the emancipation which is often bound up with great inner difficulties. This chapter tries to give us insight into the problems which Luther brought into the monastery because of his past and which determined his struggle for an individual relationship to God, or (to use Erikson's formulation) to his own identity.

According to Erikson, Luther's struggle always had an element of dichotomy. Chapter III begins thus:

> At its height, Luther's rebellion centred in the question of man's differential debt of obedience to God, to the Pope and to Caesar – or rather, to the multitude of Caesars then emerging. At the beginning of his career another and, as it were, preparatory dichotomy preoccupied him: that between the obedience owed to his natural father, whose views were always brutally clear, and the obedience owed to the Father in heaven from whom young Luther had received a dramatic but equivocal call.

Erikson remarks that in his public utterances Luther offers the material for the same investigation that Freud later undertook for himself – namely, the investigation of the neurotic components of his intellectual search. With this the direction of Erikson's investigation is defined as well. He feels out the relationship between father and son in order to find the clue to the neurotic components in Luther's search in a similar way. He knows that there are only a few reliable facts about Luther's childhood, but he believes that his clinical experience permits him – and indeed even enjoins him – to recognize 'major trends', even where the facts which are otherwise put at his disposal in a normal analysis are not all available.

He now arrives at the following picture: Luther did not have a happy childhood. His father, an active and ambitious man, was of peasant origin, but wanted his son to go further in the world than he had done, even though he had already moved one step up the social ladder when he became a miner. His son was to 'study' and to study law. Then as now, this study was a means of access to the possible 'higher' professions. So Martin would not need, as Erikson points out, to dirty his hands with mud and soil, an aspect which was bound to interest him particularly as analyst, in connection with a man like Luther, whose speech was frequently so 'anal' in its imagery. Erikson thinks that the father's exaggerated ambition was probably influenced by the fact that he had a brother who had brought shame on the family in many ways. This might also have been one reason why the father was so strict with the young Martin. We all know fathers who are continually thinking that they can discover in their sons signs of a threatened failure, which has already become fact in some other member of the family. Luther's father was certainly strict; like many fathers in those days, he struck his son, but that was because of over-tension, and out of fear of failure.

> Here I think is the origin of Martin's doubt that the father, when he punishes you, is really guided by love and justice rather than by arbitrariness and malice. This early doubt later was projected on the Father in heaven with such violence that Martin's monastic teachers could not help noticing it. 'God does not hate you, you hate him,' one of them said (p. 54).

In the context of our investigation, we quite obviously have to do here with one of the most important angles of Erikson's book. Early experiences in childhood also stamp the person's later relationship to God; or, to put it differently, here we come up against the neurotic components we have already mentioned in Luther's religious struggles to arrive at a proper relationship to God. The character that is formed in youth influences a man's whole life, and that includes his religion as well. What this meant for Luther is brought out by Erikson in the following sentence (p. 58): 'According to the characterology established in psychoanalysis, suspiciousness, obsessive scrupulosity, moral sadism, and a preoccupation with dirtying and infectious thoughts and substances go together.' And according to Erikson, Luther had them all.

A child's relationship to his mother of course is part of his early impressions. What about Luther in this respect? His mother too often struck him, and struck him hard, and it was to this, according to Erikson, that Luther traced back his later scrupulosity in the monastery. Because she beat him until he bled for stealing a nut, he was unable to palliate his later sins to the faintest degree. She even increased the pressure on his soul brought about by his father. Luther admits that from his youth up he could only hear the name of Christ with terror, 'for I was taught only to perceive him as a strict and wrathful judge' (p. 67).

Yet on the basis of his clinical experience Erikson believes that in his earliest years Luther must have had another impression of his mother as well. 'Nobody could speak and sing as Luther later did if his mother's voice had not sung to him of some heaven' (p. 69).

His positive and healthy relationship to nature as well as his mystical tendencies reveal an area of spiritual health that very probably allows us to deduce an early healthy relationship to his mother. Traces of this can be found in Luther's piety too, as well as in his marriage.

In all this we can therefore see that Luther was certainly familiar with the problems of the Oedipus complex in his life, and that his difficulties with his father must, technically speaking, be viewed in the framework of that complex. Or, to put it differently, in the analytical view Luther's struggle is the normal struggle that takes place in the development of every young man, which has to be gone through if he is to arrive at genuine, mature manhood.

One of the first things which becomes comprehensible in this context is Luther's strict conscience. For a proper understanding of Luther's life, it ought to be said that in this respect he is typical of his period. According to the ideology of his time, man was a sinful being through and through, and had only one remaining hope, before the last and probably impending judgment to find mercy 'before the only true Identity, the only true Reality, which was Divine Wrath' (p. 72). Seen in this light, Luther's struggle in the monastery has a number of different facets. It was a struggle for a better understanding of the gospel, and with it for a better understanding of God's relationship to man. At the same time, however, it was a struggle for a different view of man and his identity; and for Luther that meant finding his own identity, as well as formulating a new ideology for his time.

On this basis, in his relationship to his parents, Luther's character took on a sharper outline in the course of time. His school years, with their canings and secret schoolboy pranks, increased his sensitivity as well as his drive towards rebellion. The later years which he spent in the school belonging to the Brothers of the Common Life, with their humanism and their music, strengthened the positive sides of his character. When he was seventeen he entered Erfurt University. He had a precocious conscience, was filled with the fear of death, but also showed that he could be a good friend. He was not a 'merry' student; he was inclined to brood, which earned him the nickname 'philosophus'. He worked hard, lived in a 'Burse' – a kind of hostel – and as student arrived at a certain identity. He studied Aristotle eagerly and discovered an ideology, to some extent, in Occamism, the doctrine which maintained that knowledge and faith, philosophy and theology, were mutually exclusive. But for Luther Occamism did not solve the unsolved problems of his youth. The reverse is nearer the truth – it actually made his inner crisis more acute.

Then came the critical year 1505, a year in which the problem of 'obedience – to whom?' became acute. What was to happen? Should he become a lawyer and fulfil his father's dreams, perhaps make a good marriage into the bargain? In the calm that followed his exams he was sunk in a kind of crisis, brooding over death and the last judgment. In the middle of term he asked for permission to go home. Erikson supposes that there was a 'clash of wills' between father and son; and this supposition is not without reason in my own view, although it is extremely unfortunate that no reliable reports exist about this decisive event in the relationship between father and son. Probably Luther hinted at the possibility of entering a monastery and his father's answer (of which his son was later to remind him) was that he did not consider Martin suited for the monastic life. No doubt he thought that he would fail to realize his ambitious plans for his son, and for his son's marriage as well. Luther must have known that his father would have liked to see him married. When he did after all marry, many years later, he explained the step as being first and foremost to please his father.

On 2 July, on the way back to Erfurt, he was surprised by the famous storm which finally impelled him to enter the Augustinian monastery in Erfurt. Curiously, he did not tell his father beforehand.

Erikson devotes pages to his discussion of this step. He tries to analyse in every detail what must have gone on in Luther's mind, especially stressing the obscure and ambivalent features which were bound up with his decision. Heroically courageous though this step may seem to us today, it was by no means so in those days, and certainly not for Luther at this period of his life. The only act of heroic courage he could have shown – namely to tell his father his decision himself – he did not perform, according to Erikson; he only wrote to him when he was already behind the monastery walls. Erikson sees the importance of this step as lying primarily in the fact that Luther had to take it if he wanted to arrive at inner independence.

His father and the rest of his family could not reconcile themselves to the decision; his father rebelled against it. It was only after two of his sons had died that his anger ebbed away, under this stroke of fate. But he was still angry at heart, and at bottom Luther, who took the view that this state of affairs should be accepted, held it against him. But Erikson doubts whether Luther 'meant it' so seriously. For him it was rather an essential dramatic step, in order that he might grow up in relation to his father. Erasmus and Calvin chose a similar path at the same period. Luther later saw in it the hand of God, which planned to bring him into clear conflict with the pope by this means.

This chapter shows that in Luther's struggle for identity his relationship to his father was of vital significance, and that two factors played an important role in this connection – on the one hand the (compulsive-obsessive neurotic) pattern impressed on him in childhood, and on the other his strong vitality. His entry into the monastery was not, as it proved, sufficient to solve his difficulties. The monastery at most provided him with a moratorium in which things could go on maturing and in which he found time to arrive at the appropriate solutions.

Chapter IV, which is headed 'Allness or Nothingness', temporarily interrupts Erikson's account of Luther's inner development in order to draw our attention to a number of fundamental aspects which are indispensable for a proper understanding of what went on in Luther's mind. Here the problems involved in the search for identity are in question, as well as all the possibilities of a diffusion of identity. In the monastery Luther became 'anonymous' and in this situation he was happy for a time, though this later proved to be the calm before the storm. Beneath the surface a struggle must have begun between destructive-repressive and constructive-progressive forces.

Luther's struggle can be described as a diffusion crisis. He stood before the abyss of nothingness. Characteristic of a crisis of this kind is the lack of a normal sense of time, the quickening of shame over 'what one is already sure one is' and about 'what one may become', the avoidance of physical intimacy with others (Luther used music in order to find a solution for this problem) and the preference for a negative identity (the repudiation of an earlier identity). Often it is a question of 'allness or nothingness', a clinging to 'compulsive scrupulosity and obsessive rumination'. These signs of adolescent crisis are markedly present in Luther. In the course of the chapter, Erikson then makes an interesting comparison with the life of Hitler, whose inner development (in as far as it can be reconstructed) also shows clear characteristics of a similar crisis. He compares Hitler's political ideology with Luther's theology, which provided an ideology for him and for his time. Erikson therefore tries, as we have already indicated, to present Luther's struggle in the monastery as a struggle for maturity through the finding of a theological ideology. Luther believed that he stood before the abyss of nothingness, and that 'theology is the most systematic attempt to deal with man's existential nothingness by establishing a metaphysical Allness' (p. 105). In these circumstances theology can in adolescence represent a contribution to maturity. This naturally implies that the psychologist views the role of both theology and religion purely functionally. He does not get to the point of putting the question of truth; or rather, he would probably hold this to be wrong in principle. The only thing that we can say is that he concedes to religion a vital importance in the growth towards maturity, or in other words accepts religion as an essential element in human life, wherever the problems of his 'existential nothingness' enters man's orbit. Erikson therefore takes up a fundamentally different standpoint from Freud. For him religion is by no means a residue of infancy; it is a component of maturity.

But at the same time it is noticeable that the formulations used by Erikson point to a quite particular type of religion, and it is this which he obviously has in mind when he is talking about religion in general. In religion he is concerned with man's place in the whole. Man overcomes his 'existential nothingness by establishing a metaphysical Allness'. The words are reminiscent of Rümke, and of Fromm as well, even though there the echo is less clear. We shall see later that when Erikson is talking about religion he, like Rümke and Fromm, thinks of the particular type of religion which we called natural religion – the religion that belongs to man *per se* – and that he tries to fit Luther into this framework as well. And here in my opinion he misunderstands certain things about him.

How does a man find identity?

For Erikson the beginning is already to be found in his first contact with his mother. In this contact 'the "basic trust" is born which is of essential importance for the whole structure of life' because it 'becomes the anchor-point for all the developments which culminate at the end of adolescence, in the establishment of psychosocial identity'. Adolescence and earliest childhood therefore belong on one and the same axis. This 'basic trust' implies mutuality, and from the point of view of religious psychology this is of essential importance. 'Basic trust in mutuality is that original "optimism", that assumption that "somebody is there", without which we cannot live.' Here the face, the smile, recognition, play an important part. 'One may well claim for that earliest meeting of a perceiving subject with a perceived object (which, in turn, seems to "recognize" the subject) the beginning of all sense of identity.'

When we read in the Bible about seeing God 'face to face', and about the light of God's countenance shining upon us, this obviously belongs to the same sphere as 'basic trust', – not in the sense that man flees from life into an infantile stage, but because life is built up on the very first foundations. Erikson (p. 114) sees adolescence in the following way:

> At that point, an ideological formula, intelligible both in terms of individual development and of significant tradition, must do for the young person what the mother did for the infant: provide nutriment for the soul as well as for the stomach, and screen the environment so that vigorous growth may meet what it can manage.

Religion now assumes a particular place among ideological systems. It does not only provide nourishment, it 'restores the earliest sense of appeal to a Provider, a Providence'. It therefore apparently includes the Other, the face of God, as well. 'One basic task of all religions is to re-affirm that first relationship.'

It would be helpful for us to keep this formula in mind. For the question arises: is religion this 'basic trust' with the possibility of making the rational aspect which it implies personal? This is the theory which we came across in Rümke and which is hinted at by Fromm, when he holds personal faith in God to be a secondary element in religion. Or is this one particular type of religion, which is paralleled by another, whose main characteristic is from the very outset the I–Thou relationship which the basic trust then presupposes? This is for me an essential problem into which we must enquire more closely and which, as we have already said, ought to be one of the main themes in the discussion between psycho-analysis and theology.

Erikson's question is now: how is this fundamental unity destroyed? In his answer he points to the father's role. At the moment when the child ventures to detach itself from the mother and seems to begin an autonomous existence, fathers 'if they know how to hold and guide a child, function somewhat like guardians of the child's autonomous exist-ence'. But they can also be a jealous god and let the child sink into the pit of shame, through which the seed of rebellion is sown in them. The father's voice can be a positive element in the child's sense of identity, but he can also burden it with feelings of guilt, so that it hides its face and gets the feeling that its father is turning his back on it. We already saw the role which Luther's father played in his son's life, and how the boy projected the problems he experienced in his relationship to his father on to God. This was the cause of his greatest religious difficulties when he was struggling hardest for identity. Erikson remarks here (p. 120): 'For there is something which only a father can do, which is, I think, to balance the threatening and forbidding aspects of his appearance and impression with the guardianship of the guiding voice.' It ought to have become clear here that one of the central factors in Luther's struggles in the monastery was that his father had not fulfilled this function suffici-ently; and precisely because of that, the discovery of God's Word was for him bound to be of vital importance.

Chapter V leads us into the very heart of Luther's struggle. It is called 'First Mass and Dead Ends'. Erikson begins this chapter by emphatically underlining the way in which we ought to view the monastic life at Luther's period and its importance for Luther himself. We have already said that at that time – we need only think of Erasmus – it exerted the function of a 'cultural moratorium'. In addition the Augustinian order was rich and held in high regard, and was known for its learning. Luther 'chose one of the best organized, most sincere, and least corrupted parts of the church – and joined an organization, furthermore, which offered a flexible career'. But we must remember at the same time that with this choice Luther rejected the path that his father had devised for him and consequently with the monastery he chose 'a negative identity'.

It is now important to discover what influences were brought to bear on Luther in the monastery. Here (p. 126) Erikson points to the following facts: First, Luther must have experienced the regimented life in the monastic community 'like a repetition on a grand scale of the earliest maternal guidance'. It was a self-chosen seclusion, full of healing tranquillity. According to Luther's own statement, the devil was very quiet during his first year in the monastery. In a moratorium of this kind it was easy to put off explosive decisions. But furthermore, the monastery life incorporated the novice in a particular system of indoctrination which – just like modern systems of the same kind – was designed to aggravate the young person's identity diffusion and then to heal it. In Luther's case this meant that he had to rule his rebellious nature and wanted to do so; but that this attempt led to his gradually developing 'compulsive-obsessive states characterized by high ambivalence. His self-doubt thus would take the form of intensified self-observation in exaggerated obedience to the demands of the order.'

It was probably unavoidable that trouble should brew in this particular monk, with his nature and his past: a crisis was on the way, and it broke out at Luther's first Mass. The first Mass was a great festival in which the whole family took part. Two decisive events played a part on this day. During Mass Luther underwent an anxiety attack, and at the end of the festal dinner his father openly and angrily attacked him. At the Mass Luther, in his own words, stood directly face to face with God. And during the dinner his father spoke words which were the equivalent of a curse. Luther was deeply affected. He despised his father, yet he could not cast aside as unimportant his father's words, in which he thought he heard the voice of God. Erikson writes (p. 141): 'Incredible as it seems, at this late date Martin was thrown back into the infantile struggle, not only over his obedience toward, but also over his identification with, his father.' He tried to find the father both in God and in his own father but found a true relationship to neither of them. '*To be justified* became his stumbling-block as a believer, his obsession as a neurotic sufferer, and his preoccupation as a theologian.' In other words, on that day Luther was confronted with the fundamental problem of his life through his encounter with God and with his father; and his disturbed neurotic relationship to his father laid bare a complex of feelings in him which was bound to lead to a disturbed relationship to God as Father as well. We therefore find ourselves here entirely within the framework of Rümke's hypothesis, according to which unbelief (and we can see here the painful form in which unbelief can manifest itself) can develop because of disturbances in the child's relationship to the mother and father figures in his life.

It is understandable that from that day onwards the healing aspects of the monastic life were for Luther a thing of the past.

> This regression and this personalization of his conflicts cost him that belief in the monastic way and in his superiors which during the first year had been of such 'godly' support. He was alone in the monastery, too, and soon showed it in a behaviour that became increasingly un-understandable even to those who believed in him.

We know that in these years Luther displayed pathological symptoms. Erikson talks about 'a borderline psychotic state in a young man with prolonged adolescence and reawakened infantile conflicts'. He suffered from acute anxiety, he was a compulsive-obsessive neurotic, he had hallucinations, was sceptical and suffered from strange fits. On the basis of his analytical experience Erikson (p. 143) interprets this situation as follows:

> Today we would feel that such an attack might be the internal result of stored rage in a young man who is trying to hold on to his obedient, pious self-restraint, and has not yet found a legitimate outer object to attack or a legitimate weapon with which to hit out about him.

Erikson has no reason to doubt Luther's greatness in all this. He sees him as 'a young great man, sickness and all'. Extraordinary conflicts, with everything that this implies, do not exclude greatness; on the contrary, they are the genesis of greatness. In this context Erikson again introduces his own wisdom about life, which makes his book so valuable.

It can be said without exaggeration that Luther ran himself aground in this conflict. He was unable to find God's grace, even through an exaggerated obedience. Erikson now enters into the different aspects of the conflict, which emerge as the crisis grows, concupiscence, for example.

We shall leave this on one side, however, and turn to the main lines of Luther's development. The nadir approached: God became more and more the dreaded father in whom no trust could be felt, and Luther more and more became the son who allowed himself to be carried away by hate and who began to blaspheme. But then a new path emerged. The fatherly adviser and protector who helped him to find it was the famous vicar-general of the province to which Luther's monastery belonged.

It seems to me that Erikson is right when he maintains that the contact with von Staupitz has a twofold significance. For Luther he was the positive father figure who gave the young monk in his crisis the feeling that he was understood, and his reaction towards Luther was a positive one. In addition he let Luther preach and lecture because he was apparently convinced of his pupil's talents. Both aspects were equally important for Luther, from the angle of his mental and spiritual difficulties.

Chapter VI is headed 'The Meaning of "Meaning It"'. Erikson describes how Luther found his solution. It is the longest chapter in the book. Here Erikson gives of his best, using psycho-analysis both to penetrate the great and far-reaching problems with which Luther had to struggle, and to make the solution comprehensible.

At the beginning of the chapter Erikson first mentions Luther's journey to Rome in 1510. His behaviour in Rome 'seems to indicate a last endeavour on his part to settle his inner unrest with ceremonial fervour, by the accomplishment of works' (p. 167). It is also typical of Luther that he apparently hardly noticed the beauties of the Renaissance in Rome at all. This journey was followed by the intellectual preparation for the great verbal explosion which was to take place a few years later. These years were necessary in Erikson's view, because Luther in his 'compulsively retentive' way (he suffered all his life from constipation) needed a time for contemplation before he was able 'to say in one and the same breath what he had come to really *mean*, what he really had thought through' (p. 171).

Erikson first of all shows that what Luther had gone through was not a personal affair but was part of a 'psycho-historical' development. He was experiencing the end of an epoch; mediaeval man was gradually losing the identity which had been founded on faith. Like so many great men, Luther was at once the leader and the victim of an ideological process.

At this point Erikson maintains an original view of the theological development of Christianity from its origins onwards. In the earliest, Pauline period, there was identity on a vertical line; the horizontal dimension of human life did not count. Then came a period with a 'double citizenship', one in heaven and one on earth, i.e., a split identity. An epoch followed in which man in the horizontal was viewed as a sinner who could only acquire a true, acceptable identity in and through the church. This was the period of the Roman Catholic church, with its own theology and philosophy. Human identity was discovered in the hidden face of God as well as in the face of man revealed by God in Christ. From Augustine onwards everything that we are as man and will be was viewed as the gift of God. Thomas Aquinas then stressed the rational identity of man more strongly; but in Aquinas life is too stylized, and he fails to answer and satisfy the great personal questions of conscience, or the needs of the masses.

Luther received his education during the post-Thomist period, when the dispute about realism and nominalism (represented by the figure of Occam, who was so significant for Luther) came to the fore; there was also a trend towards mysticism. Ideologically, the meaning of these tendencies was an attack on the 'sense of identity' and a certain doubt, therefore, about the ultimate questions of human life. Combined with this 'ecclesiastical-theological' movement, the influence of the Renaissance made itself felt, that 'ego revolution *par excellence*', in which man discovered himself and the world. It was a liberation, but for most people it left the inner frontier, the sphere of 'the negative conscience' or, to put it another way, 'existential despair' completely untouched. Luther's place in this 'psycho-historical' development was now, according to Erikson, that he solved the Renaissance problem with Renaissance tools, but also on the foundation of the Jewish-Christian heritage, which is 'inherent' in the negative conscience.

For Erikson, accordingly, Renaissance and Reformation lie on the same axis. We must of course ask whether it is doing justice to Luther to 'place' him as Erikson does. Here a quite particular view of religion, which is characteristic of the book, already makes itself felt – namely, the one answer to 'existential despair' as well as to Luther's position in the religious world. We shall discuss this at the end of the chapter.

After his journey to Rome, Luther went to live in Wittenberg, where he preached and lectured until his death. This activity has two significant aspects.

First, he is now no longer forced to be silent. He is able to speak.

Erikson pointed out at the very beginning how important the word and the voice were for Luther in his search for identity. In speech he could fulfil the potentialities that belonged to his nature and he was able to enter into a proper relationship to his fellow men. In this way he came to himself. Perhaps we might even say that in this way some of the anal problems which were so characteristic were solved, for these problems arose precisely because he had up to then been unable to express himself and suffered from the inability to form relationships.

Secondly, by studying and preaching Luther arrived at new, liberating insights and found, as it were, a new approach to God as Father. Erikson traces this approach by way of the text of Luther's lecture on the Psalms, where his theology and 'ideology' developed into perceptions which he later ascribed to the 'revelation in the tower'.

We might therefore say that there were three factors which set Luther on a fresh path at the very nadir of his struggle: the experience of a positive father figure in the vicar-general, von Staupitz; the liberating opportunity to fulfil himself through speaking; and study, which brought him into touch with the positive, fatherly God, who addressed him through his Word, Christ, thereby showing him his countenance of love. Psychologically, it is significant that Luther believed that he received the decisive revelation of this truth in the *cloaca*, the privy. He experienced everything whole, body and soul. There is no doubt that, now that he was able to speak and was permitted to do so, he was a highly impulsive personality. Moreover Erikson maintains (p. 199) that 'A revelation, that is, a sudden inner flooding with light, is always associated with a repudiation, a cleansing, a kicking away'. We cleanse ourselves from the dirt of the old life. We could also draw on Erikson's view of ideology, according to which ideology serves both as the object of devotion and also as a means of repudiation. Nor must we forget here that anal images play a large part in Luther's vocabulary.

Erikson is then concerned to show psychological parallels to the growing theological insights which Luther acquired in these years.

1. He points to the fact that Luther found identity in an evident combination of passivity and activity. He learnt to accept that his own abandonment and guilt, listening to the Bible, and prayer were all surrender to God. From clinical experience we know that it is only through total passivity that a man can regain his active position in the face of nothingness, in order so to be saved. In this context Erikson then offers an interpretation of Luther's relationship to God and to Christ which, in my opinion, quite ignores the I–Thou character, together with his

guilt and the reconciliation in Christ. As Luther saw it, he was able in his suffering to identify himself with the suffering Christ who lives in me, and hence with the God whose countenance Christ is; and in this way he was able to arrive at a different and positive father-experience. But we shall return to this later.

We will, however, abide by the fact that Luther found his ego and his God in the moment when he dared to be passive. For the psychology of religion this is a particularly important point.

2. Erikson thinks (p. 207) that we can then compare Luther's theological progress with particular steps in the process of maturity, which everyone has to go through. These steps are: 'the internalization of the father–son relationship; the concomitant crystallization of conscience; the safe establishment of an identity as a worker and a man; and the concomitant reaffirmation of basic trust'. The rebirth which was at stake had all these aspects for Luther.

3. Luther's relationship to 'works' changed; when speaking became his 'work', 'work' took on a totally different meaning for him. 'People with "well-functioning egos" do good work if they can manage to "mean" the work . . . which they must do.' I am not quite certain whether in saying this (p. 214) Erikson does justice to the religious problem with which Luther was struggling, but it seems to me that the psychological change was necessary in order that the theological renewal could be realized.

4. At the close of this chapter Erikson remarks that Luther's negative conscience had not quite disappeared in the course of his struggle. 'It is clear . . . that the negative conscience which had been aggravated so grievously by Martin's paternalistic upbringing had only waited . . . for an opportunity to do to others in some measure what had been done to him.' This is demonstrated in the following chapter, which goes briefly into the rest of Luther's life.

The chapter heading 'Faith and Wrath' is significant. Erikson is first of all concerned with the effects of Luther's newly-won identity – and the theology he acquired with it – on his actual publicistic activity – on his many pamphlets, which deeply influenced the developments of the time, and above all on his translation of the Bible, which he began in the Wartburg. Erikson also discusses Luther's role in the peasants' revolt. Here the 'reverse' side of his character emerges. In 1525 he married – in his own words, because his father wanted him to. It is obvious that a belated identification with his father was for Luther the fundamental harmony in his life. And he gave his eldest son his father's Christian name Hans.

According to Erikson this calm after the storm must also have been a critical period for Luther. He now became a father himself, thus repudiating much of what he had acquired in the way of identity in adolescence. His melancholy and his conservative politics could be inwardly connected with this.

Erikson then gives a brief outline of Luther's 'breakdown' in his later years. There is no doubt that during this period, in marriage and in his dealings with his children, Luther realized some of the early happiness of his own childhood years. But we also know his anxiety states, his doubts, his constipation, his heart attacks. In Erikson's view (pp. 235f.) this betrays that 'in Luther a partially unsuccessful and fragmentary solution of the identity crisis of youth aggravated the crisis of his manhood'. In these years a number of infantile problems were apparently determined to make themselves felt: obscenities of all kinds, anal insults about people in authority (the pope, for instance), dealings with the devil. At the same time – it must be said yet again – we must never forget his great capacity for loving (the earlier influence of his mother?) and his simple joy in life.

Fundamentally speaking, Chapter VIII, which is called 'Epilogue', is of quite particular importance, and for this reason we shall deal with it in rather more detail. Here Erikson gives us insight into the functions and potentialities of psycho-analysis, as regards both the nature of religion and its particular manifestations, as he sees them. For our investigation it is useful that Erikson formulates the different premises of his book anew, so that they are better suited for a joint study. He takes a saying of Luther's as his starting point: a theologian is born by living, nay dying and being damned, not by thinking, reading or speculating; or in other words, faith grows in the totality of a human life, and through that totality, which includes the past, education and the impress given by earlier circumstances. Erikson's book on Luther shows us that to grow as a person is also to grow in faith, i.e., it is an entirely human process.

Erikson sees a number of parallels between Luther and Freud. Both strove to widen the sphere of man's inner freedom through introspection. Here Luther stresses prayer, which demands the same honesty that Freud expected of his patients. Both were concerned with the liberation of the conscience and with the 'wholeness' of the ego. Neither of them was prepared to accept any haggling about the things which were at stake. And finally, in both Freud and Luther a proper relationship to the child in us plays an important part.

Erikson then goes on to take a bird's eye view, so to speak, of the relationship between Luther's development and the analyst's attitude to a person's years of development in general. We already saw that Luther must have acquired the foundation for basic trust in his earliest relationship to his mother, and that this relationship was destroyed by his jealous and ambitious father. Luther was tormented by 'a lifelong shame over the persisting gap between his own precocious conscience and his actual inner state; and a deep nostalgia for a situation of infantile trust' (p. 249). We recognize this infantile problem clearly in Luther's own words. His strong feeling of guilt also probably derived from the Oedipal phase. His identity crisis was, as Erikson shows, considerably extended, but it then led him on to experience and overcome the crises of 'intimacy and generativity' that followed.

The author spends rather longer on the crisis of integrity – the last crisis in a person's life. If one compares the development outlined by Erikson with the one given by Rümke in 1933 in his lecture 'Entwicklungspsychologie und Psychotherapie' (Developmental psychology and psychotherapy) the agreement is surprising. Rümke thinks that it is possible at the end of human development (and therefore also at the end of psychotherapy) for a person to have existential experiences, about which he says the following:

> What the analytical procedure is capable of bringing about here is liberation from the last infantile ties; and it can also lift the fear of death into the consciousness. It is fear of death that lies behind the impossibility of freeing oneself from the old structure ... the inability to accept the law of 'die and become'. Thus analysis can help us to experience the whole problem of the limit-situation, can help the problems of death and suffering, struggle and guilt, to lose their infantile forms, so that the mature spirit is confronted by the *absolute* limits of human existence, and reaches the highest stage of its development by accepting and coming to terms with them.

Erikson talks about 'the questions of how to escape corruption in living and how in death to give meaning to life'. He then (p. 255) makes an important remark, which we shall have to examine critically, to the effect that 'the religionist's problem of individual identity' – this is the struggle that Luther waged – is 'the same as the problem of existential identity'. In other words, it is the same as the problem of acceptance of, and coming to terms with, the absolute limits of human existence, i.e., the overcoming of the fear of death. In Erikson's view this final crisis in man's life is in correlation to the crisis of life's first phase, the phase of basic trust – trust or mistrust towards existence as such. Or to put it in still another way, when Luther had overcome his crisis with his father, he could once more live from basic trust. Religion is accordingly basic trust in the face of existential nothingness or in the presence of death. Are we not here meeting one of the book's premises, according to which religion consists of a basic trust given with the nature of man?

The book's fascinating closing pages give convincing expression to this viewpoint. There Erikson says that 'man, when looking through a glass darkly' (a reference to I Cor. 13, that we now only see 'in a mirror dimly' but shall later understand as God understands us) 'finds himself in an inner cosmos in which the outlines of three objects awaken dim nostalgias'. The word nostalgia conveys that religion is seen here as being man's longing for his beginnings, a view which is constitutive for a particular type of religion. What, then, are the three objects for which, according to Erikson, man yearns? The first is the 'maternal matrix', to which man feels himself drawn through 'the simple and fervent wish for a hallucinatory sense of unity'. Man must know that he is accepted and that the 'split of autonomy' is repaired. The object of the second nostalgia is 'the paternal voice of guiding conscience'. Guilt and reconciliation are connected with this; man wants to be saved.

> Finally, the glass shows the pure self itself, the unborn core of creation, the – as it were, preparental – centre where God is pure nothing: *ein lauter Nichts*, in the words of Angelus Silesius. God is so designated in many ways in Eastern mysticism.

For Erikson these three images are the most important religious objects. 'Naturally they often fuse with one another and are joined by hosts of secondary deities.' Now, the way in which we view these nostalgias psychologically is important. The return to earliest experiences can also be a regression, in the sense of a flight, and can thereby be unreal, neurotic, an illusion. But Erikson sees another possibility. 'Religions partake of man's ability, even as he regresses, to recover creatively.' For 'they keep alive the common symbols of integrity distilled by the generations'. The ego does not become weaker through this, as Freud maintains that it does; it actually becomes stronger. In this connection Erikson (p. 259) points to dreams, which are also a regression in a sense; and yet dreaming is a healthy and necessary activity. Dreams, as Erikson interprets them, can help a man further, if they rest on a faith, a trust, which the man already has and not on one that he is still searching for.

A good conscience provides that proverbially good sleep which knits up the ravelled sleeve of care. All the things that made man feel guilty, ashamed, doubtful, and mistrustful during the daytime are woven into a mysterious yet meaningful set of dream images, so arranged as to direct the recuperative powers of sleep toward a constructive waking state.

The dream can turn into a nightmare and can cast the unstable ego even more deeply into confusion; but it can also rest on the activity of the healthy, unconscious ego as it seeks to show the searching ego the way to light. If I see the matter correctly, the lines followed by Jung are being pursued here.

Now, 'Religions try to use mechanisms analogous to dreamlife . . . to offer ceremonial dreams of great recuperative value.' Here we have to ask what medium they use for this. Erikson's answer is: 'I assume that it is the smiling face and the guiding voice of infantile parent images which religion projects on to the benevolent sky.' And this 'benevolent sky' is then 'the unborn core of creation, the – as it were, preparental – centre where God is pure nothing'.

In this light Luther's struggle can be seen in very simple terms. It was guided by nostalgia. Erikson writes in this connection: 'The original faith which Luther tried to restore goes back to the basic trust of infancy.' And through this basic trust he found the right relationship to the unborn core of creation, God, who can only in the negative formula of mysticism be termed pure nothingness. 'Peace comes from the inner space', Erikson writes towards the end of this chapter. In the course of his argument his opinion emerges that mysticism offers as it were immediate access to this 'inner space', but that another, more indirect way to the divine mystery stands at man's disposal in the historical religions, by way of their images, with their reminiscences of mother and father.

It was necessary to give a relatively detailed account of the contents of Erikson's book because it is an impressive example of the contribution that can be made by psycho-analysis to a psychological clarification of the religious life. But I am very conscious of the fact that I have not done justice to the wealth and profusion of the ideas which the author develops in his study. In the framework of our investigation I have had to confine myself to bringing out as far as possible the broad lines of his account. Up to now I have, as it were, scattered the odd critical remark in the margin. Now, however, with an eye to the whole, I should like to try to formulate my judgment about the book in more detail.

Erikson attempts to illuminate Luther's religious development within a certain period of time with the means offered by psycho-analysis. It is understandable that the material at his disposal is one-sided and limited. A considerable part of his book therefore rests on speculation, as he himself points out more than once. I will not go into this point, but will merely remark that the picture which he gives seems to me to be in many respects an illuminating one. It does at all events prove an author's right to open up analytical access to the religious life in this way.

Let me now mention a number of points which occur to me as having a bearing on the questions we are asking in our investigation.

1. This book is an important step forwards in the development of psycho-analysis. It is this in the first place because it deals with the empirical investigation of a particular patient and is not (as is so often the case in Freud and Jung) a discussion about religion in general, in which one often asks whether experience is not being used to make particular theories held by the author acceptable. In Erikson we are conscious of his constant desire to test the theory, and that is indispensable for real scientific work on specific material.

From a theological point of view I would supplement this by saying that I rate it as positive that Erikson writes about religion in his book without any 'prejudices', or at least without negative prejudices. I cannot judge whether, from the analytical side, he might perhaps be thought to be charged with too *positive* a prejudice. Pfister's book about Zinzendorf, which we have already mentioned, is also an empirical investigation of a historical personality; but unfortunately it cannot be declared guiltless of a certain 'prejudice'.

For us, the book is therefore a good example of the way in which psycho-analysis can make its contribution to the development of the psychology of religion. Moreover, it strikes me as a theologian that Erikson feels no need at all to deny religion an autonomous place in the life of man, or to 'explain' it on the basis of other, non-religious motivations, as Freud does, though, like Fromm, he only has room for the one type of religion he supports. The greater open-mindedness with which he approaches his theme is a great step forward.

2. In consequence, the contours of the contribution which we may expect psycho-analysis to make in the field of the psychology of religion now emerge more clearly in Erikson's book. It becomes clear that analysis seeks to find out what share unconscious factors, stemming from the infantile phase, have in the development of the religious life. In the Freudian school there was an inclination to assess this contribution as a

negative one, because it was viewed as infantile. Erikson shows that certain factors derived from the earliest relationships are essential for human development and hence for religious development too. 'Basic trust' as well as the internalization of the father–son relationship (which was first negative in Luther and which he was able to make a positive one with the help of von Staupitz and his reading of the Bible) are essential elements here. But their meaning as well as their possible distortions still have to be more closely investigated.

3. In this way Erikson's book touches on a whole series of themes which are important for a discussion between analysts and theologians.

I am thinking here first of the importance of basic trust, an element in existence which the child receives through its first contact with its mother and which constitutes a fundamental condition for later life. Rümke and Jung also consider this to be extraordinarily important.

If I see the matter rightly, natural theology or, better, philosophical faith (Jaspers) is rooted in this basic trust. Philosophically one could talk about ontology in this context.

Erikson shows that this basic trust implies a relationship to nothingness or, more specifically, to death. The assumption of death is bound up with trust in being. This is an idea which Jaspers maintains in connection with his reflections about the limit-situation. In the same context, we also come across the idea that *sin* does not so much mean disobedience or rebellion as *alienation*, alienation from the origin, from (real) being.

It is also significant that, starting from basic trust, Erikson develops a view of how the individual historical religions are to be explained. The basic trust determined by a man's earliest contact with his mother is directed essentially towards the unborn core of creation, the pure nothingness that is God, the benevolent sky. Mysticism without images is the highest form of religion. Particular religions are projections of childish parental images on to this centre, this nothing that is God. They are thus, says Erikson (p. 259), crystallizations of this trust, 'ceremonial dreams of great recuperative value'.

When we deal with trains of thought like this, we are really moving in the sphere of religious philosophy, where there is an obvious relationship to Hegel, for example. Hegel maintains that religion has at its disposal through the imagination (in the image) the same thing that philosophy (which for him is obviously rooted in an ontological mysticism) deals with in conceptual terms. The relationship of Western metaphysics to mysticism and its *via negativa* are well known. Erikson mentions Oriental mysticism in this context, but he might equally well have mentioned the same type of Western mysticism. Oriental thinking about religion does actually move in this direction. Radhakrishnan writes in his book *The Hindu View of Life* (1927): 'Our intellectual representations differ simply because they bring out different facets of the one central reality' (p. 27). One further point seems to me important in this connection. Both in Erikson and Jung, the view taken of religion is partly determined by the religious implications of therapeutical work. Man's growth to maturity, to himself, is experienced as a religious event, and the human help which is received in the process has a religious character. It aims to help man to find his place in the mystery of life. The sentence of Rümke's we have quoted above really says the same thing. To become adult is to become man in the sense of self-realization; and this self-realization is 'divine' in kind; it can be termed a realization of God in us. We could see this clearly in Jung. Erikson does not say it expressly but a view of this kind is no doubt part of the perspective of his thinking.

It is therefore understandable that an enquirer like Erikson should try to come to terms with the problem of religion from a viewpoint which is more or less familiar and determined by his work. But it is a question whether the type of religion that stresses a nostalgic longing for the origins of man's life does justice to the wealth of human existence. Would it not be possible for man's being itself to imply not only a relationship to himself but also a relationship to the other? And that there is accordingly a type of religion which functions within the same framework? Or to put it another way, natural religion is not the only kind; there is another, which cannot be traced back to the first, as Erikson thinks, but which constitutes an autonomous religious type.

A further subject for our discussion would therefore have to be whether there is not a second type of religion which would have to be placed parallel to the first, and whose relationship to the first also has its own particular contours in the light of psycho-analysis, i.e., in the framework of man's psychical development.[1]

One of the essential characteristics of the second type of religion seems to me to be what Martin Buber has called the I–Thou relationship, the relationship to the God who is 'experienced' as a person, who speaks to man as a person, makes a 'covenant' with him and sees him as a partner. This I–Thou relationship can take various forms: it can be described for

---

[1] This observation applies to Western culture. The 'primitive' religions, Islam, Hinduism, and Buddhism all pose problems too, and psycho-analysis can make a contribution to their solution as well.

instance in terms of king and people, or lord and servant, or creator and creature, or father and son. The problem is now whether this relationship fits into the framework of basic trust. Erikson asserts that it does, for Luther rediscovered basic trust through his reading of the Bible, in the course of which the God–man and hence the God–father relationship in his life took on another colouring. Erikson writes (p. 259) that 'the original faith which Luther tried to restore goes back to the basic trust of early infancy'. In his view Christianity is marked by an exaggerated stress on the mutual interaction of initiative and guilt, as well as by an undue emphasis on the divine fatherhood–sonship. But he considers that the mother plays a central role in this type of religion, even if in the background.

In my view this assimilation of the two types of religion is not possible. Certain elements which are essential to the I–Thou relationship are then excluded. I am thinking of elements which are determinative for biblical religion: covenant, guilt, forgiveness, reconciliation, etc. My idea of this kind of religion implies a whole series of things which do not fit into the type expounded by Erikson.

1. Religion is not only connected with nostalgia. It is also an essential element in the life of man if we see that life as a life in relationship. This is of fundamental importance, especially for the father figure in man's life. There is no doubt that one aspect of the father–son relationship is that the father is internalized and lives on in the conscience, and – if this happens in a positive way – gives a meaning to adulthood in the framework of basic trust. But in the parable of the prodigal son we are told in a classic way that, beside his internalized form as conscience (which speaks to us in the foreign country), the father is also a fellow-man, the companion to whom the son knows that he owes a duty. He stands before him as a debtor who is forgiven. Relationship to the father is also a time of apprenticeship in which a man is initiated into the pattern of fellow-manhood. In my opinion Erikson has failed to see that this pattern played an essential role in Luther's struggle with God. God is also the great Other, with whom Luther has to enter into a fresh relationship, and who has made it possible for him to do so through the reconciling sufferings of Christ. There was more at stake here than an internalizing of the father-figure in a positive conscience.

2. My view implies, further, that in therapeutic treatment the thing that matters is not merely to help the person to find himself and to become mature. Another aspect is to help man to enter into mature relationships with other people. One can, after all, say that through the

reduction to the therapist-patient relationship (in which the therapist systematically dispenses with reactions which are normal in the usual dealings between people) it becomes possible for a person to set aside disturbances in the process of emancipation from his parents, and to arrive at a mature relationship to his fellow-men. The therapeutic process has obviously two sides, first to acquire selfhood, and secondly to arrive at 'the other'. Luther does not only find God in his 'basic trust'; he can now enter into relationship with him as the great Other as well. Erikson would undoubtedly agree that both aspects are present in therapy; I am afraid, however, that he only associates religion with one of the two facets.

3. My view and Erikson's imply a certain idea about God and about the pictures of God formed by the different religions. For Erikson, religions are projections of childish parental pictures on to a benevolent heaven. Mysticism has a direct access to God which is only available to specific religions through images. According to a saying of Paul Tillich's in his book *The Courage to Be* (p. 180), there is a God above God, the God of pure nothingness, as Angelus Silesius calls him. In my view man exists within being, and he seeks access to being again and again through mother images which remind him of his original 'basic trust'; but through these images he is directed to the mystery of the 'inexhaustible cohesion of life', to use a phrase through which my teacher de Graaf tried to express the theme of religion. But at the same time man exists in relationships, and in these relationships he comes, through the proclamation of the Christian faith, into touch with God, the Other, who addresses him and who wants to enter into a bond with him. Man carries into his relationships the pattern created in his relationship to his father. Projections unavoidably play a part here, as Luther's example has shown us. But equally unavoidably, this relationship acquires its own reality in the adult life, a reality which is quite different from Erikson's 'inner cosmos', with its nostalgias and projections.

It is of course difficult to decide how the two pictures of God – the ontological picture and the dialectical one – are related to one another. Erikson would like to persuade us to an identification of the two in a third image of God. But we cannot make up our minds to this on the basis of our human data. The unity of the two pictures is a secret which God keeps to himself. We only know of two ways in which we can encounter him.

On the level of our thinking the two lie along the same axis. God as Father points back to the God of being. Even in our own experience of

God we experience continuity, but on the level of our faith, our own relationship to God, the connection between the two pictures of God is a strained one, as history, and present-day theology as well, evince in many ways.

My feeling is that a closer investigation of the way in which the relationship of the two comes into being in our own lives could make this contradiction comprehensible. That would be one important subject for a discussion with psycho-analysis.

4. Still another point needs closer discussion and consideration. Ruth Benedict and her school have made us familiar with the idea of 'cultural patterns'. On the basis of the patterns which develop in the first years of life, the different elements of a cultural pattern are linked together in the framework of a 'culture'. Erikson's work also moves along the same lines. He made a contribution to a view of this kind in his book *Childhood and Society* and it also plays a role in the background in his book on Luther.

As far as the type of religion and the picture of God that matches it are concerned, we are justified in the hypothesis that basic lines are laid down in the first years of a person's life and that these are of vital importance for his later religion and experience of God. The example of Luther has shown us that his struggle for a deeper understanding of God as Father was connected with the commanding position assumed by his father at home; and that, in the background, a different feature of his religion was apparently linked to the earlier relationship to his mother, which remained concealed in this patriarchal type of family. Could certain characteristics of biblical religion – stress on the sovereignty (and perhaps the fatherhood) of God, for example, or obedience and trust, possibly even the prohibition of images – be perhaps connected with the pattern of relationships in the family?

In a book like *Brieven aan mijn kleinzoon* (Letters to my grandson) by Abel Herzberg we see this pattern clearly and also intuitively sense its connection with the special characteristic of biblical religion. But in this case ontological 'religions' and ontological-philosophical systems would also have to 'match' particular cultural patterns in which the father does not play the dominating part. This is undoubtedly so; but then one would have to go a step further and try to find out how far certain types of theology, as well as striking alterations in the theological field, are connected with alterations in the cultural climate. I am thinking of a number of hypotheses: for example, is there a connection between the existence of feminine elements in Catholic devotional life and its liking for natural theology in addition to the theology of revelation? Is there a connection between Barth's attempt to awake biblical devotion to new life, and the patriarchal elements in Switzerland's cultural pattern? J. A. T. Robinson talks about disappearing faith in the 'God up there' and pleads for a 'horizontal' faith and a humanizing of the church's preaching. Is this not inwardly linked with what the German psychiatrist Mitscherlich, referring to our Western culture, calls in a fascinating book 'On the way to the fatherless society'? I have discussed this point at some length in my book *Gott in vaterloser Gesellschaft* ('God in a fatherless society').

This is of course important material for a discussion about the problem of truth, as well as the relativism in religious life which is connected with that problem.[1]

---

[1] There is an interesting critical discussion of Erikson's book by the church historian W. J. Kooiman in *Nederlands Theologisch Tijdschrift* 20, 1965–6, pp. 38ff.

8

Pastoral Care in the Light of Psycho-analysis

The preceding chapters have indicated that there has been a revolution in the thinking of psycho-analysis about religion. A negative attitude has been replaced by a positive one, even though we can see at a closer glance that there are still plenty of questions demanding an answer.

In this chapter I should like to introduce the reader to a book which does not only manifest this positive attitude to religion as such, but in which the writers attempt to show the opportunities and difficulties of pastoral care. Our choice might have fallen on other books, but this one seems to me particularly representative of the change we have indicated. Its authors are Louis Linn and Leo W. Schwarz and its title is *Psychiatry and Religious Experience*. The writers briefly indicate the book's purpose in the preface. Its aim, they say, is 'to show how the insights of psychiatry and religion may be used for the relief of human suffering and the release of creative human energies'.

It is noticeable that the psychiatric aspect is dominant in this aim. Now, the goal of all medical activity, and certainly of psycho-therapeutic activity, is to relieve human suffering and to release creative energy. The two writers evidently want to analyse how far religion can be seen under the same aspect. It is an aspect which is frequently expounded in the United States. Responsible statesmen put the question, for example, whether and in how far the churches can be brought in to help solve the increasingly pressing problems of mental health. The question is not unknown in the Netherlands either.

Moreover, though it is of course important that there should be such a positive relationship to religion in these circles, we are bound to ask whether this is the way to do justice to the nature of religion (and the

Christian faith in particular) and hence to the nature of pastoral care as well.

It is also an important point that the authors do not confine themselves to abstract terms and theory. They take their stand firmly on the foundation of experience, discussing their theses on the basis of numerous cases drawn from practical experience. With these writers we no longer find ourselves in the field of cultural philosophy; we are concerned with the practical cultural system.

The biographical facts given on the dust cover suggest that both authors are Jewish in origin, and that one of them is a psychiatrist and the other a rabbi. In America there are many contacts, and even genuine co-operation, on the pastoral level between representatives of the different creeds. The pastoral pattern is dominated by the idea that all religions subscribe to the same kind of 'activity', and that on the pastoral level they are therefore comparable. Consequently a book about pastoral problems written by a rabbi or a minister finds readers far beyond the author's own group. It is symptomatic that the book we are considering talks deliberately about the clergyman as a 'religious leader' and outlines a picture of his role which European readers would first like to ponder over. For in thinking about the clergy the European is accustomed to include the ministerial 'office' and not to see this office without the three 'offices' of Christ, as prophet, king and priest. In the dialogue we have in mind in our present book, this whole question of office and the ministerial role will undoubtedly have to be an important theme. But I ask myself whether a more empirical approach to pastoral work (which is the aim of pastoral psychology) will not involve certain consequences for theological reflection, as well as for the moulding of the pastoral 'pattern'.

With regard to our American book, the term 'religious leader' is very probably connected with the authors' Jewish background, where the rabbi's relationship to his congregation is really seen as that of 'leader', because of the pragmatic approach to his work. It must not be forgotten here that there has never been a state church in America and that thinking in terms of offices and institutions is therefore alien to the American mind. In the basic pattern of church life in America stress lies on the local congregation, with all that that involves.

In drawing on this book for evaluation in my investigation, I do so in order to show that I think it symptomatic of the changed climate of opinion. It is free from resentment towards the church or the clergy, and its relation to both is critical in the positive sense. Obviously there is a demand for closer co-operation between the two professions, even if we are still only at the stage of testing the ground. But the book is characterized by its continually expressed conviction that clergy and psychiatrists must be aware of their varying roles and above all that the clergyman must not view himself as a kind of psychotherapist.

As a theologian, however, I am struck by the fact that in spite of this positive commitment on the part of the authors, the clergyman's real 'concern' is not sufficiently clearly seen. Apparently we need even more empirical investigations into the nature of religion and, in that connection, into the activity of the minister or priest. Here we again come up against the phenomenon that the Christian faith and the work of the clergy in a Christian church are seen from the perspective of one religious type, the one which we have called natural religion. For example, in the definition which serves the authors as guiding line for their book they write:

> In our view religion is first and foremost the repository of a moral code . . . Religion enshrines the belief that if one obeys the code certain important satisfactions ensue, the chief of which is immortality. Religion stands also for the belief that the universe has a purpose and that it is a purpose favorable to man. This belief in turn presupposes the existence of an organizing principle of some kind, which is commonly called God. Finally, religion is associated with a kind of emotional experience which is taken as revelatory of the true nature of the universe, as proof, in a word, of the existence of God.

For the consciousness of religious people in general – and especially for the ones whose faith belongs to the so-called biblical type – this definition is a somewhat arbitrary list of purely fortuitous, and sometimes even contestable, facets. The real essence is lacking. The definition was evidently drawn up by an 'outsider'. In saying this we are repeating what we have already established in previous chapters.

As far as the content is concerned, I should like to pick out the following points. In chapter I, which is headed 'The Domains of Psychiatry and Religion', the subject is their mutual relationship. The two deal with what are certainly different spheres, but, the writers say, they have certain 'concerns' in common. They instance the moral crisis of our time, as well as the conflicts and suffering of contemporary man. But the psychiatrist is primarily a doctor. The authors know that Freud worked from the hypothesis that religion and religious morality are negative elements in our culture. One group of analysts under the leadership of Karl Menninger, however, maintains that 'religious faith may not only help to control human aggression, but may foster life by inspiring compassion and love'. Moreover at certain places Freud shows a more positive attitude to religion, when he is dealing with particular clinical cases. (We discovered the same thing in his correspondence with Pfister.) The authors themselves discuss various cases in their book in which, they claim, psycho-analysis 'enhanced a person's capacity for religious faith'.

In chapters II and III, which deal with religious developments in childhood and adolescence, the authors very noticeably stress that religious factors can influence the complicated emotional growth of these two stages favourably. Of course they are not blind to neurotic reactions. Their opinions rest on experience and they make an important contribution to the deepening of our knowledge in this field, even though they do not always, in my opinion, go deep enough and are for me often too superficially focused on actual practice. But the fact that they ascribe such a positive significance to religion is important.

For us chapter IV is of major interest. It is called 'The Basic Principles of Religious Counselling' and rests on the supposition that the roles of pastor and psychiatrist differ fundamentally from one another. They make a shrewd assessment of the real state of affairs when they claim to have noticed that the clergyman either underestimates or overestimates himself, ascribing to himself a kind of 'saviour' role. He ought to be alive to the unconscious factors in his relationship to the members of his congregation. He is often experienced as a surrogate father; and the problems of transference also play a part in his work. He cannot always be 'permissive' like the psychiatrist, who is permissive by virtue of the role he plays. Nor is he a 'social case-worker'; he is a priest and a pastor, a symbolic figure. 'His authority and power derive from something greater than himself. In this setting his techniques are those of moral guidance, prayer, and confession.' This comes out even more clearly in the following quotation:

> Now the religious leader shares with the psychiatrist and the case-worker an attitude of sympathy and respect for the individual – and for his family – but his relationship to him differs from theirs in that it is based upon a religious faith and a spiritual interpretation of man and society. It differs also in that it involves moral judgment and forgiveness. And those things are not just applied at random, but require the particular skill or set of skills that are the outcome of a particular kind of training – training, one might say, of mind and heart.

These words illustrate a growing awareness of the meaning of the minister's activity, as well as the readiness to judge it increasingly highly. I have merely one objection which I should like to make clear through the following quotation. At the beginning of the chapter the authors describe the 'religious leader's' chief task as being 'the inculcation of a religiously based moral code' and 'inspiring courage in people in times of stress and giving them comfort in times of sorrow'. Here the clergyman's role is seen in the same framework as the therapist's: his function is to act as an emergency helper in situations of stress. It is true that he must not try to be a therapist himself; but when it is a question of his unique contribution to the psycho-social team which the authors have in mind, they describe that contribution (in the context of a particular case) as follows: 'This woman was provided by the church with human contacts and recreational outlets, and the guidance of a religious leader who represented a parent figure to her.' It is very valuable for the physician to point to this aspect of pastoral work – and the pastor should also be conscious of the latent possibilities here. But this does not exhaust pastoral work; its focus is quite different in kind. Religion is a particular relationship between man and God, and man also has his difficulties in this relationship – indeed sometimes there simply have to be such difficulties. The life and work of the prophet Jeremiah are an apt example. It is dangerous to think primarily of comfort and encouragement in connection with religion. Religion is an autonomous sphere of life, which should not be seen merely under the aspect of its usefulness in situations of distress.

Chapters V–X are concerned with various fields of pastoral care. The authors obviously take as their starting point the pragmatic discussion which we have just indicated. Chapter V, 'Religion in Sex and Marriage', begins with the question:

> What, then, can religious leaders and institutions do to stem the corrosive forces in our environment? More concretely, what can religious counseling contribute to the resolution of present-day problems of sex and marriage? What can it do to strengthen the unity and stability of the family?

Here the clergyman has a great responsibility. He easily gains access to people, but he has to learn to think and work in a team. Various opportunities are listed (divorce, birth control, the sick partner, 'interfaith' marriages, etc.) and much advice is given. The same is true of the extremely practical and positive chapter on 'Understanding Illness', which contains the important sentence: 'Mature religion, as we understand that phrase, while it preaches faith and optimism in the face of life's uncertainties, is not based on childish wishful thinking.' A special chapter deals with 'Facing Bereavement'. It starts from the interesting investigations of the American psychiatrist Erich Lindemann about bereavement and gives important information and advice about facing personal loss. The writers point out that, in such situations in particular, feelings of transference deserve special attention. I would, however, add a question mark after the sentence: 'The idea of immortality is one to which the religious leader can confidently appeal in giving comfort to the bereaved.' Here it would seem to me that in their knowledge of the realities of the religious life the authors are allowing themselves to be guided by too one-sided a picture.

In an American book it is not surprising to find a chapter on conversion. Both the religious situation and the development of the psychology of religion make that understandable. The writers maintain the interesting view that conversion is to be traced back to a mystical longing for unity and means a revival of the oral phase, which does not for them mean a regression into that phase, even though they see the dangers. Here again we come up against the importance of 'basic trust' for the development of the religious life, and the particular patterns of feeling which are connected with this and which are also important for religion. We have already frequently seen that psycho-analysis can offer us important information and points of view here.

The two final chapters deal with the situation of the elderly (where the authors give valuable information and good advice) and with the more specialized work in psychiatric hospitals, with the armed forces, in prisons and in universities. The essential importance of further research and better training in all these areas of life becomes increasingly clear.

All in all, this is a book which shows clearly how far the revolution among psycho-analysts has gone; and it also indicates in what detailed ways psycho-analysis can illuminate and support pastoral work. But this too is a book which, for all its qualities, shows the necessity for a wider and deeper knowledge of the varying character of religion, as well as the nature of the pastoral problem, if we are to achieve really fruitful co-operation. Here too, in the field of practical pastoral care, the subjects which have to be discussed by psycho-analysts and theologians are clear.

9

Conclusions

After we had considered Freud and Jung we drew up a provisional balance about the transition from the first period to the second in the development of psycho-analysis. Now that we have concluded our account of the second period, let us glance back at the whole, so that we can draw some conclusions from our investigation.

I hope that it will have become clear to the reader that the second period can be aptly classified by the word 'revolution'. We have been dealing here with a different climate – perhaps even with a different type of psychiatrist. Freud and Jung were, it is true, primarily therapists, doctors and scientists; but they felt themselves to be prophets and teachers as well; and on the basis of their specialist knowledge they threw their own opinions into the scales, not only when dealing with their patients but also when considering a great variety of social and cultural problems. And in spite of the greatness of their achievements, they did not always exert this influence on the basis of sufficient knowledge of the field which interested them at that particular moment.

The psychiatrists of the second period, on the other hand, do not see themselves so much as prophets and teachers. They are primarily scientists who, when they are pursuing psychological research into religion, feel the need to inform themselves further in a sphere which is new to them. They present their theories more in the form of hypotheses; but since as psychologists they develop new points of view in this sphere, these very hypotheses open up unexpected perspectives. Consequently theologians gain the impression that increased attention to these hypotheses and an examination of them could give the study of religion new impulses and thus lead to a fruitful discussion between the two disciplines.

We shall therefore now try to bring out clearly some of the points that have already emerged in what we have said up to now, listing a number of conclusions arising from our investigations, with a view to this prospective discussion between theology and psycho-analysis.

1. The most noticeable thing up to now is that the theologian constantly gets the impression that the psychologist is operating with a one-sided picture of religion. For him, religion is apparently that part of the inner life which we theologians normally term natural religion. But theology knows another kind of religion as well. This can be defined in widely varying ways and is considered to be the Christian (and hence often the legitimate) religion.

But I must add that theology does not go away empty-handed. In nineteenth-century philosophy of religion, writers again and again operate with a general concept of religion in which Christianity is a particular manifestation. In the twentieth century, however, it has become increasingly obvious that the differences of structure between the different religions are far too fundamental for such a view still to be upheld. Nowadays, therefore, different structural types are distinguished from one another – the primitive religions, the prophetic religions, etc. – and scholars try by way of various hypotheses to find the clue to particular links between the various types. A convincing example of this method is K. A. Hidding's *De Evolutie van het godsdienstig bewustzijn* (The development of the religious consciousness), in which he distinguishes between three different structural types.

Now I believe that in the West we have to do with one type of religion which has come to be called natural religion in the course of history; and with a second type, which takes its bearings from the Bible and which manifests itself in the various forms of Christianity (and sometimes Judaism as well). This is distinguished from the first type by a series of characteristics, some of which we have already mentioned: we said, for example, that the I–Thou relationship was the most important. Both types are of equal contemporary importance in the West and they live together in a remarkable symbiosis in which negative and positive influences alternate.

If a dialogue between psycho-analysis and theology is really to take place, then exhaustive information about these two types of religion is essential. This is the only way of arriving at a common way of thinking.

2. This is also the only way of making fruitful a closer investigation of the great hypothesis which modern psycho-analysis has to offer us: that the growing child's relationship to its parents contributes to its later

religion. We saw that the revolution we have mentioned consisted primarily in the fact that today's analyst no longer judges this contribution as being a purely negative one; he now differentiates, putting the negative and the positive potentialities side by side. He starts from the idea that religion as such represents an essential aspect of human life.

Erikson (who has gone furthest in this field) sees as positive potentialities the basic trust which has grown up in the child's relationship to its mother, as well as the internalizing of the father figure in the form of a 'positive conscience'. In his study of unbelief Rümke registered a series of negative potentialities.

The problems on which investigation has to concentrate seem to me obvious. We must first have a more or less complete picture of the two types of religious life that are in question, a picture accepted by both sides (perhaps in the form of a provisional working hypothesis). We must then discover from the history of their development at what points the various elements of both types emerge (and with what potentialities, including potential disturbances); the way these elements evolve in the succeeding phases; and finally, how the elements can be on the one hand differentiated, and on the other hand connected with one another.

One problem among others that will arise is that natural religion, i.e., basic trust, develops organically, from the inside (unless it is preserved by the child in the form of images offered by its surroundings), whereas the Christian faith reaches the child through the people who bring it up. A subject of investigation here might well be the mutual influence of training and natural religion. On the other hand, we must find out how the child's relationship to its father also links up with particular elements in Christian education, or how it may in certain circumstances stand in the way of a healthy development of the Christian type (as it did in Luther's case). Moreover we must not forget that Christian education already intuitively attempts, in the case of particular elements, to link up with what has already developed in the child, so that in this way it does not convey the Christian type of religion in its pure form. I am thinking of belief in God as the providing Father, which plays a much less important part in mature faith than it does in 'Sunday school' teaching. A further difficulty here is that not only do fathers and mothers in each case exert a differing influence; their sons and daughters also experience that influence in different ways. Unconsciously we much too often hold the boy's development to be the normal one.

These are only a few openings for an investigation into certain things which have not yet been discovered, or into possibilities that have not been considered up to now.[1] The meaning of mother and father for the growth of the child is not only complicated and difficult to visualize clearly; it is also rich in potentialities and accompanies the whole life of man like a warm but sometimes shrill melody. Father and mother contribute their own special themes to the melody, but these themes also melt into one another as the music sounds. For religious development in particular, it seems to me important that although we are able to distinguish the two themes, both together determine the key in the melody of life. Erikson points to the fact that father religions have their mother churches. He believes that the one theme is heard through the other, even if to a varying degree. The special features about this fact demand closer investigation. The picture of the fatherly God of the Bible also has motherly features at some points; and conversely, natural religion's picture of God continually shows points of contact with a dialogistic relationship. Even more fundamentally: being is never without a sense of relationship; and the Other, God as the Other, raises the problem of being, of our own being. Perhaps an investigation of the differing importance of the two parents for the child's growth, as well as their importance as a whole, might throw new light on problems like these.

3. Here we now seem to have arrived at the point at which a hypothesis which finds its supporters in cultural anthropology ought to be tested against the sphere of our present cultural life as well. According to this hypothesis, religion is absorbed into the cultural pattern and is therefore in constant interplay with other elements of human life. We have already pointed to some possible connections in what we have already said. It seems to me that it would be of the greatest interest to make a closer empirical investigation of the influence of male and female factors in the various Western cultural patterns, together with the typical viewpoints associated with them that dominate philosophy and theology.

4. A further important point, mentioned in the last chapter, was the possiblity of a discussion about the different practical aspects of pastoral care, and perhaps about co-operation in certain fields. It is clear that psychiatry can perform considerable service in the pastoral sphere, even though that sphere has an autonomy of its own. Its knowledge of people, its insight into the problems of human relationships, its experience in the training of therapists, its help among groups of clergy in the consideration of more difficult pastoral cases (on the lines of the groups of general practitioners called together by Balint, the psychiatrist, to discuss

[1] I am thinking here for example of Winnicott's theory of 'transitional objects' (the toy rabbit, the doll), which help the child to form its sense of relationship.

their difficult cases) – all these things can be of great importance in the future in bringing about an improvement in the quality of pastoral care.

5. Finally it should be pointed out that in the preceding chapters a series of individual problems have been touched on which require further explanation in some future discussion. We can think of the interpretation of the mentality of primitive peoples, the meaning of image and rite, the question of the growth of conscience, and the problem of guilt. Others were not mentioned at all – the nature of fear, for instance, or the importance of church and group, the problem of secularization, etc.

Two points must still be mentioned before we conclude this section. First of all, although psycho-analysis had begun to play an important part in our society once the initial resistance had been overcome, in recent years it has once more come under fire. I am of course thinking here of the criticism raised by phenomenological psychology, but actually far more about the objections proceeding from the side of modern empirical and statistical psychology. Doubts have been expressed about the scientific nature of psycho-analysis, partly because its theories (which rest on the therapeutic situation) are difficult to verify; but also because other scientific hypotheses seem to shake the foundation of these theories. Eysenck's criticism, which attacks psycho-analysis at these two points, is the expression of a feeling of widespread uncertainty about this discipline. I have the impression that the psycho-analysts (who, as far as I can see, take these critical misgivings seriously) will be able to defend the scientific nature of analysis and even to deepen its basis; but if our discussion is to be a fruitful one, we must be aware that psycho-analysis has not the undisputed position that outsiders often attribute to it (cf. p. 7).

In the sphere of theology too all kinds of things are astir and with a view to our discussion we must try to explain the points – often fundamental ones – where there seems to be uncertainty. Our partners in the discussion would otherwise not be in a position to carry on a real discussion with us.

I do not think that I am viewing the present crisis of theology (and the churches) in unduly simple terms when I say that the uncertainty proclaimed itself in the last century with Kierkegaard. In the atmosphere of confidence, general as well as ecclesiastical, which prevailed in those days, he tried by his activity to draw attention to an element of inescapable insecurity. This uncertainty could be generally sensed during the First

World War and afterwards. In the Netherlands Roessingh was moved to write by a change of mentality, and Karl Barth embodied a part of European feeling about life when, in his commentary on the Epistle to the Romans, he tried to interpret the apostle Paul's great utterance from the perspective of a Kierkegaard and a Nietzsche. As against this inner uncertainty, in which they felt themselves at one only with Kierkegaard, Roessingh and Barth apparently found support in tradition and in the church, as Roessingh evinced in his right-wing modernism and Barth in his *Church Dogmatics*. The theologians who raised their voices during the Second World War and afterwards seemed to extend the uncertainty to tradition and the church as well. Bultmann's demythologizing and Bonhoeffer's recognition that the people of our time (ourselves included) are no longer responsive to the tiny residue of 'religion' within ourselves, destroy a series of supports for human life which have helped for centuries to overcome the unbelief that dwells in the midst of all belief. In his book *Honest to God* the Anglican Bishop Robinson expresses the feeling that he is bound to testify to a great uncertainty in the inner centres of his faith. With this he seems to accentuate an uncertainty which fills tens of thousands and which in its inarticulate form is apparently experienced as a crushing load. Tillich too has shown that most religious words and images have lost their power and that we have to try to make their content our own in a new way and using new words. The image of God is no exception. We have to learn to find God in the depths, in 'the shaking of the foundations', or we shall not find him at all any more. Another American theologian, van Buren, maintains that in the gospel we really only have to do with Christ, the man in our own human history. Many plead for a faith 'in the horizontal', or urge that we should find it in love of our fellow men.

A religious crisis such as this cannot be solved by psychological means, but with the help of psychology we can certainly try to make certain aspects of it comprehensible. I myself have no doubt that from the beginning the uncertainty was concentrated on the very centre, on belief itself. Kierkegaard's life was already dominated by the question of what belief really is. His question is: who am I as a believer? Erikson would say that in the present crisis it is a question of the believer's identity. He has taught us that our identity has to do with the society that lends an identity, as well as with an ideology that helps us to arrive at identity. But although society today knows practising Christians, and perhaps also adherents of the churches, it has no pattern, no identity for the believer. We therefore have to achieve our identity by our own methods. But here the church does not supply us with an ideology. It has done this right down through the centuries, through its theology and liturgy; but this ideology – witness Bultmann and Robinson – now has no efficacy; we no longer live from it. And we have no new ideology to give us support and to create a sense of identity. It is true that we are not quite without anything at all. We find support in the vague consciousness that our uncertainty is a good thing because we sense it in others as well, and that this uncertainty can reveal new possibilities of identification. We listen to Bonhoeffer and Robinson, but we also, as it were, listen to what is behind them.

If this is a more or less adequate representation of the situation, it seems to me that there are two important viewpoints with which psycho-analysis, above all, can help us. The first is that uncertainty can only be overcome if it is expressed, and expressed as openly as possible, as it is by Robinson in *Honest to God*. Repressed uncertainty has a destructive effect. We must deduce from the reactions to Robinson's book that in our world a great deal of inner insecurity was repressed by the sense of obligation to conform to the ecclesiastical forms of the day – its forms of liturgy and tradition, the picture people have of faith and the church. The overtone which could be heard in the word faith was evidently '*must*'. Faith and the church are fixed elements in a cultural pattern and this determined the picture which many people have of these two entities. These people certainly know that faith has something to do with a highly personal decision, but the doubt which is essentially bound up with it (and which the New Testament, for example, testifies to) can find no real place in their lives. They do not know how to cope with it, they suppress it, with the result that their faith becomes no true faith at all. For faith has the overtone of 'you *may*' – and here I am convinced that we can learn something very important from psycho-analysis: that the path to true life (and in this case to true faith) can only be found when what is suppressed is made conscious and so enters into relationship with other 'islands of experience'. In this way it can also be expressed and takes on the concrete form essential for conversation and hence for growth and integration, i.e., acceptance and 'use'.

Here we can learn from Luther, from the analysis which Erikson makes of his struggle. According to Erikson (p. 205), Luther first took a step forward when he accepted his doubt, when in a profound sense he dared to be passive, without attempting to hold on to his insecurity with the courage of despair. 'What he had tried so desperately and for so long to counteract and overcome he now accepted as his divine gift – the sense of utter abandonment, *sicut jam damnatus*, as if already in hell.' We have already mentioned that von Staupitz played a positive role at this point. Communication with the other is a quite essential element; it is significant here that the German word to communicate, '*mitteilen*', literally means 'to share with'.

I have mentioned the example of Luther deliberately, because I believe that the whole problem of identity, in the significance which Erikson ascribes to it in the context of Luther's struggle, has validity for our own times as well. According to Erikson, Luther did not only find a new identity for himself; he found one for his period as well.

In reality our whole Western world seems to have stuck fast in an identity crisis. Our religious struggle is part of this Western identity crisis. Erikson talks (p. 20) about ideology as the world image which gives a basis for the sense of identity, as the 'unconscious tendency underlying religious and scientific as well as political thought'. For those who have an understanding of these things, the religious crisis reveals a clear relationship to everything that is going on in existentialism as well as in the most widely varying forms of modern life.

Can anything be said about this 'unconscious thinking'? Could it be that our identity lies in the fact that we know we are on the search for identity in as much as we are breaking out of the 'shell' (Jaspers), are on the wrong track ('tracks which generally end abruptly on overgrown and untrodden ground' – Heidegger), are condemned to freedom in order to be man (Sartre), are on the road like Abraham, nomads 'not knowing whither we are to go' (Epistle to the Hebrews), and are moving like tight-rope walkers? In his sensitive book *Profielen van geachten* (Outlines of thoughts), W. Leendertz (one of Kierkegaard's followers) compared the dogmatist, i.e., the believer, with a tightrope walker who is playing with freedom at a dizzy height (Kierkegaard). If this image reflects the 'unconscious thinking' of our time, through which we are supposed to have a 'sense of identity', then a few facets stand out which are not without significance for the religious sphere.

In this case the theme of our 'ideology' is not, as it is with Luther, the God–man relationship in the form of justification by faith, not works. And the theme which many of us viewed as the fundamental theme of the twentieth century – the question of the meaning of life – does not seem to me central either. The central theme is rather that we are balanced between liberty and bondage, between authentic existence and inauthentic existence, the experience of being, not as firm ground beneath our feet, but as a dialectical 'letting go' and simultaneous seeking for something to hold on to at the edge of an abyss, where we go on without having any clear direction.

We might now ask: why do we not jump down from our tightrope? It seems to me that the answer must be: because it *has* to be like this, and because we are also balancing between hope and fear, in a mistrustful basic trust that we shall *succeed*, indeed that this balancing act in our relationship to our fellow-men and to God (about whom, however, we can say hardly anything specific) contains within itself unexpected and fearful potentialities.

Psycho-analysis can in my opinion make still one more contribution in this situation. I have already said that psychology cannot solve any religious crisis. That crisis must be solved from the sources over which religion itself disposes: the relationship to God, the thinking through of that relationship, the articulation of doubt, the common search and common prayer, the listening, the being open to the Spirit. But psychology can try to shed light on the situation and make it comprehensible.

We have already said that in the present religious crisis part of our culture's identity crisis is working itself out and that this is comparable with the crisis of Luther's period. This is not chance; there are reasons for it. Can anything be said about these reasons?

Because of my lack of specialist knowledge, I do not feel competent to answer this question, but I would like to point hypothetically to *one* aspect, which I hope might take on a clearer outline through a closer investigation.

What strikes me about the modern theological literature we have mentioned is its rebellion against the aspects of belief and the church which Jaspers so aptly calls the 'shell': the state church with its hierarchy (Kierkegaard), mythology (Bultmann), the fixed premises (Bonhoeffer), the established forms and ideas (Robinson). Bound up with this is the need to accept only what is genuine and what fulfils its function and is not offered as tradition. One needs very little training in psycho-analysis to see that here our relationship to the previous generation is working itself out. But it is not so much healthy resistance towards the 'fathers' that is being expressed; under normal circumstances that leads to a critical appropriation of tradition and thus to a healthy cultural transmission. What we find here is rather an unwillingness, and hence an inability, to identify with the 'fathers'. The 'fathers' give the impression of being shut up in the 'shell'; people do not find in them the living quality of true faith. They do not want the 'shell', but see no chance of identifying themselves with its 'faith'. This leads to the rejection of the shell and, as far as belief is concerned, the need to undertake one's own journeys of discovery in order to find the God in the depths (Tillich), to experiment (like modern art), to be genuine and to accept lack of security as an essential element in the human condition (existentialism). Behind the crisis of these years, therefore, I see the inability of fathers to give their sons the chance for identification. In Erikson's phrase (p. 120), they are apparently inadequate 'guardians of the child's autonomous existence'. If this is so, then the identity crisis of our time is showing the effects of our being 'on the way to a fatherless society', in Mitscherlich's sense. We must be careful not to oversimplify, but one factor is very probably that this shift in our cultural pattern also alters the content of the religion which has been detached from the 'fathers'. Many people feel that the changes in the theological climate mean a lapse from the path which Karl Barth followed in his theology for so many years. Is this not connected with the fact that his patriarchal type of religion no longer quite fits our gradually changing pattern, in which the 'fatherly' elements have become obscured? In this case the increasing prominence of 'family' aspects (the Lord's Supper, brotherly love, unity) as well as a certain mysticism (the God in the depths, the Oriental renaissance) could perhaps be understood as the chance for receptivity to other elements – *pre-fatherly* elements, as it were, in human development.

We can only say these things very hesitantly. They are highly speculative. But they are in principle capable of verification and can perhaps even, with reservations, make certain developments comprehensible, so helping us to be less strained and more tolerant towards the present and the future. In my book *Gott in vaterloser Gesellschaft* ('God in a fatherless society'), I have gone more deeply into this very problem and I shall come back to it in more detail in the second part of our present study. It is my belief and my hope that God is with us to the end of the age. We change, but he is always the same.

PART TWO

Religion in the Light of Psycho-analytical Theory

Phases and Patterns: The Oral Phase

I

Introduction

The spheres of religion and the church are undergoing a radical crisis in our society. Theologians have noticed this for many years, but recently everyone with eyes to see has become dismally conscious of it. When I asked a Swedish pastor to describe the situation in his church in a single word, the answer he gave was 'confusion'; and this is probably true of every country in the Western world.

Alienation from the churches has taken on undreamt-of dimensions in the Netherlands. Even in West Germany, where a short time ago 98% of the population belonged to some denomination or other, there is now talk of a steadily growing stream of people who are leaving the churches. But even among people who belong to one or other of the churches religious observance is decreasing irresistibly. In the parish of 's-Geavenhage the number of people attending church services declined by a third in nine years; the number of candidates for confirmation actually diminished by as much as a half in the same period of time. The same process is going on in the Catholic church as well. Here the rapidly receding number of vocations is a striking phenomenon which must give us food for thought.

Apart from the crisis of organized religion, we can establish that there is a mainly spiritual crisis as well. A theological proposition such as 'God is dead' suggests the fundamental shifts that are going on. Books with titles like *Orientatie* (translated as *New Ways in Theology*) or *Het einde van de religie* (The end of religion), both by J. Sperna Weiland, or *Het einde van het conventionele Christendom* (The end of conventional Christianity) by W. H. van de Pol, are best sellers in the Netherlands. In the churches too a conflict seems to lie ahead: conservatives are confronted by radicals – the identity of the church in twentieth-century society is becoming a problem. The question is whether the real choice is not between 'comfort and challenge'. Moreover, parallel to the churches, a widespread sub-culture is developing among young people which is increasingly taking on the features of a counter-culture. This sub-culture is developing quite individual and new religious manifestations, to which the traditional churches are now really quite unable to give any answer at all.

Here *confusion* really is the only true and appropriate word.

In our present book we will try to discover whether a certain order and system cannot be picked out of this confusion. In my book *Gott in vaterloser Gesellschaft*, which appeared in 1969, I tried to show that a series of profound alterations in the religious and ecclesiastical field find their explanation in the spreading industrialization of our Western society, and above all in the 'fatherlessness' of our pattern of society and culture which this industrialization produces. Psycho-analysis and the cultural anthropology of Margaret Mead and her school (which is based on psycho-analysis) have given us certain insights which can help us to make clear the way in which these changes in the social and cultural patterns can influence man's personal and social life – and hence his personal religious and church life as well.

In this book I am going one step further. I want to defend the proposition that in the phases of development which psycho-analysis has demonstrated as belonging to the early years of life, certain patterns are 'released' which, in later life, exert their influence to a greater or lesser degree, appearing as models for education and culture in man's common life. The whole panorama of mankind's religious life, from the so-called primitives down to present-day man, therefore reflects particular phases of development which have been pointed out by analysts such as Freud and Erikson. Sometimes they appear in 'pure' form, but often in all kinds of combinations as well. A large part of this book is devoted to the clarification and substantiation of this thesis.

In view of the confusion which besets us at present, I am not going to confine myself to a particular stage in the past, but will try to trace how far my working hypothesis is capable of bringing some degree of order into this confusion. I am here linking up directly with my book 'God in a fatherless society', and particularly with the 'fatherless' pattern of our culture. In my opinion we have entered a cultural phase which might, psychologically speaking, be called adolescence. It is therefore essentially a completely new phase, which also faces the church and religion with totally fresh problems and perspectives. In my book *Neue Wege kirch-*

lichen Handelns (New paths of church action) '*Planning of Change*' I have already pointed out that the church must be able to render an account of this situation which is changing so rapidly. I believe that in this present book I have developed more clearly certain lines of approach which to some extent emerge in my earlier study. I am thinking particularly of the pattern of the exodus experience (which I have discussed in *Neue Wege kirchlichen Handelns*) as being fundamental for an understanding of the present situation.

This book developed in the course of recent years as the result of a process whose milestones are, as it were, my two earlier studies. I am convinced that I have described the basic proposition with which I am working most clearly here. I know that it still appears highly hypothetical, which is to say that it has not up to now received sufficient support and is probably in need of correction. But it is my hope that it will be accepted as a proposition by other scholars in this field and will stimulate them to a closer investigation.

A Contribution to the Psychology of Religion

It will have become clear by now that in this book we are working in the field of the psychology of religion. Our starting point is the reflection that psychology – and especially the psychology of religion – is capable of bringing a certain order into the confusion. But how are we to define this capability?

In a very simplified way, we might say the following: The natural sciences bring order into the confusing multiplicity of natural phenomena by showing the links connecting one phenomenon with another, so providing an explanation for them. In the same way psychology is a science which brings order into the confusion of the phenomena of man's psychic life, by discovering connecting links there too.

For the psychology of religion, religion is an often confusing complex of manifestations of the human psychic life; and psychology also seeks to show connecting links, so as to create order. Now, there has been considerable resistance on the theological side, down to the present day, to the psychological investigation of religious phenomena. We can give different reasons for this. Some theologians fear a certain relativism, which could find an entry into the religious life if religious manifestations are investigated as if they all had the same scientific status, without enough attention being paid to the question of whether they are founded on truth, i.e., whether we believe them or not. Other theologians maintain that religion was never concerned with the observation of what goes on in our psychic life; its concern is orientation towards God. For these people the psychology of religion is a sterile contemplation of one's own navel. I am convinced that this resistance will disappear in the years to come. For the objections which are raised against this branch of the subject are the same as the ones which were once levied against historical research into religion. Then too people talked about the danger of relativizing and the degeneration of religion. The historical study of religious phenomena has meanwhile made its way and is accepted practically everywhere. I am convinced that the same thing will happen with the psychology of religion. For the dangers which people are afraid of here can be averted and cannot have any effect on true and authentic faith. Whereas the advantages of research into the psychology of religion, if it once really gets under way, are obvious and clearly demonstrable. The confusion must give way to order and we must arrive at an understanding of the reasons behind the confusion. This is too important a factor to be pushed aside lightly.

Let us first look at the question of where we can best start in the present situation of the psychology of religion.

The First Years of Life

A provisional investigation shows that the influence of the first years of life on religious development is probably very considerable. Freud even sees religion as not much more than something left over from the experience of early childhood. His pupil Erikson changes the negative meaning of Freud's statement into a positive one when he says that in religion the 'basic trust' of the earliest years of life is preserved. In my book *Gott in vaterloser Gesellschaft*, I have tried to show how much the religious problems of many modern people (I am thinking primarily of Kierkegaard and Nietzsche) are connected with experiences drawn from the early years of childhood.

As we saw in the first section, two psychiatrists maintain opposing views on this point. Freud starts from the proposition that religion is a residue of infancy which has to be overcome in maturity. Man has difficulty in freeing himself from the emotional complications of the child–father ties. The Dutch psychiatrist Rümke, on the other hand, in his book *The Psychology of Unbelief*, wanted to win acceptance for the thesis that it is unbelief, not belief, which is a disturbance in development. Belief in the sense of a basic trust belongs to the nature of man.

Perhaps it is an instinct. Many disturbances are conceivable, however, through which belief can be transformed into unbelief. This kind of basic trust is clearly parallel to Erikson's, which is awakened in the child through its ties with its mother and which accompanies it throughout the rest of its life. In his discussion of the disturbances, Rümke does not go into the genetic aspects, but they are evidently presupposed in his account.

Here we come up against the working hypothesis from which we shall start in this book. The bond with the mother – and we would add, with the father – is of essential importance for religious development. Our aim is to support this hypothesis by a number of examples, and thus to make it seem a probable one.

One of the ideas by which we should be guided is that the structural distinctions between the religions (about which there is so much talk today in research into the history of religion) are connected with these early childish relationships. Here we would above all support the theories developed by K. A. H. Hidding, who is Professor of the History of Religions at Leyden.

Certain premises are linked with this approach and we should examine these first of all.

1. Human life as we know it is impossible without development or growth. Everyone has a body which is in the process of growth from birth onwards. We are guided by instincts which make us take nourishment, which enable us to go on living, or which impel us to propagate ourselves and thus to protect the human race from extinction. These phenomena must have a reason, the unknown x, which has given rise to so much philosophical reflection down the centuries. People talked about a *vis vitalis*, the vital principle which is at work in all these manifestations; or quite simply about nature, which for example influences the process of healing in sickness. In his book *Levenstijdperken van de man* (The phases of man's life), Rümke picks up ideas developed by Minkowski and Goethe, and talks about a 'primal hormone' which, for example, affects the individual organism through the hormonal system and must be understood as a kind of 'entelechy' in Aristotle's sense. Differences in the genes, for example variations in the speed of growth, could be explained by this hormone.

2. Development must be seen as the realization of a plan. Rümke sees the foundation of a plan of this kind in the *mneme*, the memory, where it is stored for the individual and for the species as well. Thus the human

body is the realization of a plan fore-given from the outset with development.

3. In his publications on developmental psychology, Rümke has constantly stressed that development takes place in phases, in the course of which, he believes, evident transitions from integration to disintegration can be shown. These 'waves' can be established particularly in the sphere of the psyche; but parallels can also be shown in the structures belonging to the physical sphere.

4. One presupposition is derived from depth psychology. In the animal world there appear to be particular situations which act as 'releasers' in the development process. Ducklings will not enter the water and do not learn to swim unless an older duck precedes them in a particular way and swims ahead of them in the water. Perch, for example, only lay eggs in a particular situation which acts as a 'releaser'.

The term 'releaser' is of essential importance for my account, so I must go into it somewhat more closely. It is well known that children acquire all sorts of things from their parents in childhood. Erikson believes that motherly warmth is essential for the grown-up's later sense of identity because it gives him the basic trust which is indispensable for that sense of identity. In *Young Man Luther* he writes that Luther lacked an element that was essential for his inner growth because he had to dispense with his father's glance and his father's word. It is reported of so-called 'wolf children' – children who have been exposed and brought up by wolves – that when they were discovered years later they were lacking something because of their lack of relationship to their parents; and this could no longer be made good later. The father is necessary for the formation of conscience, for example.

It can therefore be said that the environment – and in the first place the environment of the family, with all the influences which are associated with it – is necessary for the growing child if the potentialities latent in him are to come to fulfilment. I think that we can therefore maintain that the child's ties with its parents (and perhaps with other people as well) act as a 'releaser' in his development in the same way that particular factors act as releasers biologically among animals. We could even term culture the total sum of the potentialities which have been released in man by his environment. It may be noted in addition that a particular culture can deprive man of the releaser or can rebury certain budding potentialities. We can sometimes see a (pseudo-) debility in children brought up in poverty, for example; or we discover that, in children such as Luther, certain potentialities have remained undeveloped because of a one-sided upbringing.

The questions we face in our investigation are obvious. We must discover what importance the father and mother have as the releasers (and perhaps also as the 'repressers') of particular religious potentialities in the child's life. That is one of the main points of our investigation.

What is Religion?

One of the most difficult things about any investigation in the field of the psychology of religion is to decide what definition of religion we should start from. For there are a great number of these definitions. I do not want to enter into an endless and fruitless discussion, so I will start from a distinction of structure which is usual in modern phenomenology of religion and then see how far that takes us. I am thinking of the two (or really three) types of religion which Hidding distinguishes in his writings. We will simply mention them here and come back to them in more detail later. Hidding includes in the first group the so-called naturalistic religions in which God is worshipped as the all-embracing unity, as 'the unique mystery of reality's endless being'; in these religions God reveals himself primarily in images. The second type comprises the religions in which God is worshipped as the creator, who makes, determines, rules and commands all things. These are the religions of the word. Alongside these two types Hidding sets Christianity as the third; but he maintains that it has not yet revealed its deepest nature and that it therefore still has a future ahead of it. This is an idea to which we shall return at the end of the book. We shall start from Hidding's typology (which is incidentally supported by other people too, in a somewhat altered form) because it gives us the chance of emphasizing more clearly our working hypothesis about the importance of the early relationships of childhood for religious development. For we are hoping to prove that there is a parallelism between the child's relationships to both parents and the two first named structures. And it would then seem obvious that these parallels are not chance ones, but go back to a genetic connection.

Some Methodological Problems

In this study we want to link up closely with psycho-analysis, especially with Freud and his school. And here certain problems crop up with which we must concern ourselves first of all. The initial difficulty is that psycho-analysis and psychology of religion talk different languages, at least they still do at the moment. The analyst talks about the child's relationship to its mother in terms of the relationship to an object: the mother is an object of love for the child. The psychology of religion enquires into the religious elements in this relationship, or into its qualities, and talks about security, sometimes even about security in Being (as Being is manifested in the mother). It is true that an understanding can be reached between the two over terms like trust and surrender, and some-times over such expressions as the dissolution of the ego or the oceanic feeling, but a translation is necessary; or rather, the psychology of religion has to try to investigate the religious content of the analytical formulations. We still have to learn how to go about this task of translation.

In this connection we must not lose sight of the fact that psycho-analysis is a medical discipline and one that had its origin in the nine-teenth century, so that its views have a strongly somatic orientation. It therefore has a preference for using biological patterns, and likes to start from parallels between man and the animal. We must discover how far our religious 'groupings' fit in here.

A second problem is, how are we to arrive at the facts? This is an important question, above all with regard to the first year in a child's life, where we have to discover the religious content of the relationship between mother and child. Originally the analysts derived their knowledge about development during the early years of life from psychotherapy. As we all know, man suffers from amnesia with regard to these years; that is to say, he is unable to remember them. He therefore has to try to reproduce the unconscious material by means of association (through dreams). Expedients such as LSD also seem to make it possible to lift early repressed material into the consciousness. But there are really no direct means of access to the earliest experiences of life.

None the less, attempts were made quite early on to find confirmation of these 'memories' through the empirical observation of children. And many analytical theories were actually borne out by these observations. The existence of an oral, an anal and a genital phase need no longer be doubted. The behaviour of children provides unequivocal proof. Re-cently the child's very first experiences in its relationship to its mother have also been the subject of investigation. In the Netherlands, Bowlby has become especially well known in this field, but in specialist circles the investigations of Anna Freud and R. A. Spitz also have their special importance. We shall later be drawing particularly on Spitz's book about the first year in a child's life. In the same context we might draw attention to J. de Wit's dissertation *Problemen rond de moeder-kind-relatie* (Problems in the relationship between mother and child), which is a good introduction to this field.

A Survey of the Phases

The development of the early years can be divided up into phases in different ways, depending on the point of view adopted. An attempt to map out development from the aspect of the degree of intelligence produces one division; if we start from the aspect of manual dexterity, we arrive at another. But it will very probably emerge that the two things do not deviate a great deal. The development of the child's life evidently takes place in waves, a fact which Rümke also had in mind when he talked about psychical development as being continuous movement, in which integration and disintegration alternate with one another. It may therefore be said that religious development in the child's life is not something isolated; it is connected with the rest of its development and hence with the phases of that development. We use the vague word 'connected' deliberately, for it is difficult to form a clear picture of what the connection really is without a more exact investigation. For this reason we believe that in our investigation we can proceed from the psycho-analytical division into phases.

1. We find the most important thing about these phases in Freud. He starts from the standpoint of the development of sexuality. One aspect of sexuality is obviously erotic behaviour towards the other sex, behaviour which is concentrated on reproduction. On the other hand it also has the aspect of a more diffuse libido. If we remember this fact, we can understand how Freud arrives at his division into phases on the basis of the sensitivity of particular 'erogenous zones' in the child. In the first nine months the baby's mouth is particularly sensitive to feeling, and this made Freud talk about an 'oral' phase. It is followed by the 'anal' phase, because at this period the anus is especially open to stimulus. The third phase is the genital one; as the word suggests, it is now the sexual organs which are excitable. The latency phase follows, during which there are, as it were, no clearly identifiable zones, and the whole is completed with puberty. Now man advances to maturity; that is to say, he arrives at full sexuality.

Although sexuality is certainly the determining point of view in this division, Freud is clearly aware that the development takes place in waves. Particular psychical characteristics are associated with the sexuality, for these phases involve various ties with other people, and above all with the child's parents. In the oral phase stress lies almost exclusively on the bond with the mother, whereas in the anal phase the first withdrawal from the mother appears, and in the third, genital phase the child is drawn in a particular way by the parent who is of a different sex from himself. In these phases therefore we can talk about particular patterns of feeling and behaviour, and can do so with some degree of certainty if we take into account the fact that aggression also plays a particular – and different – part in every phase. Freud has sometimes been reproached with a kind of pansexualism. I think that what we have said shows that this is a biased view.

2. Erikson shows even more clearly that the psycho-analyst's division into phases is linked with particular patterns of behaviour. He is a modern pupil of Freud's who takes over his division into phases, merely using different conceptions to characterize them. His determining viewpoint is not the development of sexuality but the development of the sense of identity. In this way he arrives at eight phases which run through to old age. As far as the first three are concerned (the ones which primarily interest us) the main terms he uses (apart from oral, anal and genital) are trust as against mistrust; autonomy as against shame or doubt; and initiative as against guilt. For us it is important that Erikson – even more clearly than Freud – does not derive his point of view from one particular characteristic. With these terms he introduces a complex of feelings and modes of behaviour which can really best be termed a 'pattern'. We shall go on to show that in the closer working out of this classification of the phases, Erikson says that the particular feature of every individual phase is the appearance of a new complex of feelings and actions.

The Influence of Cultural Factors

Our thesis is therefore that during the developmental phases of childhood, particular patterns are 'released', and that particular religious patterns (or structures) develop in conjunction with them. We deliberately use the somewhat vague phrase 'in conjunction with them', because we are not yet at the stage of being able to say how this connection ought to be conceived of. I hope that we shall be able to explain this in the course of our account.

But here we come up against a problem which we must first examine more closely. At first sight it seems as if the division into phases had a purely biological basis. This is especially true of Freud, who in listing the phases puts all his stress on the development of sexuality. But cultural anthropology has shown that this is wrong. Natural, biological data do not appear in pure form in a single culture area. They are absorbed into a particular cultural pattern and are thus in some particular way re-moulded, perhaps also assimilated or 'experienced in a new way'. In reality, therefore, we do not know the natural data at all; we only know them in their multifarious cultural forms. The result is that we can never determine where the borderline between the natural and the cultural lies. We can at most attempt to test our suppositions against evidence drawn from the animal world; but the animal world does not always supply unequivocal material either. In the seal world, which Walt Disney presents to us so vividly in his film, we come across Oedipal situations; but these are evidently not general in the animal world.

It would seem as if the further we proceed in human development, the more cultural factors are mixed with natural ones. We shall see this very clearly when we are dealing with the Oedipal phase and adolescence. But even in the earlier oral and anal phases we can discover the influence of cultural factors.

This fact complicates the testing of our thesis as well as its application. We make our distinctions and thus attempt to bring order into the motley collection of religious phenomena through a division into phases which has grown up within a Western cultural pattern. One thing is urgently necessary: a dialogue with research workers from other culture areas who are attempting to develop a division into phases within their own cultural patterns – of course with the help of the psycho-analytical method (which is itself however strongly influenced by the West).

It is now already possible for us to draw certain conclusions. For one thing we will have to resist the tendency to see even the oral pattern (to take an example) in unduly simple terms. In oral cultures, with their naturalistic religions (to adopt Hidding's view), cultural influences are possible (and often demonstrable) which go back to father experiences very close to those of *our* Oedipal phase. If our thesis is correct, this must influence pictures of God. We must hence be prepared to differentiate sharply. We then discover in addition that our cultural pattern is changing and has probably always done so. We must hence differentiate even among ourselves. It is not difficult to discover, for example, that there are cultural and religious differences between Catholics and Protestants, and it will be permissible to suppose that these are connected with one another. It is even very probable that we are at present involved in a transition to an entirely new pattern, which is already exerting its influence on religious and ecclesiastical life. In my book *Gott in vaterloser Gesellschaft* I was primarily concerned to win acceptance for this theory with the help of material drawn from many fields. I shall be coming back to this problem in detail in the chapter on the adolescent phase (see pp. 285ff. below).

We must therefore establish that in view of the variegated reality of religious life, our initial thesis is an over-simplification. The details will have to be investigated, and then various differentiations and corrections will have to be made. My account does not therefore aim to be exhaustive. Its goal at the moment is to win acceptance for a particular thesis about the phenomenon of religion. But I am entirely conscious of the limitations of my account, and in what follows I shall again be pointing at the appropriate points to the limitations of its scope.

2

The Special Character of the First, Oral Phase

Erikson's View

It may be said that the dominating view in modern psychology in general is that the first phase of life – which Freud called the oral phase – has to make an essential and also a specific contribution to the child's development. In the study I have already mentioned on 'Problems in the relationship between mother and child', J. de Wit analyses the theories which are valid in this field and relativizes the one-sidedness which is sometimes to be found in them. In my view, however, his book is really based on the same conviction as Freud's.

But what is this specific contribution?

Here again different definitions are possible, and these are connected, as we have said, with the standpoint from which the development of the child is viewed. If we investigate the development of its intelligence we will arrive at a different definition from the one which will emerge if we take the motoric system as the guiding line. We are concerned with the child's religious development. In my opinion we get most from Erikson's definition when, in the search for the growth of identity, he terms the real thing that the mother contributes in this first phase the conferring of trust. The basic trust that comes into being through contact with the mother is for Erikson a fundamental element in the growth of identity. We must therefore ask: what can we learn from Erikson as regards our investigation?

We must begin, however, by noticing that it is apparently difficult to see the intrinsic nature of this phase completely. Even if we do not confine ourselves to a particular area as our guiding line, such as intelligence or the motoric system, but take a much more comprehensive one such as human identity, we still seem bound to a medical (and hence very particular) definition of the question. Psycho-analysts, it becomes clear, are doctors, and this influences their investigations into developmental psychology in a very definite way. We cannot therefore simply take over their formulations without more ado; we will have to 'translate' them in the framework of our own enquiry.

I am thinking here of René A. Spitz's investigation *Vom Säugling zum Kleinkind* (*Naturgeschichte der Mutter-Kind-Beziehung im ersten Lebensjahr*) (From baby to toddler. The history of the relationship between mother and child in the first year of life), one of the best known studies from the analytical side. In his survey of the subject (p. 23) he says that he wants to find out what happens between mother and child. He is therefore going to try to discover how the relationship helps self-preservation, and the ways in which it contributes to the unfolding of the psychical and physical regions of the personality. In my opinion this is to say too little, because in this phase the child achieves more than just this; he is already laying a foundation for his later maturity. The child must also be seen as the being who is taking his first steps on the road to adult life. We must therefore also ask: what contribution to maturity is made by what happens between mother and child? This is Erikson's question; and he maintains that through the quality of the mother–child relationship a foundation is laid for the sense of identity, which is for him another word for maturity; a foundation, that is to say, in which 'trust' is awakened.

There is no doubt that Erikson is right. But we have to ask whether he too is not working within the framework of a particular medical question as well, for maturity can also be thought of as independence in the sense of emancipation from the parents. Now, from this aspect, the road to maturity already begins in the very first months of life, for one of the most important aspects of the first period is the process of emancipation. The child has to learn to be alone, to wait for its mother, to be disappointed by its mother, and so forth.

My point of view is therefore as follows: the child is part of a development from the very beginning in the sense that immediately after its birth it begins to grow in the direction of independence. That is to say, it grows in order to emancipate itself from its mother and perhaps from its father, on the basis of a slowly altering relationship to its parents. I am mentioning this last point deliberately, because the process of emancipation, as it is generally called today, is, taken as a whole, a complicated matter. It is a kind of swing of the pendulum, away from the mother, back to the mother, with stress falling increasingly on the emancipation. The nature of the relationship also alters gradually. Harlow's famous monkeys are a good example of what I mean. Harlow is an American scientist who, among other things, carried out experiments with monkeys. He shut these monkeys up in a cage with substitute mother-figures – dolls to which the monkeys could cling. Some of the dolls were even equipped with nipples that produced milk. The dolls differed from one another, some of them having a kind of fur, others merely being covered with cheesecloth. It emerged that the monkeys went on exploring trips but clung to the 'dolls' (though not so readily to the 'cheesecloth' ones) when they were afraid of some danger. We do not need to enumerate all Harlow's many experiments, but can confine ourselves to his main observations.

1. The process of emancipation is unmistakable. The animals are on the way to discover reality and first of all the reality of the external world. But in the case of a child it will certainly be permissible to presuppose the reality of the inner world as an exploratory field as well.

2. If an animal feels unsafe or is frightened, it again looks, in certain circumstances, for the bond with its mother. This bond communicates serenity. We can indicate the meaning of the word serenity by saying that the mother helps the baby monkey to accept and assimilate the insecurity of facing reality alone.

3. A baby monkey gradually dares to stray further away from its mother and also gradually seems able to stand more insecurity. Apparently the capacity to accept and assimilate the insecurity grows. We therefore see that the development that takes place in the years of childhood is a continuation of the process that begins at birth. The beginning is a symbiosis; the path of development is a dissolution of that symbiosis, and the end is independent being.

The important question for us now is: what does the child find in the bond? Or, to take our example, what does the baby monkey discover when it clings to the mother doll? Erikson's answer is: (basic) trust. But what is basic trust? Erikson's 'trust' is actually comparable with what Rümke also calls trust in his well-known book *The Psychology of Unbelief*. For him this trust is the real beginning of belief, and he starts from the proposition: 'The whole of life is based on a trustful belief' (p. ix). But he then terms belief 'something we consider true' and therefore something we do 'regardless of being unable to supply a sufficiency of intellectual reasons for it'. It becomes clear that he has *perceived* something – the same thing that Erikson means by his 'trust', only he formulates it in my opinion much too intellectually. Incidentally he returns to this intellectual formula when he introduces Monakow's 'religious instinct', which is closely connected with trust. In all this, I would say, he is moving in the right direction. For at the basis of our existence there is a fundamentally positive attitude towards reality, and this attitude, Erikson shows us, is awakened through the child's relationship to its mother.

Let us again for a moment consider Harlow's experiment. In trust, certain aspects can be distinguished which make it easy for us to perceive its religious meaning. What can we discover from the monkeys?

1. A certain *delight* in reality: through their 'trust', their curiosity and frankness – one might even say their courage – grows. Probably 'trust' manifests the will towards health, so that through contact with the mother a certain natural disposition is strengthened.

2. 'Trust' implies the sense of ultimate security (it is safe with its mother). Through trust we also acquire the foundation on which we are able to stand, 'the courage to be', to use a phrase of Tillich's.

3. To possess 'trust' also means that one can absorb and then integrate (negative) experiences. The capacity for integration is therefore closely connected with trust, although inherited disposition probably also plays a part. Harlow's experiments show clearly that fear of newly introduced objects is 'stood' better by animals with 'trust'; and on p. 94 of his book de Wit points to Hebb's experiments, which show that 'emotionally deprived' dogs (animals whose 'trust' has never been awakened) are apparently unable to learn to avoid an 'electric hedgehog' which gives them a shock when they touch it. That is to say, they cannot integrate this frightening experience in the normal way.

4. But to have trust also means not being overwhelmed by one's own negative impulses of fear or aggression. In his book *Childhood and Society* Erikson writes (p. 220) that 'the general state of trust, furthermore, implies ... that one may trust oneself and the capacity of one's own organs to cope with urges'.

5. Finally, trust is the capacity for receiving love. Erikson points to the quality of the relationship between mother and child and its great importance – among other things, in developing the capacity for giving love oneself later; the capacity, that is to say, for entering into deeper ties.

In Freud the term *satisfaction* plays a great part in the mother–child relationship, on the child's side. In the motherly warmth, at the mother's breast, the child feels satisfied. Emphasis here is on the relaxation which we can observe in the child. But in German the word satisfaction (*Befriedigung*) has a deeper note – the echo of the word 'peace'. And psychologists, watching a 'satisfied' child, have also used the word 'bliss'. In the five characteristics we have mentioned the conception of 'peace' takes on a particular outline. Originally it was a religious term. The biblical word is *shalom*, the word for the bliss of the End-time, the time when we shall be blessed. It is remarkable in this connection that the word bliss should often be used for profound oral satisfaction as well.

It is therefore not a mere assertion when we say that the heart of the relationship between mother and child is religious. The word 'trust' is full of religious connotations.

There are plenty of examples in religious literature – in the poems of Jan Luyken, for example. He tries again and again to convey in words the same feeling which we described when we were discussing the child's basic trust, in connection with the relationship between mother and child. In his poem 'Van de rust der zielen' ('The rest of souls'), Luyken describes how fearless his heart is though the wind rages through the forest, and the waves of the sea roar, and the storm breaks. He goes on:

> The storm that beats without
> Can find us unafraid
> Let but the heart be filled
> With utter peace within.
> The utter peace within
> Subdues the storm without.

Let me also quote some lines from another poem which show that for the poet God has the qualities of a mother:

> Each tells and testifies of that first being
> As of his mother and his nature's ground.
> This is the source from which our journey issues,
> This is the teeming womb from which we come ...
>
> Thou source and root of all our being,
> Put in our hearts a thirst for thee,
> To new life may our wills awaken,
> And all have ears for thee alone.[1]

[1] English readers may think of the poem by John Quarles:
> Long did I toil, and knew no earthly rest,
> Far did I rove, and found no certain home;
> At last I sought them in His sheltering breast,
> Who opes His arms, and bids the weary come:
> With Him I found a home, a rest divine,
> And I since then am His, and He is mine.
>
> *Translator*

It would be inappropriate to compare these poems with what we said about Harlow's experiments, but the parallels are unmistakable. These verses are about the search for rest, for trust, for peace. They deal with the possibility of integrating negative experiences – both outward experiences and inner ones. Luyken finds God to be the origin, the point where man is at home, the place of trust and peace. This religious vocabulary points clearly to what Erikson understands by the phrase basic trust, with its religious core. There are other examples of similar parallels. We find the same ideas in the poetry of Spieghel and Henriette Roland Holst. We also find them in Spinoza's philosophy, when he talks about an *amor intellectualis dei* – the intellectual love of God; and Spinoza's *Ethica* is a classic testimony to 'basic trust'.

These parallels make it permissible for us to conclude that the relationship between mother and child has a religious core and that certain religious experiences point to the 'basic trust' of this relationship. We hope later to be able to bring evidence to show that a particular religious kernel is 'released' in the relationship to the mother, and that this kernel develops with man himself.

Aspects of Emancipation

First of all, however, we must return to the essentials of the first phase. We have seen that two aspects of this phase are of decisive importance. The first is: the child emancipates itself from the mother. It leaves the symbiosis with its mother and observes her as an object in the external world. When the child follows her with his eyes, when he gives his first smile, these are (as Spitz rightly stresses) the first signs of 'relationship to an object' and thus signs of the emancipation process. The fear which, as we know, can be established at the age of eight months, belongs to this. The second aspect is the experience of oneness, of security. Here two factors play a great role. The first of them is the taking of nourishment. We already pointed to the association between 'bliss' and oral satisfaction. In feeding – especially from the mother's breast, but even from the bottle – the child experiences the secure oneness with the mother – an oceanic feeling, we might say. Later the child will try to repeat the same experience by means of transitional or 'intermediate' objects, which it puts in its mouth and strokes – its thumb, its rabbit, its teddy bear. Later still sweets or cigarettes have a similar function, though to a lesser degree. The other factor which plays a part in the experience of oneness is the skin, the body, and above all the warmth which it radiates. Harlow's monkeys opened our eyes to the great importance of this fact. But we know from catastrophes like the floods which took place in Holland in 1953 that the nearness of the (secure) mother figure, who presses the child to herself, is of the greatest importance in the endurance of frightening experiences. We all know how the knowledge that our mother was at home gave the experience of 'home' as such its enduring stamp. If our mother was not at home, home gave us no feeling of security.

Now, it is an important fact that tensions can arise in this process of emancipation. Harlow's experiments showed this clearly. Fright leads to 'fight' or 'flight'. The absence of the mother causes fear, and this fear leads to aggression or to a despondency which can sometimes have depressive features and can be characterized as 'flight'. Frightened animals attack or withdraw. In the first phase of the child's development we can see the same manifestations quite clearly. Children bite, scream, howl and sometimes become apathetic.

Recent investigations have shown that negative influences can emanate from the mother to the child even in the earliest months. The mother can be over-protective (generally out of fear) and can thus arouse fear in the child, which sometimes leads to bottled-up aggression. The mother can also give the child insufficient protection or can be aggressive towards him, and can arouse fear and aggression in this way too.

This makes it clear that even in this first phase the child experiences its mother in two forms, which in later phases can lead to two mother images. On the one hand he experiences the *good* mother, the figure who provides peace and love, the figure with whom the child feels secure, with whom he forms a unity and from whom he receives nourishment and warmth. But there is also the *bad* mother, whom the child experiences as aggressive and loveless, with whom he feels insecure, the figure who is often not in control of her negative impulses and with whom the child can actually have a feeling of destruction, even of being devoured. The history of religion has made us familiar with the picture of the fostering mother goddess; but also with the very different image of the devouring and threatening goddess. In this first phase, with its oral characteristic, the unconscious fantasies of the child can only have an oral character: the 'bliss' of oral satisfaction, and the fear of being devoured itself.

Remarkably enough, psychiatry calls the fears of this first phase 'ontological anxieties'. In his book *Clinical Theology*, Frank Lake repeatedly talks about ontological anxieties when he is referring to 'separation anxiety' (fear of being separated from the mother). In his book *Identity: Youth and Crisis* Erikson talks (p. 82) about the sense of basic trust which grows out of contact with the mother and calls it 'the ontological source of faith and hope'. This means that in its relationship to its mother the child learns to experience its most fundamental relationship to reality. It is a matter of 'basic experiences' of being and non-being, of the experience of nothingness.

In this connection we have talked about a religious core in the relationship between mother and child. Perhaps we could even talk about metaphysical experience here. When Heidegger puts fear at the centre of his philosophy, and calls this fear, fear of nothingness and above all fear of death, or when he goes on to say that human life is characterized by the fact that being escapes us, these are experiences which are prepared for in the child's relationship to its mother.

Psycho-analytical studies have taught us that fairy tales are the deposit of mankind's primordial experiences, the experiences which man had when he was a child for the first time. Now the primordial fear which emerges in all fairy tales is the fear of being abandoned by the mother, or by the parents (in the wood or at home), and of then being devoured by some evil figure (the giant, the wolf). Nor is it chance that in the ideas which man has about death, we find the image of the jaws of death, or the jaws of the grave. The experience of death is apparently prepared for in the child's relationship to its mother.

In the famous scene in the 'Gloomy Gallery' in the second part of Goethe's *Faust* the poet describes Faust's journey 'to the mothers'. Here the relationship to the mothers is experienced entirely along Rudolf Otto's lines as a '*mysterium fascinans et tremendum*'. The scene is a clear parallel to the duality of the mother images which, as we have already said, are to be found in the history of religions.

The trust in which Erikson sees the nature of religion therefore grows out of a positive experience in relation to the mother which, as it were, conquers the negative one. In this experience of oneness, the oral aspect therefore plays an important role, but so does the sense of touch – feeling the skin and stroking it. Remarkably enough this tactile aspect again plays a dominating role in later life. In his book *Totalité et infini* (Totality and infinity) Levinas devotes a number of interesting pages to the caress (pp. 235ff.). He writes (p. 236): 'The caress is directed neither to a person nor to a thing. It loses itself in a being which dissipates itself as if in an impersonal dream, without will and even without resistance, a passivity, an almost animal or infantile anonymity, long before death.' In religious imagery we find trust expressed in tactile terms, by means of metaphors like the guiding hand of God, or the everlasting arms.

Phases of Emancipation

Emancipation takes place in phases. We discovered earlier that Harlow's monkeys dared to venture further and further away from their substitute mothers. They had, as it were, to grow into an independence based on trust (the second phase, the one following the oral phase of 'trust', is for Erikson the anal one, and its most important characteristic is autonomy). This is no different in people. The child grows gradually into independence by means of particular transitional stages.

One important element in this process of emancipation is provided by the 'transitional objects' which D. W. Winnicott investigated. In his article 'Transitional Objects and Transitional Phenomena' (1953; repr. in *Collected Papers*, 1958) he writes about the phenomenon familiar to us all: the child that sucks its thumb; the rabbit it takes to bed with it; the teddy bear with the rough fur that it presses to itself. All these are particularly important when the child is going to sleep, but they also serve as a protection against other frightening situations as well. They play a part in the life of the smallest child and can be reverted to later whenever the child is afraid and feels left to itself. (They can also in certain circumstances develop into fetish objects.) Winnicott believes that these objects represent a particular experience of reality that lies between the primary narcissistic experience of infancy and the objective experience of the adult. It is a transitional phase, which makes frustration bearable. The mother understands this and tolerates the illusion.

According to Winnicott this is a kind of intermediate reality, such as we later discover again in art, religion, in the world of dreams and in creative, scholarly or scientific work. As far as religion is concerned, this seems to me open to dispute. It is true that religion is familiar with a particular experience of reality which goes beyond ordinary experience, but this does not lie between a libidinously coloured and an 'objectively hard' reality. A *true* religious experience of reality includes the 'hardness' and penetrates it, as it were. True religion does not therefore spring from the need to defend oneself against reality. Here Winnicott is really saying the same thing as Freud. Let me make myself clear here: I am not saying that there is not a whole series of religious experiences which have to be explained in this way, or that religion does not frequently have this function; but fundamentally the religious experience of reality is different from the experience of reality found in transitional objects.

We start from the presence of a religious core in the child's relationship to its mother. This relationship develops into a certain autonomy, and with this the religious core develops as well. But it must be clear that in many cases this development does not run its course undisturbed. The bond with the mother has such a deep significance that fixations crop up, sometimes even fixations which call on transitional objects for help. It is also possible that the development does not proceed equally far in every life, or in every culture, so that the bond with 'more primitive' levels of development is more easily preserved.

Thus it is also possible that there are primitive religions in the sense that primary feelings towards the mother (and perhaps the father) play a more obvious role than they do in our Western culture, with its twentieth-century religious forms and usages. This is one of Freud's initial themes in *Totem and Taboo*. It undoubtedly deserves closer investigation. We can think of the use of amulets, for example which, worn on the body, are supposed to guarantee the person's safety. We might ask here: does a person *know* that he is safe with an amulet of this kind, or does he feel safe? If we see amulets as transitional objects (as I think we must) it should be clear that feeling plays a decisive part. The same applies to the bones of dead martyrs, which are preserved and venerated as relics. For the awareness of the believer, a healing power emanated from them. This 'veneration' was probably more strongly rationalized later, the primary feelings being correspondingly weakened. But the intermediate reality indicated by Winnicott seems to me even more clearly traceable here. The same can be said about water from Lourdes, or the custom of putting a crucifix into the hands of the dying.

I believe that from this angle we can gain insight into the meaning of images in religion. In religion the image is also an 'intermediate or transitional object'. Rationally speaking, the image can be seen as a representation. But even superficial observation shows that the emotional side is much more important. The image makes the deity present. In his book *The Meaning of Religion* W. Brede Kristensen shows that in Greek religion it was not the classical images of the gods – the ones we have in our museums – which were the most important; it was the xoana, crudely fashioned pieces of wood or stone which were roughly reminiscent of the human form but had no clearly recognizable arms or legs, and not even heads. Even when the sculptor's art was at its zenith, these images were venerated. They represented the deity.

In the same way the Virgin Mary is represented by a statue or picture. It is carried about, it is decorated with flowers, candles are placed in front of it. And there are innumerable accounts of statues of the Virgin which have allegedly spoken. The icons of the Russian church too are the representations of a different reality. The believer uses them in prayer.

3
A Particular Type of Religion

Introduction

What we have said up to now suggests that there is a particular type of religion, with its own religious problems, founded on the 'basic trust' which is formed in the first phase of the child's development, in the complex problem of ties and emancipation. It is a type in which the person who has been cut off from the basis of his existence seeks to find union with this basis once more; he tries to experience it and to explore it. The levels on which this happens are varyingly material (and sometimes varyingly abstract). That is to say, in the different manifestations of this type of religion we can discover a development from the material to the abstract, in the sequence given below.

Primitive Religion

The naturalistic religions mentioned by Hidding stand at the beginning of this development. These are also often called primitive religions. They are concerned with the total cosmic unity in which man and the world participate and which becomes visible in a particular place – an image, an altar, a spring, a tree, etc. Man experiences and discovers this all-embracing unity in the cult, through which he overcomes his separation from the cohesion which is the foundation of his existence. He develops this unity in myth, through which he also finds the way back to the unity. Psychologically, the telling of the myth, like the telling of fairy stories in the life of the child, may perhaps have the function of objectifying experiences of the 'uncanny' (we remember Otto's description of the numinous – the holy and divine – as a '*mysterium fascinans et tremendum*'); and in this way these experiences are given a less emotional form. Through myth we penetrate the mysteries and thereby learn, in a sense, to live with them.

In this context magic might be described as the artifices whereby the unity of man and world is organized and harnessed to particular purposes (healing, the chase, etc.). It is clear that in these religions it is hardly possible to talk about a precise demarcation of the three entities, myth, cult and magic. The relating of myth is a cultic event and magic is an extension of the cult.

We must of course be careful not to see the structure of this type of religion in unduly simple terms. In the development of human life, elements which are only latent in other phases of development in these cultural patterns, can crop up and take on a colouring of their own within the primitive structure. We might think of phallic symbols, for example. At first sight they do not belong to this type of religion at all. They are clearly male, whereas the religious type that is based on the pattern of the first developmental phase is female (maternal). But in these naturalistic religions the phallus is not a symbol of autonomy (second phase) or masculinity (third phase); it is a symbol of fertility and is hence interchangeable with female fertility symbols. An element which accordingly emerges in a later phase and which must therefore remain latent within these religions, nevertheless cannot be denied; it is too deeply rooted in human life for that. But instead it takes on a meaning derived from the legitimate pattern of the first phase.

One important aspect of this type of religion is the attitude to death. Whereas in the religions of the word which Hidding mentions, death is an element which is the enemy of life (we remember what Paul has to say about death), in the naturalistic religions death is incorporated in life; it is one aspect of life and belongs to the cosmic unity. In his well-known book *Het leven uit den dood* (*Studiën over Egyptischen en Oud-Grieksen Godsdienst* (Life after death. Studies in Egyptian and ancient Greek religion) Kristensen says (p. 17) that among the Egyptians death actualizes one element, and indeed the most important element of all, in the self-revelation of life. In Hinduism too death has become one element in cosmic life through the idea of reincarnation. Along the same lines, in a particular modern experience of death, death's importance for man is represented in female symbols which express the continuity of life and death. Death is compared with the womb or is represented by a sleeping female figure, as in the two famous statues of sleeping women, Dawn and Night, which Michelangelo created for the Medici chapel in Florence.

Hinduism

In Hinduism belief in cosmic unity dominates. In the more developed forms of Hinduism we can even ask whether we have to do with a religion or with a philosophical doctrine about life. That is why Radhakrishnan, the well-known Indian philosopher (who was also President of India for some years), calls one of his books on Hinduism *The Hindu View of Life*. The all-sustaining vital principle reveals itself in gods who are experienced as 'pictures', that is to say as approximations, and not as something definite. There are also gradual transitions from a more primitive popular belief, in which 'the reality' of the gods predominates, to a more spiritual philosophical faith, which stresses the pictorial character of all talk about the gods. Let me quote from Radhakrishnan's book (pp. 19f.):

> The Divine reveals itself to men within the framework of their intimate prejudices. Each religious genius spells out the mystery of God according to his own endowment, personal, racial, and historical. The variety of the pictures of God is easily intelligible when we realize that religious experience is psychologically mediated.
>
> It is sometimes urged that the descriptions of God conflict with one another. It only shows that our notions are not true. To say that our ideas of God are not true is not to deny the reality of God to which our ideas refer. Refined definitions of God as moral personality and holy love may contradict cruder ones which look upon him as a primitive despot, a sort of sultan in the sky, but they all intend the same reality.

Religious Humanism

It is only a short step from a man like Radhakrishnan to religious thinkers like Eckhart, Spinoza, Hegel and, in the Netherlands, H. T. de Graaf. De Graaf expressed his views on religion in *Om het eeuwig Goed* (On the eternal good), a book which he published in 1923. He writes (pp. 142f.):

> The idea which is more widespread than anything else in religion is the notion of an inexhaustible life which maintains itself in individual things in spite of all growth and decay. The gods of the fields who die and rise again, the hero who overcomes Bluebeard, the winter that petrifies life, the symbols of death and resurrection – these things fill all religions with the idea of life's continuance. This life is something inexhaustible, something which cannot be grasped or unfolded in any one thing, an object of veneration for the individual and the group, which experiences its own deficiencies and cannot confer growth on itself. This discovery gives man his place. It fills his heart with reverence and makes him proclaim this inexhaustible good. In many manifestations all this falls apart at once; but in the relationship of man and mankind to what is beyond man and mankind, the ruling principle is *the urge to seek and maintain his place in this inexhaustible bundle of life*.

In a view of this kind about the principle behind religion, the different religions become attempts to bring out this single truth. What Radhakrishnan expresses by the phrase 'they all intend the same reality', Hegel sums up in the sentence that what religions possess in the form of different representations, exists in philosophy in the form of the concept.

We therefore see in religious humanism the final stage of a development which can probably best be termed a 'spiritualization'. In this development the concrete symbols which as 'intermediate or transitional objects' communicate the experience of unity are spiritualized; and in this way an almost completely image-free experience of unity comes into being. Karl Jaspers' philosophical faith, in which the believer becomes conscious of the 'comprehensive' through 'cyphers', is a good example of this almost imageless experience of unity. In this development the cult is no longer stressed, and myth and magic continually decline as well. Their place is taken by explanation through the word, and its most important goal is ultimately to evoke the stillness in which man then experiences the wordless unity.

At the close of his study de Graaf devotes some impressive sentences to the voices which typify the religion of the future. He mentions among other things the Barchem movement, about which he says: 'The condition of a return to the origin has led the movement to a remarkable form of community, to the quiet hour of dedication.'

The final possibility which is open to man if he wants to achieve the experience of unity is negative theology, the abnegation of all 'symbols' or words. In the history of Christianity negative theology has played an important part in the development of mysticism. We find a modern form of negative theology in Cornelius Verhoeven's book *Rondom de leegte* (On emptiness), in which he talks about contemplation (pp. 202ff.). In his opinion through contemplation we can find 'the godhead, the expectation that a meaning can be given to emptiness'. In another passage he writes about

> ... a religious attitude or really a way of looking into a methodically purified emptiness, beyond panicky religious bustle. It is a positive attitude, because through purification and hope the emptiness partakes of a fundamental, endless significance ... Contemplation is hence the opposite of projection ..., contemplation is directed towards an unnamed and unnameable wealth of meaning which transcends every meaning that is consciously conferred and is hence anticipated as a gift from the emptiness. Towards this reality one can only be filled with unimaginable hope, because every reality is completely different from the potentiality that is imagined or aspired towards.

J. L. Springer deals with the same ideas in his stimulating book *Waar, wat en wie is God?* (Where, what and who is God?).

The Crisis of Religion

One particular problem in the framework of our study is the fact that this type of religion has at present arrived at a crisis. We can only go into this in summary form and will content ourselves with a few observations.

We are living at a time which, we are told, is going to bring about the end of religion. Some people see in this development 'traces of Bonhoeffer'. They mean by this that in his *Letters and Papers from Prison* Bonhoeffer intuitively sensed this crisis in advance and reduced it to a provisional formula. I deliberately say that the formula was a *provisional* one. Many people have the impression that a fundamental alteration is taking place on the deepest level in man's relationship to reality, and they know that this is the *religious* level, the place where religion is to be found. But it seems to be particularly difficult to express the nature of the change in a satisfactory way. I should like here to go somewhat more deeply into the way in which Han M. M. Fortmann deals with the problem of religion in our modern culture in his great four-part work *Als ziende de Onzienlijke . . .* (As seeing the invisible). Before his untimely death, Fortmann was Professor of the Psychology of Culture and Religion at the University of Nijmegen. In his view the problem of religion today is closely bound up with what he calls 'shrunken' perception. He believes that we must rediscover the way to the full perception which we still find among primitive peoples. This must be introduced into the contemporary consciousness of modern man by means of a second 'primitiveness'. In this second primitiveness we should acquire a feeling for the place where we ourselves stand, and for the value of symbols, and hence for the place and value of the sacrament. Fortmann sees the possibility of religion for modern man cut short by the 'shrinking' of his perception; and he wants as it were to 'save' religion by giving it back its old basis – though in a new way – in an 'unshrunken' relationship to reality. My difficulty with this argument is that I can form no clear picture of this second primitiveness. Fortmann gives the impression that he has difficulty himself (and indeed sometimes begins to doubt himself and his own views) whenever he tries to express himself somewhat more clearly and positively. Because of this, his four-volume work rather gives the impression of a constant defence. He is very illuminating, and continually stimulates his readers to new reflection, but his own position does not emerge very clearly in the process. He tries to indicate it briefly in a short paragraph headed 'For the last time: the problem of projection' (Part 3b, pp. 310ff.). But even here he does not seem able to find the right words. He asserts that there is 'no objective world without perception'. 'We still live', he goes on, 'in an animated world with expressive qualities.' It is true that there are no longer any gods whom primitive man 'perceives'. But the feelings, the forces that they represent continue to exist none the less, even if man believes that he can exclude them from his life through 'science'. According to Fortmann we have not only sacrificed the gods to our 'scientific struggle'; we have also sacrificed God himself to the 'neutralization process'.

I must confess that although I can see the contrary arguments which Fortmann is attacking, I cannot gather any clear picture of the position from which he himself is mounting his attack. What strikes me is the emphasis he lays on the two forms of cognition, where his renunciation of the one form is just as emotionally based as his preference for the other. According to the first form of cognition, the world is dead and neutral, a 'shrunken' world. According to the second it is animate. Today we continually meet this emotional evaluation of the two forms of cognition. I will not go into the phenomenological ideas found in foreign literature, but will merely point to J. H. van den Berg, who has treated this subject in many different strains, probably most clearly of all in his short study on *De Dingen* (Things). In this book he deals with the two cognitive structures, the structure of so-called objective perception and the structure of the true, living knowledge in which one does not stand aloof from things but as it were participates in their life. Fortmann also talks about a participating perception. Here we can also refer to the various publications of G. van der Leeuw a few decades ago. (I am thinking in particular of his book *De primitieve mens en de religie* – Primitive man and religion.) He also distinguished between two fundamental structures, primitive man's 'participation mystique' and the objective scientific knowledge of the average secondary schoolboy, as he somewhat ironically puts it. He took over this distinction from the well-known psychologist and student of the history of religions, Levy-Brühl.

The striking thing about this idea is the stress on participation; but it seems impossible, apparently, to make this adequately clear. It is on the one hand the protest against a kind of alienation and on the other nostalgia for the experience of oneness, for the primordial (in the sense of what belongs to our origins), for the undivided (over against the division into what is often called subject and object). In the context of our book we can say: nostalgia for the maternal, for the oneness of the first phase.

I believe that at the present time we are actually experiencing a crisis of religion in the sense that the pattern of the first phase (which, as we have seen, has a religious character) has drifted away from us. In a certain sense we are experiencing the end of religion. But we must say more clearly what we mean by this. I see it as follows: we are losing the forms, the symbols which provided a kind of transitional object in which we preserved the 'basic trust' of the first phase. The basic trust itself – the foundation for later development laid in the earliest phase – does, it is true, remain, and lives on, even if without clear contours, in the pattern of a later phase; it is absorbed into it. Shortly after the Second World War there was a great deal of talk about 'secularization'. The problem that people had in mind was that the cultural territory dominated by the church was diminishing. People discovered that cultural spheres were acquiring their own autonomy, and that the church was increasingly losing its function. Writers like J. de Graaf, A. T. van Leeuwen and Harvey Cox have ascribed a positive value to this development. They see it as a disappearance of the relics of 'religion' and a greater opportunity for a de-sacralized relationship to reality, closer to the faith of the Bible. It is understandable that the discussion about 'secularization' has gradually died away. People have grasped that secularization does not even now mean an attack on belief; on the contrary it liberates belief from a certain impediment – from being equated with a series of 'religious' customs and views.

It is clear that secularization as such does not mean any advance for belief, but – as the writers I have mentioned have undoubtedly grasped – there is a certain relationship between secularization and the belief's structure. In *Totalité et infini* Levinas says that in the eyes of the other – i.e., in the relationship of man to man (this is the structure of the third phase as it is realized in the structure of biblical faith; we shall come back to this in detail later) – things are undoubtedly merely things, so that there can be no question of a religious experience of oneness with total reality. Here I see a parallel to Heidegger's view in *Being and Time*, where relationships between people are given the function of 'equipment'. They thus do not come into question for religious experience either. Our Western, secularized culture therefore embodies an experience of reality which fits into the structure of the biblical faith.

If this is true – and I am convinced that it is – it will be permissible to say that Fortmann is heading in a direction which is at least open to dispute when in his great study 'As seeing the invisible' he rebels against our Western culture's 'shrunken' experience of reality (as he calls it) and pleads for a 'second primitiveness'. We shall go more closely into the problems of the present religious situation in the next chapter. Here we will only note that there will always be a connection between 'basic trust', i.e., 'religion', and faith, in so far as no faith in God is possible without this trust. Even faith is founded on it. Anyone who has not learnt to trust cannot trust God or obey him in the biblical sense either. Fortmann could therefore be right in his dissatisfaction with the 'shrinking' process (a study of the question ought to differentiate more closely between its essential components). But to plead for a 'second primitiveness' on the basis of this dissatisfaction does seem to me a dubious matter. Fortmann does not seem to have taken sufficient account of the unique structure of the biblical faith.

In our consideration of these problems we must not forget that, historically, Christianity on its entry into our Western world found its deposit in various *religious* forms. It picked up the already existing '*rites de passage*', it organized itself on the basis of existing local communities, it built its churches on the foundations of heathen temples, and even built them with the stones of those temples, long seeing them as 'the house of God'. In short, just as the father is on the one hand experienced in the maternal form of the family and on the other hand has his own emotional valuation over against these feelings, so Christianity is historically present in the forms of religion although it breaks through these forms at the same time. Today we are experiencing the tension between the two aspects very clearly, and we are sometimes in danger of forgetting that a complete separation between the two is impossible, because each is the premise of the other. The inner contradiction belongs to the nature of the Christian faith, which Tillich once accurately defined when he termed 'the Protestant principle' 'a form of grace and criticism' (see for instance *The Protestant Era*, ch. XIII).

An understanding of the importance of this inner contradiction is extremely important for a clear view of the potentialities and limitations of the psychology of religion in the study of Christianity. Psychology investigates psychical phenomena, it directs its attention to events or experiences, i.e., to the formal aspects of faith which become visible in the reality of the psyche. In so doing it often overlooks the fact that it is viewing faith as religion; whereas although it is certainly true that faith is religion, it is at the same time 'criticism of religion' and has its own anti-religious structure. The protest of the dialectical theologians Barth and Brunner was justified in so far as they reproached the psychology of religion with viewing Christianity as religion, as a kind of experience of oneness, and of neglecting the individual structure of faith. This book is built up on the idea that there is an essential difference in structure between religion and faith. But it also shows, I think, that, perhaps for that very reason, the psychology of religion has its own particular functions.

4

Some Particular Aspects of the Present Religious Situation

If we look back for a moment to the train of thought we have pursued up to now, it becomes evident that we have already pointed several times to particular aspects of the present religious situation. We saw that among scholars like Fortmann, there is an evident desire for 'oneness'; and furthermore that a process is taking place in our culture which is often termed secularization. Secularization is marked by the development of an experience of reality whose structure is less 'maternal' (or religious) and more 'paternal' in character. We shall go more deeply into this process later.

First of all let us look a little more closely at some aspects of this situation. Paul Tillich makes an important contribution to a better understanding of its fundamental motivations. His way of pursuing theology is apparently symptomatic, though it is important for a better understanding of his ideas to remember that he is influenced by German Idealism, and above all by Schelling. His emphasis on oneness and the importance of the symbol is closely connected with this. In his *Systematic Theology* Tillich tries to give the Christian faith a place in this oneness through the methods of correlation, without doing violence to its special character in the process. This attempt of Tillich's is not, in my view, successful; but this does not mean that his books do not contain important viewpoints which give us a deeper understanding of the fundamental motifs of the twentieth-century religious situation.

I am thinking of his book *The Courage to Be*, in which he treats one of the fundamental themes of modern 'religion'. The book is about courage, but in essence it is concerned even more with a fundamental ontological experience from which this courage grows. He approvingly quotes Spinoza's saying that 'self-affirmation is participation in the divine self-affirmation' (p. 33). Tillich contrasts courage with the anxiety which arises when human self-affirmation is threatened by non-being. Later (p. 68) he writes:

> The anxiety which, in its different forms, is potentially present in every individual, becomes general if the accustomed structures of meaning, power, belief and order disintegrate. These structures, as long as they are in force, keep anxiety bound within a protective system of courage by participation. The individual who participates in the institutions and ways of life of such a system is not liberated from his personal anxieties but he has means of overcoming them with well-known methods.

We therefore see that anxiety is overcome by participation, and we discover that here Tillich arrives at the same result as Harlow in his experiments, or what we were able to conclude from Jan Luyken's poems. Courage is a self-affirmation which comes into being on the foundation of 'and yet' and 'in spite of'.

There are good analyses of modern culture in chapters IV and V, entitled 'Courage and Participation' and 'Courage and Individualization'. In the former Tillich defines his theology as follows: 'The self-affirmation of the self as an individual self always includes the affirmation of the power of being in which the self participates' (pp. 91f.). And: 'The courage to be is essentially always the courage to be as a part and the courage to be as oneself, in interdependence' (p. 92). He is concerned with 'the courage to affirm one's own being by participation' (p. 93). In chapter V he points to the fact that in modern existentialism (which interests him especially) there is a courage of despair – we could also say, a courage without participation (I would remark that the supporters of existentialism do not know any participation). In chapter IV he points to the danger of modern collectivism. He wants to overcome it and sees a possibility of doing so in the religious roots of the courage to be. He writes (pp. 152f.):

> ... and this means that every courage to be has an open or hidden religious root. For religion is the state of being grasped by the power of being-itself. In some cases the religious root is carefully covered, in others it is passionately denied; in some it is deeply hidden and in others superficially. But it is never completely absent. For everything that is participates in being-itself, and everybody has some awareness of this participation, especially in the moments in which he experiences the threat of non-being.

What Tillich is saying is clearly evident from Harlow's monkeys: in threatening situations we need courage to be, and we acquire it through participation.

Tillich is concerned with a twofold root. In ch. VI he calls mystical experience on the one hand 'participation in the ground of being' which creates the courage to be, and on the other 'the personal encounter with God' which embraces 'both mystical participation and personal confidence' and in this twofold way also lends a courage to be. Here we find in Tillich the double structure mentioned by Hidding, but he also sees the connection of the two structures, which is in its turn linked with the connection between the two phases in which these structures are rooted (see also p. 254 below).

The important thing in Tillich is now that both roots in his opinion lead down to a deeper root. He talks about an absolute faith, which makes it possible for a person to have the most radical doubt and the courage to be that overcomes the meaninglessness which surmounts both mystical experience and the divine-human encounter. By this Tillich means an experience which has left all symbols behind it – and therefore theism as well, he says. 'It is the accepting of the acceptance without somebody or something that accepts. It is the power of being-itself that accepts and gives the courage to be' (p. 179). It is my belief that we must use the word mysticism here, in spite of Tillich's own opinion, which we have just quoted. It is certainly not mysticism in the usual sense, but it is a particular type. I believe that here we have strayed close to the negative theology which today has also left clear traces in the work of Cornelis Verhoeven, a fact to which J. L. Springer, for example, points in the book we have already mentioned, *Waar, wat en wie is God?*. Tillich talks about a God above God:

> Therefore [absolute faith] is both the courage of despair and the courage in and above every courage. It is not a place where one can live, it is without the safety of words and concepts, it is without a name, a church, a cult, a theology. But it is moving in the depth of all of them. It is the power of being, in which they participate and of which they are fragmentary expressions (p. 182).

Here we meet in Tillich a conspicuous aspect of the religious situation of our time. He professes a negative theology, which combats the traditional images not only because they try to express the inexpressible, but also because they hide what has become essential for us today: the experience of radical emptiness and desolation, of comfortless alienation and absurdity. He shows how for many people an authentic humanity implies the courage for radical doubt and for meaninglessness. The answer to the radical doubt and meaninglessness does not therefore lie in mystical experiences or theistic encounters of faith. The only answer is the act of going on living, the courage to be which rises out of bottomless depths, where being itself is experienced namelessly and without symbols.

In this context it seems the obvious course to take a look at Zen Buddhism, which is also a typical modern religious manifestation. For a while it had great influence among certain groups of intellectuals and artists. Today it plays a role, together with other trends, in the 'counter-cultures' of the hippies, etc. The interest in Zen Buddhism differs from the interest with which the religions of the East were approached earlier, and which found expression in theosophy, for example. At that time uneasiness over the dogmatic rigidity and disunity of Western Christianity played a considerable part. The interest in Zen has a different background. Here it is more a question of discovering a courage to be which no longer finds a mainstay in any concept. In the sphere in which we are moving here a concept fulfils the same function as a symbol. It helps man to be free, to have courage to be, without the support of (direct) participation. But as long as man still needs the image, he is not yet quite free. In Zen Buddhism man now learns to let everything go – concepts as well – in order to be free. He must learn one thing especially (and here learning is more than an intellectual taking possession): what one might call the jump into space. (At this point we come close to what we have just said about Tillich's negative theology – that being and non-being are no longer to be distinguished from one another.)

We might say that man must learn to participate by no longer participating – that is to say, in emptiness. In *An Introduction to Zen Buddhism* Daisetz Taitaro Suzuki writes (pp. 53f.):

> Zen is not all negation, leaving the mind all blank as if it were pure nothing ... There is in Zen something ... which ... knows no limitations and refuses to be handled in abstraction. Zen is a live fact. ... To come into contact with this living fact ... is the aim of all Zen discipline.
> Nansen (Nan-Chuan, 748–834) was once asked by Hyakujo (Paichang, 720–840), one of his brother monks, if there was anything which he dared not talk about to other people. The master answered, 'Yes'.
> Whereupon the monk continued, 'What then is this something you do not talk about?'
> The master's reply was, 'It is neither mind, nor Buddha, nor matter.'
> This looks to be the doctrine of absolute emptiness, but even here again we observe a glimpse of something showing itself through the negation. Observe the further dialogue that took place between the two. The monk said:
> 'If that is so, you have already talked about it.'

'I cannot do any better. What would you say?'
'I am not a great enlightened one,' answered Hyakujo.
The master said, 'Well, I have already said too much about it.'

It is impossible to say anything logically about the state of the inner consciousness; it has to be achieved before one can carry on a reasonable conversation about Zen. Words are simply an indication of the state of being. They can give us an idea of what it is like, but we must not expect to receive the clue to the whole thing. First we must understand the spiritual attitude which is behind the way the Zen masters act. They do not talk such apparent nonsense or make such silly statements (as one might perhaps describe them) simply out of caprice. Their statements have a firm basis of truth, acquired through profound personal experience. The systematic exploration of the nature of truth winds through all the seemingly crazy acts like a scarlet thread. In the light of this truth, even the movement of the universe has no more importance than the flight of a midge or the movement of a fan. The aim is to see the focus, the spirit which penetrates everything, and that is absolute cognition without any sign or shadow of nihilism.

> A monk asked Joshu, 'What would you say when I come to you with nothing?'
> Joshu said, 'Fling it down to the ground.'
> Protested the monk, 'I said that I had nothing; what shall I let go?'
> 'If so, carry it away,' was the retort of Joshu.
> Joshu has thus plainly exposed the fruitlessness of a nihilistic philosophy. To reach the goal of Zen, even the idea of 'having nothing' ought to be done away with. Buddha reveals himself when he is no more asserted; that is, for Buddha's sake Buddha is to be given up. This is the only way to come to the realization of the truth of Zen. So long as one is talking of nothingness or of the absolute one is far away from Zen, and even receding from Zen. Even the foothold of Sunyata must be kicked off. The only way to get saved is to throw oneself right down into a bottomless abyss. And this is, indeed, no easy task (pp. 54f.).

Zen Buddhism exerts a constant attraction in Western Europe (it is true that it seems to be less popular at the moment, but that could alter at any time). This attraction can be explained by the fact that for Zen the important thing is to estrange man from reality, and we are apparently involved in a similar process of estrangement in our secularized culture. Zen Buddhism, it is said, offers the Western European the chance to find something to hold on to in this process. It helps him to accept the process and even to integrate it. But because Orientals and Europeans come from completely opposite spiritual backgrounds, the acceptance is more difficult than is often thought. The Oriental wants to be released from being; in Buddhism being is unmasked as suffering, and man has to extinguish his desire, even eradicate his self, if he is to liberate himself from that suffering. Alienation is therefore on man's side an active process which – and this is also an essential point – can only be completed through a series of reincarnations. The European experiences estrangement as a process which descends on him and to which he would like to call a halt or 'take in hand' himself, because he experiences his life as something unique, as a creation aimed at fulfilment. For him, consequently, in contrast to Zen Buddhism, estrangement is something negative. It is true that it is possible for us Europeans, just like the Orientals, to unmask being as mere appearance – we can discover a tendency to this among ourselves here and there, and with it a latent Buddhism. But the active attitude of the European towards reality, which is directed towards autonomy and achievement, is based on 'basic trust' (compared with the 'basic mistrust' of the Oriental); and this will probably make for inner difficulties.

In his voluminous *Clinical Theology*, Frank Lake makes a number of observations (pp. 241f.) which shed light on the background of the European predilection for Zen. If this predilection is more than a superficial impulse, it has deep – and early – roots in human existence. Lake, who is a psychiatrist by profession but who is very interested in religious problems, tries in his book to convey more insight into the so-called 'schizoid personalities' who are to be found in great numbers in our modern society. In his opinion, the fundamental problem with which these people are struggling, because of their earliest experiences of life, is the problem of participation and separation. They can for example display a 'commitment anxiety' because they have not properly assimilated the trauma of the first separation from their mother. In his practice Lake has discovered schizoid symptoms among many patients who 'have taken up Zen Buddhism'. Many of them are looking in Zen for 'the void of non-being', apparently because they are afraid of 'participation in being'. In a sentence we have already quoted Suzuki writes: 'The only way to get saved is to throw oneself right down into a bottomless abyss.' Apparently many Europeans feel a need for this because they have early on lost faith in the fulfilment of being.

Throughout the whole of his book *Als ziende de Onzienlijke*, which we mentioned above, Han M. M. Fortmann is concerned with the question of the possibility or impossibility of religion (or unbelief) in our modern society. For him it is a problem of 'shrinkage', which makes a religious life impossible and which has to be overcome by a second 'primitiveness'.

It might be said that out of his own inner dissatisfaction Fortmann has worked on the results of secularization, which for him means that the character of our culture is now entirely determined by science and hence by technology. The separation of subject and object which is fundamental to this process is coupled with a shrinking of our relationship to reality which, in Fortmann's opinion, makes religion impossible. For if all projections have to be withdrawn, as Sierksma suggests in his book *De religieuze projektie* (The religious projection), we cut religion off at its roots, since the religious man lives 'as seeing the invisible', to borrow the title of Fortmann's splendid book; and he does so through images. For Fortmann, symbols belong to the very nature of religion (he is evidently thinking here of the structure described by Hidding, which we are considering in this section); and since we have of course grown out of primitive religion, with its symbols, we have to look for a second primitiveness. Anyone who has read Fortmann's book *Hoogtijd* (Thoughts on Feasts and Fasts) knows that the source of his religious life is participation in the ritual of the Catholic church. But he has pointed to various ways in which our cultural group could achieve a renaissance of second primitiveness, although, as his book shows, he is constantly hindered by his critical objections from identifying himself completely with it. He points to Jung's views on the symbol, and to the pre-scientific unity of subject and object in philosophical phenomenology; and in *Hindoes en Boeddhisten* (Hindus and Buddhists) and above all in *Oosterse Renaissance* (Oriental Renaissance), both of which appeared shortly before his death, he draws attention to the newly awakened interest in Oriental techniques of meditation with all their ramifications. If I see the matter rightly, Fortmann is dealing with the same fundamental problem as Tillich in *The Courage to Be*, i.e., confrontation with the alienation from 'basic trust'. And this means confrontation with the 'shrinking' process in religion, with the radical emptiness of life. In *Oosterse Renaissance* he gives some indications of what this shrinking process means: the incapacity to go on seeing things as simply as a child, the inability to lead a relaxed life, the loss of the inner life, estrangement from the body, lack of contemplation, insufficient knowledge about the unity of being, obsession with one's own ego. We must conclude from all this that we Europeans do not sufficiently possess or seek the experience that reactivates the original 'basic trust'. In our city culture, stamped as it is by science and technology, there are far fewer opportunities to reactivate basic trust than there are in a rural form of life. If we say that we have become alienated from *nature*, this really means, in my view, what Fortmann is indicating here. The things which we use have become factory-made tools which no longer remind us of the fellow-men belonging to our own village or our own family, who once made the things themselves. 'Anything old' is so fashionable today partly because we can participate purely emotionally in a world in which we were once at home – a world which has disappeared but which can be recaptured in feeling. Our achievements are often achieved simply for achievement's sake – almost compulsively, without the liberating warmth of the appreciation which they once earned for us at home. Professional advancement or a rise in salary are often only a poor substitute for this. And the prosperity we bask in is without any relation to a giver who is well-disposed towards us. For that reason our very prosperity is sometimes positively boring; it is too much of a good thing.

Where things hinder us from participating in the warmth of community, they throw us back on ourselves. We are estranged from what is human, from what we once experienced at home in our earliest relationships. Things therefore alienate us from our first basic trust and hence from a religious attitude to life. Here we come up against the same problem which Frank Lake discovered in his 'schizoid personalities'. The question therefore arises whether the things we meet in the subcultures of youth (but not only there) in the form of 'sensitivity training'. drug-taking, the 'love-in' and so on, are not an attempt to regain something of the basic trust, even if the methods used are more or less artificial. Fortmann, with his immense sensitivity, has I think pointed to the connection here in *Oosterse Renaissance*. But we have to ask how far what is being offered is more than a mere substitute, and whether it is a question of regression without the prospect of maturity. I have the feeling that Fortmann himself points in the right direction here. In an impressive epilogue, four pages long, which he wrote on his deathbed for *Oosterse Renaissance*, Fortmann talks about the 'bright light' which can illumine us in death. The epilogue deals with various questions, all of which deserve closer discussion and reflection, but I will confine myself to our present context and merely mention that he starts from a great experience of light in the decisive hours before death, in which the little things of life are experienced in a totally new way. This is a very different attitude, therefore, from the approach of the East. He remembers a poem by Jaqueline van de Waals in which everyday life 'since she knows it' is also different and more intense. Moreover Fortmann's experience of light is founded on his liturgical experience, or we should perhaps say, on his experience of the community in which he felt 'at home'. He even talks about the liturgy as if it were his mother. In the decisive hours basic trust suddenly develops into a power which gives us hope. The two evidently belong together.

We must pay particular attention to the word 'decisive'. Fortmann, I think, wants to express in this way the fact that we are totally dependent on ourselves and are totally alienated from the normal. We experience the exodus from our familiar country, the journey into the unknown, into the wilderness. Now the thing on which everything depends is that the community reactivates basic trust, hence calling hope into being. In the exodus experience of dying, therefore, basic trust takes on the aspect of hope for the man who stands within the community of the church, where he can participate in the light, because he encounters God there. We already saw in Harlow's monkeys that it is participation which makes them set forth once more into the 'wilderness' of the cage with a 'courage to be'. One could also term it the hope of not being left in the lurch by their mother. Erikson too translated 'basic trust' by 'hope' at certain points. In Fortmann it is the great darkness of the deathbed to which his basic trust reacts with the great experience of light. On the last page of his epilogue he writes:

> For the person who has once encountered God, the question of 'the next world' ceases to be interesting. The person who has learnt to live in bright light is no longer tortured by the problem of whether the light will also be there tomorrow. A child who lives under the warm and loving protection of his mother never thinks to ask whether his mother will look after him tomorrow as well.

The darkness of dying which is overcome by the experience of light is its loneliness and inescapableness. Basically it is the same darkness that confronted Harlow's monkeys. And they too found their trust in a renewed and deepened participation, so that one might also say that it is the profundity of the limit-situation which releases the experience of light rather than practice in reaching such experiences.

This I think also throws light on the tenor of Fortmann's *Oosterse Renaissance*, in which he maintains that we could learn much from the spiritual experiences of the East, so as to achieve the 'second primitiveness' of his earlier book *Als ziende de Onzienlijke*. If I see the matter rightly, exercises, in the sense in which he means them, can undoubtedly make a certain contribution, but to render an account of the situation into which we and our civilization have strayed is much more important.

According to the most sensitive minds of our time, we in the West are really living in the limit situation of an exodus. True and authentic religious experiences can be born solely through a deeper experience of this reality. Only then will 'feasts and fasts' (to take the sub-title of Fortmann's book *Hoogtijd*), as well as the renewal of contemplation, which is under discussion in so many circles, receive true inspiration.

We shall hope to go more deeply into the problems of the present religious situation at the end of the book.

5
Some Fundamental Observations

The Problem of Individuation

One of the basic problems of this type of religion is individuation. How does the individual detach himself from his matrix? What does this mean, and what is the relationship of the individual to the whole? These are the questions which are of fundamental importance in the framework of this type of religion. Individuation is experienced as a great mystery and often too as a kind of transitional phase. The Dutch psychologist Heymans believed that the individual disintegrated after death and returned once more to the great whole; he expounded this as a philosophical system in his 'psychic monism'. Indian thought about man continually tends towards similar ideas in varied form. Belief in reincarnation (that is to say the idea that we shall one day arrive at perfection, when the wheel of birth stands still) reflects a negative evaluation of individuality. These ideas about human individuality express the longing one day to be absorbed into the whole. The meaning of the individual lies outside himself, namely in the whole for which he is destined and from which – as is expressly presupposed – he has proceeded. Hegel is really saying the same thing when he sees the process of history as a path of the spirit which proceeds from the Other Being and returns to itself via the numberless individuals that people the stage of history.

The nature of religion can also be determined in line with the same trend of thought. My teacher H. T. de Graaf defined religion as man's urge 'to seek and maintain his place in the inexhaustible cohesion of life'. This sentence shows us that within this type of religion there is a fundamental tension between being an individual maintaining separateness, and participation, absorption into the unity of the whole. Spinoza calls the *determinatio* a *negatio* and de Graaf calls sin 'self-seeking'. Here we are concerned with some of the experiences which, as we have seen, are part of the primal experiences of the first phase. But this is significant, for in the first phase there is as yet no real experience of the other as other – as yet no I–Thou relationship in the sense in which Buber talks about it.

The Problem of the I–Thou Relationship

How ought we to conceive of the relation to the other in the structure of this phase? As far as I know there has as yet been no investigation into the small child's experience of the other, of his fellow-man; but everything points to the fact that only as life goes on do we grow to have an experience of the other as a counterpart, a being with a will to whom we have an ethical relation in Levinas' sense, i.e., an I–Thou relationship.

There are apparently two possible ways of experiencing the other. First he is for us the person in whom we participate, with whom we are together, with whom we feel at one and with whom we experience safety and security. The skin and glance of the other are important elements here. This other person can also affect us negatively, by withdrawing or by meeting us with negative feelings. He (or she) then delivers us over to the nothingness that threatens to swallow us up and to destroy us. Childish fantasies and primitive ideas of God can apparently reflect a negative experience of the mother, i.e., an experience belonging to the first phase of human development.

Parallel to this is a second experience which is already heralded, if I see it correctly, in the experience of autonomy. This belongs to the second phase, with its cleanliness training, but only takes on clear outline in the third phase, in which the child is confronted with another person's will, his father's. This experience fits into a relationship in which the other confronts us, in which he is experienced as alien, and as one who has a secret in which we cannot participate, or only to a certain degree. In this relationship the word, which bridges the distance and abolishes alienation, also plays a dominating role. *Doing* something together is more important than merely *being* together. One could compare the father–son relationship in this phase. In his *Neurosenleer* (Theory of Neuroses) R. C. Kuiper talks (p. 62) about 'going out in the car together, catching fish for the aquarium together in the brook, playing football together, and looking at something interesting together'. Finally, it is a question of a relationship in which we are challenged and in which (we remember Levinas) appeals are addressed to us.

In relationships between people therefore we have to do with two patterns which are 'released' in the first and third phase of the child's development. Of course these two patterns are also to be met with after the years of childhood, in the adult person, where they lie parallel to one another and amalgamate with one another. The two possibilities are different stresses which play a varying strong role in every human relationship and which are often clearly visible in it. Thus common work in the office can be given colour by the experience of being together (we have only to think of the pleasure of seeing one another again after a holiday); or the being together of two lovers can be deepened by the act of doing something together.

If two patterns really do play a part here, that will of course exert an influence in the religious field; and we shall come back to this in more detail. We have already pointed to the fact that the contrast between religion and faith made in present-day theology of the Bonhoeffer school is especially illuminated by the difference between the two patterns. In religion emphasis lies on *being together* with God, on experiencing God through particular forms such as liturgical usages, prayer, singing, dance, etc. Faith, on the other hand, is knowledge of a call addressed to us, as if – to use a familiar Old Testament expression – we were to appear before the face of a king. What we experience here is the distance, Kierkegaard's 'qualitative difference', Barth's 'line of death'. As a subject, one cannot really share a relationship with a king. The king calls upon us, he commands us and we have to obey. We shall come back to this in more detail when we deal with the third phase, the relationship to the father.

6

Summing-up and Transition

Let us see how far we have come and where we stand at present. We can sum up what we have achieved up to now in a number of theses.

1. Our point of departure was that the phases in the child's earliest development 'release' particular patterns (or structures in Hidding's sense) which determine the rest of life.

2. In the first oral phase, basic trust is released through the child's relationship to its mother. This basic trust grows in the mutual play of bond and emancipation, and its essence is knowledge of ultimate security (certainty).

3. The experience of the mother has two aspects. There are good mothers who guarantee security, and also aggressive mothers who inspire fear and let the child down. In this way 'ontological anxiety' or 'basic mistrust' arises, parallel to the basic trust which can be termed a positive experience of oneness with being – the mother.

4. There are 'transitional or intermediate objects' in the relationship to the mother and in the relationship to God which make them (emotionally) present, so that they can be participated in by way of these transitional intermediate objects.

5. In our own time we have to do with a crisis of religion which goes back partly to the influence of other patterns and partly – as a result of this – to the loss of our capacity for experiencing oneness in the religious forms.

6. Christianity lives in religious forms on the one hand; but it is also aware of the tension between religion and the call of faith.

We shall now go on to a closer investigation of the second, 'anal' phase in the child's development, especially considering its significance for the sphere of religion. We should remind ourselves once more, however, that the patterns released in the phases of development are determined culturally as well as biologically and that there are no purely oral patterns. In the oral cultural pattern, traces of other phases are often to be found as well.

The Anal Phase

7
The Unique Character of the Second, Anal Phase

Introduction

In psycho-analytical theory – in Freud, but perhaps even more clearly in Erikson – the phases of child development are not only distinguished from one another; they also form a coherent whole. Each phase provides its own stone, as it were, for the building of human identity. These stones fit together without a gap. The one presupposes the other. For the one phase cannot well be completed before the preceding one is finished. The second phase, in which skill or ability is called upon, can only be successfully completed in proportion to the basic trust which has been acquired by the child in the first phase. The first phase is therefore the presupposition for the second and third phases which, according to Erikson, centre on initiative.

With this development a development also takes place in the child's relationship to his parents; and this is important for religion. For it can be established that the child's relationship to his parents prepares the ground for its relationship to God. Now, in the process of emancipation from the parents, in which the relationship to God gradually develops, the religious relationship also acquires its own structure and colouring, just as does human identity. We have already pointed out that there are different religious structures or patterns which are connected with the difference between the phases and which, together with the differences in the educational and cultural patterns, lead to the historical or personal differences which we know. In this study we want to try, with the help of this thesis, to classify and clarify the religious situation's motley variety. The connection between the first three phases produces the following picture:

1. In the first phase we are concerned with a 'basic trust' which makes it possible for the child, on the foundation of the oneness that is associated with it, to recognize itself as being separate from its mother.

2. In the second, anal phase it is a matter of a growing sense of being *able to do* something. The extension of this sense comes about through cleanliness training which (on the foundation of the basic trust) develops a certain feeling for independence or autonomy, though in the framework of the mother–child relationship this is obviously related to the mother. This sense of independence rests to a large extent on motherly encouragement and approval. Achievement therefore strengthens autonomy, above all in the sense that the child feels that it has acquired status with its mother.

3. In the third, Oedipal phase, the point is *to want something by oneself* (to have initiative). But here too the child's will is obviously related to its parents – in the boy's case, to the father particularly. Relationship to the father is the framework in which the child can talk about wanting something himself. In this relationship stress lies on the father as the other, over against the son and in certain circumstances above him. Here, as we have seen, we are touching on a relationship of a different kind from the relationship to the mother, in which participation is paramount.

We can therefore establish that in the first years of life a coherent whole is released from patterns which will all play their part in later life, although in different cultures and in different people the stress can lie in different places, so that the structure of the whole can also vary.

The Second Phase

We will now look at the pattern of the second phase, here too taking Erikson's ideas on the subject as our starting point.

(*a*) As we know, psycho-analysis terms this phase the anal one; that is to say, a different erogenous zone, the anus, now becomes the centre of attention. In this phase it is important for the child to have some achievement to show, because in that way it can obtain praise. According to Erikson the capacity now develops to 'let go' and to 'hold on', and to be the master of both.

(*b*) Erikson stresses how much the pattern of this phase has penetrated the cultural life of the West. He points to the kind of person we frequently meet who feels the compulsion to be just as thrifty and exact in matters of love, time and money as he is in his excretions.

(*c*) This phase also has its own, anal problems. The child can already fight for its autonomy, it can be rebellious and refractory. The mutual relationship of child and adult can according to Erikson be subjected to a heavy strain.

(*d*) This phase has its own emotional and mental correspondences, especially in the form of pride (in himself and his capacity), doubt (of his own abilities) and shame (at his own ludicrousness in the field of what he can do).

(*e*) In this phase the first foundations can be laid for a compulsive personality, for an over-manipulation of the self. This develops under the pressure of the child's relationship to its parents.

(*f*) As far as religion is concerned, the first phase leads to 'basic trust', according to Erikson, but the second to 'law and order'. Law and order are necessary, he says, but they must not be exaggerated. The contribution of this phase to religious development is therefore discussed only by the way – as a necessary limitation of autonomy. We will go into the religious aspects involved in detail.

The Cultural Factor

All this shows clearly the importance of upbringing and with it of the cultural factor in this second phase of development. A particular cultural pattern, with its own ideals of upbringing, has a great importance in the complexes which we in the West call anal problems and the anal pattern. Observations have shown that in primitive cultures cleanliness training does not play nearly so important a part as it does with us. Children often teach one another to disappear briefly into the bush. Moreover differences can be shown even within our Western cultural pattern. Protestant countries are generally more strongly influenced by this ideal in their upbringing than Catholic ones. We must therefore note that in this book we are proceeding from a pattern that only enjoys validity in a particular culture area and we shall try to find out how far this pattern materializes in particular religious manifestations.

The Other Relationship to the Mother

One important thing is that an alteration takes place in the child's relationship to its mother in this phase. Up to now she was its source of 'trust' – we remember Harlow's monkeys. Now, especially because of the cleanliness training, the relationship takes on a new emphasis: the mother expects something from the child. If he fulfils her expectations he is praised. Otherwise he is made to feel 'small'. The mother urges the child on and because of this he already develops a certain kind of superego. This superego has a different colouring from the superego of the third, Oedipal phase which, as we know, develops in relation to the punitive and admired father, though the two will later fuse together. I have the impression that although psycho-analysts of course understand that the roots of the superego go back further than the Oedipal phase, the complications of this process have been very little investigated. I assume that this 'maternal conscience' plays a considerable part in the formation of psychosomatic syndromes. Psychosomatics have already frequently pointed to the influence of the superego in the genesis of a number of syndromes and it can also be established that the mother plays an important part here (particularly noticeably in asthma, for example); so it would seem obvious to assume that this contribution is made primarily through the formation of conscience.

My thesis here is once more that in this phase – just as in the first one – particular patterns are released which make an important contribution to human identity. One must remember here that the child's relationship to his mother, with its dialectic of bond and emancipation, goes on existing; but it now acquires a new aspect, through the child's feeling that he is able to *do* something. We might say that the general trust of the 'basic trust' takes on a particular emphasis with an element of *self-confidence* based on ability.

In the first phase the dialectic of bond and emancipation brought with it a dialectical and, as it were, paradoxical relationship between 'basic trust' and 'basic mistrust'. In the same way self-confidence relates in a dialectical and paradoxical way to the fear of *not* being able to do something and then – and this is important – of standing alone; for the child fears that he will be rejected by his mother. The relationship to the mother therefore remains an essential element in the pattern of this phase. Autonomy always functions within the framework of this relationship, as it were, as well as on the basis of the 'trust' which it contains. We can compare the behaviour of Harlow's monkeys, as they cautiously and yet bravely leave their mother, knowing that they can always return to her.

The pattern which is introduced into human life in this way (and which we can thus call an anthropological pattern) therefore has its centre in the phenomenon of being able to do something, by means of certain achievements; just as in the oral phase the pattern had its centre in the phenomenon of oneness and separation, and hence in 'basic trust'. The first phase reveals certain aspects about this centre which are characteristic of the phase; and in the same way the anal phase too has several aspects of this kind, which we shall discuss in more detail.

The features of the anal pattern include:

(*a*) The dialectic of activity and passivity. This is a phenomenon to which J. Groen and the other authors of the psychosomatic study *Het acute Myocardinfarct* (Coronary thrombosis) draw attention. In his essay on the structure of personality Treurniet explains that patients who have had a coronary thrombosis differ from other people in the following ways:

> They cannot do anything by halves. Every task they take up is for them of vital importance. It is always a question of all or nothing. This means that certain impulses proceeding from the deeper levels are warded off. As a result they are never really able to admit without fear to any of the needs indicated by the dangerous collective term 'passive' – are never able to admit to being dependent, inactive, childlike, feminine, etc.

Compulsive activity, with a secret longing for passivity, for security with the mother, is characteristic of the behaviour pattern of the anal phase, and the connection between this kind of neurotic conflict and the problems of the anal phase has also been clearly recognized.

(*b*) The dialectic of independence (autonomy) and dependence is directly connected with this. We shall be unable to understand the child's desire to do something himself and to be 'big' (a desire which can also be discovered in many grown ups, such as the coronary-thrombosis patients) unless we sense the longing for dependence that it conceals. Such a longing has of course to be suppressed, but it can appear at certain moments.

(*c*) The dialectic of defiance, shame and doubt. Another tension in the anal phase and the anal pattern is the dialectic of pride in the achievement produced and doubt of that achievement – doubt which is mixed with shame. If on the basis of his own capacity the child has to expand his basic trust into self-confidence, it is obvious why doubt and shame (on exposure) are so often to be found besides pride in this phase and pattern, for the child still possesses so little on which he is able to base self-confidence.

In the context of these three forms of dialectic, the anal pattern now displays a number of aspects which were not present in the oral pattern. In the anal phase the child is about to do something or rather to achieve something. Defecation, which puts an excessive emotional strain on the child in the context of cleanliness training, is not primarily a technical achievement. (Erikson accordingly places this type of achievement in the learning phase – during the child's period at school – which he calls the 'industry' phase.) It is rather a creation, a letting-something-appear-from-ourselves – a *pro-ducing*. It is consequently comparable rather with bearing children and it is worth noting here that in German a journalist will sometimes derisively say that he has 'shitted out' an article; and a writer often calls his book his 'brain child'. Making, in the sense of creating or producing, is an important aspect of the anal pattern 'released' in this phase, and plays an important role in our present-day culture especially, as we shall see.

The second important aspect is that the child – and later the adult – acquires a *status* through these achievements. To achieve a status is, as we all know and as many American novels about the life of business men show especially clearly, a decisive factor in modern man's existence. We now discover that this fits into a quite particular pattern: the status which the child acquires consists of being big in his mother's eyes, and of being able to reckon with her praise and encouragement. The word status therefore has an emotional meaning and must be seen in terms of a mother figure through whom one knows oneself to be recognized and at the same time secure. In my opinion this throws clear light on the way the concept of status functions in our cultural pattern. It evidently often has a strongly emotional importance. To achieve a certain status gives great emotional satisfaction, above all – and this is now understandable – in relation to the group in which one hopes to reach this status. To acquire a status means to be accepted by people of whose acceptance one is not certain. One feels valued for one's achievements; and this means leaving behind uncertainty, which was ultimately only insecurity, in order to submerge oneself in the security of the group, without whose 'love' one cannot live.

The third aspect which represents an essential element in this pattern is the idea that with the excretions something dirty and impure is eliminated. This notion develops during this phase under the influence of cleanliness training – or perhaps it is an inborn idea which only crystallizes then (for this question see what René A. Spitz has to say about the baby's playing with excrement). Through cleanliness training this idea is absorbed into the superego, into the first levels of our conscience: the dirty and impure must be thrown off and avoided.

This makes it clear that this concept has a function in the same pattern as achievement. They occur together and are connected with one another.

We hope to show later how this makes particular religious manifestations comprehensible. I am thinking of both Pharisaism and Puritanism.

The fourth aspect means that in this phase – and hence in this pattern – fear of being thought small or dirty plays an important part. One sometimes talks about shame or guilt cultures. In this case shame belongs to a culture in which this pattern is strongly accentuated, and guilt to a culture in which the third pattern, with its relation to the father (and the associated growth of conscience and feelings of guilt) stands at the centre. Japanese culture, for example, belongs to the first form and European culture to the second. But we must in my opinion note here that in Western society too, with its status requirements and its pressure towards 'achievement', shame plays quite a large part.

To be ashamed, then, is connected with the fear of standing alone and feeling defenceless. It is really a particular kind of fear of the loss of security and love. It is therefore something fundamentally different from a sense of guilt, which is rather fear of punishment and thus fear of losing love. Helen Merrell Lynd has pointed to this aspect of the sense of shame particularly in her book *On Shame and the Search for Identity*. She writes (p. 67):

> Contrasting the emotional concomitants of shame and guilt, Piers says [in *Shame and Guilt*, pp. 11, 16] that the unconscious, irrational threat implied in shame anxiety is abandonment, in contrast to the fear in guilt of mutilation. 'Behind the feeling of shame stands not the fear of hatred, but the fear of contempt which . . . spells fear of abandonment . . . the deeper rooted shame anxiety is based on the fear of the parent who walks away "in disgust", and . . . this anxiety in turn draws its terror from the earlier established and probably ubiquital separation anxiety.' Important as is Piers' emphasis on the different kinds of anxieties that are the outcome of shame and guilt, it seems to me probable that the anguish of the experience of shame is not so much the fear that isolation or alienation will be the *penalty* for the shameful act as that the experience of shame is itself isolating, alienating, incommunicable.

And in another passage she says (p. 47):

> Thus shame, an experience of violation of trust in oneself and in the world, may go deeper than guilt for a specific act. . . . With every recurrent violation of trust we become again children unsure of ourselves in an alien world.

We find similar ideas in Erikson's book *Identity and the Life Cycle* (pp. 68f.)

> *Shame* is an infantile emotion insufficiently studied. Shame supposes that one is completely exposed and conscious of being looked at – in a word, self-conscious. One is visible and not ready to be visible; that is why we

dream of shame as a situation in which we are stared at in a condition of incomplete dress, in night attire, 'with one's pants down'. Shame is early expressed in an impulse to bury one's face, or to sink, right then and there, into the ground. This potentiality is abundantly utilized in the educational method of 'shaming' used so exclusively by some primitive peoples, where it supplants the often more destructive sense of guilt to be discussed later. The destructiveness of shaming is balanced in some civilizations by devices for '*saving face*'. Shaming exploits an increasing sense of being small, which paradoxically develops as the child stands up and as his awareness permits him to note the relative measures of size and power.

Shame and pride are therefore opposites and that presupposes the possibility of 'being able to produce something', of having 'achieved something'. In *The Nature and Destiny of Man* (the 1939 Gifford Lectures) Reinhold Niebuhr says that human pride (in the sense of arrogance, not in the sense of a justifiable sense of one's own value) is the essence of human sin. For him pride is the lust for power and glory; he connects it with the basic insecurity of human existence: 'The self is afraid of being discovered in its nakedness' (Vol. I, p. 220). On this basis guilt then comes into being as the objective and historically visible consequence of sin.

The fifth aspect is displayed in the relation of man to himself in the framework of this pattern. Man can doubt, and can doubt himself; that is to say, he can doubt his own abilities. This is often associated with a tendency to suppress such doubt, which can lead to the formation of a compulsive personality. Erikson points out (pp. 72f.) that the 'compulsive personality' (which he says is often called 'anal' in psychiatric literature) has its normal aspects as well as its abnormal exaggerations. When the compulsiveness is compensated by other things he thinks that it is 'useful in the administration of matters in which order, punctuality and cleanliness' play a part – as long as it is not too strong. But it is often difficult to remain a master of the rules. And then the compulsive character develops.

We therefore discover that in the anal phase a large and important area of life opens up. A pattern is released which is marked by its stress on doing, organizing, ability and cleanliness. But through this very fact a strained relationship is produced between doubt and shame on the one hand and self-confidence and pride on the other. This is a pattern which throws light on man's ego, and which Erikson hence rightly characterized by the word autonomy. In this experience of the self, i.e., in this autonomy, two possibilities have to be distinguished from one another. Either the ego is experienced as being embedded in a secure relationship in which it helps to establish its self-confidence, or it feels isolated and is exposed to the fear of standing alone and of having to assert itself alone.

If we ask about the significance of this phase (and hence this pattern) for religion, the answer is really to be found in this second possible course of development. A perversion of religion or a breach with it becomes possible through the fear of isolation.

8

What Light does this Phase Shed on Religion?

The Pharisee

Our aim is to show that the analysis of the anal pattern which we undertook in the last chapter facilitates the understanding of a number of religious manifestations. First of all let us look at the phenomenon of Phariseeism, which is familiar to us from the gospels.

The negative judgment about the Pharisees found in the gospels is probably too one-sided. In the light of the prophetic preaching of Jesus and his disciples, this negative judgment is understandable, but from the historical and sociological point of view, the Pharisees performed important services to the Jewish people. They gave linguistic form to the Jewish character and tradition, lent them a certain impress, and preserved them.

Among their fellow-countrymen the Pharisees were characterized by a clear pattern. In my view this pattern corresponds to the structure of the pattern of the second developmental phase, i.e., the anal pattern. We can also sense the dangers involved in this pattern from the gospels.

First of all, the status idea is very noticeable. In the gospels this plays a particular part in connection with the Pharisees. In Jesus' discourse denouncing the scribes and Pharisees (Matt. 23.5–7) we read that 'They do all their deeds to be seen by men; for they make their phylacteries broad and their fringes long' and that they 'love the place of honour at feasts and the best seats in the synagogues, and salutations in the market places, and being called rabbi by men'. It also emerges that the status concept is a question of relation as well; it points to the group (the mass of the people) who accept the man and give him a certain security. Through this group the Pharisees now seek a status with God. Another noticeable thing is that *achievement* has an essential importance in their lives. Jesus reproaches them with tithing 'mint and dill and cummin', with 'straining out a gnat' and cleansing 'the outside of the cup and of the plate' (Matt. 23.23–26). This is an expression of their exaggerated feeling for *order*. The Pharisees are compulsive personalities, they cannot overlook anything. Every *i* must be dotted and every *t* must be crossed. Here we have the picture of constrained, frightened people who suffer from their consciences (the superego). The lack of cleanliness attacked in v. 26 seems to me to fit into the same pattern. To produce certain achievements by means of cleanliness training is obviously connected with cleanliness and order. Doubt fits into this context too, as we have already seen, and especially self-doubt. Thus the Pharisees in Matt. 23.16–22 are characterized as people who try to make sure, down to the most ludicrous details, when an oath is binding and when it is not. One can understand that this kind of person is of immense importance for a nation that is living under a foreign power and is in danger of losing its sense of its own identity. But at the same time there is a great danger that the religious relationship may be perverted. Jesus draws the Pharisees' attention to the most important law, which they are neglecting – clemency, mercy and faithfulness. We might also say 'love and liberty', or, with Augustine, *ama deum et fac quod vis* – love God and do what you like. Erikson points out how often, in individuals and groups, the letter of the law kills the spirit that makes the law (*Identity and the Life-Cycle*, p. 73).

On the basis of what we have already said above, we should like to underline that the autonomy of the second phase is only 'normal' when it develops on the foundation of the first phase's basic trust and within its framework. If this does not take place, because the basic trust functions insufficiently, fear and doubt of the self will turn autonomy into a perverted self-justification – in the religious sphere as well, as the example of the Pharisee shows.

This phase therefore lays the foundation for the 'superego' whose genesis is generally placed in the third, Oedipal phase. It develops in the third phase out of the need to form an ideal, as well as out of fear of punishment; and in puberty it can grow into an independently functioning conscience, which has more or less lost its infantile features. But anyone who thinks that he can already discover traces of the superego in the anal phase is right: under the influence of cleanliness training *a clear feeling develops that 'you must' and 'you must not'*, which means roughly the same as 'I am condemned to do this . . . if I want to be accepted'. Cleanliness training is associated with the mother's praise and acceptance, and also with the fear of losing status. Now, we can observe in many modern people the compulsion (prompted by unconscious fear) to achieve something. That is to say, these people have to earn love (like the Pharisees) and consequently they cannot be free, and they cannot be passive. The Pharisee is in a certain sense the 'manager' in Jewish society at the time of Jesus.

The Pharisee is obviously the person who *has* to be pure, who *has* to fulfil the law in its every detail, in order to earn God's love and to acquire a certain status with him, and hence with the people. In his book on Luther Erikson has brought out the anal problems in Luther's struggle to find a proper relationship between faith and works. Here his father evidently had more influence on the problem than his mother.

This can all be summed up in the formula that the second phase sees the transition from confidence to self-confidence, and that the two to-gether are of essential importance in life. In the Pharisee this unity of confidence and self-confidence was broken. Self-confidence became desperate self-assertion in the face of fear and self-doubt.

Puritanism

Puritanism is the second religious manifestation which we can make comprehensible with the help of our analysis of the anal pattern. Puritan-ism was not a unified complex in Christian history; it was an important religious and ecclesiastical movement with a number of different aspects.

In his well-known book *The Protestant Ethic and the Spirit of Capitalism*, the sociologist Max Weber investigated the connection between a re-ligious group (and in the first instance Calvinism which, as we shall see, is closely related to Puritanism) and the rise of capitalism. In doing so Weber was not so much thinking of large-scale modern capitalism; he rather had individual, early middle-class capitalism in mind.

Weber writes that money plays a part all over the world, but that capitalism is unique in that it is nothing more than a rationalized striving for gain. Industry and trade are separated from one another, and profit and loss is rationalistically calculated. Further characteristics are free labour and exact calculation. It is therefore a middle-class, a bourgeois capitalism; but the bourgeois is not the free 'burgess' of the Middle Ages but the modern Western employer (p. 24).

Sociological research now sees a connection between religious de-nomination and secular profession. Here Weber offers statistics drawn from the German state of Baden in 1895. At that time 37% of the population was Protestant and 61·3% Catholic. But 69% of the pupils of the *Realgymnasien* (the more scientifically orientated secondary schools, which must be distinguished from the grammar schools) were Protestant and 31% Catholic. In the *Oberrealschulen* (which also had a modern rather than a classical bias) 52% were Protestant and 41% Catholic. In his dissertation *Gezin en Schoolkeuze bij Handarbeiders* (1968) C. E. Vervoort points to the analogous situation in the Netherlands. Investigations have shown that Catholics display relatively less interest in the *Hogere Burgerschool*, which means relatively less interest in the natural sciences, whereas the reverse is true in the case of the grammar schools and the arts. Weber points out (pp. 39f.) that Protestants (and particularly certain branches of them) had a special preference for economic rationalism, whether they were the majority or the minority group. This was not true of Catholics, either as a majority or a minority group. This, therefore, has nothing to do with chance historical circumstances. It was associated with a kind of life regimented by religion. We find among Quakers and Anabaptists a clear, strict way of life, a certain unworldliness, and a strongly developed and intensive turn for business. The same might be said of the German Pietists (p. 42).

What, now, does Weber mean by the spirit of capitalism?

He characterizes it by a quotation from Benjamin Franklin: 'After industry and frugality, nothing contributes more to the raising of a young man in the world than punctuality and justice in all his dealings' (p. 49); and Weber speaks a little later (p. 51) of 'the ideal of the honest man of recognized credit, and . . . of a duty of the individual toward the increase of his capital'. This stress on status, possessions, order and exactitude is, as we have said, typical of the anal pattern. It is a morality, a sense of duty (cf. the superego of this phase). A remarkable feature, moreover, is that people were forbidden to enjoy money. A person must in all circumstances be moderate and clean. Weber stresses emphatically that this was a rational way of life in which order, prudence and sobriety were paramount. This morality is a professional ethic, rooted in a sense of duty.

Weber thinks that it derives from the Reformation – not so much from Luther (whose underlying tradition was a more agricultural form of life) as from Calvin and the Reformed sects who carried on 'this – worldly asceticism'. Here he includes Calvinism, Pietism, Methodism and the Anabaptist sects, as well as the English puritans.

Weber finds belief in predestination one of the most striking features of the religious pattern of these groups. Predestination implies that a person's acts are not really of decisive importance and that his status is dependent on God. We could sum the matter up by saying that these groups stress autonomy, with a strong feeling for status (which is conferred by God – this association is quite common in the anal pattern, as we have seen). The fact that we have to do here with the pattern of the second phase also becomes plain when we see that belief in predestination is bound up with the problem of certainty. In the attempt to acquire status, doubt (including self-doubt) cannot be repressed in the anal pattern. In Pietism doubt plays an important part; and in the Netherlands we need only point to the 'Gereformeerde Bond' ('the Reformed Covenant'). Status in God's eyes always remains an uncertain matter. In Calvinism the problem is often solved by assuming that success here on earth is proof of God's blessing. This view still comes out in the American attitude to money and to social success.

Weber deals with this problem too in his book. He writes (pp. 110ff.) that wherever people hold the doctrine of predestination the question arises, whether there are sure signs which allow a man to deduce whether he belongs to the elect or not. One way of achieving certainty here was ceaseless exertion in one's daily occupation. It is true that good works are not a way of achieving blessedness, but they are a token of election. 'They are the technical means, not of purchasing salvation, but of getting rid of the fear of damnation' (p. 115). Systematic self-examination is therefore continually necessary.

This, therefore, is a type of religion which differs from the religion of the oral phase. Here it is not a question of oneness with God or participation in him. In so far as we can talk of oneness at all it is a question of participation from a clearly defined distance. Brotherly love, for example, says Weber (pp. 108f.) merely serves the glory of God. It is therefore remarkably matter-of-fact and impersonal, a kind of service designed to aid the rational organization of the social cosmos surrounding us. Or in other words, the feeling of oneness with God or one's neighbour plays no part in a *love* of this kind; detachment is paramount. In modern times we find the same kind of belief in the theology of Karl Barth, which also constantly stresses the 'qualitative' distance between God and man and particularly mistrusts feelings of oneness with God.

It would seem as if Pietism (and the Reformed Covenant) broke with this type of religion. But in my view it only attempted to correct it. The pattern was not destroyed; it is just that an attempt was made to meet a certain need for 'oneness' within this same framework. I believe that

Weber is therefore right to point with such emphasis to the parallels with the traditional type of Calvinism. Methodism, an outpost of Pietism, supports works and a methodical way of life as a token of election. Among the sects we find a similar morality in the quiet, sober and extremely conscientious way of life of the Baptists and Quakers, to which Weber points (pp. 144ff.). All this has therefore anal references. One and the same pattern characterizes all the different types, a pattern marked by the clear need for self-control, asceticism and the rule of reason. What, now, is the characteristic mark of the ethics of economic commerce here? How does this kind of employer carry on his everyday life? The English Puritan Richard Baxter, one of the most important representatives of this ascetic Protestantism, wrote a series of books on which Weber bases his investigation of this question (pp. 156ff.). In his *Saints' Everlasting Rest* and *Christian Directory*, Baxter points out that the Christian has to be very careful about money and possessions – he must not 'enjoy' them – he must not waste any time and must work hard in order to balance all the temptations of the 'unclean life' (an expression typical of the anal pattern). Work is even a holy end in itself. Unwillingness to work is, as Weber puts it (p. 159), symptomatic of the lack of grace, whereas a man's application to it is 'a proof of his state of grace through his conscientiousness' (p. 161). Puritanism 'has the highest ethical appreciation of the sober, middle-class, self-made man' (p. 163). Thrift is highly regarded and to build up capital through savings is a work well pleasing to God. According to Weber the secularized middle-class spirit widespread above all in England, the Netherlands and the United States has developed out of this pattern and this morality.

When we remember Erikson's definition, we see clearly that this is the pattern of the second phase. The emphases are the same as they are in Erikson. Man has to live for the sake of *achieving* something. He must on the one hand *cast away* the impure and dirty ('the unclean life') and must *hold fast* to money (which, as we shall see later, has a central significance in the anal pattern). His *status* with God and the world (the group) must mean a lot to him too. His life must be characterized by *order* and punctuality. And all these things are permeated by a strong feeling of *independence* (autonomy; the attitude of 'I'm the king of the castle'). Moreover beneath the surface one senses a distinct feeling of *doubt* (of one's own value and capacities).

We see that in this type of the religious life, as Puritanism represents it, the educational pattern of the second phase exerts its influence. In my opinion the connections here are not as direct as Weber would like us to believe. He thinks that a direct line leads from Calvinism to capitalism – or, to be exact, to a particular early capitalist morality. I myself would say that as society develops a particular class of people grows up; that a particular pattern of upbringing (morality) evolves in this class; and that in that pattern of upbringing certain religious aspects stand out (for example, a particular *relationship to work*, which has a religious bearing, as Weber shows so clearly in Calvinism and Puritanism). From this point a line of development leads back to the daily practice of trade or profession, which in these groups actually does have a capitalist character. It is also a remarkable fact that the capitalist ethic of early Calvinism is still strongly stamped by a mediaeval mentality. This is a phenomenon to which Tawney points, for example, in the book which we shall be considering under this aspect presently. In its educational ideas too Calvinism in its early days is closer to mediaeval humanism than it is in later centuries; we have only to think of Calvin's Geneva.

Let me point to one other important phenomenon. Weber brings out the unique way in which the groups he is dealing with handle money. It must not be enjoyed, and the relationship to money is rationalized, as he puts it – in a certain sense even purified ('the clean life'). Freud had already discovered the anal significance of money, and psycho-analysis in its later stages confirmed his discovery. Money plays an important part in our society too, as well as in the morality of many groups; but it also has a prominent place in the personal views of many people belonging to our own time. We shall therefore come back in more detail to the religious significance of money.

In his book *Religion and the Rise of Capitalism* (1922) R. H. Tawney subjected Weber's theories (which dated from 1902) to a closer investigation. His starting-point is somewhat different from that of Weber, who was really writing a treatise on the religious and ecclesiastical origins of capitalism as an ethic. Tawney, on the other hand, deals with mediaeval Christianity, the Reformation on the continent, the Church of England, and Puritanism, discussing their different ideas about economic life and their links with commerce.

According to him mediaeval life has an agrarian pattern. Possessions mean the possession of land. Interest and credit are by their very nature sinful. Only Jews were allowed to practise usury. Avarice is a sin as well. In a pattern of this kind capitalism is actually impossible. Tawney goes on (p. 66):

The essential facts were simple. The Church sees buying and selling, lending and borrowing, as a simple case of neighbourly or unneighbourly conduct. Though a rationalist like Bishop Pecock may insist that the rich, as such, are not hateful to God, it has a traditional prejudice against the arts by which men – or at least laymen – acquire riches, and is apt to lump them together under the ugly name of avarice.

Or in other words, something like capitalism grows up because a kind of middle class grows up too – but it cannot develop fully.

Tawney then shows that at the Reformation something in the nature of an economic revolution took place. It was the period of financial *condottieri*. He writes (p. 88):

> Compared with these financial dynasties, Hapsburgs, Valois and Tudors were puppets dancing on wires held by a money-power to which political struggles were irrelevant except as an opportunity for gain. The financier received his payment partly in cash, partly in concessions, which still further elaborated the network of financial connections that were making Europe an economic unity. The range of interests in which the German banking houses were involved is astonishing.

We see, therefore, that there was as yet no question of a middle class but that the agrarian pattern of society was being superseded. There was as yet no capitalistic ethic; we have rather to do with financial dynasties, like the Fuggers.

As far as the Reformation and its leaders is concerned, Luther belongs to the process of dissolution of the old pattern, because he rebelled against the Pope and the power of the Catholic church; but on the other hand he still belongs entirely to the old agricultural ethic: he is on the side of the princes, repudiating the peasants' revolt and the usurers as well. Luther's background is, according to Tawney (pp. 111f.), the traditional mediaeval agricultural society, 'a natural, rather than a money, economy'. Trade and traffic in money only occur by chance. They are not forces which keep the whole system going. We have to do with a society which is opposed to the entrepreneur, a striving for gain, and an unceasing competition which shakes the stability of the existing order.

In Calvin the situation is different. He fits into the framework of an urban society and accepts the rules of commercial life as far as credit and interest are concerned. According to Tawney (p. 117) he develops the view that 'Good works are not a way of attaining salvation but they are indispensable as a proof that salvation has been attained.' God is to be glorified, not only through prayer but through action. In Calvinism, the stress is thus on achievement, as well as on order, prudence, cleanliness and discipline. This gave the life-style of the middle classes of Western Europe its stamp. There are still obvious traces of it today among Protestants of the Calvinist tradition in France, the Netherlands and Scotland. But this means too that there is no place in this way of life for economic libertinism, i.e., for profiteers and hoarders.

Tawney then goes on to deal with the Church of England, which obviously stands under the influence of the traditional mediaeval pattern of society. In this pattern the landowners (or the English nobility) played an important part. The landowner stood quite apart from the economic problems of a changing society. In this situation the Church of England's only policy was to keep quiet – something which took a bitter revenge later, in the nineteenth century especially, at the period of the Industrial Revolution. According to Tawney the church could not give inspiration and guidance in the face of the immense economic reorganization because it had neither inspiration nor guidance to give. 'The spiritual blindness which made possible the general acquiescence in the horrors of the early factory system was, not a novelty, but the habit of a century.'

The last long chapter deals with Puritanism. In Tawney's view its essence is will – will organized and disciplined and inspired (pp. 201f.):

> To contemporaries the chosen seat of the Puritan spirit seemed to be those classes in society which combined economic independence, education and a certain decent pride in their status, revealed at once in a determination to live their own lives, without truckling to earthly superiors, and in a somewhat arrogant contempt for those who, either through weakness of character or through economic helplessness, were less resolute, less vigorous and masterful, than themselves.

Puritanism crystallized in the different free churches, and it was members of these churches, like the Baptists and Quakers, who as the leaders of commercial and industrial undertakings dominated public life. They patently represented the middle class in urban society. Tawney characterizes the Puritan as follows (pp. 229f.):

> Called by God to labour in his vineyard, he has within himself a principle at once of energy and of order, which makes him irresistible both in war and in the struggles of commerce. Convinced that character is all and circumstances nothing, he sees in the poverty of those who fall by the way, not a misfortune to be pitied and relieved, but a moral failing to be condemned, and in riches, not an object of suspicion – though like other gifts they may be abused – but the blessing which rewards the triumph of energy and will. Tempered by self-examination, self-discipline, self-control, he is the practical ascetic, whose victories are won not in the cloister, but on the battlefield, in the counting house, and in the market.

The Puritan is characterized by a particular morality which Tawney stresses in some detail. Let me quote a few sentences from pp. 241-4:

> Luxury, unrestrained pleasure, personal extravagance, can have no place in a Christian's conduct . . . The Christian life, in short, must be systematic and organized, the work of an iron will and a cool intelligence . . . Success in business is in itself almost a sign of spiritual grace.

An industrious life of this kind is something like religion; it is a life in God's service and lived to his glory.

In Weber and Tawney, therefore, we come across the same fundamental ideas. Tawney has merely a better sense of history's complicated ramifications. The basic proposition of both writers is: capitalism and Puritanism live from a certain set of ethics which are connected with a certain economic development, with a certain social class, and with certain religious motivations. Both breathe the same air and are rooted in the same pattern of upbringing.

It can be clearly established that here we have to do with the structure of the second phase in the child's development. The deepest roots of both capitalism and Puritanism are to be found in the anal pattern.

Secularization

We have seen that the second developmental phase contains a particular problem. The child develops a certain autonomy, but it develops it on the basis of the participation of the first phase (basic trust, oneness and security with the mother). There is the danger that the autonomy may not be organically anchored in the basic trust or may detach itself from it: the autonomy breaks out of the basic trust and tries to find a ground of its own. Religiously speaking, this leads to a breach with religion or to its perversion. We can say that the tension between autonomy and participation, which is integral to the relationship of the two, is so heightened that autonomy receives too one-sided an emphasis, so that participation – and hence the religious pattern – recedes into the background.

In my opinion this has taken place in the transition from the agrarian to the urban pattern of society. Traditional religious forms fade or disappear and the middle-class citizen (and with him the 'manager') takes the stage. Paul Tillich talked about the middle-class spirit as 'the spirit of the finiteness which rests within itself'. This transition to the urban middle-class pattern is an aspect of the phenomenon of secularization which in my view has received too little attention. Apart from the influence which modern scientific development has certainly had upon the traditional religious consciousness, and apart from the social changes through which large groups have become separated from the church, the process of secularization also has a cultural component which is connected with the shifts in the pattern of upbringing, and is consequently also linked with changes of stress in the various developmental phases.

Our common life is increasingly dominated by the pattern of modern capitalist society. This pattern is for its part rooted in a pattern of upbringing: children have to be educated for life in this society early on. It seems to emerge with increasing clarity that the second phase of development, the anal one, is given a strong emphasis in this educative process. We would add that the pattern of the fourth phase as well – the phase for which Erikson's main term is industry – plays an important role in this upbringing. But this phase has links with the second one.

We have seen which elements play a part in this anal pattern of upbringing. They include achievement, status, doubt in oneself, a feeling of shame (more than a feeling of guilt), stress on the 'unclean' element in sexuality (the taboo), the compulsive *having to* work and fear of enjoyment. We would add two elements which are stressed by existentialist philosophy: insecurity, and the being condemned to freedom – two elements whose roots in the anal pattern can be recognized without much trouble.

The compulsive element about this pattern in the lives of many modern people means that a rebellion against the pattern as such can be sensed in the midst of our society – especially among young adolescents; and this rebellion presents itself as a kind of alternative culture. The characteristics of this alternative pattern are: rebellion against a culture based on achievement, an aversion to earning money, the sweeping aside of sexual taboos, and the almost compulsive will towards enjoyment. These are aspects which we met earlier in the phenomenon we called a counter-culture.

One evident aspect of secularization is therefore the pattern of urban middle-class life, which is taken to excess in the 'city' pattern, with the manager as central figure, and a counter-culture as an alternative pattern.

9

Religious Problems in the Pattern of the Second Phase

In the last two chapters we indicated the most important aspects of the anal phase of the child's development; and we took Pharisaism, Puritanism and secularization as first instances of the significance of the phase for the religious life. We will now go more closely into certain problems which this pattern poses for the religious attitude to life. These problems are: money, product and production, technology, and people who have had a coronary thrombosis.

Money

We already saw in the last chapter that money (and above all earning money and dealing with it) plays an important part in the pattern of the second phase. Certain traces of this can be shown in Christianity particularly. The gospel already distinguishes between serving God and serving mammon. In Puritanism the value attached to money plays an important part, as we have seen. In modern society, however, money and the possession of money has become so much a matter of course that it is difficult for us to acquire the detachment which is necessary if we are to consider the religious problems involved. Here I should like to look at one of the few books which deal with the problem of money from the theological point of view, James A. Knight's *For the Love of Money*.

Freud gives an important stimulus to a modern investigation of the problem of money in his article 'Character and Anal Eroticism', which appeared in 1908 (*Collected Works*, Vol. IX). One can well understand that the connection which Freud traces in this article between money and anality seemed ludicrous at first. Today no one finds it surprising. Incidentally in colloquial speech (which is known to be in some respects the spontaneous expression of unconscious fantasies) there is a whole series of metaphors and phrases which show this connection very clearly. We talk about 'being filthily rich', 'throwing money about like dirt', money being 'down the drain', to take a few examples. Freud points out in his article that there are certain people whom we could characterize as orderly, thrifty and obstinate. He shows that holding back his stool can apparently give a child pleasure. According to Freud the people we have just mentioned have grown to be what they are through a sublimation of anal eroticism. Their 'decency' is, as it were, a continuation on a higher plane of their aversion from dirtiness. The same can be said, *mutatis mutandis*, about thrift. And obstinacy still reveals something of the child's reaction to the urgings of its parents. One could therefore say that money is a sublimated form of defecation and that it has a comparable function in the anal pattern. It is remarkable too that money only acquires meaning in the child's life when it reaches youth. The 'experience' and 'estimation' of money therefore plays an important part in the pattern of the second phase; or, to put it another way, money is associated, or can be associated, with very deep emotions. Knight's book gives a whole series of examples.

(*a*) Knight first of all describes the strong influence of money on our feelings of anxiety (p. 13). In a world of tensions and sudden changes, he sees the pursuit of money as largely based on the hope of finding something which will be like a magic amulet, and will provide emotional security. This leads to a competitiveness in which success (becoming rich) becomes a form of self-endorsement, solid evidence of 'power' both in our own eyes and in those of others.

Knight writes this with an eye to American society, in which these manifestations are obvious; but his analysis brings out general human requirements. In other societies as well money is a way of suppressing anxieties of the kind indicated by Knight. In America and Europe, for example, money can be used to overcome the fear of 'not belonging'. A person may try with the help of money to gain access to a particular group and to be accepted by it. The fear of not belonging is really nothing other than the child's fear, in its second phase, of being worthless and rejected in the eyes of its mother (represented here by the group).

(*b*) Or to put it another way: money is power – through money one can achieve a great deal. Knight (p. 16) points out that in our society whoever has money has reputation and power. He therefore thinks that the need for wealth is connected with the need for power, and with the will towards power about which Nietzsche and Alfred Adler wrote. It is not difficult to uncover the roots of this necessity: children feel almighty in a primitive way because of all the things that they are already able to do. All their lives they still have a faint remembrance of this, and they long to experience the feeling once more.

In the gospel of Luke (12.16–21) we can read the parable of the rich fool who heaps up all his possessions and then says to himself: 'Take your ease, eat, drink, be merry.' He thinks that his possessions have *insured* him against every kind of insecurity. He feels as if he were almighty. But God says, 'Fool! This night your soul is required of you.' Jesus calls the man a fool because he expresses such immature, childish ideas about his own power. When the gospel of Matthew talks about serving two masters, God and mammon (6.24), it means that mammon (i.e., money) represents power for people. In *L'Avare* Molière describes superbly how deeply this feeling of the power of money is rooted in human life. Avarice is simply the fear of losing this power.

(*c*) The miser also shows how closely money and the body are originally related to one another. He has a positively physical relationship to his wealth. He has to play with it, let it slide through his fingers – grasp it sensually, so to speak. The analogy to the way the child plays with excrement is obvious. Even expressions like 'my money's lying at the bank' or 'he just sits on his money' illustrate our need to 'feel' the sense of power through this visual imagery.

(*d*) Money therefore gives us a feeling of security, as Knight showed in the first passage we quoted. It is the same security that the amulet gives, the same sort of safety that the mother's security represents. In the Middle Ages, when land gave this security (and was hence forcibly defended) the Jews were forbidden to possess real property. Consequently they had to acquire security by means of money – which incidentally had the advantage that it could more easily be taken with them if they had to flee persecution.

(*e*) It is understandable that in spite of the relationship to the body and especially the anal region (or probably because of this very connection) in some cultures money is 'dirty', something inferior. This feeling is also deeply rooted in our culture. The aristocrat can be poor and look down on the earning of money; and in fact he often has his own attitude to it. He does not cling to money so much and parts from it more readily. In cities like Amsterdam and Rotterdam the gap between professional people, like lawyers and teachers, and groups which make their money through commerce and industry can still be felt. (It is significant that the expression 'to earn money' is less used among professional people.) Earlier, this gap was in fact very wide indeed. Many people can still hardly believe that earning money plays so important a role for doctors too.

The Bible also talks about earning money. The epistle of James talks about the rich 'fattening their hearts' (James 5.5). The special feature of Puritanism was to free money from this 'impurity'. It was permissible to earn money, but not to enjoy it (this attitude plays an important role in American society), or to hoard it, using it as a 'possession' for giving security. One had to 'do' something with it. American generosity towards good causes is connected with this. In so far as the Puritan attitude to money is still detectable in our modern capitalist society, it can be recognized in the following attitude: a clear distinction is made between the use of money for personal and for social purposes, or putting money in the bank, which in a primitive sense prevents us from enjoying it. In this way money is cleansed of its taint, it is deodorized. It still gives security, but in quite a different way from the one Molière describes.

(*f*) We see a particular aspect of money when we give it away. This can release deep feelings in us which were originally connected with anality. Anyone who gives money away undergoes a certain tension. It is as if something had been severed from us. We can see the same thing when we give away a dress or a suit. It is difficult for us to see someone else wearing a piece of clothing which we have worn ourselves. To give money away can make us anxious. It is a reduction of our security and confidence in ourselves, since it is connected with a reduction of power. The phrase 'penny wise, pound foolish', which is applied to people who get excited about a trivial amount but throw away large sums, applies to particular 'anal' types of people, as every psychoanalyst knows. This indicates how hard it is to handle power. Absolute rulers are often suspicious in small things, but when it is a question of something affecting their power in a wider context, they are positively naïve, if not infantile. Shakespeare observed this aspect of a ruler's life very acutely.

Gifts of money suggest that people are trying to exert power over others by means of presents, that is to say through money. In the anal patter the child frequently tries to acquire power over his mother through the 'gift' of his achievement. Money sometimes plays the same role in human relationships. We often see children distributing sweets in the playground, so as to win friends.

It is not difficult to discover the important religious and pastoral problems that emerge here. For basically, dealings with money have a great deal to do with a religious attitude to life – the gospels already point this out. It is really a semi-religious activity, or an activity similar to a religious one; one which is frequently connected with profound feelings of anxiety and power, as we have seen. That is to say, money can put people in bondage. But the religious person, particularly, is free, or can be so. He seeks and finds his 'being', his power and security, in God and from God. We can reduce it to a formula: show me how you deal with money, and I will tell you what God means to you.

The conclusion, accordingly, is: we can possess money but money must not possess us. We do not have to view money as if it were dirty. It is true that it has anal connections, but what is physical does not deprive us of freedom – on the contrary, the liberty of the children of God involves matter-of-fact, free dealings with the body, and hence with money as well.

The problem here is that in the anal phase we take a first step on the road to later maturity, that is to say in the direction of autonomy. This also means that we experience for the first time what it means to be without maternal security. We need assurances against fear; we need self-endorsement. In the anal pattern of life money plays an important part here, since for many people it fulfils this very function. At this point we are faced with a religious problem. A person with a mature faith can do without assurances and self-endorsement; for the supporting foundation is provided by the basic trust which lies at the heart of this faith, and by belief in God's commission. We shall be dealing with this last point later, in the context of the third phase.

Product and Production

I believe that these two words, which are central to our present-day social and personal pattern, also have important religious and pastoral aspects. I am thinking for example of the figure of the artist, who plays an important part in every culture, and whose relationship to religion and the church is evidently fraught with considerable difficulty – again in almost every culture. I am thinking too of the fact that because of the altered rhythm of life and work in our industrial society the meaning of product and production has changed; and this again has important consequences for religion.

In general we can say that product and production give a person the feeling that he is something, that he is capable of something and has an identity. It is under this aspect that Erikson sees the significance of the second phase for the child's development. Cleanliness training, one of whose features is the displaying of some product, is an almost indispensable link in the person's growth to maturity and identity. It awakes deep feelings in the child which, it seems, are really of decisive importance throughout his life. This becomes comprehensible when we remember why the clergy frequently envy doctors. The latter see the result of their work in far more concrete form. The clergyman is much more uncertain. The radio chaplain's complaint that he has no real contact with his hearers in his work is illuminating. In spite of the many letters he receives, he never has a real *feeling* for what he is actually doing.

The product evidently awakes in the producer positive (and perhaps also negative) feelings. He views it with satisfaction and sometimes with pleasure. He enjoys touching it. When a writer has his book in printed form in front of him, he likes to pick it up and turn over the pages. There are painters who hate to part with their pictures and who like to know where they are hung and if they are appreciated properly. Psychotherapists are increasingly aware of the importance of handicrafts and hobbies. Everyone wants to show what he has produced and wants to hear a judgment about it. Many people are bad at hearing criticism. It is also understandable that production is often linked with feelings of doubt. Nearly every artist has periods when he is possessed by the idea that what he has produced is valueless. These are feelings which extend far further than the product itself; they revolve round the question of our value as writer or painter. Doubt of the product is linked with doubt of ourselves. The well-known psychiatrist J. H. Plokker wrote a dissertation called *Geschonden beeld* (Distorted picture) in which he deals with visual expression in schizophrenics. He writes (pp. 101f.):

> The artist needs publicity, however strong an individualist he is and however distinct his personality. He is dependent on the attention of his fellow-men. To respond with deathly silence would amount to a mortal blow. Praise is of course best, but even scathing criticism is better than no criticism at all . . . For the artist, response is a vital necessity, however much he plumes himself on being 'above' other people and their little world, and superior to all criticism.

It must by now be clear that these are feelings belonging to the pattern which is 'released' in the anal phase of human development.

This becomes still more evident when we pay more attention to the *process* of production than to its result. In this process we again have to do with various feelings deriving from the anal phase. Observations among children show that evacuating the bowels can be associated with a feeling of satisfaction. One can sometimes even talk about an 'orgasm'. A climax is reached by way of a particular tension.

Now, artists also report that the creative process is associated with the feeling of being caught up in a tension through which they can lose the feeling of space and time. The creative artist feels intensely active and sometimes arrives at a climax, as in an orgasm. At the same time he is passive as well; it is as if the product (the poem, for instance) goes through him and out of him. Poets or painters consequently often do not 'know' what they are doing; they simply 'splash the paint about' (Karl Appel). Nor can they talk about it. They are not themselves conscious of the things that other people find in their work.

A creative artist of any stature therefore works from a combination of basic trust and self-confidence (autonomy). Because of this self-confidence he is generally an individualist and a nonconformist. But basic trust is necessary because he must be passive if the product is to come into being. Nearly every artist has therefore a touch of the feminine about him. That is to say, among other things, he must also be able to 'enjoy'. Few artists are puritans.

In discussing the social function of the artist, Plokker maintains the view that the artist is close to the feelings present in all of us, the only difference being that in him they are not so repressed. He reveals these repressed feelings in his work, and if he does not do so too openly, but in more or less veiled form, the reader or observer is able to identify himself with him because he recognizes his deeper life in the artist's work. But if the process is too open, the shock of recognition is too great and the work of art has a repellent effect. This has been the fate of the 'modern' artist throughout the centuries. It is therefore understandable that in a puritanical culture particularly the artist has difficulty in finding his proper place. France, especially Paris, has always been fruitful ground for artists. This is much less true of the Netherlands.

In the religious and ecclesiastical field the artist poses particular problems. As we have already said, he is an individualist and a nonconformist, but this is not the only reason why he generally has little interest in the church. Life and creation are in him such a unity that one could say that he finds the trust on which his life is based in himself rather than in the usages of religion and the church. I believe that this makes it possible to understand why artists are in general not very active in the traditional ecclesiastical and religious spheres. But the artist is not as a rule anti-religious; one might perhaps even say that the deeper levels of his life are in fact religious. Moreover he is frequently interested in religious feelings and customs. I would explain this by saying that in his life he has developed a sense of 'leading' which is obviously connected with the religious sphere. But it must be stressed that his interest in religion in its ecclesiastical and institutional forms is purely platonic and that he needs the church more for his artistic production, than as something to which he can belong actively.

The craftsman must be mentioned as well as the artist when we are considering the subject of product and production, for like the artist he makes something of his own. We can think of the carpenter or cabinet-maker, the tailor or dressmaker (couturier), the gold or silversmith – the townsman in general, as he emerged as a particular group in our West European society at the end of the middle ages. Between this group and the artists there are some remarkable agreements and differences.

1. Both groups display pride in what is produced, which is a sign of an emotional relationship to the product. In both groups the producer is also emotionally involved in the productive process. He is completely absorbed and 'forgets the time' in the process. Individualism is clearly a feature of both groups, by way of the link between the basic trust of the first period with the 'trust' acquired in the productive process. The autonomy to which Erikson points in connection with the second phase is in actual fact an important word for both groups. One could say that when Tillich defines the middle-class spirit as 'the spirit of the finiteness that rests within itself', it is this autonomy that he means – the autonomy which is so strongly connected with the trust proceeding from the product and therefore with dependence on the individual self.

2. There are, however, important differences as well. For the craftsman, trying and measuring plays an important role. He is an orderly man who among other things has to know how to divide up his time, so that he can deliver his product punctually. Because of this he is emotionally bound in a quite different way to his product, which is, after all, not his artistic creation but is made according to a commission and takes account of particular instructions. He therefore enters less into the enjoyment of his product, and in the productive process it is less a question of his letting his productions go 'through' him and allowing them to emerge from himself. He lacks the passivity, the feminine element which we noticed in the artist. The process of production has consequently a less 'orgastic' colouring and is channelled towards enjoyment

to a far lesser degree. On the contrary, the painter's 'splashing the paint about' is out of the question for the craftsman, who is confined to clear, orderly procedures. Erikson points out that in the second phase of childish development the character traits of order, exactness and cleanliness can come into being because they are so closely connected with the creating of a good product. The 'law and order' mentality has its roots here.

It is therefore understandable that Puritanism could grow up in a group of this kind, with its own pattern of culture and upbringing; and it is a quite particular Puritanism, with an unconscious detachment from what is 'dirty' and from the enjoyment of the physical and emotional aspects of life. The good artisan is decent by nature; he represents the ideal of the 'decent' life.

This also has certain consequences for religion and the church. It is significant that the middle classes link the functions of religion and the church very closely with their need for order. They experience both as positive orderly elements. In primitive societies, religion has a clear function. Religious usages uphold the sacral order. They are, as it were, a bulwark against chaos. It could also be said that through religion the middle-class citizen anchors his – always unsteady – autonomy in trust in the sacral order. Without religion and the church he feels threatened in his existential security. That is the reason why in the liberal middle-class society of the nineteenth century there was a constantly ambivalent attitude towards church and religion. On the one hand these people took an aloof attitude to the primitive and 'unenlightened' faith of the church; but on the other hand they conceded to the church a clear function because its faith protected the still immature masses from false doctrines through which order might be violated. The efficacy of church and religion guarantees the order which preserves society and without which no good life is possible. They thus remove the threat of chaos. This is the church's 'comforting' function, which is so often mentioned in modern sociological literature, in contrast to its 'challenging' function. Investigations have shown that in the church the need for 'comfort' is particularly great, especially among the laity.

In all this the problem of the value to be ascribed to sexuality plays an important part. It is not chance that the problem of sexuality has at present moved so emphatically into the foreground, as a rebellion against the anal cultural pattern. As a rule, we believe that the experience and evaluation of sexuality is a moral problem. But really it is a question of the classification of the pleasure associated with sexuality, and the right to that pleasure – and the people who support a freer attitude towards sexuality are usually very well aware of this. For the liberty for which they are pleading is not the right to a kind of libertinism, but the freedom for another experience of sexuality, sometimes also for a deeper experience of the body and the physical.

In the anal pattern the body is primarily an instrument which has to be 'fit' because it has to be able to produce certain achievements. Here learning how to cope with the body primarily means learning to use the body rightly. Man's ego is the body's active counterpart. Today people plead for a different experience of the body and try to 'discover' it in a different way, namely as a way of mediating experiences which we have first to accept passively before we can evaluate and integrate them. We therefore long to be passive and to be allowed to enjoy this passivity. Sexuality is experienced as a play of activity and passivity, and as the enjoyment which is bound up with it.

This longing is a rebellion against the attitude to the body we have already mentioned, in which sexuality (in the meaning which it has now acquired) cannot develop and really ought not to develop, because the longed-for and defended passivity is a threat to the constantly shifting autonomy of the middle-class citizen, who seeks his identity in activity. Personally and socially, people who advocate this 'free' sexuality seem to constitute a curious but understandable threat to others who take their bearings differently. Two patterns, and indeed two worlds, clash in the persons of the artist and the middle-class 'manager', for example. The Rotterdam novelist Herman Robbers brings this out very well in his novel *De bruidstijd van Annie de Boog* (Annie de Boog's Betrothal).

We ought not, therefore, to divide the sexual revolution which is under discussion from the rebellion which we can see everywhere against the order which is felt to be imposed on us and which is not inwardly accepted. This order appears to be embodied in the 'Establishment' and in big business, and it seems to smother creativity and play – in short, elements which are non-anal and non-compulsive – and with them an inwardly freer sexuality.

We can therefore distinguish between two groups of people in the anal pattern. In both groups achievement, product and hence a feeling for autonomy (based on possible self-doubt) plays an important role. In the group consisting of middle-class people and artisans this leads to a view of life clearly based on order, with the typical Puritan characteristics of non-enjoyment and thrift. In the other group, the artists, passivity and the creativity associated with it plays an important part; today this group includes many young people, as well as older ones who are searching for alternative patterns to the 'middle-class' view of life. Noticeable here are an atrophying concept of order, stress on enjoyment and sexuality, as well as a very relaxed attitude to money.

Preference for this alternative to the 'anal' pattern understandably brings with it a dissolution of the traditional pattern, which was impressed on middle-class society. The growth of small concerns into large-scale capitalist industry seems to me a decisive factor here. The extensive division of labour, the assembly line, the introduction of the computer, and the important place assumed by administration in connection with it, all mean that for the worker the final product towards which he is working has moved out of sight altogether. The individual no longer sees the result of his work, and the emotional relationship of the producer to his product no longer exists. We only see the result of our work indirectly, through promotion, 'rises', or a product's success on the market (which incidentally no longer exists as a *market* at all). For that reason the doubt which exists as a permanent potentiality in the anal pattern is visibly increasing in modern society. Anxiety, psychosomatic illnesses, a general reduction of inner freedom and an increasing tension are the results. The need to withdraw from this pressure finds visible expression in the use of sleeping pills and every kind of stimulant, as well as in participation in group experiences, the practice of meditation, Yoga, etc.

We are experiencing the end of the middle-class age in Tillich's sense. It is hardly possible to talk about 'a spirit of the finiteness that rests within itself' any more. The middle-class citizen has become a restless neurotic, and his finite world no longer gives him any rest.

Technology

Modern technology is generally considered to be one of the most important elements in the secularization of the Western world. Harvey Cox's widely-read book *The Secular City* (which Cox also calls Technopolis) shows clearly how much the pattern of man in the city dominated by technology differs from the original religious pattern of village society. It cannot be denied that from the religious point of view technology has a decisive importance for modern man and that its influence is connected with the different patterns which we are considering in this book.

Erikson does not mention technology in his treatment of the anal phase. It is true that he gives 'industry' as one of the typical features of the fourth phase, but he connects it more loosely with the development of the technical mastery of toys and of objects. But on the basis of this connection it can be said, I think, that in the fourth phase the foundation created in the second phase is developed further. Technology is one aspect of the 'producing' of the second phase. It is its systematic summing up, the planned working together with a differently organized production on a larger scale. In other words, technology develops out of skilled craftsmanship. Consequently we must treat it here in the context of our account of the second phase.

In an evaluation of technology the first striking thing is that the attitude towards it differs in America and Europe. In America judgments about the development of technology are positive. It is the country in which new gadgets work immediately, in which one tries out new technical discoveries as quickly as possible – we have only to think of the computer or space travel – the place where inventors like Edison are reverenced as heroes, and where theologians like Cox give technological development a kind of religious consecration or at least a carte blanche. In Europe we are certainly familiar with a positive attitude of this kind, but over here there seems to me to be a marked reserve towards modern technical advances. As early as the First World War, Walther Rathenau talked warningly about a 'mechanization of the spirit'. In Germany at that time Ludwig Klages, to name only one, was a fanatical opponent of every form of technology. The philosopher Heidegger also had an obvious anti-technical tendency. Technology is seen as being a threat to 'culture', a danger to the life of the spirit. The beginning of Huizinga's book *In de schaduwen van morgen* (Shadows of tomorrow) was on everyone's lips when it came out in 1935 and it seems to me typical of the feelings about technology in certain quarters in Europe. The first chapter is called 'Voices of Decline' and it begins:

> We are living in a mad world. And we know it. No one would be surprised if the madness suddenly degenerated into a frenzy which would leave poor European man behind in a condition of stupidity and idiocy. The motors are still running and the flags are still flying, but the spirit has gone.

In 1918 Huizinga had incidentally expressed his views about technology in *Mens en menigte in Amerika* (Man and the masses in America). He writes (p. 118): 'How, in our highly developed modern society, is the life of the spirit to escape degeneration, the levelling down and the mechanization which are so intimately linked with commercialization?'

What strikes me about these words is the unspecific character of their unrest and also the sweeping accusations which Huizinga levels against technology. Its influence – which undoubtedly exists – is not empirically investigated and statistically proved. He is simply frightened of it and rejects it emotionally, instead of subjecting it to a closer investigation. Expressions like the tower of Babel, which European theologians sometimes apply to modern technology, are on the same lines.

In more primitive societies the reaction to technological advances is generally very different. Even before the war Hermann Keyserling pointed to the phenomenon of the 'technologized primitive'. Experience teaches that 'primitive' people – even in Western society – are not only fascinated by modern technology; they are particularly clever at dealing with technical devices. They are quick to learn how to handle cars and aeroplanes and they make good drivers and pilots as well.

Let us now go a little more closely into some definitions of technology. First of all let us consider Martin Heidegger's article 'Die Frage nach der Technik' (The question of technology), which appeared in 1954 in *Vorträge und Aufsätze* (a collection of lectures and essays). It is worth mentioning that Heidegger talked about technology in several of his books. In this particular article he writes that the nature of technology cannot be summed up as belonging to the instrumental field. The latter is a producing, a bringing forth, whereas technology is a revealing, a bringing to view, what the Greeks call *aletheia*, unconcealment or truth. Technology is therefore a particular kind of producing, or revealing. The word technology, which means not only handicraft but also art, shows that man knows two ways of producing things, on the one hand through art, '*poiesis*', and on the other through what we call technology.

Of course what we call modern technology is not a producing in the sense of *poiesis*. It is a producing on the lines of craftsmanship, as we described it earlier. Heidegger now goes more deeply into this modern technology. According to what he says it is an 'engine technology' with which man confronts nature. When he produces, he no longer co-operates with nature – with wind, rain and sun; he challenges nature, mining coal and iron and transforming them into energy which he stores. Thus farming no longer means 'giving the seed over to the forces of growth; it has become a motorized nutrition industry'. The essential difference from earlier times is for Heidegger that today man no longer participates in nature as he did in the days when he used windmills or scattered the seed on the ground. The German word for planting the fields is *bestellen* – to order, as one orders a loaf of bread from the shop. That is to say, man confronts nature as an autonomous being. According to Heidegger a *Ge-stell* now comes into existence, a structure of being (of thinking and acting) which comprises a particular kind of human behaviour with regard to existing things, himself included. The real becomes in modern technology the 'stock' or content, and so Heidegger gives the name *Gestell* (i.e., structure of being in the sense we have just indicated) to 'the challenging claim that rallies men to order what reveals itself as "stock"'. Through this behaviour towards things and himself which Heidegger describes in the word *Gestell* (his expressions are often almost wilfully individual) man has taken a road from which it is hard to turn back. Everything he does and does not do is determined by this behaviour. In Heidegger's view, a certain 'belongingness' develops – man is in danger of going wrong over the thing that is revealed and judging it wrongly. Or to put it more simply, he is in danger of not seeing things correctly and of making false judgments. This is *Geschick*, 'destiny', to use another of Heidegger's words. He means that through the influence of modern technology on our lives (or on our spirits) it is our destiny to become estranged from our origin, from the genuine, from the truth (the true 'disclosure'). We no longer participate in the original natural unity with nature. Nature becomes 'stock', the object of our exploitation. Or, as he writes on p. 34, the man who makes everything his object and is finally threatened with becoming a mere object himself 'spreads himself in the guise of lord of the earth'. He makes himself completely autonomous, free from all participation, with the result that he really never again encounters himself, that is to say his nature.

Now salvation from this situation is possible if we arrive at a deeper understanding through a process of reflection, that is to say in art. Heidegger believes (pp. 43f.) that it is in the field of art that the decisive clash with technology will have to take place. Our questionings are an expression of the dangerous situation in which we stand, in which, because of all the different techniques, we no longer see the nature of technique itself; the more we think about the nature of technique, the more profoundly the nature of art reveals itself to us as a great mystery.

In this essay Heidegger is really dealing with the fundamental problem of his philosophy, the search for participation (in being). He complains about 'forgetfulness of being' and believes that the metaphysics of the West provide proof of it. But I have the impression that here he is overlooking the fact that all metaphysical statements are essentially 'images' of the experience of being, of participation. Henri Bergson expounds this convincingly in his impressive lecture (delivered in 1911) on 'Philosophic Intuition'. I am certain that the problem with which Heidegger is struggling lies rather in the fact that for him these images have lost their power. He is suffering from loneliness and fear, and since fear is for him apparently fear of separation, loss of security in participation, he tries to put the blame on the way in which we deal with things, in this case technology. But we may ask whether the reason is not a quite different one, namely his own powerlessness really to experience things as things. Is it not rather the case that he has not apparently gone through the necessary process of detachment sufficiently, and has therefore remained bound to things in the wong way? In this article (and in all Heidegger's work incidentally) we can sense something of the nostalgia for the whole-ness of life: nature as he conceives it is for him an image of lost unity. Heidegger is an example of modern, intellectually and technically edu-cated man, who meets the autonomy (and the dizzy freedom) involved in these attributes with a sense of fear; he lives in the pattern of the second phase, and through his one-sided stress on lack of security expresses his nostalgia for the first phase of all.

In Heidegger we encounter the ideal of culture and upbringing which was current in Germany during the nineteenth century and at the be-ginning of the twentieth. In this ideal, the bond with the maternal element plays an important role. The father was primarily experienced as authori-tarian and patriarchal, so that nostalgia for the maternal (the first phase) cost the individual an undue amount of energy. I dealt with the same problem in my book *Gott in vaterloser Gesellschaft*.

A still more eloquent example of the criticism of technology levied by Heidegger can be found in Ludwig Klages. At the end of *Die Grundlage der Charakterkunde* (1910ff.), for example, Klages gives vent to his wrath over the stereotypes and mechanization of life, over the decline of our Western culture in America, as well as over the American enslavement of the 'free citizen', who cannot escape the influence of the press and its financial backers. He rebels against the role of reason, which shatters and fragments the life of the spirit, against Christianity, which destroys the unity of life through its laws, and against the activism which 'enriches' our life with machines. Klages is impelled by a strongly emotional attitude towards unity, and by a prereflective experience of the soul and the personality. He pleads for a 'sense of the universe', which experiences the world as a constant ebb and flow of primordial and animate images, and which is directed towards the past, towards life's maternal matrix into which man will return. We may point here to the elements which we saw were typical of the pattern of the first phase: the experience of the primordial images and of participation. Ludwig Klages' fanaticism is directed against the loss of these elements.

The Dutch poet A. Roland Holst seems to me to be related to Klages in the emotional character of his poetry. In his book *Over den dichter Leopold* he compares mankind with the crew of a convict ship who are 'condemned to hard and degrading labour without any sight of the outside world, in a huge and smoky prison, lost men, who no longer know that it is the soul against whom they are defending themselves in fear and frenzy; men who through their apostasy bring down on themselves their former hopes and enthusiasm in the wrathful negatives of despair and confusion'. We remember Plato's picture of the cave in which fettered and blinded men, fallen from truth, also have to pass their lives. On board the ship in Holst's book there are also poets, among them Leopold, whom he stresses particularly. They are people who participate in a different reality, which they often make spring up before us in deeply suggestive images. Holst is just as fanatical as Klages when he is talking about the loss of these elements.

Let me quote some verses out of his book *Een winter aan zee* (A winter by the sea) which reflect his view of life. The elements of participation and the primordial images are clearly evident.

> Early sunders now, and oft
> in alien blizzard,
> the dying that of old
> communed with love. Since Troy's day
> deadly revenge raves
> from world's end to world's end.
> Black in the winter cold
> stand the turrets of dreams.
>
> Lion in fading light, dying
> there in the lonely dunes
> this very day. The bitter eye
> dims and the mane
> flurries the sand. Over the sea
> a tower of clouds still burns
> as dragons breathing fire
> guard the Eternal's retreat.

In Roland Holst rebellion against historical development is often a rebellion against the city. In a well-known poem cities like Babylon and London become demonstrations of this world's shipwreck and abandonment. It is a revolt against 'Technopolis'. Klages raised his accusing voice against this Technopolis as early as 1926 in his little book *Mensch und Erde* (Man and the earth). He writes:

> The rapids and waterfalls, even Niagara itself, have to feed power stations; forests of factory chimneys tower above their banks and poisonous waste products from the factories pollute the pure water of the earth. In short, the face of the continents is changing gradually into a single Chicago, with some farming here and there!

In these words we can sense the deep longing for primal participation in a first, unspoilt natural reality. It is significant that Harvey Cox has a totally different evaluation of this Technopolis. In his view man only really becomes man at all in a city like this. Before, he was merely in bondage to the primitive forces of nature.

We mentioned Tillich in connection with the first pattern; but in this context it is interesting to go into the ideas which he develops about Technopolis and about 'The Technical City as Symbol' (see *On the Boundary*, p. 16). We saw when we were dealing with Tillich in connection with the oral phase, that the fundamental pattern of his thinking is the pattern of the first phase, and that one of its keywords is participation. For him there is something equivocal about life in the modern city. On the one hand the city where one lives gives a kind of security against the 'uncanniness' of the reality in which we live. (We note that security is the norm against which the city is measured.) On the other hand the technical house and the technical city remain alien to us; objects have had their own lives taken from them, and no Eros can link them again with our lives.

Thus according to Tillich a new 'uncanniness', a horror of the frozen world, develops together with the freedom of the technical world of things. Primal participation is therefore withdrawn from us in the city. Tillich is on Klages' side, not Cox's.

Is it possible to put the problem of technology in a more adequate way, so as to arrive at a responsible evaluation of it?

Technology proceeds from the autonomous action of 'second-phase' man. (We remember that Erikson puts 'industry' into the fourth phase, with respect to its technical mastery, and that this fourth phase evidently goes on building on the foundations laid in the second.) Here we have to do with the problem of a new relationship to the mother and hence to maternal representatives, such as nature, etc. In the first phase the child participates physically in the mother; but in the second phase, in which he is learning to stand on his own feet and to do things for himself, the mother is more in the background and is often physically no longer present. She lives as it were hidden in the 'basic trust' with which the child is standing on his own feet and thus experiencing its autonomy. But, as we saw in our treatment of the Pharisees, a perversion can develop – a perversion of the religious relationships which develop out of the basic trust. It is a perversion when man does not feel free because of this relationship but because of his achievements. He gains his confidence from the consciousness of being able to manage alone with the help of what he can do. In other words he gains his confidence from self-confidence, from his feeling of power. It is clear that this is a perversion of the original religious relationship, which also means a perversion of the child's original relationship to the mother. So this perversion inevitably involves a feeling of alienation from the mother, the origin of life as we know it from the first phase.

This raises the question whether the feeling of estrangement which many people have, when they think about their lives in a society dominated by technology, is connected with 'mechanization' or with the perversion which comes from the sense of power. I doubt very much whether anything in the nature of 'mechanization' really exists. When we think of the spread of electric light, the almost universal use of central heating, or the bicycle or modern motor boat – and all these mean a profound intervention of modern technology in our lives – can we say that human life is enslaved, frozen and mechanized, along the lines of Heidegger, Klages, Tillich and Roland Holst? Is it true that various things in our lives change because of these technical interventions. Our contact with light, fire, the road and water is no longer so direct, or our experience of them is different. We are, as it were, at a distance from the things which we once experienced 'shoulder to shoulder'. But for that very reason, does this not mean that we have the chance of a less primitive and probably a deeper relationship to the reality in which we live, one more in accord with human dignity, because we are freed from the frustration and the toil of our earlier contacts? Technical achievements have led our lives out of 'primitiveness' and they have acquired many new and fitting possibilities in the process.

It is my conviction that the true alienation of modern technology is its seduction to power, i.e., the alienation is in the potential perversion. The objects of nature can become objects in which we experience our power, and they lose their aspect of belonging essentially to our lives; we no longer participate in them. They lose their 'maternal' character, their original symbiotic aspect. We are not alienated from nature because we take electricity from her and store it in power stations, as Heidegger thinks. The alienation is that we are totally absorbed by technology, that we experience our autonomy in our technical achievements. In the gospel the rich fool is mocked because he has forgotten the limitations of the power he owns through his possessions. In the twentieth century the technical fool ought probably to be mocked because of the power which he feels because of his technical advances. This is how technology seduces primitive peoples. They are suddenly able to *do* a lot through their cars, their aeroplanes and their modern weapons. It is not mechanization that threatens their lives. I believe that it is here that the threat of modern technical development for the spiritual life of the West lies as well. Life in and with technology can wrench us out of the vitally necessary foundation of our lives in 'basic trust', which finds generalized form in religion. It can give us a perverted feeling of power and can intoxicate us by means of other potentialities which we cannot ignore. Our question is: are we inwardly able to stand the seduction to power offered by technology? It is not so much mechanization that can poison our spirits; it is the power of mechanization.

We see here, therefore, that Cox is not worried by mechanization. Indeed he has an eye for the positive sides of technical development, because they make people free for a more worthy human life. Such an evaluation is entirely in accord with the American cultural pattern. There emancipation plays an important part: America is still the country in which one can live a free life, far away from European tyranny. It might also be said that Cox sees that through technology the way is prepared for another kind of participation, one which does not depend on the primitive maternal basis of life but on one's fellow men, one's companion, the common community of men. *The Secular City* is full of hope. He calls it hope in 'a new inclusive human community' (p. 145). For that reason technology can be felt in America as something which binds people together. American astronauts have again and again declared how deeply they felt their undertaking to be an experience shared with all the people who were involved in the project, in whatever function. Trade secrets are not carefully guarded in America as they are with us in Europe; they are shared as much as possible.

In the first part of his book Cox continually contrasts traditional religion with the pattern of life in Technopolis. This is essentially a liberation from a restricted outlook, reactionariness, stagnation, injustice and lack of liberty. For Cox it is therefore essentially *more biblical*. Here we come up against the problem of the pattern which is prepared in the third, Oedipal phase. We shall come back to this in more detail in the next chapter.

What we have said ought to have made it clear that Cox's book represents a typical American view of the problems of modern technology. This view, we must emphatically stress, decisively rejects the European outlook we have described. In the American view nostalgia for primal participation, with its primordial images and the religion that is bound up with them, is unworthy of man and unbiblical.

We have therefore tried to show that modern technical development must be fitted into the framework of the second (and perhaps the fourth) pattern, if we want to gain a clear picture of it and to offer a responsible contribution to the solution of the outstanding questions. One of these questions is without any doubt the religious problem posed by modern technology.

It is quite obvious that in our culture technology conjures up the problem of religion. Technology is not in my view anti-religious in itself, but it influences our religious line of conduct (or to be more exact our religious attitude). It does so in the first place because it exerts an evident influence on modern man's sense of autonomy and is thus in a position to pervert his religious attitude to life. And it does so secondly because it breaks through the closed pattern of life found in primitive religion and causes a breach with the original religious participation.

This influence, then, can be clearly shown in the religious field. Bonhoeffer's stress on modern man's coming of age is an example. In his view man is no longer living in the closed circuit of a world in which God fills up the gaps – man has become autonomous, he has come of age. Bonhoeffer's words have had a remarkable effect. He evidently expressed a feeling about life which was already present in latent form, and made it conscious and capable of articulation. It would seem that because of this a new religious pattern is emerging which is at the moment being more closely investigated in all kinds of ways. I have tried to make a contribution to the exploration in my book *Gott in vaterloser Gesellschaft*.

Fortmann in his books touches on a problem which is closely connected with the origin of technology. He maintains the view that our modern culture is evolving a new kind of perception in which, under the influence of modern science, things are only seen as objects (he means, for our technical activity) and which makes an emotional participation in the reality of things impossible. He is convinced that through this process religion (which is based on this emotional participation) is shrinking increasingly; and that is why he pleads so emphatically for a second primitiveness.

We shall come back to Fortmann's work in more detail later, when we have fully developed our 'phase' theory. At this point let me simply make a few provisional remarks. Fortmann has obviously clearly experienced and visualized one of the many aspects of the position of religion in twentieth-century society. But I ask myself whether the solution of the problem to which he points can lie in the return to a second primitiveness. For Fortmann, the most important aspect of religion is the opportunity of participating in the divine mystery through liturgy – we have only to read his book *Hoogtijd*. In *Oosterse Renaissance* he terms this mystery 'light'. Liturgy is for him a learning to live with the light as a reality or, to put it differently, learning to participate in the Godhead (p. 66). A careful reading of the epilogue (pp. 64–7) will enable us to see that this experience of light, this participation, has two sides: liberation from pressure (tension, darkness) and liberation from the fear of being left alone (above all in the hour of death). If we are reproducing the book's argument correctly, Fortmann is concerned to regain the basic trust which drives away the tension and fear. In his opinion a religious renaissance is accordingly to be expected from a return to the pattern of the first phase. If I see the matter rightly, a return of this kind would certainly be a positive contribution in so far as we have to break through a potential perversion; but it could never be the last word. On the contrary, it would even involve certain dangers. I am convinced that basic trust is an indispensable element in every religion, but it must exert its function in the patterns that follow the pattern of the first phase. It would therefore be impossible to stand still in the forms and images of the past, or to return to them. I hope to be able to show in the present book that since we are at present existing in the fatherless pattern of society and culture which I have talked about in 'God in a fatherless society', we have arrived at the pattern of a further phase of human development. In this phase we are unavoidably confronted by new religious problems which we cannot solve by withdrawal from them and by a return to a second primitiveness.

I am therefore also sceptical about attempts to look for the solution of today's religious problems in a renaissance of (historical) mysticism, perhaps in the more primitive form of drugs, astrology or a 'love-in'. For me that is a retreat from the challenge of the present and hence a sign that we have not yet come of age. In so far as in these forms people are protesting against the oppressive patterns of the present, they obviously have importance in pointing a way towards renewal; but they are not the solution.

An important problem which crops up here is the relationship of this modern development to the religious pattern which we meet in the world of biblical faith. Cox and the Dutchman A. T. van Leeuwen (in his book *Christianity in World History*) see the two patterns as belonging at two ends of the same line. Modern secularization is connected with the biblical pattern in so far as both, in Cox's words, result in a 'disenchantment of nature', a 'desacralization of politics' and a 'deconsecration of values'; that is to say, both break through the primitive religious pattern. We therefore do not need to lament secularization, like some of the people who are worrying about the decline in church life and the fading of the church's pattern for existence. We must rather ask whether the biblical pattern is not concerned with quite different things, indeed whether the traditional pattern does not stand in the way of the further workings of the true biblical view of things. On the other hand secularization can hardly be said to be a step in the direction of the kingdom of God. Since it is rooted in the second pattern, it at once conjures up difficult problems. Secularization is certainly a liberation from the primitive religious pattern with which the Bible also has to do. But its stress on autonomy can also, as we have already indicated, lead to a perversion of the religious relationship.

We shall, however, only be able to talk about this adequately when we have treated the pattern of the third phase in more detail. In this phase it is a matter of the relationship to a Thou (the father); and here *belief* comes into its own, as well as religion.

Intrinsic to the third pattern is a tense relationship to the religious pattern of the first phase; and this emerges from the developments of modern theology. We have only to think of the prohibition of images or symbols; of Barth's sharp rejection of religion; of the ideas which Bonhoeffer developed on the subject; and of certain American publications by Cox, Gibson Winter and others, which attack the traditional pattern of the churches which might be called religious, in order to make room for another pattern, whose nature is related to belief. Secularization has therefore the same 'concern' as the biblical pattern, but in itself it is not at all 'more Christian' than the religious pattern. It at most creates 'a possibility of . . .'; but it can also be a danger. Autonomy can seduce us to a tower of Babel, to what Niebuhr calls the sin of pride – for him *the* sin of modern man. The desire 'to be as God' is the great danger to which man is exposed in both the Old Testament and the New. Or in other words, the autonomy of the second phase is from the standpoint of the phase that follows only to be accepted in correlation with a relationship to a 'Thou'. We shall return to this later.

The Problems of the Person who has had a Coronary Thrombosis

In 1965 a group of Dutch scientists (J. Groen and others) published a psychosomatic study of coronary thrombosis entitled *Het acute myocardinfarct*. This gives a striking picture of the psychology of patients suffering from this heart complaint. Here, as we have already said, we come up against the problems of the second phase as we have already met them: the tension between participation and autonomy. And in this, I would say, we have to do essentially with an important religious (and hence pastoral) problem. I think that there may be related problems in other psychosomatic illnesses.

Patients suffering from what is known as a psychosomatic illness try to solve particular psychic (neurotic) conflicts through a physical ailment. In my book *Pastoral Care in the Modern Hospital* I have written in some detail about the pastoral care of patients with stomach ulcers, coronary thrombosis, asthma, and rheumatoid arthritis. Other illnesses might be mentioned as well. People who investigate this field know that here one starts from a hypothesis which has to be closely investigated in every case, indeed they admit that besides psychical factors other, physical ones can influence the genesis and course of the illness, and so they concentrate on a 'multi-causal' diagnosis. In the case of someone suffering from a coronary thrombosis, this means that besides possible psychic factors, we must also take account of weight, diet, etc. Here we are confining ourselves exclusively to the psychic factors, which are in the forefront of the book we have mentioned above.

The coronary thrombosis is a physical complaint in which the coronary vessels of the heart are attacked by a thrombosis which affects the nourishment of the heart muscle. Physically, the causes to be looked for are faulty diet, not enough exercise, excessive smoking, arteriosclerosis, high blood pressure and an inherited tendency. Very probably factors like overstrain, insufficient rest, and other aspects of the so-called manager diseases play an important part. It is an illness which is typical of our Western culture.

The research team we have mentioned starts from the hypothesis that coronary thrombosis occurs in people with a particular neurotic personality structure, in (or often after) a particular 'stress' situation. In their book they start from the question: what stress situations and what personality structures are characteristic of the people who suffer from this complaint?

First of all they list a number of situations which often trigger off a coronary thrombosis: a birthday party or a family celebration; a funeral; a piece of distressing news; being unjustly passed over for promotion; and pent-up anger. These are all situations in which the vital point is whether the patient can 'cope', can come to terms with it, or rise above it. The autonomy of the second phase becomes very noticeable here. As far as personality structure is concerned, it was once characterized in masterly fashion by a patient who was recovering from a coronary thrombosis and who set up eleven requirements for membership of an imaginary coronary-thrombosis club:

1. Your job comes first. Personal considerations are of secondary importance.

2. Go into the office in the evenings, as well as on Saturdays, Sundays and holidays.

3. If you don't stay at the office in the evening, take your briefcase home full of papers. That will make it possible for you to expose yourself again to the day's burdens and worries.

4. Never say 'no' to any request – always say 'yes'.

5. Accept every invitation to conferences, dinners, assemblies, etc.

6. Never eat in peace and relax – see to it that you always have a conference over lunch.

7. Fishing and shooting are a waste of time and money. You will never be able to bring home enough fish and game to justify the expense.

8. It shows you aren't taking your job seriously if you take the whole of the leave owing to you all at once.

9. Golf, bowls, billiards, cards and gardening are a waste of time.

10. Never delegate responsibility – always carry the whole burden yourself.

11. If you have to take a business trip, work all day and travel overnight, so that you can keep your appointment punctually the next morning.

Emphasis here is obviously laid on the fact that *we do everything ourselves*, and indeed that we *have* to act like this, not because other people tell us to do so, but because of an inward compulsion. It is the compulsive need for self-affirmation through achievement, in order to experience autonomy and thus self-confidence. That is the problem of the second phase.

It emerges from the book we have mentioned that these coronary-thrombosis patients are often personalities who at a deeper level have to cope with particular tensions and conflicts in their lives. On p. 58 we are told:

> The fundamental mood is hard to define, but one might characterize it as exaggeratedly restless and harrassed, with a tendency to abrupt changes of mood, from boisterous exhilaration to the deepest depression. At the centre is the fear of being small and powerless, the fear of foundering altogether, and also fear of the coronary thrombosis; at least this is the impression one gets.

This means that in the depths of the personality there is an evident tension based on a quite particular anxiety. This tension seems to have two sides to it (pp. 61ff.):

> The superego has a number of characteristics . . . one is the striving for greatness, partly as an ideal, partly as a necessity, in the form of barely veiled fantasies about omnipotence and invulnerability. 'I am a self-made man . . . I can do anything . . . nothing can happen to me . . . I really like to do everything myself, for other people only do it wrong.' . . . But there is another and quite different element as well . . . an intense striving for what is quite small and a longing to identify oneself with it . . . This has to be vigorously warded off because to give way to this longing . . . is so tremendously dangerous . . . There are therefore two positions which lead to an intra-psychical conflict and hence to neurosis, because they are mutually exclusive.

What we have here is hence a tension between autonomy (the wish to do something oneself and the desire to be 'big') and on the other hand participation (to be small and passive). That is to say, it is evidently the problems of the second phase which take these people captive. If one projects these problems on to the situation of the second phase, it emerges that at the deeper levels of their existence these people have remained the little children who have to seem big in the eyes of their mother (and sometimes, later, their father), and who have to produce achievements; and this is associated with the fear of being small – a fear which is never free of strong desire in that very direction. These are people with 'big mouths and small hearts', as a patient expressed it when he was being examined. Through the superego these two sides of the situation determine the compulsive behaviour of these people.

It would be worth while to investigate how far the problems of the second phase influence the genesis of other psychosomatic illnesses as well. There are certainly sufficient indications that such an influence exists.

When we view the problems of these people under the aspect of the psychology of religion, the first thing to note is that the 'manager', with his striving for autonomy on the basis of his achievements, is often an anti-religious person, but that on the other hand through his secret longing for what is really primitive security he expresses a hidden religious longing. I think one might say that what American sociology calls the desire for comfort (which the churches have to satisfy, not only in the view of their members, but also in the opinion of many outsiders) has its roots in this problem. This explains why many supporters of the churches and many outsiders have such a conservative view of the position and task of the church in modern society.

This is an important problem for pastoral theology, as well as for quite general thoughts about the function of the church and pastoral care in contemporary society: what is the church's task, and what are the possibilities open to her among modern people and in modern society – people who stress big achievements so emphatically but at the same time doubt their own capacities and see few chances of arriving at any degree of self-knowledge in this sphere?

It would be valuable if more attention were devoted to this problem in the discussion about secularization.

Youth Today

At this point we must also say something about the problems of present-day youth. We shall later go into these in more detail, but here, in the context of the second phase, a particular aspect of the problems of young people emerges quite clearly.

Our modern cultural pattern is, as we have said, a strongly 'anal' one. We live in a world in which achievement, autonomy, activity – but also self-doubt and Puritanism – often determine behaviour in a compulsive way. The remarkable thing is now that a considerable number of adolescents – and with them different groups in our society who in a certain sense display a particular trend – are apparently developing a counter-pattern; the word already used is a counter-culture (cf. Theodore Roszak's book *The Making of a Counter Culture*). This group has a series of opposing ideals. They are against a culture based on achievement, and their attitude is characterized by passivity, feminine behaviour, sexual freedom, and going round in 'scruffy' clothes. Let me quote a few sentences from the February 1969 number of the former periodical *Dux* (a monthly for 'youth and world') describing visits to a pop festival in Utrecht and to the 'Paradiso' on the Weteringschans in Amsterdam:

The floor was dirty. An irrational world, perhaps a symbolic protest against our rational society. Young people camping in the centre of a technical world (p. 48). . . . Children are discovering earlier and earlier that their fathers (and gradually their mothers too) only work for money, while they hate work, become ill, ugly, unattractive, lacking in imagination, dishonest and aggressive, and finally go to pieces because of it . . . (p. 68).

To put it more generally, here we are faced with a new picture, which is to be traced back to the rejection of the parental pattern. When we look at it more closely we are struck by a great problem of loneliness and helplessness. These are therefore 'anal' problems, primarily doubt in oneself. The important thing now is how we are to evaluate the new pattern that is presenting itself here. Does it mean a flight from the 'anal' pattern into primitive ones, or does this youthful behaviour, this counter-culture, herald a renewal of our culture? We shall come back to this question too in more detail. Here we shall confine ourselves to a few provisional observations.

It is not difficult to point to manifestations which fit into a more primitive pattern. I might name the relatively anonymous 'togetherness' which is characteristic of so many assemblies of young people and which also clearly shows oral (and hence primitive) features, such as common chatter, drinking and smoking. The stress on free expression which dominates in this counter-culture is also noticeable. In his book *Jeugd en welvaart* (Youth and prosperity) Beets links this with the 'free association' of psychoanalysis. It is probably a kind of letting off steam. In a lot of it, it is easy to recognize the longing for the identity diffusion which is connected with the lack of stimulating opportunities for identification in our society; but it is also linked with the need to retreat from an all too emphatic and compulsive identity profile. There is a need for security and warmth. In this connection Beets points to the factors which emerge in a fatherless society.

Summing up, we can say that there is a group which has no contact with our anal cultural pattern, because it sees it as compulsively neurotic; and this group is now experimenting with counter-patterns. The question is, what does this counter-culture mean for the future?

IO

Summing-up and Transition

At the close of this section let us briefly sum up the most important insights we have gained, first noting in a few sentences how far we have come and where we stand at present.

1. A particular pattern is 'released' in the second phase of the child's development as well. The characteristics of this pattern are: status, shame, self-doubt, an avoidance of what is dirty, and autonomy.

2. The influence of this pattern can be seen in Pharisaism, Puritanism, and in the problems connected with secularization.

3. The religious problem is linked with particular aspects of this pattern – attitude to money, stress on the product and on producing, the development of modern technology, the personality structure of people who have had a coronary thrombosis, and certain manifestations of the sub-culture of young people.

We will now turn to the third phase in the child's development and to its significance.

One important problem is the way in which what has been acquired in the one phase is used in the phases that follow. We have seen that 'basic trust' is the presupposition for the autonomy of the following phase, but that this autonomy can also assume perverted forms. It can now be established that if the basic trust is to function well in the second phase (i.e., if there is to be no perversion), then that phase must continue this trust. But this is only possible if it is preserved in particular ways. It must not atrophy. We must not forget the way in which the phases and their patterns dovetail. Similar problems arise at the transition from the second to the third phase. But here too we must remember that basic trust remains the fundamental condition for human life. Consequently the problem of its continuation in the forms destined for it must be noted in this transition too.

Finally, we remember our observation that in all this we must take account of the fact that cultural factors determine the pattern of this phase as we have elucidated it.

The Oedipal Phase

II

The Particular Character of the Third, Oedipal Phase

Introduction

I should like to introduce this chapter with a few observations. I have misgivings about a number of important facts here, more than was the case in my treatment of the two previous phases.

1. First of all, I am afraid that the way in which I shall be treating this phase does not exclude the possibility of misunderstanding. We are moving in the sphere of the Christian faith and the danger that theologians or believing Christians will reject a psychological (and above all a psychoanalytical) treatment of what is for them the most profound truth in their lives, cannot be rejected out of hand. The relationship of man to the God in whom he believes – that is to say, the God whom he worships, trusts and serves – is for him something unique. He talks about the revelation of this God, meaning that through it a relationship is set up which enters deeply into his life, is irreplaceable and hence has a unique significance. In every religion man's relationship to his God is in this way a unique matter. It rests on the sacred mystery which man tries to describe more closely through the term revelation. To use the word revelation is not to explain the mystery; on the contrary, it only makes the inexplicable nature of the mystery clearer. In my book *Gott in vaterloser Gesellschaft* I wrote (p. 46): 'This is a mystery which psychology naturally tries to solve – by means of the projection hypothesis, for example. But the believer himself feels that ultimately the mystery eludes psychology's grasp.'

For the psychologist this relationship and the mystery of revelation is a psychological datum which he tries to fit into a coherent whole with other data, with the aid of psychological hypotheses, such as projection. It is understandable that the theologian, like the believer, can feel that this is a threat. For does not this infringe the unique nature of his relationship to God, and so in certain circumstances explain the whole mystery away?

Here we come up against the same objection which, as we have already said, was once raised against the study of the Christian faith as a historical manifestation. Then too people felt that the unique character of the relationship to God was threatened, and it seemed as if the whole mystery might be going to be explained away. We will therefore have to react to the objections to psychology in exactly the same way as we react to the objections which were levelled against the historical study of Christianity.

I believe that we can hold on to two things. First, the Christian faith has a number of aspects which can be linked up with other data, not merely historically but psychologically. In my book *Gott in vaterloser Gesellschaft*, I have explained how our society's trend towards fatherlessness (the well-known hypothesis of the German social psychologist Alexander Mitscherlich) exerts a profound influence on various spheres of faith: on the picture of God, for example, or the relationship between belief and unbelief, the function of tradition, and so forth. It can only be a gain for theology too to take account of the study of these interactions. Secondly, as far as the explaining away of the mystery is concerned, we discover when we look more closely at the best known example of it (Freud) that he tries to explain the one mystery by another. When Freud explains the mystery on the grounds of the infantile bond (with the father), his explanation only points essentially to another mystery – that of the relationship between father and child. We have already seen (pp. 159f.) that the mystery of religion is really already existent in the relationship between mother and child (the 'basic trust' which is one of the things to which Freud indeed also points). We would hence rather say that the sacred mystery already proclaims itself in the infantile bond and that, where development is normal, this develops into a mature relationship to God. But what Freud noticed is that development is frequently not normal, and that the person then 'stays put' in an infantile relationship. We are bound to say that he is right in this; but by establishing the fact he has not, in our opinion, explained the mystery away. The ultimate thing eludes psychology's grasp.

We therefore note that it is the task of religious psychology to fit religious manifestations into already known coherences, but psychology must be aware that for the believer the religious relationship conceals a mystery. Psychology can of course include this mystery in its investigations – not every statement made by believers eludes closer enquiry;

but its starting point must be respect for the mystery. That is to say, it must recognize that the believer has a right to his mystery. Or, in other words, true faith need not feel threatened by psychology. We hope in the following pages to show that a closer psycho-analytical investigation of the Christian faith is capable of illuminating various aspects of it (can make them comprehensible, and can perhaps explain them); but that it is not capable of infringing the mystery. Indeed precisely through what it has to say about these aspects, it can throw more light on that mystery.

2. I then have doubts about the scope of the analytical concepts and viewpoints in our field. The focus of *our* enquiry is a relationship, the relationship of man to a reality which he calls God. Psycho-analysis is interested in a totally different aspect of man: his maturity, his identity, his emergence from the pattern of childish behaviour and feelings. Here his relationships do indeed play a part, but analysis is not as interested in the unique nature of those relationships as we are. This has up to now been no problem, for the child of course does not stand outside his relationship to his mother. But the situation now alters. As we shall see, the father brings a new element into the child's life, particularly into the son's. This new element is a different kind of relationship from the one which the child has up to now had with his mother. For us this new relationship is of essential interest because it is the medium through which it becomes possible to enter into a new relationship to the divine reality. This has escaped Erikson, for example, for whom religion is one aspect of basic trust. He continues to be interested in the growth of human identity, but the fact that this identity also grows towards an I–Thou relationship as something new, plays no part in his writings.

We cannot therefore use analytical viewpoints and conceptions more or less as a matter of course, as we have done up to now. We must deepen them and explore their value for our investigation.

3. I have in addition doubts about the Oedipus complex of the third phase, which a closer investigation would suggest must be seen highly critically. There is no doubt that the discovery of the Oedipus complex in our cultural sphere was of inestimable value for the investigation of neuroses, but when we want to make use of it for *our* enquiry, we will have to start from the fact that it too is a product of our own cultural pattern. Malinowski already pointed this out many years ago in his collected studies *Sex and Repression in Savage Societies* (1927). Even in the oral and anal phases, as we saw, the way in which the mother treats her child is not only determined by biological or general human factors; it

also involves elements connected with the culture in which the mother is living. In this respect she follows the traditions of her cultural pattern. In the third, Oedipal phase this is very clear. Not only the structure of the complex discovered by Freud, but also the fact that he ascribes such importance to it, is due to the nineteenth-century cultural pattern of the West, as well as to the Jewish milieu in which Freud grew up. Freud stresses the father–son relationship, and in so far as the problems of the girl in these years are discussed at all, they are judged in accord with the structure of the Oedipus complex. Living as he did in a one-sided, male-orientated culture, Freud did not have a clear eye for the woman's particular problems and potentialities.

We must therefore adjust our minds to the fact that, when we are considering the significance of this third phase for religion, we have to do primarily with an account of the phase which is plainly culturally determined (and also limited); and that the religious pattern can therefore be more varied than this account would suggest. I would even go further: our picture of adolescence and maturity is obviously culturally determined as well. It is one-sidedly male and pushes the woman's problems and special potentialities too much into the background. In what follows we shall start from the traditional picture of the third phase (as we did in the case of the two previous phases) and talk about the religious pattern on that basis, so that we can then try to enter into the woman's problems in so far as the state of the investigation can help us to do so.

We will now treat the Oedipal phase in the same way as the two previous ones.

We saw that what is called the oral phase – based on contact with the mother – 'released' a pattern which rests on the basic trust with which man begins his journey through life. It also builds the core of what theology calls *religion*. In the 'anal' phase that follows, a pattern develops which is marked by a rising feeling of autonomy, on the basis of the child's achievements. From a religious point of view this means that man tries to emerge from his security in order to stand on his own feet. But on the other hand he cannot live without the feeling that his supporting foundation is securely based. In the phase which we are about to discuss, a new and different pattern develops. Its especial characteristic is the relationship to the father, who is now discovered as the one who confronts us, as it were. Just as in the second phase basic trust, the heritage of the first phase, is presupposed, so this third phase cannot be conceived of without the development of a certain still immature sense of autonomy in the child. The discovery of the other as a 'counterpart' is only possible on the basis of a certain independence on our side. As we shall see, this phase is a very important one for religious development. According to Erikson, all the phases are necessary for the development of a sense of one's own identity, since every phase builds on the previous one. It is true that particular traumas and fixations can exert their influence and make the normal integration of factors belonging to the different phases difficult. We then have to do with neuroses, with false dominants, or with particular paradoxes of behaviour. It is obvious that such developmental disturbances also have an effect on religious development as well. We have already drawn attention to the perversion of the religious relationship.

The Third Phase

First of all, let me once more outline a few general facts about this phase. Its name is not quite fixed. If one starts from the erogenous zone at the centre of the phase, one talks about the genital phase (in boys, who are still given more attention than girls in psycho-analysis, one talks of the phallic phase). If, on the other hand, the starting point is the fact that the relationship to the father introduces a new element into the child's (son's) development, the term used is the Oedipal phase – a reference to the relationship of the boy (and later king) Oedipus to his father in the famous Greek saga.

As far as the first term is concerned, Freud discovered that the boy now discovers his genitals as an object of pleasure and this is for him important. The girl, on the other hand, wonders why she has no penis (the so-called penis envy). A new erogenous zone therefore develops, and this plays an important role in the emotional and mental life, kindling, for example, an evident sexual curiosity, among other things.

In the family – and that is the second aspect of this phase – the child's relationship to his father becomes important. The father now plays a part of his own in his children's lives, his relationship to the boys being of particular interest. Freud as we know characterized this relationship as the Oedipus situation. P. C. Kuiper describes it very well in his *Neurosenleer* (p. 52):

> His feelings towards his mother are ambivalent. A strong desire and warm love for her is threatened with destruction because the son has to share her with another and feels that she has disappointed him. What is the little boy's attitude to his father? He hates him and would really like to kill him. Is this not the psychological view? No, it is not as simple as that. The little boy is

mad about his father, with whom he can drive the car, catch fish in the pond for his aquarium, play football, and look at interesting things. His father knows such a lot and can talk about so many things. Father has such delightful hobbies and the work he does every day is so frightfully important. What would the family do without him? The boy knows very well what it means to have his father there, and he loves him. But there is another zone of feeling too. Imagine what would happen if Father didn't come home one day. Well, then he would look after Mother. That would hardly work at the moment, but it would be possible before very long. The child has as yet no distinct sense of time, and his mother often tells him, 'You are my big boy.' So here there are ambivalent feelings, a difficult situation for the boy. The most varied factors can kindle feelings of disappointment and enmity, the secretly present death wishes towards the father can flare up for some trivial reason and the child can be drawn into severe inner conflicts to which he will react with feelings of guilt.

What Kuiper describes here gives us a good insight into what is developing inside the child. First of all there is a superego, an initial form of the later conscience, with the two well-known components of the ideal ego and the primitive, forbidding ego, – the way in which the father takes form, as it were, in the child himself. And secondly there is a feeling of guilt, especially because of his aggression and the fear of punishment that is associated with it. We remember that in the second phase shame stands in the foreground; in this phase it is guilt.

Freud devoted the most intensive study to the Oedipal phase, which is quite understandable. If one wants to penetrate into the deeper strata of man's nature, one must begin with the less deep and hence more accessible levels. We already find initial insights about the previous phases in Freud, but the great discoveries there were only made later. We also get the impression that Freud was particularly fascinated by the problems of the Oedipal phase because he discovered in the course of his autoanalysis that the great problems of his own development lay here especially.

Erikson does not differ essentially from Freud about the significance of this phase, but he gives a more colourful account of the phenomenology of its pattern. He points to the child's freer locomotion and his pleasure in initiative, and underlines the aspect of 'intrusion' in this phase. In his book *Identity. Youth and Crisis* he gives an account of this intrusive mode. He says that the child (and he is obviously thinking primarily of the boy here) wants to intrude: into space with his vigorous locomotion; into the unknown through consuming curiosity; into the ears and minds of other people by the aggressive voice; into other bodies by physical attack; and – often most frighteningly – in fantasy he thinks of the phallus intruding into the female body. He goes on to say that in this phase the male and female roles clearly diverge, so that something like a conscience with feelings of guilt develops and the child adjusts himself to figures with whom he can identify.

We can therefore establish that in this phase a coherent pattern of feeling and behaviour develops which in the child's life superimposes itself, as it were, on the first two phases – not in order to push them aside or destroy them, but in order to absorb them and as it were to expand them into a new pattern with a different centre. This is the case in a normal development, at least. We must not forget that fixations on to patterns that have already been gone through (or on to individual elements in them) are possible, and this means disturbances in the development. We must also remember once more that cultural factors play an important role here.

Let us now look more closely at this pattern, especially trying to show its importance for religious development, since this is our goal. One important element must be particularly stressed. On the basis of the autonomy of the anal phase, a second pattern of relationship to the father now crystallizes out of the existing pattern of relationship to the mother. We have already pointed out above that this can be shown in the boy's development above all. We shall come back to the girl's development separately.

In the first phase, and in the second one too, the child's relationship to his mother is marked by the experience of participation, the discovery of oneness and hence security. In the very first experiences of life, the consciousness of another person apart from ourselves probably did not exist. We experienced something like an 'oceanic feeling' (Romain Rolland's phrase in a discussion with Freud), a symbiosis which is also experienced physically. It is only gradually that the mother comes to be experienced as a particular person apart from and outside ourselves. But although the mother increasingly becomes someone different, the sense of participation dominates the child's experience of her. The basic feeling in contact with the mother is safety, security, and the knowledge that we belong to her. The little brother or sister, and even the father, are experienced in the same way at first. Then the autonomy of the second phase also develops in the framework and on the foundation of the family as a protected whole, and especially on the basis of the mother (of 'basic trust'). When we remember Harlow's monkeys (see pp. 159f.) we know what is meant here.

In the third phase a different pattern develops out of this, in the child's relationship to his father. As well as participation, a *counterpart* comes to be an element in the relationship with the other; this is technically known as the I–Thou relationship. Now the father represents an individual, mysterious figure within the totality of the family. In the experience of the boy's world, he appears as the powerful figure who can threaten but who can also evoke admiration. A relationship arises which can be compared with the primitive magic relationship between king and subject. The father can be felt as someone very close but at the same time as someone who is remote and unattainable. Thus the sense of the Other arises, someone who is at the beginning not merely 'our counterpart' but is also above us, an Other whose being combines power and capacity. *Potestas* (power) and *potentia* (capacity) have the same root. In Kuiper's account the effect of this deeper experience is clearly traceable in the boy's life.

Thus in these years the boy's world of experience is marked by a number of ambivalences. He thinks that he is big (autonomous), but in relation to his father he is small (dependent); he can already do a lot, but compared with his father what he does is still very little; he admires his father very much but is also afraid of him; he feels himself to be still a child (in his identity as a four-year-old) but he wants to be like his father. These ambivalences show that the child's relationship to his father is different from his relationship to his mother. With the father there is no participation and no security, or only participation and security beyond the cleft of a detachment. Father and son are not to be understood as a totality, like mother and son. And if the relationship is a totality at all, it is different from the one shared with the mother, more a question of doing things together, of companionship, rather than being together. Any older person who examines his own feelings will discover that this difference can be traced right through to maturity.

For the purpose of gaining a certain insight into the meaning of the cultural pattern, it is fruitful to compare these discoveries with Emanuel Levinas' observations about the relationship to the Other in his well-known book *Totalité et infini*. Levinas distinguishes two kinds of metaphysical thinking, one which proceeds from totality and the other which proceeds from a relationship (which for him always means a cleft) to the other. The analogy with our experience of father and mother is obvious.

Levinas now gives a number of important emphases to this relationship to the Other.

(*a*) It is marked by a counterpart on either side, by a being face to face; there is no totality, there is a cleft, a 'rupture'.

(*b*) Language, the word, is of essential importance; relationship is only arrived at through the word.

(*c*) Like ourselves, the Other is a being with a human face – which is to say that looking at the Other is of essential importance in the relationship.

(*d*) This looking at the Other is ethical in character – it is connected with power, with the possibility of killing him in certain circumstances (by this I imply that looking at the Other means that I recognize the Other who is my counterpart).

(*e*) The face of the Other is also an appeal; it unveils the Other's wretchedness, his hunger and nakedness. This creates a difference of level in the relationship. The Other comes from above and from below; I am dominated by a master. Could we here perhaps think of the paradox of the suffering Messiah in the Old and New Testaments? We shall come back to that presently. But the structure is important: expressions like 'appeal', 'above', and 'below' are fundamental.

We do not even need to point to an analogy. The relationship to the pattern of the third phase is obvious. The pattern Levinas draws is the one that is 'released' in the third phase, in the relationship to the father. I and the Other are divided by a cleft, there is no totality; differences of level and the possession of power play an important role in the relationship; word and glance are fundamental. The latter reminds us of what Erikson says in *Young Man Luther* about the importance of face and voice in the relations between father and son (pp. 100, 111f.).

Levinas is incidentally obviously thinking of Old Testament structures and he also repeatedly draws on pictures from the Old Testament as a comparison with the characteristics of this pattern. (He is a Jew himself and teaches in a Jewish school.) We shall of course come back to this point.

In his relationship to his father, however, the son does not experience totality and duality in the radical form in which Levinas contrasts them. The son feels profoundly secure with his father too – at least at the beginning. Kuiper also brings this out in his account of the Oedipal situation. Perhaps the difference between the Jewish and the traditional Western cultural pattern plays a part here. The Oedipal phase also represents a transition in the continual process of emancipation which the child undergoes. On the one hand the father, together with the mother, is the basis of security in the family, but on the other hand he also causes the separation, as we shall see in a moment in a quotation from Vergote. It can be said that this separation opens up the road to puberty, and hence the way to maturity, in which emancipation from the family as a whole has to take place. Another process takes place on the way to maturity as well, namely the constant diminution of the difference of level between father and son. In the Jewish pattern this diminution is not as strongly marked as it is in (present-day) Western society. In the West remembrance of the father's special power is still inherent in the uniqueness of the son's relationship to him. But in the Jewish pattern, if I am right, this remembrance continues to exist much more intensively. This, I think, explains why Levinas stresses the cleavage and the difference of level between the two so much. In the West the ideas of companionship and a common human destiny play an increasingly important role.

Up to now we have only talked about the third phase in the context of the father–son relationship. But, as I have said, we shall also try to enter into the problems of the third phase in the girl's life and to pick out the features that could be of significance in the religious field.

In an article called 'The Oedipus Complex in Women' (in *The Development of the Mind*) the Dutch analyst Jeanne Lampl-De Groot tries to shed more light on the girl's psychological development in the third phase than Freud found it possible to do, with his one-sided interest in the boy. In Freud's view, in the third phase the boy abandons the love for his mother which he has cherished from the beginning, because he feels threatened by what Freud calls fear of castration. This fear is supposed to originate in the period in which he experiences the anatomical difference between boy and girl (which he had probably known about earlier) as a punishment inflicted by his father. In the first phases of her development, the girl knows the same love for her mother as the boy. She too has to abandon this love, just like the boy. But in the girl's case this is not caused by the fear of castration but by its reality. She experiences herself as a woman, that is to say, she identifies herself with her mother and 'loves' her father just as her mother does. She wants to be a mother too and plays with dolls.

I believe that more cultural factors play a part in this process than this account would suggest. Let me try to explain things in my own words so as to crystallize out these factors. How can we define the problems of boy and girl in another way?

In the oral and anal phases the mother means solicitude and care for both boy and girl; that is to say, she gives warmth and security. On the other hand at particular moments when she is 'cross' she is also a threat;

she represents the danger of being left alone and of being devoured. Both boy and girl, however, have already experienced something of the fascination of autonomy in the anal phase (see what Erikson has to say about the second phase); they have felt what it means to stand on one's own feet and to be 'capable' of something. Following on that, in the third phase a series of new experiences is a burden that oppresses the child's life. When Erikson calls this phase the phase of 'initiative', he is certainly indicating the direction in which these experiences tend, but he does not bring out the intensity of the experiences which both boy and girl go through at this period.

Let me name some of the factors. Boys and girls both discover that boys can do more than girls. Boys are *more powerful*. The difference between what is expected of boy and girl is taught in the greatest detail in upbringing up to this point. Margaret Mead has pointed out more than once how early and how forcibly parents and teachers impress on children that boys can do more, and are allowed to do more, than girls. This experience is now strengthened by a discovery in a sphere which, as a new erogenous zone, already excites the child's attention sufficiently: the genital zone. In his genitals the boy possesses something with which he can do all sorts of things that a girl cannot do. Moreover it is an area which seems to be particularly interesting, because the parents make such a mystery of it. The autonomy of the second phase is positively spurred on through this zone, in which the child can 'compete' with its parents and can seem to be already 'big' in relation to them.

But all this does not take place painlessly. Through this new step on the way to grown-up existence, both boy and girl lose the familiar security with the mother, and in the framework of this phase they both want to win it back. The boy behaves like a little man, like a father, and wants to protect his mother (which really means to draw her to him); and in a childish way the girl sees her mother as sharing the same destiny. She identifies herself with her mother and plays beside the boy with her dolls like a 'little mother'. They are both still small, but in this way they behave as if they were already to some small extent 'big'.

In all this, the father is now playing a new part in their emotional life. In the first two phases he was, as it were, one with the mother; he too gave security and warmth. Now the threat, which earlier on could sometimes emanate from the mother figure too, becomes more clearly concentrated in the father. Father and mother together have something which is connected with the genitals and with having children, with the secret of being grown up. But they shut the children out from this region.

This can give the impression that the father is taking the mother away from the children, as if he grudged them the mother who meant so much to them earlier. Mother gave us warmth, that is to say she let us feel that we were important to her, that for her we were not 'unimportant little children'. Sometimes it seems as if the father, who can do so much and who is so big and powerful, wants to keep us small and unimportant by shutting us out of the mother's life – as if he grudges us the instrument (to use a technical psycho-analytical term) which we think is so important. He can be 'dangerous', attacking the substance of our being, just as earlier on the mother could be 'dangerous' too when she was 'cross'.

On the other hand the father can mean a great deal to the child in a positive sense too. If the threat does not play a part in the relationship (and the child can contribute a great deal to this through his own behaviour!) he is actually the person who enjoys enormous respect, with whom the little boy loves to do all kinds of things (see Kuiper, p. 288) and through whom the boy is already given a foretaste of what it is like to be big (identification and the forming of the ideal). And with her father the girl already senses something of what it means as a 'little woman' to draw the attention of a man to herself; and in this way she already feels how splendid it will be when she is one day grown up.

I hope that this account of the Oedipal situation is more or less correct and that it explains the specific emotions of this stage, which are both intense and confusing. Perhaps I may add a few comments.

1. This phase is not a purely biological occurrence, marked by the same characteristics in every cultural sphere. On the contrary, it is saturated with cultural factors. It is not a matter of course that boys should be taught that they are more important than girls; or that the sexual should be veiled in mystery; and that consequently the difference between being small and being big should be so intensely felt as it is with us; or that father and mother should so obviously have a sphere of their own, closed to the children, and that the father should therefore be experienced in the double tension of threat and admiration.

2. On the basis of this account we can try to say something more about feminine identity, which develops on the basis of this upbringing in the cultural pattern to which that upbringing belongs. We see that this identity comes into being, partly through identification with the mother, and partly because a particular role is assigned to her by the man. In the third phase, as we have seen, the girl identifies herself with the mother who has children and looks after the family, and who confers warmth

and security. In my book *Gott in vaterloser Gesellschaft* I said the following about the woman's identity in a paternalistic and male society: 'The woman is the foundation of life. In order to be able to exist, male society needs the woman. She must be fruitful . . . she must bear children, she must bring them up and must look after their clothing and food generally' (p. 14). We could also say that in this way the woman acquires her identity in the oral phase and preserves it in an oral cultural pattern or on an oral (sacral) cultural basis. She is the representative of the sacral order which is seen as existent in every society, she is the realization of a kind of being in which we share through participation, that is to say she does not enter our lives like a 'Thou' from whom we are divided by a cleft. This has certain consequences for sexual contacts. For the man, the woman is the one in whose being he participates. We talk, for example, about sexual community, in which oral aspects (kissing and caressing) play an important part. The woman experiences this in a quite different way. In her view society – and especially man in this society – assigns her a role which demands that she be there for the other, and which embodies the expectation that she will be the pillar of order, as the basis of society. She, the woman, must consolidate the family. In a period in which paternalistic structures are being demolished, it is this role above all against which many women rebel.

3. In the Oedipal phase, therefore, the girl experiences her father in a different way from the boy. For the boy the father's punitive and ideal functions take priority, and through these he becomes a 'Thou' for the boy, as it were. We have suggested above that the father – with his capabilities and with the threat he embodies – can let us feel how 'small' we still are, and can on the other hand also communicate something of the splendour of our later 'bigness'. In relation to her father the girl will become conscious of her being as a woman; he rouses her feminine identity, though in still immature form. That is to say (again we are talking about our own cultural pattern) she experiences her father as the one who expects her to be there for him, in order to be together with him, in order to let him participate in her being. The situation is therefore not the same as it is with the boy, with whom his father undertakes all kinds of things; with the girl it is more of a 'social' togetherness. Philosophically one might perhaps say that this is already a realization in immature form of what we call the (sacral) order of being as the foundation of human co-existence. We shall come back to this presently when we discuss the question whether a different experience and picture of God (with a correspondingly different type of religion or faith) can be

shown to derive from a different father experience in man and woman (cf. pp. 275 ff.).

We can therefore conclude that the third phase in the child's life also 'releases' a pattern with a structure of its own. In this structure the other is experienced as a counterpart, as an I–Thou relationship (to use an expression of Martin Buber's, who was of course also a Jew). We must stress in this connection that this pattern is built up on the basis of the second phase, in which the child arrives at an immature sense of autonomy on the foundation of 'basic trust'. Out of this autonomy the child now develops the sense of its own identity in its relationship to its father. The fact that the father looks at us is linked with a process of recognition. His glance – and the common play with his son that follows it – lends the boy a (male) identity. It is interesting that our language should express the fact that we know the characteristics of this glance. We talk about looking up to someone or looking down on him. It is clear that in this way we strengthen the person's identity. He stands in a social relationship to us either on a higher or on a lower level. This, in other words, is his *status*, and status and identity are closely connected with one another. We might add that the fact that the father punishes his son, undertakes things with him or acts in common with him, as Kuiper puts it, must be seen as a clear recognition of identity. In this way the father lets his son feel or share responsibility. In this way he makes him another, in the sense of the thou who is his counterpart, a partner. We see from Kuiper's account that this is the way the boy experiences it as well.

We find a confirmation of this view of the relationship between father and child in the Belgian writer on the psychology of religion, Antoine Vergote, who is a professor at the Catholic University of Louvain. In his book *The Religious Man* he speaks about a negative aspect in the relationship between the two (pp. 18off.):

> The father jerks the child out of his dream of indistinct harmony . . . He separates the child from the mother . . . Thus he learns to become himself, a distinct and autonomous being.

In my view Vergote is here looking beyond the second phase, in which the first step towards separation and autonomy is already taken. Through contact with the father this development continues. Vergote goes on:

> The father is the one who recognizes the son. To recognize means to accord someone his own personality. . . . The recognition is made by the word. . . . Recognition is . . . the intentional creation of a conscious bond

with another . . . In the same way, the father, by his word, recognizes the child. This word is not necessarily spoken, it may be transmitted by the language of significant behaviour.

The different structures indicated by Levinas can be clearly recognized here.

The third phase in man's development therefore leads to a new pattern with a new structure. Its characteristics are: the other can now also be a Thou, a counterpart; he is no longer merely the one who gives security. Through his experience of his father, man has the chance to experience 'father figures', like the king (God might also be mentioned in this context), as being powerful, punitive, threatening – but also admirable and worthy of imitation, i.e., as opportunities for identification. In the relationship to the other the face, the glance and the word play an important part. New features of this pattern are the conscience, as well as the sense of guilt, whereas the relationship to the other is dominated by the appeal, the call which goes out to me from the other.

We must not forget one thing. Vergote points out in his book (p. 181) that the father's word 'assumes tender sentiments but goes beyond them'. It is not only autonomy that finds its continuation in the third phase; it is also basic trust, with its experience of participation. We shall see later that because of this a bond that is fraught with tension is forged between religion and belief in the religious sphere.

Up to now we have especially stressed the 'counterpart' aspect, along Levinas' lines. But if we look briefly at the quotation from Kuiper's book, we see that the relationship to the father also has the aspect of what is *common* to the two (just as in the case of the mother), and that in this way the relationship to the father displays a certain ambivalence. Really every mature experience of the other has these two sides to it. We feel both the detachment and the bond. What is remarkable in this connection is that the feeling of what is in common predominates to the degree in which the number of the 'others' grows. The group experience is primarily a motherly experience, a new experience of the family, and the sphere of its feelings. The father figure has therefore obviously two aspects. Together with the mother (and the children) he constitutes the family; both together create a home in which the children participate in the experience of being together and doing things together. On the other hand the father is the one who is felt by the children (and especially the boys) as being above them and as their counterpart.

Cultures can be distinguished from one another because they put the stresses differently in the field of relationships. There are cultures in which detachment is especially stressed. There are patriarchal structures in which an absolute ruler holds sway over his subjects. But there are also cultures in which the common life of ruler and subject stands in the foreground; this can often be seen in small primitive communities. But we repeatedly discover that the counter-stress is not lacking either. Even in the case of the tyrant there is still a feeling of a bond existing between the absolute ruler and his subjects, and even in small societies there is still a certain distance between the two. That is an important factor for the religious sphere. Stress on the gap between God and man fits the pattern of the third phase in our culture. But we see all the same that a certain bond is constantly stressed here too, in particular religious forms, such as worship, or it may be in certain mystical elements in a particular devotional trend. We shall come back to this in the next chapter. In all this, cultures with mixed patterns present a special problem; we might instance the Babylonian/Assyrian culture, in which a primitive (oral) basic pattern displays evident authoritarian (paternalistic) aspects.

12

The Structure of Religion in the Pattern of the Third Phase

Introduction

In his book *De evolutie van het godsdienstig bewustzijn* (The development of the religious sense) Hidding compares the historical-prophetic group of religions with the nature religions; these two groups are primarily distinguished from one another by their different picture of God. The deity in the prophetic religions is in Hidding's view spirit (he defines it more closely as will). This deity is apparently experienced as a king on whom man is dependent as a subject. This divine king rules and commands so that on man's side the religious relationship is experienced as obedience. A God of this kind is worshipped as creator, but stress does not lie on the act or system of creation; that is to say, these religions are not primarily interested in an explanation of the world. The main stress lies on the fact that through creation God shows himself as the Mighty One who stands above man and the world. In these religions the prophet is a central figure – the man called by God, who calls men in God's name. The call of God through the prophets plays an important part here.

In his book, Hidding does not enter more closely into the complications of this relationship between God and man. Nor does he discuss the fact that in a structure of this kind, with its stress on obedience, the problem of guilt is strongly emphasized in the life of faith and in theology. But guilt fits unmistakably into this structure.

Judaism and Islam are undoubtedly religions with this structure, but so is Christianity in my opinion. Hidding, however, maintains the view that Christianity, with its special type of Christology, has a structure of its own. This structure has not yet fully emerged, because Christianity has not yet sufficiently detached itself from the structure of the second group, which is not in conformity with its character; this is a problem to which we shall return later.

Hidding therefore calls these religions historical-prophetic, his aim being to express the fact that in these religions reality is not experienced as nature but as a reality with a past, a present and a future. Nature knows nothing of these three aspects; it has a cyclical character – that is to say, it always repeats the same pattern. There is consequently no eschatology in nature religions, as there is in historical-prophetic ones.

In my opinion the following point must be added to this. Nature religions are also natural in the sense that they are 'inborn' – they develop out of the natural relationship to the mother. The basic trust which stands at the centre of these religions is fore-given with the nature of man and can only be destroyed through a developmental disturbance in the relationship to the mother. It is hence not by chance that when Rümke is considering basic trust in *The Psychology of Unbelief* he is inclined to talk about a religious instinct.

The historical religions such as Judaism and Islam certainly grew up on the basis of the natural relationship to the father as well, but it was not a definite development. Here a historical personage, a prophet, had to enter the scene in order that a religion might develop within the pattern. Unlike the nature religions, religions of this kind have a founder. They therefore also have a different kind of revelation from the nature religions, in which the mystery is rather unfolded through symbols, rites, etc. In the historical religions, on the other hand, the breach with reality takes place through a call, an appeal from another and transcendent reality – from a mystery. We can hence say that these religions have a historically demonstrable beginning, on the basis of a particular cultural pattern. We shall now look a little more closely at some important religions of this type, drawing on the pattern of the third phase to help us.

The Jewish Religion

In his now famous book *Israel. Its Life and Culture* Johannes Pedersen gives a good account of the social and religious pattern of the Jewish people.

At the centre stands the father figure. We only have to think of the patriarchs, who exerted a kind of absolute rule over their tribes, or their clans or families. Pedersen shows how later in Palestine life in the towns was dominated by the men (I, p. 44): 'It is the man who acts outwardly and represents the family. Behind him stands the woman, whose sphere is in the house and within the circle of the family, and who does not appear independently in public.' The heart of the family or tribal community is the (tribal) father's house (p. 51). He is the master of the house, that is to say, he exercises power: the father's will is law (p. 63). The word father means authority. In the Old Testament the word is closely related to the word command.

The figure of the king must not be overlooked in this pattern either. According to Pedersen it developed out of the figure of the 'chieftain'. The stories in the book of Judges can give us an impression of this. We can follow the transition from chieftain to king in the stories about Saul and David. In the nature religions the king is primarily a 'mana' figure, half divine, half mythical. He can heal the sick, he is a priest, and one who preserves life. We can discover these characteristics in the Old Testament too. The oldest texts let these primitive naturalistic elements shine through; they can be discovered, Pedersen thinks, in spite of later Jewish revision. In later Yahwism, however, the king evidently becomes a vassal (or son) of God, and he himself has a whole series of vassals round him. His centre of gravity is the power which rests on the bond between him and his people. The army and the possession of land play an important part in the exercise of this power. The king's will is decisive, and can sometimes degenerate into despotism. Pedersen then conveys an excellent impression of the factors which had a decisive influence (III, pp. 33–106). The power of the king, he says, really rested in part on the position of the 'elders' in the towns, who were responsible for upholding law and order. The king was a man of great authority, 'a superman of inconceivable strength of soul' (p. 83).

Two things especially must be noted here: 1. Pedersen continually points to analogies with the Arabs. Jews and Arabs have apparently a related social pattern. 2. II Kings 22.19 (RV) describes the courtiers as 'those that saw the king's face'. Levinas stresses the importance of the face in the relationship of an I to a Thou.

When we look at the structure of the father–son relationship, we discover in it the elements which we have already mentioned: guilt, punishment, forgiveness and reconciliation. The parable of the prodigal son is a good example. There too stress lies on the guilt and not on the shame. If we submit ourselves to the impression made by an Old Testament narrative, like the story of David and Bathsheba, we shall find the same basic motifs there too.

Within this structure, therefore, the sons play an important part, both individually and in relation to one another, as the Old Testament clearly shows. The father's authority is bound to lead to considerable tension among his sons. The Oedipus problem is perhaps the most noticeable thing about the pattern of Jewish society. Nor is it by chance that this plays such a central part in the work of Freud, who had a Jewish up-bringing. The Oedipus situation is the situation of the crown prince. A crown prince knows that he is soon going to take over the father's place. He cannot wait – understandably enough from a human point of view – and he is therefore envious of his father. He wants to push him off the throne and to kill him. The relationship between David and Absalom is the Jewish parallel to the situation between Oedipus and his father.

What is striking about the structure of this social pattern is the rivalry among the sons. I see this as being due to the fact that since the sons cannot direct their aggression against their father, they seek a way out, as it were, through their quarrels with one another. Pedersen suggests an explanation of this kind when he writes (III, p. 72):

> The king's sons, as we see from the history of David, were attached to the palace but had a certain degree of independence, and might sometimes cause their father trouble enough. There does not seem to be any question of a participation in the government in conjunction with the king.

Even in the Joseph stories we see how aggression towards the father can be turned against the 'favourite' son.

I also see this as a phenomenon which is connected with the pattern's essential structure. The continual flaring up of tensions between the Moslem leaders in the Middle East, the frequent sharp conflicts in Judaism, and the schismatic disputes among Calvinists also have a structural cause, in my opinion.

It has become clear that aggressive actions like this are only possible when the father offers a certain scope for them in the structural frame-work (see the Absalom stories). If the father's authority makes itself felt, the sons are silent.

This social and cultural pattern also has its own particular type of religion. Side by side with the nature religions, Hidding sets the historical-prophetic group. Here there is no question of a God who represents the mystery of being and in whose mystery man participates by way of symbols, in the cult. In the historical and prophetic religions we have a God who gives the law, who demands obedience, and who is, above all, will.

We find a religious pattern of this kind in the Old Testament. In

Judaism God is the Father who is experienced in just the same way as the father is experienced in the family and in society. The pattern of father and son, and the relationship between king and people, find their continuation, emotionally speaking, in the God–man pattern and the God–people relationship. We have already seen that the feelings of the first pattern are projected on to the relationships of the second. There are a number of important aspects to be taken into consideration here:

(*a*) God is continually the one who calls and appeals: the word is of essential importance in the relationship.

(*b*) God and people are joined together by a unique covenant: at the centre of this covenant stands the law.

(*c*) 'To stand before God's face' is an important element in this relationship: God reveals his being through his countenance.

(*d*) In this relationship, which is characterized by the law and hence by obedience, the elements of guilt, punishment, reconciliation and forgiveness are in the forefront; here again we can point to the story of David's transgression against Bathsheba.

(*e*) We therefore have to do with a pattern whose basic structure is determined by an I and a Thou. Historically, a structure of this kind develops on the basis and in the context of the pattern of a nature religion. Pedersen, in my opinion, demonstrates this convincingly. The Jewish religion, however, has in principle a structure of its own. We can think here of the way in which, in the child's development, the third phase develops on the basis of the first and second. It too has a patttern which is clearly distinguishable from the two others.

We will now go more deeply into the problems involved in the Old Testament picture of God; or, to put it another way, into the Old Testament (or Jewish) experience of God. One particular feature is always picked out in the literature on the subject. We are told that Judaism's picture of God is marked by its stress on power and authority. God is the king and the creator, who with his power stands above dependent man. Pedersen, for example, calls Yahweh 'the leading will . . . , the mighty royal ruler . . . , creator of heaven and earth, . . . the guardian of . . . law and tradition, . . . the leader of all the world, and the God whose law all were to obey' (IV, pp. 611f.). On pp. 623f. he speaks of the fear of Yahweh, the fear of his power and authority, the total subjection to him which is an essential part of the God–man relationship. God is 'a strict father' (p. 626). This is the qualitative distance between God and man to which Kierkegaard and Barth later pointed so emphatically.

We must supplement this, however, by saying that as well as the qualitative distance, common activity and the nearness of the father give a particular colouring to the relationship between father and child. Kuiper indicated this clearly in the passage we quoted earlier. The father is a part of the family and, as well as the emotions of fear and separation, he also conveys particular feelings of safety and security; he has, as it were, motherly attributes. This side of things also appears in the Old Testament picture of God (and in other religions), though Hidding has not, in my view, grasped this sufficiently. Just as in family life, there are particular forms (places and opportunities) where this aspect is experienced with special force. A pilgrimage to the temple meant for the devout Jew what a birthday means for a family. The same may be said of Holy Communion or Sunday worship for the Christian (and we may also compare the function of the Ka'ba in Mecca for the Moslem).

The devout but unreflective man experiences God in these forms – his hymns show this. It is only when a man later thinks about the character of this 'presentation', knowing as he does that God (Christ) is in heaven and man on earth, that he comes to ask how he ought to understand this experience. The discussion about the presence of Christ in the Eucharist is comparable with Solomon's prayer in I Kings 8.27ff., where he asks whether God can really dwell on earth, if even heaven cannot contain him. There the worshipper solves his problem by pointing out that God has said his name should dwell in his house. Here we come up against an aspect of this particular religious structure: 'signs' of God's reality are to be found in the reality that is visible to us. These signs are not the symbols that belong to the structure of the nature religions and which actually represent the divine reality. In the temple, in worship, we are together with God, without this fact diminishing the qualitative distance. There are 'forms' which bring him so close that they allow the feeling of 'doing something together' in spite of the 'fear of the Lord'.

In the Protestant sphere this aspect of the religious structure is developed in more detail in the doctrine of the Holy Spirit. It can be historically demonstrated in Pietism, for example, as well as quite generally in mystical movements such as the '*Bevindelijkheid*' of the Reformed tradition (a devotional movement with a strong emotional stress; one of the meanings of the word *bevinding* is mystical experience). What is in question here, therefore, is the experience of God's nearness. I think that in this context we can compare this more spiritual experience very well with the sense of the nearness of God in the Law, in the mezuzah, etc., which belongs to the religious pattern of Judaism.

·   ·   ·

In Pedersen's description of the Jewish picture of God, God's power and authority is therefore greatly accentuated. But I doubt whether this view is quite correct. It is true that the texts talk unequivocally about God as king, as well as about his remoteness from men. But there is also another aspect: God is experienced as a God who is bound to his people in suffering.

In my view the Old Testament image of God is partly stamped by the experience of the people in the dispersion. This book is built up on the proposition that the believer's picture of God reflects a pattern derived from his own development, because he cannot do anything else than project on to his God the feelings about particular key figures which emerge in the course of this development. In the Old Testament pattern it is primarily feelings springing from the father–son relationship which influence the relationship between God and man. But is the father–son relationship in the Jewish family sufficiently characterized when we point to the father's authority in the family group? I do not think that it is. In the Jewish family the father is also the one in whom the suffering of the people becomes visible and who, in the family, takes the lead in bearing suffering and in coming to terms with it. Jewish humour is typical of this. It is a man's humour – the father's humour. In his humour the Jewish man shows that he sees himself as a sufferer, and that he accepts suffering. It is through this very humour that he keeps a vista open towards the future; he does not simply let things take their course and he by no means makes light of the situation in which he really is. Through humour and the joke he creates for himself and the people round him a kind of breathing space in which he can more or less live. Thus the father holds the family together in the dispersion through his care and love; he can wait in faith and meanwhile makes plans for the future. In his *Brieven aan mijn kleinzoon* (Letters to my grandson), Abel J. Herzberg gives us an impressive description of his father (chap. II). He describes him as he saw him as a child: a silent man, who lived somewhat apart and at a distance from the family, but who could none the less enter in a quiet way into a profound contact with other people. He was a man who 'did not know in what direction things would develop', and who evidently conveyed to his children through his life something of the hopelessness of the dispersion existence. He talked in 'jokes'. Everyone knows what a joke is, but no one can define it. A joke in the deeper sense is something quite different from a mere pleasantry; it is not merely 'funny'. It is humorous, which is something more profound. The examples which Herzberg gives show that the humour of the joke make reality more bearable. 'The comfort's a bit thin, but the smile is worth something too . . .' Or, a little further on: 'It's obvious that it's quite unimportant what one decides, since whatever one does turns out to be the wrong thing.' The 'joke' shows that we are always being 'made a fool of' but that we can still smile at the fact. 'If someone met him (my father) in the last years of his life and asked him, "How are you?" he answered, "Don't tell anyone, but I'm really dead; only the Holy One, blessed be his name, doesn't know yet."'

In *Fiddler on the Roof* Sholem Aleichem's character, Tevye the dairyman, is shown as the poor *'schlemihl'*, the 'born loser', the comic victim of life's mischances. He helps some rich Christians who have got into difficulties, but grasps the humour of the situation when they later forget him. Tevye is the man who knows from experience what suffering means, but who, with the help of his faith, grows through suffering into what could perhaps be dignified by the name 'wisdom', but which in more everyday language we could also call a wry humour.

We meet these people who bear the stamp of suffering everywhere in the Bible, especially in the Old Testament – in Moses' parents, in Moses himself, in the father of the prodigal son in the New Testament.

The dispersion has scored deep furrows in the pattern of the Jewish people. They came to know the dispersion in Egypt, then in Babylon, then through many centuries of foreign supremacy, and finally, for about nineteen hundred years after Christ, life without a country of their own. Under these circumstances a very particular family pattern was bound to crystallize out, and its characteristics are still evident today.

If we start from the proposition that the picture of the father can also, out of the pattern of the family, be 'projected' on to the deity (or, to put it another way, that deep personal experiences also make the revelation of certain aspects of the divine mystery possible), then we ought accordingly to find the traces of the dispersion experience in the Jewish picture of God. God is then not merely the Mighty One, but also the one who knows what suffering is, who suffers with his people and does not leave them alone in their suffering. We Western Europeans, who do not have this experience, will have difficulty in perceiving certain features in the picture of God and in estimating their value properly. I ask myself, for example, whether contemporary Christians can enter emotionally into the experience which a Jew has when he hears the words from the beginning of the Ten Commandments: 'I am the Lord your God who brought you . . . out of the house of bondage.' Passages like Isaiah 40 or some of the psalms have a profundity which it is difficult for us to enter into. My reservation about Pedersen's account is that he stresses this aspect of the Old Testament experience of God too little.

Apart from the fear of God, the devout Jew is always filled with the confidence that God will not let him go. Herzberg (pp. 27f.) says that his father 'was not an orthodox man but he was a believing one. He believed with complete confidence in the existence of God ... in the revelation on Sinai. And he believed in the power of prayer.' Herzberg tells how his father was convinced that prayer was essential as well as bombs if Hitler was to be defeated. The messianic faith of the Jewish people is in essentials this trust in God in extreme and concentrated form. In the first pages of his book Herzberg tells the story of the Passover eve (which commemorates the exodus from Egypt) and lets us sense how the profound confidence in God's help gives this occasion its atmosphere.

The experience of the dispersion is the experience of suffering, and because of it, suffering in the relationship between God and man (or the nation) takes on its special meaning. God is especially with us in suffering, just as when we were children it was in suffering that we felt the depth of the community with our parents in the family. In suffering above all, God is the one who is to come, our hope, the one who unleashes the End. Of course sin and punishment also play an important part in the re-lationship to God in the context of reconciliation – Isaiah 40 begins with the mighty words of repentance for unrighteousness – but the experience of suffering is central, above all in Deutero–Isaiah, the author of the second part of the book of Isaiah, which begins with chapter 40.

But the experience of the dispersion has laid its stamp not only on the picture of God but also on the whole Jewish cultural pattern. The laws about dealings with the poor bring out again and again what the Jews themselves had to suffer in the dispersion. They felt it, we might say, as a threat to their identity. Suffering in a foreign land, far from home, helplessness in the face of the ruling powers, the namelessness to which he is condemned – all this takes away from a man the essential elements, as it were, of his identity. Coloured people in the United States, who look back to centuries of slavery in a foreign country, have experienced the same thing. Freud would talk about castration. If the Jewish nation itself is meant by the Suffering Servant of Isaiah 53, as many scholars think, then this loss of identity is being presented to us in drastic terms. 'He had no form or comeliness ... He was despised and rejected by men; a man of sorrows, and acquainted with grief; and as one from whom men hide their faces he was despised ... Who considered that he was cut off out of the land of the living? . . . And they made his grave with the wicked . . .'

The classic song of the dispersion is Psalm 137. From this we learn what difficulties the Jews by the 'waters of Babylon' had in preserving their 'identity'. 'How shall we sing the Lord's song in a foreign land? If I forget you, O Jerusalem, let my right hand wither!' and 'Remember, O Lord, against the Edomites the day of Jerusalem, how they said, "Rase it, rase it! Down to its foundations!"' They identify themselves clearly with the city and the temple, and with their bond with God.

It is in this light that we have to see the meaning of the Jews' own, promised land. There, in Israel, in its capital and in its temple, the nation's hidden identity will be discovered; there the people can be and are permitted to be 'as they are'.

In his book *The Prophetic Faith* Martin Buber develops a picture of the Jewish faith which derives from the experience of the dispersion. The difference between Buber and Pedersen is astonishing. Pedersen maintains that Yahwism developed out of primitive beginnings into a religion in which Yahweh was worshipped as the 'remote authority'. For Buber the covenant is the centre from the very beginning. The elements of nature religion – the ark, the temple, sacrifice – take on a particular function within the covenant. He also brings evidence to show (pp. 49ff.) that the ark is something paradoxical because 'an invisible deity becomes perceptible as One Who comes and goes'. This paradox was accepted because the purpose of the ark, like that of the golden calf, was 'to make the leadership permanently perceptible'. The setting up of the golden calf, Buber says, is forgiven by God with the promise that his 'face' will go with the people; he interprets this as meaning that the visual character is conceded where none exists. The same is true of the Passover; 'A nomadic feast, as it certainly was in primitive times, it was transformed by the holy event into a feast of history.' Here too we have a paradox; as later generations tell the story of God's leading, they experience his historic deed as happening to themselves.

The paradox consists of the fact that an event in the past is experienced in such a way that one knows oneself to be emotionally linked with it. At the same time there are elements taken from the naturalistic Baal worship, against which the prophets especially rebel (as Yahweh's most faithful ambassadors), because Baal worship cannot be reconciled with the worship of Yahweh. In Canaan, says Buber (p. 75),

YHVH cannot remain really Lord of the people . . . in the old absolute
sense, unless He brings under His rule the domain of the new, agricultural
form of life. . . . The rallying cry 'YHVH versus Baal' is necessarily intended
to shake the religious foundation of West–Semitic agriculture: the sexual
basis of the fertility mystery must be abolished.

In this case it is not a question of a paradox; it follows from the principle
underlying the religion of Yahweh that he is not a nature God, but a God
who makes a covenant, and demands faith (obedience). If we want to
understand this covenant rightly, we must understand that it is not so
much a question of a 'remote authority' entering into a bond with the
people. The relationship between God and people is for the Jews marked
by warm devotion; it is experienced in the manifest elements of ark and
Passover and receives its quite particular impress through the experience
of the dispersion, against the background of the suffering which the
people had to endure in captivity.

One might say that through his way of depicting the Israelite faith,
Buber gives us insight into that faith from the inside outwards, as it
were. Pedersen, who primarily stresses the authority of the far-off God,
devotes no particular attention to the influence of the dispersion ex-
perience, showing thereby that, as a Christian, he is observing and
describing more from the outside.

At this point, however, we must come to one particular problem. In
the course of the centuries the Old Testament picture of God was in-
creasingly stamped by features of the 'remote and exalted authority'.
Yahweh became the creator of the universe and the ruler of world history.
In my view two factors may have played a part here. On the one hand,
the social and family pattern no longer remained so 'primitive', but de-
veloped in a systematic and authoritarian direction – we have only to
think of the growth of the court, for example. And this means that the
picture of God and the relationship to God changes – or so I would
maintain (and cultural anthropology supplies confirmation). On the
other hand, the more the people had to suffer and endure in the dispersion,
the more God was experienced as 'the Mighty One'. We see the same
thing in the sick person's relationship to his doctor. The more helpless
he feels, the more 'power' he believes the doctor to have. When we read
some of the psalms, or the book of Job, we sense that the process of
coming to terms with the experience of the dispersion meant that faith
in God's power was bound to increase. If this is true, then it is obvious
that the relationship to this almighty God will not decrease in intensity.
This is in accord with what Pedersen says (IV, pp. 668f.):

In the relation of Israel to her God there is a constant fluctuation between two goals: on the one hand, the eagerness to exalt Yahweh above everything and free him from constraint by what is found on earth, and on the other hand, a passionate endeavour to bring Israel into more and more intimate relations with him.

We shall see later that lack of the dispersion experience gives Christianity an emphasis of its own compared with the Jewish religion, even though it developed on the basis of the Old Testament pattern. Partly because of its patriarchal social pattern, Christianity almost exclusively stressed God's 'remote authority' (with which mankind is confronted as a debtor), as well as the paradox of his love. Suffering plays practically no part in the relationship between God and man. In the interpretation of Isaiah 53 it is almost exclusively the aspect of reconciliation that is picked out. We shall come back to this later.

A survey of the total complex of Jewish religion shows that its structure displays clear conformity with the structure of the third phase.

(*a*) The God–man relationship is an I–Thou relationship; the two involved confront one another; God is like a father; he is mighty, and he is both remote and close.

(*b*) The God–man relationship has the word as its medium.

(*c*) Seeing 'face to face' plays an important part in the relationship. (We have already pointed to the significance of this factor in connection with Erikson and Levinas.)

(*d*) The God–man relationship is a moral one; its most important attributes are: call, obedience, guilt, punishment, and reconciliation.

Islam

Islam is a convincing example of a religion whose structure is the pattern of the third phase. That is proved by the Koran and Islam's history. Allah the Almighty is to be honoured and feared; he will requite sin. The relationship of God to man is also established through the proclaimed word. God is experienced as 'remote authority'. In the Fourth Sura (lines 130ff.) we read:

> To God belongs all that is in the heavens and in the earth. We have charged those who were given the Book before you, and you, 'Fear God'. If you disbelieve, to God belongs all that is in the heavens and in the earth; God is All-sufficient, All-laudable . . . If He will, He can put you away, O men, and bring others; surely God is powerful over that . . . God is All-hearing, All-seeing . . . Give thou good tidings to the hypocrites that for them awaits a painful chastisement . . . Glory altogether belongs to God.

In the Sixth Sura (1f.) Allah is praised as the creator on whom men depend:

> Praise belongs to God who created the heavens and the earth and appointed the shadows and light . . . It is He who created you of clay . . . He knows your secrets, and what you publish, and He knows what you are earning.

Man owes God obedience; he is judged by God, the Last Judgment playing an important part. He must do his duty in everything. The Sixth Sura continues (70f.):

> Say: 'God's guidance is the true guidance, and we are commanded to surrender to the Lord of all Being . . . Perform the prayer, and fear Him' (70f.).
>
> Say: 'Come, I will recite what your Lord has forbidden you: that you associate not anything with Him, and to be good to your parents, and not to slay your children because of poverty . . . and that you approach not any indecency . . . And that you approach not the property of the orphan, save in the fairer manner, until he is of age. And fill up the measure and balance with justice . . . And when you speak, be just, even if it should be to a near kinsman. And fulfil God's covenant. That then he has charged you with; haply you will remember' (152f.).

Now and then we find in the Koran the same characteristic terms as in the Old Testament: 'to see his face', for example, or '(Abraham's) covenant with Allah', as well as the paradox that Allah can be very near to man in his house. (What is meant is the Ka'ba in Mecca; see Sura 2.125.) The sentence in Sura 50.15, is characteristic here: 'We are nearer to him (man) than the jugular vein.'

In his book *The Christian Message in a Non-Christian World* H. Kraemer talks about what he calls the riddle of Islam and then about its 'core' (pp. 220f.). He thinks that it is a radically theocentric religion.

> God's unity and soleness, His austere sovereignty and towering omnipotence are burning in white heat within Islam . . . Allah in Islam becomes white-hot Majesty . . . The surrender to Allah . . . has that same quality of absolute ruthlessness.

Kraemer points to the curious fact that there is also a Moslem mysticism but that he can find no adequate place for it in this religion. In his opinion Islam is thoroughly unmystical and anti-mystical. He thinks that mysticism was a reaction to the terrors of 'The Day of the Lord'. It was Ghazali, he believes, who turned mysticism from 'a very important element in Moslem religious life into a recognized part of the great orthodox system'. Unfortunately he does not say how this was possible. I ask myself whether it might not be said here that stress on the 'remote authority' of God inescapably evokes the longing for his presence, without thereby diminishing his sovereignty. We have already mentioned that it was Calvinism, in all its strictness, that gave rise to '*bevindelijkheid*', the typically Calvinistic form of mysticism. Here we come across the phenomenon to which Kuiper points in his passage about the Oedipal situation. Perhaps Kraemer is conjecturing something similar when he connects this mysticism with fear of 'the Day of the Lord'.

An important question in all this is whether there are factors to explain why particular cultures and religions have this one-sided stress on the strict father. In my book *Gott in vaterloser Gesellschaft* I have cited certain remarks of J. Bastiaans in which he suggests that in surroundings in which, because of poverty and anxiety, the mother's emotional bond with her children is not as strong as it should be, the father has to make his contribution to the child's upbringing through more severe punishments and prohibitions; and this results in an intensification of the Oedipal problems. In fact we find the strictest forms of patriarchalism among the nomad peoples of the Middle East, where Islam has its roots. The Jewish religion developed in a similar environment. The influence of the cultural factor therefore evidently makes itself felt here, a hypothesis which deserves our attention.

Finally, let me point to the fact that Islam differs from Judaism in some typical ways, although there are analogies between the two at certain points. The Moslems lack the Jewish people's experience of the dispersion; they therefore have a different father experience (the fathers differ, understandably enough). And this influences the religious pattern. For example, the suffering which plays so great a part in the religious pattern of the Jews (we have only to think of the book of Job) is not mentioned in the Koran. Its picture of God hardly includes the element of 'suffering-with' at all; it is much less flexible. The Koran knows nothing of a God who hears the complaints of his people, as in the Old Testament. Even the word 'reconciliation' is missing. It is true that there is talk of forgiveness, but it is only granted on certain conditions. What is also lacking are the Deuteronomic laws, with their principle of helping the unfortunate because the Israelites too were outcasts in Egypt.

Christianity

We cannot go into all Christianity's many aspects here, so we will merely sum up a number of important points about it, in this way illustrating the thesis of our book, and especially our hypothesis about the pattern of the third phase.

We are therefore starting from the hypothesis that the biblical structure is connected with the pattern of the third developmental phase. The essential features of this structure and pattern include: the I–Thou relationship; the gap between the I and the Thou; the father's authority (the father figure); the medium of the word; and the experience of guilt. Let us look at the following three aspects:

1. For decades scholars have been pointing out that Western European culture is based on two roots, Hellas and Israel. Our Western pattern of culture and upbringing has therefore certain classical (Hellenistic) elements, as well as Christian ones. The result is that biblical elements are sometimes experienced and expressed in the different framework of Greek or Hellenistic thought. I am thinking of the experience of God, or a phenomenon like human love. In Western culture the biblical experience of God is very often *religiously* experienced (i.e., not through faith, in the sense of the I–Thou relationship) and also *religiously* (philosophically and idealistically) formulated. The I–Thou relationship of the third phase is, as it were, submerged by the religious experience of the first phase. We have only to think of the various ways in which natural theology (which, as we know, is the theology belonging to the 'basic trust' of the first phase) has influenced theological and philosophical thinking in Christian history. In his study on *Platonismus und Prophetismus* (Platonism and prophecy), Johannes Hessen has treated the problems of the relationship between the two elements historically. Attraction and repulsion alternate, and though continual attempts at a synthesis can be shown (we have only to think of mediaeval Catholic theology, or of philosophical Idealism), this synthesis has met with constant – and often very vigorous – resistance. The Reformation and the dialectical theology of the twentieth century are pregnant examples. The most obvious one is of course Hegel's philosophy. For him the duality (the I–Thou relationship, for example) is by nature a unity. Hegel traces everything back to a unity encompassed by the totality. The basis of his thinking is 'basic trust', and his thinking itself is this trust's creed.

As a rule a synthesis is in fact attempted, but it does not always lead to a perfectly complete and consistent system. The work of Thomas Aquinas, the great mediaeval Catholic thinker, is an example. He combines nature and the supernatural, reason and revelation, into a single system, though trying the while to preserve the proper nature of both. In Part I of his *Summa Theologiae* he deals with the relationship between

God and creation. In Question 2 he discusses the problem of how the existence of God can be proved. In Article 2 he writes, in connection with this proof:

> From effects evident to us, therefore, we can demonstrate what in itself is not evident, namely that God exists . . . The truths about God which St Paul says we can know by our natural powers of reasoning [Rom. 1.19f.] – that God exists for example – are not numbered among the articles of faith, but are presupposed to them. For faith presupposes natural knowledge, just as grace does nature and all perfections that which they perfect. However, there is nothing to stop a man accepting on faith some truth which he personally cannot demonstrate, even if that truth in itself is such that demonstration could make it evident.

In Thomas, therefore, it is a question of a unity where the joins are still visible – and this incidentally is true even of a philosopher like Hegel. Thomas's proof is not at all so remote from Hegel's idea that philosophy owns in the form of the concept what religion possesses in the form of the (emotional) idea. The only decisive thing is the way in which the relationship of the two is judged.

In Augustine's thinking we are constantly aware that he has arrived at Christian belief by way of Neo-Platonism. In his *Confessions* (VII.20) he describes how the writings of the Platonists had convinced him of the greatness and truth of the existence of God, but that as a result he had become 'puffed up with knowledge', so that though he had seen the goal, he had missed the way to it. He only learnt that way through Christ, who put love into his heart on the foundation of humility. Augustine therefore combines in his life the 'both . . . and' of philosophy with the 'either . . . or' of theology, although he gives the latter the preference.

Calvin continues along the same lines. He admits that the philosophers had a certain knowledge of God but it was a very incomplete one. The true knowledge of God must be found elsewhere. In Book II of his *Institutes* (ch. 11.18) he says that where it is a question of knowledge of God, and especially his fatherly benevolence towards us, on which our blessedness rests, 'the greatest geniuses are blinder than moles!' He goes on:

> Certainly I do not deny that one can read competent and apt statements about God here and there in the philosophers, but these always show a certain giddy imagination.

They are like men who see the landscape of their life briefly lit up by a flash of lightning, but who are not able to gain from it enough knowledge for the rest of the way and who have 'never even sensed [the] assurance of God's benevolence towards us'. They must be perpetually filled with an immeasurable fear.

There is therefore at bottom an evident tension between the classical, philosophical, religious and biblical elements of belief in our Western cultural pattern and hence in the pattern of our religion. This tension can be sensed right down to contemporary philosophy; Karl Jaspers, for example, again and again sought an opening to Christian theology in his 'philosophical faith', but felt forced to arrive at the saddening conclusion that the theologians always break off communication at the critical moment.

2. Unlike the Jewish people, Christianity has no dispersion experience and this can be demonstrated in the religious pattern. It was stamped by the patriarchal cultural and social pattern in which it developed. 'Remote authority' dominated the picture of God. Man is in the first place a debtor towards this authority, and because of this the necessity of reconciliation is emphatically stressed. Anselm's theology (which also had a great influence on the thinking of the Reformers) is an eloquent example. K. Strijd devoted a dissertation (1958) to an analysis of Anselm's doctrine of the atonement in his famous book *Cur deus homo?* ('Why did God have to become man?). He comes to the conclusion that Anselm lays too much stress on the 'honour' of God, as well as on the *necessitas* connected with it, i.e., the (double) necessity that God should carry out his plan for man and yet that the penalty be exacted; which is as much as to say that 'it was not seemly for God to leave sin unpunished or to forgive *sola misericordia*, simply out of mercy' (p. 146). For clarity's sake we may quote from *Cur deus homo?* (I. 12, 13):

> It is not fitting that God should forgive something that is disordered within his kingdom. . . . There is also something else which follows if sin that goes thus unpunished is forgiven: viz., God would be dealing with the sinner and the non-sinner in the same way – something which is unsuitable for Him [to do].
> (13) Therefore, it is necessary either for the honour that has been removed to be repaid or else for punishment to result. Otherwise, either God would not be *just* to Himself or else He would not have the power to do the one or the other – heinous things even to think.

In Strijd's view this is not really in accordance with the Bible; and he is right. Anselm sees the *love* of God too little in the sense of mercy. The clear influence of the authoritarian, patriarchal cultural pattern makes itself felt. On the other hand I would be inclined to say that all statements about the atonement in traditional Christian theology have something indistinct about them because of the shifts in the cultural pattern. On the one hand we have the God who must be propitiated or reconciled (*satisfactio*) and on the other the God who himself has reconciled the world with himself out of love (*misericordia*). As an example let me quote a sentence from A. M. Brouwer's book *Verzoening* (Atonement): 'Since God is holy love and the moral order of the world is founded on his holiness, sin cannot be forgiven without this order being upheld. Christ does this through his life of obedience unto death.' In this sentence we again come across Anselm's *necessitas*, but in confused form. It seems to me as if this *necessitas* is given another meaning in the Bible from the one it has in Anselm through God's solidarity with his people as they suffer under the dispersion.

The result is that for many people in the West the atonement takes on the colouring of something forced on us. Simon Vestdijk once wrote that he did not ask anyone else to perform an act on his behalf and he therefore refuses to recognize it. We could also say that if God – on the basis of a cultural pattern – is primarily experienced as a 'remote authority', there is a danger that man will feel himself merely as an 'object' and will only experience grace in the God–man relationship against the background of arbitrariness. In the *decretum horribile* of double predestination, this danger is obvious. The arbitrary aspect of the biblical picture of God cannot be denied – the authoritarian pattern of Oriental society gives its stamp to the religious consciousness here too; but according to my thesis the dispersion experience goes on working perceptibly in the biblical picture of God (especially in the Old Testament): God feels himself one with the sufferings of his people.

3. Christianity, like Islam, is familiar with the paradox of remote authority and the Father who is experienced as very near. It is only Calvinism, with its stress on the 'qualitative distance' between God and man (Kierkegaard, Barth) and the word as the exclusive medium of revelation, that is familiar with the phenomenon of '*bevindelijkheid*', a strangely emotional mysticism. Catholicism, with its natural theology and the mysticism that is bound up with it in religious experience, does not have this paradox.

This Calvinistic form of mysticism is directed towards God as Father, and may perhaps be connected with fear of the divine judgment, as Kraemer thinks is the case in Islamic mysticism. In his uncertainty about what his father thinks, the little boy often seeks him out in order to assure himself of his love. One of the representatives of this devotional movement was Schortinghuis, who all his life had to combat the suspicion that he had something to do with the Spinozists, the Hattemists, the Pietists and the Labadists. In one of his writings he says that it is necessary to follow Reformed doctrine, but one must know the '*bevindelijkheid*' and enjoy it 'with one's whole heart'. The following quotation from D. A. Vorster's *Nederlandse Mystiek, Protestant* shows what that means:

> The soul is marred, because she could earlier be so foolish as not to serve such a Lord. Such a soul will say, 'I want nothing, I know nothing, I can do nothing, I have nothing, I am nothing worth' (the five nothings). When the pardoned soul says, 'It was always my desire that God should be all and I nothing – O blessed Saviour, make my heart thy cradle that I may eternally be united with thee and may refresh myself in Thee . . .', Christ's death allows the pardoned one to melt into the ocean of immeasurable love.

Gerhard Tersteegen belongs to the same movement of spiritual mysticism. In one of his hymns he says:

> How sweet from earthly things to part
> And in the closet of the heart
>   To live retired with God!
> How sweet, the Lord himself to find
> Residing in our inmost mind
> And make him our abode!

From German pietism the historical line runs on to Schleiermacher, to German romanticism and to German idealism.[1]

We have seen that in Judaism and in Islam too, apart from the mystical elements, there are also 'forms' in which the 'maternal' aspect (the nearness of the Father) is experienced quite strongly. We have mentioned Christian worship and the Christian sacraments as related elements, and looked briefly at what Calvin had to say about the sacraments in his *Institutes* (Book II, ch. xiv). He begins with Augustine's definition of a sacrament as a 'visible form of an invisible grace'. This definition may perhaps remind us of the explanation of the sacrament I gave when I called it 'a sign of God's reality' (p. 261). In the word God is often only experienced as a remote power; in the sacraments he stands visibly before us, as it were; this is in accordance with Calvin's view (see here our discussion about the prohibition of images, p. 279 below).

---

[1] In the English-speaking countries Calvinism was less directly associated with a devotionalism of this kind. But we may remember the warmth of personal devotion in Bunyan – a line of approach which later found its continuation in Deturdism and Evangelicalism. The mystical element in Anglicanism was of course very much stronger. We have only to think of Herbert, or Donne who 'carried his hearers . . . to Heaven in holy raptures'. But one will perhaps link that rather with the Catholic tradition surviving in the English church. *Translator.*

13
Two Special Problems

An Investigation into the Correlation between the Image of the Parents and the Image of God

The starting point of our book was the hypothesis that a particular emotional relationship to God develops on the basis of particular emotional relationships to the parents, because God comes to take the place in a person's life which was originally held by his father and mother. We believe that the particular cultural pattern, and hence the pattern of upbringing in a culture, determines whether the relationship to the father or the relationship to the mother will receive greater emphasis later. We are living in a culture which has up to now had a strong patriarchal (paternalistic) stamp, and has so still in many respects. This fact must therefore find its deposit in the picture of God.

A number of Belgian scholars have subjected the possible correlation between the picture of God and the parental picture to empirical investigation: for it is in the pictures that the emotions crystallize, as it were. We shall go more closely into this investigation in the present chapter. Its aim was an empirical investigation of Freud's view of religion – the view that it was an infantile residue of the sense of dependence on a mighty father. Freud believed that through the mechanism of projection a picture of the father is projected on to a heavenly figure which gives man the same feelings that the real father once gave the child. In the investigation process the researchers used well-known psychological techniques such as the Q technique and free association. The first method offers the chance of illuminating particular aspects of the inner life more clearly through the ordering of particular statements according to personal preference.

The first investigation was carried out by the Jesuit André Godin and Monique Hallez, and was published in 1964 by Lumen Vitae, the well-known Catholic catechetical institute in Brussels. The *Archiv für Religionspsychologie* published a summary of this report in 1967. The Lumen Vitae publication is called *Images parentales et paternité divine*. The authors first of all discuss some earlier investigations carried out by M. O. Nelson and E. M. Jones in 1957 and by Orlo Strunk in 1959, and then go into the methods they used (the 'Q technique'). Their respondents consisted of 70 people of varying sex, age and profession, and the task they were given was as follows: 'Complete the sentence "When I think of my mother (father, God)" by one of the following: "I feel (protected, forsaken, etc.)."' In this way the respondent could choose between a wide range of possible answers, and from these the research workers were able to draw conclusions about possible correlations between the relationships investigated and the pictures made of them. They summed up their conclusions as follows (p. 105): In a Christian population belonging to a Western culture such as ours there are certain obvious trends:

(*a*) The image of the parents influences to a variable but important degree the psychical situation in which the relationship to God finds its basic structure; and in which, accordingly, the psychological attitude towards God also develops.

(*b*) The influence (correlation) of the mother image makes itself felt more frequently and more strongly in the case of men and boys; and the image of the father in the case of women and girls.

In the 1967 issue of Lumen Vitae the French scholar Jean-Pierre Deconchy published the report of his enquiry into 'Dieu et les images parentales'. His method is free association and his respondents were a group of boys and girls between the ages of seven and sixteen. He is the author of a comprehensive study which was also published in 1967 by Lumen Vitae under the title *Structure génétique de l'idée de Dieu*. Here too the subject of the investigation was a series of boys and girls belonging to the group we have mentioned. Earlier, in 1964, he had already established the same correlation as Godin and Hallez in an investigation based on the free association method. He now comes to the conclusion (p. 96) that the development of the idea of God in boys is more strongly marked by the concept of the 'Holy Virgin' (the picture of the mother or woman? He leaves that open) than by the concept of the man Christ (the picture of the father or man?); whereas in girls the exact opposite is true.

For Deconchy one of the most important points about the results established by Godin, Monique Hallez and himself is that Freud's exclusive stress on the Oedipal situation, and its aggressiveness in the relationship with the father, is open to question in the explanation of religion.

Vergote subjected the work of Godin and his group to a closer critical examination in *The Religious Man* as well as in an article which he published in 1967 in *Archiv für Religionspsychologie*. He has considerable reservations about Godin's methods, because he thinks that in selecting the most important quality which the respondents have to pick out and name in the 'Q technique', Godin concentrates much too strongly on the 'intimateness' which is a particular aspect of the relationship to the parents and to God. Godin's questions are related to help, confidence, nearness, etc. In these circumstances the results he arrives at are obvious.

For Vergote the aspects of authority and power, and the functions of judge and leader, etc., also have their importance for the image of the father. On p. 177 he sums up the result of his own investigation:

> The father has, then, a more complex image; not only does it include a large number of the maternal qualities, but it is also made up of specific qualities which distinguish the father from the mother. The qualities of intimacy and tenderness are, however, peculiar to the mother. The attributes of judge, governor, strength, are more exclusively characteristic of the father image. But in the application of these different characteristics to God, it appears that the deity image is even more complex than the father image; it includes in a still higher degree certain maternal characteristics such as: patience, depth, interiority, refuge, availability, welcome, care, sharing in man's interests, knowing how to wait. The paternal qualities attributed to God express above all firmness and directive action, such for example as the qualities of ordering intelligence, judge, power, strength, law-maker, authority, steadiness, concern with the future. The deity image results from the two parental images; it is, then, nearer to the father image than to the mother image. But the maternal characteristics are attributed more emphatically to God than are the paternal characteristics. It should be observed that everything that has been said up to now concerning these two images is equally true of the attributions made by the boys and by the girls.

We may note here that the enquiry extended to 178 people, 82 girls and 96 boys, all Catholic university students between twenty and twenty-four years of age. Vergote does not give a precise account of the method used. It seems to be most closely related to the 'Q technique', the investigators associating the suggested categories with the three images of mother, father and God.

We can conclude from this that in his investigation Vergote discovered a picture of God as father which evidently had motherly features as well as authoritarian, fatherly ones.

. . .

A number of things may be said in connection with this enquiry.

1. We discover that there is a correlation between a person's experience of God on the one hand and his experience of his parents (father and mother) on the other, although more is involved in the experience of God than primitive infantile feelings derived from the parent–child relationship. We get the impression that (in the structure of a particular pattern) primitive infantile feelings can develop into more mature ones.

2. The pattern of upbringing probably plays a role in the correlation. The question is whether just as many maternal features are to be found in the image of God held in a Calvinistic milieu.

3. The correlation that has been established is to be connected with projection. This expression is easily misunderstood, as I have already pointed out in *Gott in vaterloser Gesellschaft* (p. 124). In the religious field projection is not so much a matter of particular images or ideas; it is rather a question of feelings which, as the person develops in the process of his emancipation from his parents, also go through a certain development. These feelings therefore always play their part at a particular moment in the relationship to the God in whom a person 'believes' in the framework of his pattern of upbringing and culture (and that means here, psychologically, the God with whom he 'reckons' in his behaviour); for God takes the place in a man's life which was taken by his parents before he was grown up. These feelings can still be infantile and primitive (although we should then have to talk about a developmental disturbance); but they can also (in spite of what Freud says) have a mature character, albeit within a prevailing cultural pattern.

4. This therefore means that it is possible to trace a development in religious feelings. In my view no attention is paid to this point in the investigation, and for that reason I have some reservations about it. In the groups of people investigated, the influence of the age of the respondent in any given case was not taken into account.

I should like experimentally to develop the following propositions:

(*a*) If the rise of particular religious feelings is connected with projection and therefore with the process of emancipation from the parents, these feelings will only emerge when this emancipation process has reached a certain stage, and they will only develop clearly in adolescence.

(*b*) If it is possible, in our pattern of culture and upbringing, for us to talk about religion (in the relationship to the mother) and belief (in the relationship to the father) these too will both become particularly noticeable as the person develops.

(*c*) My own observations suggest that the religious feelings awakened in the relationship to the mother are only projected on to a providing fatherly God round about the age of eight, when the child senses that he is gradually emerging from the security of the family, even though shyly and tentatively at first.

(*d*) The relationship to faith, which is marked by call and obedience, develops on the basis of the foundation of the conscience which is set going through contact with the father; here too the projection on to God begins round about the age of eight – though also hesitantly at the beginning.

(*e*) On the child's side, talk about God is not yet related to true religious feeling; it remains in the intellectual sphere. It might perhaps be said that vague religious feelings already emerge in the unrest of the Oedipal phase, even if they are still primitive and numinous in character; but at this stage they are not tied to a picture of God. Perhaps I may point here to my article about the existence of numinous feelings among children in my essays on pastoral psychology, *Pastoraalpsychologie opstellen*. I have already written about the importance of the eighth year in a child's life for its religious development in my book about pastoral care in sickness.

(*f*) The predominance of maternal features in the picture of God can therefore be linked with the influence of the pattern of upbringing and culture, but it is also connected with age. It seems to me that the projection of maternal feelings after the age of eight proceeds more quickly than the projection of feelings associated with the father.

The Belgian investigations show us how necessary and fruitful an examination of general hypotheses can be in the field of religious psychology. This applies especially to the hypotheses with which this book is concerned. I have tried to back them up continually by empirical material but I am very well aware that a more exact and more finely differentiated investigation is needed.

The Prohibition of Images

We saw that the symbol or image plays an important part in the nature religions; it is through the symbol that man can participate in the divine mystery. In the historical and prophetic religions, in which the word is at the centre, the image is forbidden, as we have already said. Judaism, Islam and Christianity all have this prohibition. It is true that images play a large part in Catholicism, but there they are obviously correlated with the 'naturalistic' elements in devotion and theology.

What is the reason for the prohibition of images?

In my book *Gott in vaterloser Gesellschaft* I have already discussed this point, but I will make one or two observations here too. The Old Testament sees the worship of images as faithlessness towards the God of the covenant. It sometimes even uses the word 'whoredom'. In my opinion the problem that arises here is related to the problems of the third phase. In the framework of the Oedipal situation the father demands the obedience of the son; he is forbidden to partake of the maternal mystery. Could one compare the intense emotion with which the Bible and church history talk about the prohibition of images, with the emotions of the Oedipus conflict? The uniqueness of the relationship excludes all others.

This raises the question of whether and in what way God's presence is talked about in this pattern. We have already discussed this above, pointing to Solomon's prayer in the temple, and to Calvin's view of the sacraments; and in that connection we also mentioned the phenomenon of a particular type of mysticism in this pattern.

In my opinion we can make the difference clear by saying that in the nature religions the image makes the deity present, so that through the image one can partake of its mystery. In this pattern, however, we hear of *signs* which certainly point to the divine mystery and are hence able to rouse and intensify particular feelings, but their nature is not such that one has the feeling of partaking in the mystery of God; the distance is still observed. In his *Institutes* (IV. XVII. 18f.) Calvin tells us how he conceives of the presence of Christ (who 'has taken his flesh away from us, and in the body has ascended into heaven') in the sacrament of the Lord's Supper. The analogy with Solomon's prayer is very striking. Calvin goes on to say: 'He shows his presence in power and strength, is always among his own people, and breathes his life upon them, and lives in them . . . *as if* he were present in the body' (my italics). Calvin talks in this connection of our enjoying Christ 'in his wholeness'. I think one must say that *being* together with one's mother has a different character from *doing* things together with one's father (as Kuiper points out) although the word 'together' obviously points to related feelings in the two relationships.

Perhaps the word illustration could be used here. In *Institutes*, IV. XIV, Calvin says that the word appeals to the ear and the sacraments to the 'eyes' of the heart. An image or an illustration is an aid to preserving the living quality of a relationship which we have with someone; or it helps to make clear some truth. The sacrament does both, but the '*as if* God or Christ were present' remains intact; the sacrament does not become the participation of the first phase.

Thus in this pattern even the '*bevindelijkheid*' always puts the distance from God before the mystical participation in God. It is not the ontological mysticism which has the identity of God and man as both its point of departure and its ultimate end.

Differences between Man and Woman

Up to now, for understandable reasons, it is only the man's religion that we have discussed in the framework of this phase of development. We said, however, that we would come back to the woman and her problems. We know that the woman has a 'being' of her own within the paternalistic pattern. Is there then a corresponding type of religion as well? To this we must say – on the lines of this book – that our theology (that is to say, our formulation of the Christian faith) bears a male stamp.

In the Western cultural pattern the man is addressed by God as a 'Thou'. The relationship between the two is an ethical one, with all that that means: it is a matter of obedience, guilt, reconciliation, etc.

Where the woman is concerned, I have the impression that she does not fully recognize herself in this picture. For her the relationship to God is not primarily an ethical one. She is mainly concerned with the *recognition* of the relationship, and a longing for faithfulness to it. We might think of the line in Jacqueline van der Waals' hymn: 'What e'er the future brings, God's hand it is that leads me'. We could also wish for a closer investigation of all this. In so far as the woman feels herself addressed as woman, her main concern – as it seems to me – is to know that she is destined to be the *guardian* of the sacral order. If this is correct it means that the woman has her own religious experience in the relationship to God (her own image of God) and that one can probably also recognize projections derived from the relationship to her father in that image. Anyone who looks round at church life can discover, for example, that the woman is concerned with the forms, the rites, the church buildings, the images; whereas she is less interested in a theological discussion about the sermon. It emerges too that the stories in the Bible (the images) interest her far more than the actual proclamation. In this connection one can think of religious instruction in the family, and the work done by women in the Sunday schools. Whereas service in the synagogue is exclusively a matter for the man, Judaism obliges the woman to preserve the religious forms in the family. After all it is a woman, Rachel, who in the familiar story in Gen. 31. takes along the household gods. Perhaps we might say that the woman's sin is not rebellion; it is lack of care – that is to say, lack of love.

14

Summing-up and Transition

At the close of our discussion of this phase as well, let us sum up what seems to be of essential importance about its pattern in the context of our investigation.

We arrive at the following theses:

1. The relationship to the father is a new and essential element in the third phase. The I–Thou relationship and the ethical appeal which is connected with it play an important part in the pattern which is 'released' in this phase.

2. With this pattern as a basis, religions of the historical and prophetic type have a pattern of their own, with its own particular image of God and experience of him. God is experienced primarily as a person and as will; man is associated with him in a covenant relationship in which guilt, forgiveness and reconciliation play an important part. The 'qualitative' distance between God and man is one aspect; but the pattern also includes a particular 'mysticism' in which, though the feeling of distance is certainly preserved, the experience of closeness has its particular importance. Particular sacraments, places, etc., have the function of awaking and maintaining this experience.

3. There is a pattern of this kind in Judaism, Islam and Christianity. Judaism's picture of God is stamped by the experience of dispersion, whereas Islam is distinguished by the paradoxical unity of the experience of the 'remote authority' and an individual mysticism. Christianity contains various streams of development: first, links with natural theology; secondly (in connection with the authoritarian cultural pattern), stress on God's 'remote authority', the problem of guilt standing at the centre; and thirdly mystical and pietistic reactions against this.

4. Empirical investigations have revealed that there is a correlation between the picture of God and the picture of the parents in which –

contrary to what many people would expect – there is also a clear correlation with the picture of the mother.

In my book *Gott in vaterloser Gesellschaft* I expounded the view that, with their entry into the 'fatherless' age, religion and church are exposed to a new cultural pattern. I compared our pattern with the pattern of adolescence. I will now narrow that down somewhat. Up to now we have discussed three developmental phases, with their respective patterns. But there is also the adolescent phase; and that phase's pattern shows itself today in the cultural pattern of the industrial, fatherless age, in which we can already see the first signs of a new pattern for religion and the church.

The Adolescent Phase

15
The Particular Character of the Adolescent Phase

Introduction

Psycho-analytical theory interposes a distinct phase between the third, Oedipal phase and adolescence. Freud calls it the latency phase, because we have the impression that the emotional development proceeds underground, as it were. Erikson calls it the 'industry' phase. We will leave it on one side in our discussion, because it does not, in my opinion, contribute anything in particular to religious development. The 'industry' really proceeds from the 'achievements' of the second phase; and when we were considering that stage we discussed in some detail the religious problems involved in 'achievement', especially modern technology.

I will only briefly refer to the fact, which we have already briefly indicated, that about the age of eight, when the child makes the transition from home to school, i.e., the transition from the third phase to the fourth, a clear breach takes place in the child's ties with home. This results in a detectable projection (even if only in immature form) of family – and especially motherly – security on to the providing Creator-God. Many of our children's hymns show this.

In spite of all the investigations that have been made into puberty and adolescence, this phase is an unexplored field in many respects, and one in which young people themselves are constantly surprising us. I can only agree with the psychologist whom I once heard say that the definitive book about puberty and adolescence has still to be written. Of course this is a warning against reproducing certain opinions; on the other hand I feel emboldened to formulate some theories about the problems of this phase, which I think could perhaps contribute to a better understanding of its religious significance.

We have known for many years that the manifestations which we see as characteristic of puberty and adolescence are linked with our Western cultural pattern. In discussing the other phases we pointed to the importance of cultural factors in the formation of the patterns which fit them; and that is certainly true here as well. We shall therefore confine ourselves expressly to a treatment of the religious situation in Europe in the light of the cultural pattern released in adolescence. We should point out, however, that comparable developments are taking place in other cultural patterns under the influence of a speedy urbanization and industrialization – in Japan for example. So an investigation of the religious situation that is developing there could be an important check on our hypothesis.

Puberty and Adolescence

We will begin by hearing what some of the important researchers into this phase have to say about it. Let us first take H. C. Rümke, who considered the problems of puberty and adolescence in detail in his book *De levenstijdperken van de man* (1938). Rümke had already expounded his view of human development in 1933, in his inaugural lecture 'Ontwikkelingspsychologie en psychotherapie' (Developmental psychology and psychotherapy): According to this he holds the psychical development of man to be a repetition of the process from disintegration to integration; and he sees in puberty especially disturbances of regulation and integration (Rümke was a psychiatrist). He views adolescence above all as the conclusion of this process in still provisional attempts to arrive at the vital choice, i.e., at integration.

The second important writer whom we will look at briefly is Charlotte Bühler, who has written about puberty and adolescence in a number of her publications. In my opinion *Der menschliche Lebenslauf als psychologisches Problem* is her most mature book in this field, especially the first, 1932 edition. She sees man as *animal faber*, a technological animal, and more particularly as *homo faber*, man the artificer; through the unspecific and functional phase (the game) he arrives at a phase when he discovers the world and partially adjusts to it. This phase covers the years in which the 'dimensions' (the different spheres of life) increase, in which he becomes 'expansive', but in which his work is not yet specified and his decisions still have a provisional character. This is the phase of puberty and adolescence, which is followed in later phases of life by the years of true maturity, of more definitive specification, and of 'change of dominance' (in the transition to the second phase of life).

In spite of the fact that it was published shortly after the First World War and is strongly stamped by the milieu of the German youth and student movement of that time, one of the best books about puberty is Eduard Spranger's *Psychologie des Jugendalters*. Spranger wrote as an educationalist. He sees the special thing about this epoch in the life of man as being that the boy or girl is growing into the world of older people. He was particularly concerned with the problems connected with this process. For growth into the adult world is linked with particular emotions. Spranger talks about a religious feeling for life in which discovery of the ego, drawing up a plan for life, and growing into the surrounding culture and life's different spheres must be clearly distinguished from one another. Spranger has a fine sense for what the feeling for life involves; the need to be understood; reflections about the oldest questions in life – loneliness, love and death, the search for God; and experimenting with an ideology. But he also describes how, after a period of doubt and searching, young people find their place in the culture of those older than themselves as well as in the patterns which are lying ready to their hand, as it were.

Finally let us cast a glance at Erikson; for in the context of his psychology of development he has published a number of books and essays in recent years dealing with the problems of youth especially. The chief books to be mentioned here are *Young Man Luther*, *Identity and the Life Cycle* and *Gandhi's Truth*. Erikson's key name for this phase is *identity*. By identity he means that in this phase man rounds off the development of the preceding phases, and in so doing goes through the crises of the preceding phases once more, and in a new way. Through this process he finds himself and his place in the world – in his world. Both are intrinsic to the concept of identity in Erikson's view. The danger of this phase is consequently a diffusion of identity, meaning that the person fails to find himself and his place in the whole. One of the ways in which the adolescent protects himself against this danger is by forming 'gangs', often with special characteristics, in which he is able to recognize himself. If he is to find this identity, the young person is dependent on particular things. I would give as examples chances for identification (with older people and other contemporaries); the basic trust of the first phase, on which he can fall back, for he often feels so helpless; ideology – a comprehensive view of life and the world; and a 'moratorium' (a favourite word of Erikson's) so that he can find identity with a certain degree of freedom.

Each of these writers describes the picture which he has of puberty and adolescence in his own words and his own concepts; but it is obvious that the picture is the same, as far as its broad features are concerned, and that the writers therefore agree with one another in the main lines of their accounts. We can indicate these main lines of agreement by saying that the characteristics of puberty and adolescence are:

(*a*) an inner disorganization;

(*b*) the preparation for adulthood through attempts at integration;

(*c*) a religious feeling for life, which is bound up with reflection about themes such as loneliness, love, death and God;

(*d*) the forming of a plan for life;

(*e*) a growing into the world of older people;

(*f*) the finding of the self (identity) and its place in the world;

(*g*) a renewed endurance of earlier crises;

(*h*) the search for identification and ideology.

Could we say that the discovery of identity is coupled with an inner disorganization in which experimenting with adulthood is bound up with the identity problem of earlier phases which have not yet arrived at the clarity towards which they strive? In this case adolescence would have a triple direction: towards the future; towards the world; and towards the self – that is to say, towards the goal of bringing the self out of the twilight of the past into the light. One might also say that the adolescent is a proof of the thesis that true creativity (that is to say, dealings with the material presented by the world with an eye towards one's own future and the future of others) always develops on the basis of a regression. Man must return to the situation from which he started.

Spranger shows how the religious feeling for life which he believes is closely connected with the experience of a '*vita nuova*' is linked with reflections about the old, old themes of loneliness, love, death and God. These are essentially the themes belonging to the child, because they are the themes of the man who knows that he is destined (or called) to leave behind him the familiar ties of home, and father and mother. It is not chance that children like to listen to fairy stories, for in fairy stories (which are also nearly all aware of the problems of loneliness, love, death and God) the child learns to lift these difficult problems out of their threatening obscurity into the light, and to make them capable of articulation and experience, even if in an indirect way. The child identifies himself with Tom Thumb, when he is left behind in the wood by his parents and is in danger of being swallowed up by the giant; or with the seven little goats who are left at home by their mother and are eaten up by the wolf (even if they are rescued in the end). When we think about these subjects as adolescents, we gradually grasp who we are: people who are set in a threatened world without being really forsaken; so that we can find a foundation which will enable us to make a start on our way into life. Ultimately these are the themes of the first phase (we remember Harlow's monkeys), which repeat themselves in every other phase and which appear again in more exaggerated form in adolescence.

If fairy stories are for us an expression of the uncertainty and the searching of people of former centuries (as they are for many scholars); if they represent the suppressed but most vital problems in life; then we must conclude that the themes of the fairy tale and of adolescence are the original themes of religion, the primal themes of man, who is trying to find his place in the whole. Kant formulated the three well-known questions of philosophy as: 'What can I know, what should I do, and what may I hope?' If we put the famous final question 'What is man?' beside these themes, we sense that they have clearly something in common. Kant too is concerned with man's identity and hence with his place in the world.

For the adolescent this therefore means that all the phases are really present in him in one way or another, and continue to exert their influence. His life is consequently full of contradictions and tensions. Besides the nostalgia for basic trust, we find the need for autonomy and self-confidence through one's own achievements, which derives from the second phase; and the antithesis between rebellion against, and admiration for, the father, which belongs to the Oedipal phase; and all this is surrounded by the intense need to experiment with adulthood.

The Present Cultural Pattern

In my book *Gott in vaterloser Gesellschaft* I picked up what Alexander Mitscherlich has said and suggested that our present cultural pattern is determined by the fact that we are – as Mitscherlich says – on the road to a fatherless society. This is connected in my view with the circumstance that in our present-day society we have to do with so many 'puberal problems'. I would even go further and maintain that at present we are living in a society dominated by the pattern 'released' in the adolescent phase.

It is not difficult to say what Mitscherlich means by his fatherless society. With the development of large-scale industry, a pattern of behaviour develops between people in which the old relationship of authority, with its paternalistic features, diminishes, and in which functional relationships dominate. In functional relationships authority is one aspect of the function; the function is no longer an aspect of the authority, as it was earlier. Everywhere, the father figures of earlier times are losing their self-evident power, and they only retain it on the basis of the way in which they fulfil their function – and even then it is power of a different kind. We might also say (and I have discussed this in detail in my book *Neue Wege kirchlichen Handelns* ['New ways of church action']) that power is losing its sacral character and is increasingly becoming a function; and that means that it is becoming an 'objectified' power with a personal stamp. Or to put it in another way, the 'subordinate' is losing part of his emotional security and sees himself as left on his own; but at the same time he is considered as a partner to a far greater extent.

But the process is much more comprehensive than this. As the father figure in the factory, the office, the parish or the congregation disappears, the family-like cohesion and the 'motherly' quality of the group (in which the father figure dominates) disappears as well. The whole of common life is increasingly becoming a matter of working together, of mutual service, rather than something in which people feel emotionally bound to one another, and look up to father (or perhaps mother) figures. In other words the feeling underlying our whole modern society is the sense of leaving home and starting out for an unknown world on one's own responsibility. Now this is the main motif in the pattern of the adolescent phase. Our problems and perspectives in the cultural pattern are the problems and perspectives of the adolescent. In *Gott in vaterloser Gesellschaft* I have tried to discover where the corresponding traces are to be found in the field of religion and the church, starting from the assumption that cultural changes of this kind also find their deposit in religion. We know that the increasing separation from the church, modern unbelief, and the radical modern trends in religion and theology (the God-is-dead school, for example) have all sprung from these changes; we can see them as being a result of the adolescent phase of our culture.

It is worth while comparing these ideas with the observations which C. A. van Peursen makes in a book published in 1970 called *Strategie van de cultuur – een beeld van de veranderingen in de hedendaagse denk- en leefwereld* (Strategy of culture – a picture of the changes in contemporary life and thought). Van Peursen distinguishes between three phases in the historical evolution of human culture: the mythical, the 'ontological' and the functional. The mythical phase is 'man's participation in the world that surrounds him' (p. 29). The myth is the embodiment of 'an overwhelming manifestation of something, the "ontophony", the appearance of being'. On p. 33 he writes: 'In the sphere of mystical thinking there is no clear-cut division between man and the world.' This reminds us of the pattern of the nature religions which, as we saw, derives from the first developmental phase. Van Peursen calls the second cultural phase the 'ontological' one. I am sorry that he uses the word in this connection, for according to traditional linguistic usage there is in ontology a contemplation of participation in being. Accordingly, although ontology is certainly to be distinguished from mythical thinking, it can also be seen as a continuation of that thinking, by reason of the participation. Van Peursen actually emphasizes the fact that 'in the sphere of ontological thinking a clear distinction is made between man and the world, between subject and object' (p. 55). I ask myself why he does not rather talk about scientific or objective thinking; but what he is trying to say is clear. He says (p. 61) 'Subject and object find their mutual relationship on the basis of their mutual distance. But ontological thinking too knows a more negative component, man's striving to grasp power for himself.' In this type of culture, therefore, we have a pattern whose main concept is distance, the emancipation from the unity with, and participation in, the other type. Here it is not very difficult to see the pattern of the second developmental phase – man and his autonomy, according to Erikson's scheme. But at the same time we see what makes van Peursen talk here about ontology; for in the second phase of development the autonomy remains normally rooted in the basic trust of the first phase. According to van Peursen ontology develops out of mythical thinking, so that in some cases one can talk about a 'change of stress' (pp. 50f.). Thus he then goes on to talk about a 'rounding off of the subject' through the distance and not about the subject's exercise of power as such, so that the object disappears from view (cf. p. 61). This is therefore a perversion of 'ontological thinking' which is to be compared with the perversion of the religious relationship which we talked about earlier. Van Peursen calls the third cultural phase the 'functional' one, and in this, he believes, relationship above all comes to the fore. He explains what he means by this (pp. 84f.):

> In mythical thinking man had as yet no full identity ... ontological thinking arrives at a confrontation between man and the world ... in the functional forming of relationships, however, the relationship comes more to the fore than the distance, and so here the entities which are complete in themselves are opened up once more ... The identity of the person, like that of the powers and norms, is functional in nature and is formed in the relationship.

Earlier on we called our modern, large-scale industrial urban society a functional society, because in it relationships no longer bear a paternalistic stamp; their impress is functional. We expanded this idea by showing that in this way the cultural pattern bears the stamp of the adolescent phase. Van Peursen's view about this phase points in the same direction. For him, the cultural contribution of functional thinking is that it liberates us from the rigid system of ontological thinking, which is difficult to manage – from what is in his opinion an unbelievable and unreal system. Pictorially, man is leaving his home with its fixed concepts, rules and norms, and setting off on the road to a new country; and on the way he discovers the man beside him as a fellow-man, as a companion in destiny, but also as co-designer of a new world, through whose companionship all 'truths' acquire a functional character, namely in their value for the common journey and the common task of construction. Or, to put it another way, thinking can only take on a functional character in a cultural pattern which is no longer paternalistic in trend.

What I am trying to say is that while I accept van Peursen's division into cultural types as correct, I would maintain the view that he has not grasped the logical development on which it is founded. He merely says that the one type means a liberation from the other, suggesting that it is a question of liberation because human identity is pushed a little further forward in the process. Is this logic not rooted in human development, as it can be demonstrated in the different developmental phases with their pattern, a development whose impulse is the realization of identity? To this I may add that in van Peursen's three cultural phases, the third, the Oedipal phase, is not mentioned at all. This is understandable, because van Peursen is concerned in his definition of culture with man's identity in relation to the world that surrounds him; and it is the other phases he names which make an especial contribution here.

The Sub-culture of Youth

In his books *De onvoorziene generatie* (The unexpected generation) and *Cultuur en cultuurbeleid* (Culture and cultural policy) G. C. de Haas has developed certain theories about the place of youth in our present-day culture. De Haas is an expert on problems connected with youth, and his ideas deserve closer attention.

One of his propositions is that the manifestations we come across in youth today are not 'modern' as many people think; they are rather a resurgence of a kind of folklore. He points out that the sub-culture of young people shares many of the features which belonged to the bygone world of 'actors, musicians and magicians'. Young people feel and behave like the wandering scholars and the people who were once to be found at country fairs. De Haas thinks that the protest which is so typical of contemporary youth, with the ideology and the utopia that inspires it, is really camouflage. Behind it is something quite different, which finds evident expression in the way these young people behave.

> The beloved T-shirts are at home in the world of pierrots and harlequins. The black cloaks which are worn so much nowadays are the clothes of the heretical *vagantes*, the wandering scholars who were the religious desperadoes of the middle ages and who continually turn up in European history. The black cloak is a symbol of death. We can see death personified wrapped in it in many pictures. Magic and death, hell and loneliness are intimately connected, and their symbols can be found in widely different forms in the folklore of youth (*Die onvoorziene generatie*, pp. 39f.).

In character these young people are by no means so far removed from the youth movements that followed the First World War. We find the same motifs in clothing and behaviour. They simply appear in greater numbers, and are full of tension, but otherwise problems and attitude are the same now as then. De Haas cites many examples, both past and present, to show that we really have to do here with very ancient manifestations which actually belong to mankind *per se*. He points to motifs in the clothing of ancient peoples, to features in the mediaeval Fransciscan movement, to modern films by Ingmar Bergman and Fellini, to artistes in contemporary satirical revue, to modern novels like Alain Fournier's *Le grand Meaulnes*, and to certain constantly recurring motifs in children's books. He suspects that these phenomena belong to a problem of our culture, which is seeking for a way out of its inner tensions and finds it through the use of safety valves. The youth movement was a new variation on the old 'country fair' tradition (*Die onvoorziene generatie*, p. 109). Indeed, in 'Culture and cultural policy' he puts it, as far as the present-day is concerned, in the same context as the trend towards fatherlessness of our society, which makes entry into the world of older people difficult (see p. 48). He therefore links the broad motifs of the sub-culture of young people with the trend towards fatherlessness of our cultural pattern. I should like to explore this point a little more deeply in the context of our own study. Does something of the adolescent pattern which we have discussed above emerge in this sub-culture? If it does, how are we to think of the relationship to the folklore motifs to which de Haas points? One striking thing about de Haas' books is that the movements he describes are 'fringe' movements in the culture of their time and that they are, he suspects, something like a way of release for inner tensions in their culture. In saying this I think that he touches an essential point. The use of safety valves is well known as a social phenomenon. Many people have worked on them from a sociological aspect. Every culture, as the framework that gives form to the life of a particular group, has a number of rules and norms which the members of the group are in duty bound to observe but which inevitably lead to tension within the group itself. In country districts fairs were for centuries the institutionalized way of 'celebrating', that is to say of working things off. Weddings often had the same function. Everyone wants to get outside himself sometimes, and to move about outside the compulsive pattern of his everyday life. In my view there is no doubt that cinema and theatre – which both once started in the fairground tent, and which have remained essentially related to it – help to fulfil this function in our 'educated' urban society. Incidentally G. van der Leeuw (who is well acquainted with primitive mentality through his studies into the history of religion) once said, in his book *Levensvormen* (1948), that the detective story too provides modern man (who is usually unadventurous man) with an escape route. Thus every period creates its own safety valves.

I should like here to pick up what I said in my book *Neue Wege kirchlichen Handelns*, pp. 88ff., and suggest that every culture calls forth its own fringe manifestations. Every culture evokes tension in its midst through its structure, and through its compulsive organization of human relationships by way of rules, norms, social controls, the exercise of power, etc. This means that it has to constrain or forbid the striving towards freedom and 'living life to the full' (which is natural for every member of the group) by means of regulations about clothing, outward behaviour, etc. The individual is therefore forced to suppress these strivings. But this does not eliminate it. It crops up again in the individual's own fantasies, fantasies which he then projects on to the marginal figures of our culture; indeed in this way he positively creates the fringe figure: the *vagantes*, the fairground people, etc., figures which he detests and yet envies. That is the reason why he so readily identifies himself with them and experiences their life for a moment at the times when this behaviour is tolerated, in 'safety valve' customs. He 'pulls out' for a little while. De Haas means by all this that this function in our society is now practised by contemporary youth; and the facts confirm his theory. Youth today is the reaction against the 'duty' and 'ideal' pattern of our culture. It is trying to be free, to rove about, to live it up, to be 'different' in dress and the way it wears its hair. On the one hand people view it as long-haired, lazy riffraff (note the moral undertone!). On the other hand they envy it. At a distance they copy it – on holiday, for example, i.e., outside the control of the social group.

We cannot therefore really talk about a sub-culture at all; like Theodore Roszak in his book *The Making of a Counter Culture*, we have to describe it as a counter-culture. Roszak believes that technocratic America (and we might add the whole world) is evoking a largely revolutionary element in its youth. We shall come back to this point. In our context what interests us is that the safety-valve aspects of modern youthful culture are connected with what we said above about adolescence and folklore motifs.

As long as a culture is a binding unity, the use of safety valves will not emerge so clearly. They will be more concealed. If a culture loses its binding force, tensions will be more powerful and the projections on to its fringe groups will play their part. Our middle-class culture was a binding unity of this kind in the nineteenth century and at the beginning of the twentieth. Its norms and rules were a firm clamp. Anyone who suffered under these rules had his chances to escape them for a short time (always provided he was rich enough) in the form of brief trips abroad or through the 'moratorium' (to use Erikson's word) of the years spent at the university. All that was institutionalized, so to speak. Others had their 'fairs'. But many people, especially women, had to try to conform. After the critical period of puberty and adolescence the younger ones again found chances for identification in particular 'father figures', and therefore opportunities for finding their place in society as well.

We have already pointed out that in our society the father figures are fading and losing their power. In addition, the population has become more mobile and thus social control has become weaker; and young people have more freedom because they have more money. All this means that the unity has more or less lost its binding force. We therefore have to do with fringe manifestations of our culture, in which the culture recognizes its unsolved conflicts – the tensions between commands and prohibitions on the one hand, and the longing to escape them on the other. In this situation young people experience their liberation from the power of their parents (and especially their fathers) as well as the need to rebel against it; in other words the adolescent situation. In these years, therefore, young people experience the basic problems of puberty and adolescence to an intensified degree. They are searching for themselves and their place in the world. And as we already said, they come face to face in this situation with the primal themes of loneliness, love, death and God. De Haas had the right feeling when he talked (*Die onvoorziene generatie*, p. 47) about a 'nostalgia' for the lost country of their childhood with father and mother, where fairy tales first actualized the search for frail human identity in the mysteries of life; the lost country where in these years they return (regression) in order to grapple on a higher level with the same fundamental problems and to undergo preparation for the great journey of life. De Haas rightly points to the fact that these themes are also the central themes in the life and activity of the *vagantes*, the travelling actors and fairground people. They are also the themes of the great mediaeval dramas – *Everyman*, *Faust* and the rest. Indeed, is not every drama ultimately about these themes? And are not actors still the fringe figures of our society on whom we project something of our most secret fantasies? This seems to me to be especially true of film stars. Modern political revue is also essentially concerned with these themes. They are evidently the problems of our little human identity in an overwhelming culture.

We may deduce from all this that in many places on the fringe of our modern technical society the old basic religious questions of our human existence still play a part, often in veiled form, but in the sub-culture of young people quite openly and with especial emphasis. They are the break-through of the cultural pattern of the adolescent phase into the present pattern, as well as into the other pattern, founded on earlier phases, in which we older people grew up.

Before I go on let me make one comment here. We find a whole series of manifestations in our society which we can term regressive; but in many cases this cannot be the last word. The characteristic thing about adolescence – as we have already pointed out – is the very fact that at this period young people are experimenting with adulthood. Regression is always linked with the trend towards a point ahead, and therefore with the experimenting with adulthood. Young people are, as it were, struggling once more, on another level, through the themes of their childhood – and these are the primal themes of human existence. Of course there is the danger that the regression is a retreat from the reality of adult life and that the experimenting with adulthood does not therefore come sufficiently into play. We have to do with the young man or woman who wants to remain young and who sticks fast in adolescence, like the eternal boy scout of the years following the First World War.

Let me follow this up with a few remarks. It is not chance that in these years young people take up a position on the fringe of our culture, or stick fast in it. If it is true that there is a tension in every culture between the demands which that culture makes and the individual's natural strivings, then this tension must also be present in upbringing, in veiled form. Parents bring up their children with an eye to these demands – obedience plays an important part in their upbringing – but the child senses their 'discontent', to echo the title of the book in which Freud deals with this theme (*Civilization and its Discontents*). The parents themselves sigh over the severe demands with which present-day culture confronts them. They have to stand fast and work hard; they must not allow themselves any rest; they have to satisfy the demands of their environment and acquire a status, and then maintain it; and so forth. It is obvious that at the moment when the adolescent becomes free and can make his own decisions, he will live more from the 'discontent', which must unconsciously have deeply influenced him, than from the commands and prohibitions which his parents have inculcated. Psycho-analysis knows that children identify themselves more with their parents' unconscious ideas than with their conscious ones. The more strongly the 'discontent' is felt by the parents, the more radically the boy or girl will turn against the existing situation. Is this now what we are experiencing at the moment?

From this standpoint let me say something about the word 'revolution', which is constantly used by particular writers (e.g. Roszak) in connection with the counter-culture of youth. If this word makes us think of violence and the threat of overturning the existing order, it does not seem to me applicable. Of course there are revolutionary manifestations – I am thinking of the solving of conflicts through violence or of particular ideologies. But what seems to predominate is the 'discontent' and the need to work off this discontent through conflicts, among other things, and especially in confrontation with parent figures; however, this does not lead to planned and co-ordinated long-term activity; it stops at casual actions. Young people seem to be much more concerned with themselves than with the reality surrounding them. The reaction of older people is significant as well. Many of them are disturbed, but it is only very slowly that they actually arrive at real action, and then it is only sporadically and always, it seems to me, only with a bad conscience. I ask myself whether the ambivalence we have mentioned does not play a decisive role here. Older people recognize something of themselves in the protest and in the new thing that the young people are striving for. They are afraid – and this fear is understandable – that the radicalism of many younger people is unreal in so far as it does not suffice the demands of a modern society. But they also know from their own experience that these demands gradually destroy a large area of human happiness. We only have to think of modern traffic and the pollution of our environment through industry; or the many families that break up because the parents have a mania for earning money; or the women and children who are neglected because of the man's compulsive passion for achievement. I have the impression that if old and young were able to listen to one another and to themselves in their conflicts, and could recognize that they share the same 'discontent', then a way would open up by itself which would allow them to meet each other half way. In chapter 5 of my book *Neue Wege kirchlichen Handelns* I have discussed conflicts in some detail and come to the conclusion that often they are not only unavoidable, but can even be useful, provided that they are realistic and do not degenerate into ideological hair-splitting. I also believe that something which presents itself as a revolution and is really felt as such, can lead to a fruitful evolution.

At the close of this chapter let me say a few words about the interesting observations made by Margaret Mead in her book *Culture and Commitment*, in which she also considered the relationship between parents and young people in our culture area. Her thesis is that we older people often fail to read the situation correctly. She writes (p. 63):

> Like immigrant pioneers from colonizing countries, we cling to the belief that the children will, after all, turn out to be much like ourselves. But balancing this hope there is the fear that the young are being transformed into strangers before our eyes, that teenagers gathered at a street corner are to be feared like the advance guard of an invading army.

Many older people know what this fear is when they see how young people act. Margaret Mead makes it clear that it is almost impossible for young and old to live in communication with one another. We older people, she says, are living in the new technological world of today with a picture which is derived from the world before 1940. But for young people that world no longer exists. They only know *one* world, today's, which they have to conquer without the help of their elders. They are pioneers who are irritated by our behaviour and our standpoints. I understand Margaret Mead's view; after the First World War we in Europe experienced a deep cleft between the generations. Like her, I believe that the cleft is now much deeper. We really have become strange to one another and because of this we tend merely to level reproaches at one another. The decisive factor for Margaret Mead is that we are now living in a culture in which the children have to be their parents' teachers. She calls it a prefigurative culture. We are emigrants to a new country and in a country of this kind the children are the true pioneers; the parents cling much too closely to the past. The children therefore have to help their parents to find the way to the new country; they must above all show them how to go their way with inner freedom, open-minded, without the unnecessary burdens of inadequate and unproductive memories.

But Margaret Mead's discussions do not, I think, quite correspond to reality. In a new country the elders cannot have the authority of experience, it is true. But a new country, where everything is new and unknown, is just the place where there are a number of difficult problems to whose solution older people can probably contribute a certain *wisdom* – where the basic problems of being man and of living together are concerned, for example. When the Pilgrim Fathers were approaching the coast of America, they drew up a charter based on their experience in the past, in which they summed up the basic lines on which their life and their co-existence in the new country was to be based. It is simply essential for the *wise* to exert this function in a new society; only the relationship to wise men is different from the attitude to the older person who was the practical expert in earlier times. Those were father figures in the old style, with clear authority. The wise, on the other hand, are companions on the way who, because of their greater experience, can be a kind of sounding board for their younger companions. They must be able to listen and think with them. Here the earlier relationship between above and below no longer applies; it is a relationship between companions on the same road and on the same level, but with the opportunity for a clearly evident function in a special field.

This brings us up against a problem in the fatherless society into which we shall go more deeply in a special section. The fatherless society creates a new pattern of relationships, a pattern in which the others who are on a level with me can come to my side in their particular function. As we have already mentioned, van Peursen also sees a special connection between relationship and function in our cultural phase.

The New Pattern of Relationships

In the phases we have already dealt with, the relationship to the other seemed to be the most important factor, according to Erikson's view, which is the one we have followed for the most part. In the first phase it was the relationship to the mother; in the third phase the relationship to the father; whereas in the second phase, with its stress on autonomy, relationship was the power against which the child rebelled, in the attempt to emancipate itself. In the following phases, which cover the years at school (in which 'industry' stands at the centre in Erikson's view) and adolescence (in which the search for identity plays the most important role), the relationship to the other moves out of sight. It is only perceived in the problems of 'intimacy'. As a psychotherapist, Erikson in his evident one-sidedness is primarily interested in identity, which is more or less equated with the ego-strength which is always important for psychotherapists. In religion, however, the point at issue is ultimately not ego-strength but a relationship. I would therefore say that here we must not tie ourselves down to what Erikson says, but must also try to grasp the nature of this phase ourselves, especially as regards the pattern of relationships.

In our discussion of the third phase, we pointed to the view developed by Levinas in *Totalité et Infini*. For him a difference of level is an essential factor in the relationship between one person and another. The other is always below and above me in the call which he addresses to me. Two movements arise in me, he says (p. 174), one towards the height and one towards the depth of the other. I am moved both by his misery and by his grandeur. Such a view (and the context in which it is developed: we can compare what Levinas has to say about the desire to kill the other, which arises in the relationship) unavoidably makes us think of the problems of the Oedipal phase. We must therefore ask whether the last word has been spoken about the relationship of a person to his fellow-men. In my opinion we can already conjecture from Levinas' views about above and below that an 'at the same time' and a 'together' must be possible.

Erikson describes the end of the adolescent phase as a stage in which a person is capable of 'intimacy', as he calls it. The way in which he talks about this – he speaks of 'interpersonal', 'true twoness' and the possibility of 'distantiation' – shows that he has in mind contact on the basis of equality. I think that one might say that in his need for contact, conversation, discussion, common experience, etc., the adolescent is experimenting with the new way of 'togetherness'. If I see the matter rightly, we could say that the aspects of cleft, call and bond, which are taken over from the third phase, continue in the structure of this relationship, though without an above and below.

Let me go a little deeper still into the new pattern of relationships. In the relationship of this phase man experiments with a behaviour through which the other is experienced as a possible equal. In reality he is often not this at all, but the approaches to it are present. By *equal* I mean that the other is first experienced as a *companion in destiny* in the world in which we live. We are both set in this world and recognize ourselves as such. We are side by side on the basis of a common fate. But to be companions in destiny does not mean that we are together on the way. Destiny is not, for a man, the last word to be said about his existence; we take our destiny into our own hands; we try to realize the potentialities it holds; we build towards our own future. Or to put it another way, we are called to go towards the future together, not to put up with our destiny. We are bound together through our destiny and our future, and we manifest this in particular cases through the forming of a bond. In this way we actually already have the bond, essentially speaking. Consequently as people we can also direct an appeal to one another. Levinas was right in saying that the appeal is already made in advance with the face which we turn to one another. Our common human relationship is ethical in character.

This also therefore means that a future essentially opens up with the human relationship, on the level of this phase. Where people are equal, they have a common future which they have to realize with one another and for one another. That means, in the well-known formularies of present-day theology, that human life is historical and eschatological in kind and that hope is part of its basic structure.

The relationship of an I to a Thou therefore means more than a more or less fortuitous 'being with one another' as Heidegger describes it in *Being and Time*. It includes the opportunity for communication which Jaspers considers in detail in his philosophical thinking. Part of the nature of this communication, in my opinion, is to recognize our companion in destiny in the other and to mould the future together on this basis. Anyone who grasps what this means will also understand that in this communication, in this common mastery of life, part of the future is even now being realized – part of the *shalom* of the kingdom, to express it in biblical terms, a future which is achieved in the teeth of cynicism towards destiny, and despair over it. If I see the matter rightly, this communication holds within itself an individual experience of God: on the one hand in the experience of the 'secret' knowledge that we are called by destiny to the future, and are directed towards our neighbour in our loneliness and forsakenness; and on the other hand in the experience of the *shalom* we have just mentioned. I repeat, if I see it rightly, this is the experience of God with which modern radical theology is closely concerned – the God-is-dead theology, for example, and others as well. It is an experience in which Christology has a totally new function (Dorothee Sölle talks about 'substitution', for example). But it would be taking us too far if we were to go further into that here. We shall come back to it briefly in our discussion of the religious pattern of this phase.

In the framework of what we have to say about the particular pattern of relationships in this phase, let me make two comments:

1. In the new pattern of relationships the two structures of experience belonging to the two fundamental phases of childish development provide the two foundations on which the new pattern rests. In the uncertainty which marks adolescence they emerge particularly clearly. The adolescent must continually experience, in order to find and preserve his identity. The basic trust of the first phase is sought in group experiences which evidently have a maternal character. The many discussions and conversations, with their familiar companionableness, have an oral aspect. The awakening of the 'physical nature' (as one might perhaps call it) – I mean the mutual embracing, the holding on to one another, and the caressing, which seems to satisfy a certain need to feel things physically – points in the same direction. In my opinion the same need is behind the fashion for the often vulgar-seeming sensitivity trainings, which are now reaching Europe from America. They are almost a degenerate form of the first 'trainings'. In the *Gestalt* therapy carried out by Fritz Perls and others we see the deliberate attempt to undo the alienation of the body and, above all, the primary feelings which are bound up with it. In the sub-culture of young people this therapy is popular. On the other hand there are evidently also other aspects: the experience of the distance from the other; the stress on loneliness; annoyance over unwanted efforts on the part of 'a higher hand' (manipulation); as well as carefully cherished 'privacy' – all aspects of this phase which are in line with the pattern of the third phase. For an adolescent, the search for his own identity is only possible on the basis of these experiences.

2. Let me now make one comment on Levinas' observations about language and objectivity (see pp. 184ff. and a number of other passages in his book). We saw that the objectivity of things has estranged many modern people from the pattern of participation, and that because of this life has become stunted and religion no longer has any chance (I am thinking primarily of Fortmann here). Levinas maintains that this objectivity is a function of the relationship to the other, which comes into

being through the language in which I show him things and so interpret them. We come back to this in this context especially, because in this phase language really does have this express function. In the relationship to mother and father, language has to serve other purposes (to express the familiar nearness, to pass on commands, etc.). But *here* it is in the first place a way of orientation for people who live together in their world. Through language we emancipate ourselves from the primitive security of the world and recognize each other as companions in destiny and builders of the future in a world which in this way becomes for us a sphere through which we pass and material for us to mould. This is undoubtedly a painful process – we can feel with Fortmann here – for we are tied to our experience of security in the world. This is apparently a necessary step in mankind's development, just as the adolescent also has to find his way out of the security of home into a new world, together with his companions in age and destiny. The objectification through language belongs inescapably to this. Without language, orientation in the world is not possible; and this really means that we are on the way to a different kind of religion.

16

The Religious Pattern of this Phase

The theme of this book is that the religious pattern of a particular culture has its basis in a particular pattern of relationships. We saw that different relationship patterns and (on their basis) different religious patterns as well fit the oral and Oedipal phases. We have also established that a particular relationship pattern belongs to the adolescent phase; and this faces us with the question whether we can now talk about a new religious pattern too. It is not so easy to answer this question. The new pattern of relationships has not become completely established; we only see it emerging at particular places in our society. Consequently we can only talk experimentally about a new religious pattern; it is a matter of something heralded from afar rather than something that is clearly demonstrable. Traces are at most to be seen in the sub-culture, and in addition it is probably making its influence felt in the church and in general religious development. In my book *Gott in vaterloser Gesellschaft* I have tried to show that at the moment we are in a period of transition between two cultural patterns; that one can describe this period as a trend towards fatherlessness in our culture; and that the signs of such a transition are to be found in the spheres of the church, and of belief and unbelief. Traces of the new pattern were not yet clearly visible, however. I will pick up my earlier study at this point and try to take it a step further.

1. Many research workers have pointed to the phenomenon that the religious life and life in the churches is being individualized (we might particularly mention Thomas Luckmann's book *Das Problem der Religion in der modernen Gesellschaft* – The problem of religion in modern society). In my opinion this phenomenon is very closely connected with the trend towards fatherlessness of modern society. This means on the one hand a fading of all hierarchical structure, and hence an individualization; but

on the other hand it also makes possible the transition from latent to open rebellion against the authoritarian hierarchy. An individualization of this kind is therefore not a mature and definitive form of faith; its character lies in its detachment from the existing institutions, joined with experimentation with new forms of institutionalization.

2. We can therefore see groups forming (often temporarily) in which particular aspects supervene: the being together (as a reaction against the loneliness of individualization); common discussion (as a mutual exploration and as an attempt, by way of conversation, to get to know one's own situation and identity); and the search for identification figures in the 'peer-group', as a help along the road to identity. These groups are therefore both regressive and prospective: regressive because they meet a need for maternal security and thus fortify the basic trust; and prospective because they give people an opportunity through common experiment to make the new relationship of this phase jointly their own. Numerous conferences and courses in 'educational centres' are obvious examples of these provisional but important group formations.

3. A great variety of factors play a role in all this. Pre-eminent among them is the need for structuralization. In earlier patterns the individual found a structure outside his own personal sphere – the father figures saw to that. Now the structuralization has to take place from within. Exercises in Yoga and meditation, often strengthened by a stay in a monastery, have to help the individual to prevent his life from atrophying through the many impressions and stimuli, and to concentrate on certain basic ideas and feelings. In addition there is apparently a need for liberation, or an extension of the consciousness. The individual feels wedged between the many commands and prohibitions of our 'achievement' culture with its anal tendencies, and especially by the pattern of behaviour enjoined by parents and home, and furnished by them with the necessary authority. He seeks the distant and far off; he wants to roam about – literally, in far away countries (the Far East, for example, and places with a magic sound), and in a transferred sense, in the country of his emotions, in the common experience of the group (if possible to the accompaniment of music), or in some erotic bond. Of course the use of drugs must also be seen under this aspect (though there other and mixed motives are probably involved). One can float away into dream-like forms and arrive at an extension of the consciousness with the aid of fantasy. It is significant of our cultural situation that someone like Timothy Leary should connect the use of LSD with the problem of death (see his book *The Psychedelic Experience; a Manual based on the Tibetan Book of the*

Dead). The use of drugs apparently plays on the themes of adolescence: loneliness, love, death and God.

4. If I see the situation correctly, both the need for structuralization and the need for liberation continually find fulfilment in 'expression' and in the 'festival'. Both are significant elements in our contemporary culture. First of all these are typical group experiences. (Expression was once an individual matter, but it is increasingly taking on a collective character. The artist too no longer wants to be an individualist – he wants to be a person in the community.) And as group experiences they also offer – even if only provisionally – a liberation from the compulsiveness and structuralization of experience. They are the safety valves of our modern culture.

5. Particular 'leaders' play an important part in all this. These are not figures who lead a group by means of authority combined with power – we can think of the role played by a person like Hitler. They are individuals who, because of their knowledge of the situation of human life in these years, help young people to achieve a certain *Daseinserhellung* – an illumination of existence, to use a curious modern expression. I am thinking of people like Marcuse and Ernst Bloch; or Norman Brown, who is mentioned by Roszak in his book on counter-culture; or writers like Roszak himself, or Reich, the author of *The Greening of America*, or – underlying them – Karl Marx. They communicate knowledge and give advice, i.e., an ideology, to take the word Erikson uses when he maintains that the adolescent must find his identity through an ideology; but they try to beware of modern man's aversion to every (authoritarian) manipulation. One of the great themes of these 'leaders' is *alienation*, in the personal and social spheres, and in this they too are pointing preeminently to the themes of the adolescent phase which we have already frequently mentioned. Norman Brown particularly stresses the problem of death in this connection.

6. This gradually brings us to the typical religious problems of this cultural pattern. The striking thing about adolescents in our modern culture sphere is their interest in Oriental religion. Fortmann especially, with his sensitive mind, sensed this and he even expected this 'interest' (as we call it) to lead to a renaissance of our atrophied religious life. As I have already said, I doubt whether he can expect this renaissance to bring about a return to a 'second primitiveness' and a diminution of the one-sidedness of our modern relationship to reality; and even if a return of this kind were possible, I do not know whether it is necessarily desirable. But it is clear to me that the interest is really connected with a

deeper need in our culture. I am quite convinced that many people are seeking a way out of the compulsiveness and authoritarian hierarchy of our religious and church life into structuralized experiences of expansion of the consciousness and oneness with the mystery. These are offered in the Oriental religions and they play on the fourfold theme we have already named. It is also a noteworthy fact that there is virtually no interest in Islam.

7. But we must not shut our eyes to the fact that even in Christianity itself traces are to be found of the influence of the new pattern. This is true of the 'underground' or 'latent' churches, but signs are already to be found even in official devotion and theology. For a detailed discussion of particular aspects of this development, let me point to my book *Gott in vaterloser Gesellschaft*. Here I will confine myself to a number of important points, not all of which were dealt with there.

(*a*) On the basis of a different experience of God, the picture of God is changing. The father is losing his meaning as the representative of authority, of the providing power who also calls us to account. This fact is apparently connected with a different experience of fatherhood in our Western society. This development was given challenging expression in the thesis 'God is dead'.

(*b*) We discover that the relationship between God and man (or men) has a functional character. In his acute book *Hij is het weer!* (Observations about the meaning of the word 'God') C. A. Van Peursen says that in the Old and New Testaments the point is neither 'to know who or what "God" is', nor a dogmatic or philosophical theory about God; their concern is a recognition and a reaction to a proclamation. In faith, therefore, stress does not lie on the acceptance of a 'revealed' truth, but on being 'on the way' together, on a functional relationship.

If we try to evaluate this psychologically, we can say that in the first alternative, the accepting of a thing as true, man is dependent and immature; whereas the second, the common journeying, could be regarded as the first attempt at a more mature relationship between God and man. We may remember that we also connected Van Peursen's view about the functional character of our modern culture with the cultural pattern of the adolescent phase (pp. 379f.).

I myself believe that it is possible to show that there is actually less stress on theory in preaching and in theological publications; and that in the sub-culture of young people, above all, in spite of its inclination towards ideological theorization, there is a search for an experience of God which goes beyond the theory. But I also believe that what Van Peursen means by the 'recognition', which must lead to a 'commitment', to being on the road together, only exists in immature form; and its contours are still indistinct.

(*c*) We have already pointed out that the modern pattern of relationships of our time contains its own experience of God. For the religious themes of adolescence are loneliness, love, death and God. I wrote in this connection (p. 301) that this communication has an individual experience of God: 'on the one hand in the experience of the "secret" knowledge that we are called by destiny to the future, and are directed towards our neighbour in our loneliness and forsakenness; and on the other hand in the experience of the Shalom' (in the communication). Perhaps one could say that the natural theology of our cultural pattern is concerned with an experience of God as the mysterious one who calls us; and also with an experience of him as the creator of a new reality in existential communication. I believe that we can already see signs that this experience of God is beginning to reveal itself in the traditional pattern of the churches. Stress on the church's social action and on action in general as a fundamental religious category (see Nijk's *Secularisatie* and Sperna Weiland's *Het einde van der religie*); the importance of the group within the congregation; strivings to experience the cultic meeting as a mainly group event through renewal of liturgy – all these things point in this direction. But we can also continually discover that in the culture of young people the central figures and the symbols of Christianity are being drawn into the pattern of this experience of God. The American weekly *Time* (in its number for 21 June 1971) deals in detail with the Jesus revolution, which is acquiring a clear outline in the culture of the young.

It is impossible to say that the religious experience of this pattern fits straight away into the traditional patterns of church and religion. There are obviously tensions. Outwardly the main point at issue is usually the problem that the familiar formulations of the traditional pattern are under attack by the representatives of the new. Robinson began this in *Honest to God*. But we have the distinct feeling that it is really a question of a different 'feeling about life', a different 'mood', as Robinson calls it. I would like to draw attention to my book *Gott in vaterloser Gesellschaft* here.

Perhaps we can define this mood somewhat more closely by pointing out that two things play an important part in the experience of a common human destiny, which is so fundamental to today's feeling about life. In the first place helplessness. It is impossible to understand most of the manifestations of youthful culture unless one perceives that profound feelings of helplessness are often behind them. The need to talk, to unburden oneself, and the need for community are closely connected with this. Feelings of helplessness have always played an important part in adolescence, but earlier the forming of groups usually helped to overcome these feelings. Today we often have the impression that these groups rather intensify the helplessness, because the group takes on the function of a place of refuge – it encourages 'dropping-out'. Even so-called action groups among younger people often suffer from a profound feeling of helplessness and they are then frequently only short-lived. In addition suffering plays a part. In his book *The New Essence of Christianity*, Hamilton points out that for many people in our time the experience of suffering stands in the way of faith in God; and that we can already see the image of a suffering and helpless God emerging in place of the picture of the God who is sovereign and almighty. He points to Bonhoeffer. Helplessness and suffering are of course closely linked. Perhaps we could say that the part which guilt played for many people in the traditional pattern is now filled by suffering.

When we were discussing the religious pattern of the third phase we pointed to the importance of the dispersion experience for the Jews. In my opinion it could be said that the experience of companionship in human destiny is evidently related to the dispersion experience, with its two themes of helplessness and suffering. I hope to go more deeply into this in a moment, when I discuss the exodus pattern. If the situation is as I have described it, it is understandable that tensions should inevitably arise between supporters of the 'mood' and champions of the traditional pattern. These tensions will perhaps have to be fought out in the form of theological differences, but they can be traced back essentially to an underlying difference in the 'feeling about life' and to the religious experience that corresponds to this. Faith in God's power and hence in Christ as victor occupies the centre of the traditional pattern – we have only to think of the importance of the resurrection. Because of this the problem of suffering is only given a subordinate place in the life of faith. It inevitably follows that a belief in God which is rooted on man's side in the experience of helplessness and suffering, and which therefore 'discovers' the meaning of Christ for our faith in God on the basis of this fundamental experience, is bound to come up against profound resistance among supporters of the traditional pattern.

Perhaps we can define the difference somewhat more closely when we remember the antithesis expressed by the American sociologists Glock, Ringer and Babbie in the title of their book *To Comfort and to Challenge*. For the believer in the traditional pattern, faith in God's power is his 'sole *comfort* in living and in dying', to put it in the words of the Heidelberg Catechism. But many modern people feel this to be a flight from the reality that meets them as a 'challenge'. For them the comfort of faith does not lie *alongside* the reality in which they live but in the *entering into* the challenge of that reality. Hope is awakened through action on the basis of this challenge; and that offers comfort. Many people feel akin to Ernst Bloch, who has clearly expressed ideas of this kind in his books. In Bloch there is an absolute antithesis between the theology of hope on the one hand and theism, with its belief in God's power, on the other. But I would say that it is questionable whether we can uphold this antithesis in its absolute form. It is right to protest against too cheap a 'comfort', but the pointer to the mystery of God's power, even if it is power we do not see, seems to me essential for the Christian faith.

But the problem which we are touching on here cannot be solved on the basis of a rational discussion, because it is a problem of belief. That is to say, it can only be adequately solved when we recognize it and see it through in its full depth – or, to put it differently, when we are able to discover whether the comfort of the traditional pattern is really a flight from reality and its challenge. For it could well be that we have experienced the reality in which we stand differently, and that we therefore have a different 'feeling about life'; and in this way for us the comfort of faith would also have become a different one.

In fact I believe that this is actually the case. In order to clarify this theory let me introduce the concept of 'the model'. For I believe that today we use a different model of reality for our faith. The concept of the model plays a big part in science today, but I do not intend to go into that here. Here we are using the word in the wider meaning of an aid which helps us to make clear something that cannot be adequately expressed. It has the function of a picture, but in our present case it clarifies not so much visually as emotionally.

I am convinced that one of the essential elements of the traditional religious pattern is belief in an *order* in reality. Even in primitive religions, as we have seen, the cosmos has an order in which man can participate. Public worship with its liturgy has a central importance here. My thesis is that this model of reality has laid its impress on the traditional pattern of religious experience down to the present day. But in

Christianity the order was as it were transferred to God, who made earth and heaven and who will make them new again, in spite of the Fall. Perhaps we could say that one characteristic of Christianity is faith in the 'Father's house', which embraces the earthly reality that has been blighted. God is our Father, and the liturgy of our Sunday services is part of the mystery of his order, allowing us to participate in the 'Father's house', which is present in concealed form in the community of the church. The Father's house is the model of the reality experienced in the traditional pattern.

I have the impression that the experience conveyed by this model is what Bonhoeffer termed religion. At all events I believe that one of the essential characteristics of our experience of reality is that this model has for us lost its emotional power. We no longer experience reality as an order; for we have been turned out of that order. Our model is that of the exodus. We are living in the dispersion, and because of that we have come to view the word comfort with distrust. In its old meaning it points us to an experience of reality which can no longer stand up to the demands we put on it.

If we can really view the exodus model as our own, a number of things which we can notice about our time become comprehensible.

1. We discover a noticeable ambivalence with regard to tradition on the one hand, and only very few constructive plans for the future on the other. As far as the ambivalence is concerned, we see in some people resistance against giving up the old or trusting to new ideas (and even Moses has to struggle with the people in the wilderness who were unable to give up 'the fleshpots of Egypt'); while in others we find a definite aversion to the traditional: whatever comes from older people is often immediately suspect. As far as the lack of constructive plans for the future is concerned, we come up against all kinds of utopias, which show the need to get away from what exists today; but they lack clear insight into the reality of the processes in which we are involved, nor do they provide well-considered plans to make this exodus a real move into a new country. We can at most say that a few structures are gradually emerging which we must keep in mind, for the future as well.

2. We can now also understand better why the meaning of what is called life *style* is stressed so much at present. Like Hamilton in his book, for example, we can include in this the fragmentary, the experimental, the incomplete in our knowledge, the unpretentious, the awareness of the unbelief in ourselves, etc. I read in an article for Sunday School teachers that it is essential 'to be clearer about what faith, what life style

and what sense of direction we want to pass on to our children'. It is significant that belief, style and sense of direction are all named in the same breath. The word 'style' is used in an attempt to express the divergence from the earlier pattern of life, in which permanence, tradition, the fixed formulation, power and the finished and perfected played so great a role. All this fits into the order of the Father's house, into the order of the cosmos. But now we are on the move, and not nearly everything that was valid under the old order has validity now; and we know neither the way nor the future, so that we set out along the road experimentally and with inner freedom. No one knows it any better than ourselves, but we are seeking the truth together. In our modern world to be mature always means that we are better able to live with uncertainty, whereas earlier it rather meant to know what was the right thing, to have achieved a kind of certainty.

I believe that it is possible to establish that the problem of Christology (the question of the meaning of Christ for our faith) is one of the central questions of our time, both religiously and theologically. We have already pointed to the article in *Time* about the Jesus revolution. But the development of modern theology can also be characterized as a development which is distinguished by stunted thinking about God (to the point of a declaration that God is dead) and by a stronger concentration on Christological ideas. Here it is noticeable how much the humanity of Jesus is underlined and that hence (in the sense of his functional relationship to God) his humanity is held to be more important than his 'divinity'.

Before we go into that more deeply, let me make a few comments. In the traditional pattern, Christology always pointed towards God and his order – Christ was God's representative in the work which God consummated in the restoration of the order that had been destroyed. In this pattern, therefore, there was a relationship between Christ and the people who were the representatives and guardians of order in human society; it was a relationship which could not always be clearly specified but which there is no doubt can be traced in latent form. In theory this relationship is ambivalent: on the one hand Christ represents a 'higher' order, and is hence a revolutionary from the point of view of our society; on the other hand, in people's minds the order of society points to a fundamental order which is rooted in creation's deepest reality. It is clear that Paul is grappling with this ambivalence in his thinking about authority, and that there has been a continual consciousness of the equivocal character of order in Christianity. Now, it seems to me that one of the marks of the traditional pattern is that in it Christ forms a kind of background for the representatives of order, and that the church is felt by many people to be a co-representative of this order, which is regarded as having a sacral character. For ruling princes and other holders of power, Christ in some sense provided an opportunity for identification.

In the new pattern this aspect has disappeared. Our modern technological and industrial society no longer has the sense of a sacral order. Achievements and functions are the guarantees of today's order of society. It is true that there are still some forms stemming from the old pattern which have been preserved by rulers and holders of power, and in which the church also plays a certain role; in England one might instance the coronation. But such forms are increasingly taking on the character of a folklore that no longer fits our culture.

One result of this development is that today the 'revolutionary' nature of the ministry of Jesus is being discovered anew. Thus Jesus can again offer an opportunity for identification to people who no longer get on with the existing order. The *Time* article already mentioned talks about the new slogan 'Jesus is coming'. Here is a typical passage:

WANTED

JESUS CHRIST

(alias the Messiah, the Son of God, King of Kings,
Lord of Lords, Prince of Peace, etc).

Notorious leader of an underground liberation movement.

Wanted on the following charges:

Practising medicine, winemaking and food distribution without a licence.

Interfering with businessmen in the temple.

Associating with known criminals, radicals, subversives, prostitutes and other anti-social elements.

Claiming to have the authority to make people into God's children.

Appearance: Typical hippie type – long hair, beard, robe, sandals.

Beware! This man is **extremely dangerous.** His insidiously inflammatory message is particularly dangerous to young people who haven't been taught to ignore him yet. He changes men and claims to set them free.

In our world, therefore, there is a kind of suppression of the figure of Christ; that is to say, he is being pushed out of the culture which is traditionally valid into the counter-culture. When we say that one mark of this counter-culture is the fourfold theme of loneliness, love, death and God, we can well understand how the figure of Christ above all, as we know it from the gospels, fits into this theme. Christ knew not where to lay his head, he was forsaken by his own family and friends, he was concerned with the importance of love in human relationships, he founded a 'commune', he died an early death, and lived as if looking towards that death, which was for him of essential importance. In his life all this had, as it were, its ultimate context in knowledge of God. In this counter-culture Christ can offer a chance for identification to young people in an even wider sense than the above quotation brings out.

But here we come up against a problem. The question arises whether there is a direct continuity between these religious themes and the identification with Christ (perhaps we could talk about an 'imitation of Christ') or whether we ought rather to talk about a discontinuity in new form. Or, to put it another way, are we dealing here with the old antithesis between religion and faith? The question is of essential importance, because what is at stake is the problem of what the church's task should be in relation to the young people of this sub-culture; and, even more fundamentally, what place the church should have in the new cultural pattern that is now presenting itself. Perhaps the problem can also be approached in a different way. In their arguments about the fourfold problem of loneliness, love, death and God, these young people are, as we saw, searching for a more mature identity, for a view of their own about their own place in life. Can the Christian tradition, as embodied in the figure of Christ, make its special and irreplaceable contribution to the growth of the individual's faith for these future adults too, or is it merely one possible variation on the religious theme – one which can perhaps even be replaced by another?

It is my conviction that the former alternative is the true one. In order to make this clear I will try to shed more light on some important aspects of this tradition which seem to me of essential significance in this connection.

If I see the matter rightly, certain things which play a part in the problems of our present culture and society were of central importance in the ministry of Jesus.

1. One of the guiding ideas of Jesus' life was that the 'establishment' of his time, which was trying to maintain its ground under the leadership of the scribes and Pharisees, was approaching its downfall. This must have been a bond with John the Baptist, who was probably one of the many representatives of the awareness (widespread at that period) that

the End-time was approaching, because the people had fallen into the hands of false leaders. For Jesus this must have meant that God's promises were now to be fulfilled and that his rule or kingdom was imminent. In this Jesus was picking up what I have called elsewhere in this context (pp. 263ff.) the dispersion faith in God. I said there that it is in suffering above all that God is the one who is to come, that he is our hope and the releaser of eschatology.

2. Because he rebelled against the establishment, Jesus became a figure on to which the people were able to project their unconscious conflicts with existing conditions. At that time he belonged to the same kind of fringe group as the *vagantes* we have mentioned already. It can be said that in the Israel of that time a very one-sided anal culture, based on achievement, had developed under the leadership of the scribes and Pharisees. We already pointed out that in a culture of this kind profound demands for freedom and authenticity are repressed; these needs find an outlet for themselves in fringe groups, but at the same time they become a danger to the leading groups. It is plain that this is what happened in the vicinity of Jesus. How dangerous his ministry was for the leading groups can be clearly deduced from the gospels.

3. It is understandable that a group, a community, should form round Jesus, creating a counter-culture and by means of a new way of life (one could probably use the word 'style' here too) detaching itself from the old society and preparing itself for the new (the new kingdom). In the Sermon on the Mount we find what is, as it were, an attempt to outline a new pattern of life. One might say that these *vagantes* made the attempt to realize now, in the present, something of the *shalom* over against the old culture. This happened on the one hand through a clear commitment on the part of those involved, and on the other hand through the working out of the new spirit which made its way in the life of the group.

In so far the Jesus revolution still fits the themes of the sub-culture of our young people, even if we do not very often find a clear commitment there. In the ministry of Jesus, however, there is a further element which seems to me new and unique in its bearing on these themes. When we look more closely, we find that in the ministry of the great leaders about whom the Old and New Testaments tell us, we continually come across an aspect which reaches its zenith in Jeremiah, in his self-identification with the Suffering Servant of God. I mean the experience that the man who feels powerless to perform the work expected of him is none the less ready and able to accept his powerlessness, and not to withdraw from the work in which he discovers the secret of the covenant which God has made with him; that he experiences the blessing of the *shalom*, and passes on this blessing to others. At the burning bush Moses answered that he was 'slow of speech' and therefore felt powerless to convince Pharaoh; Isaiah was a man of 'unclean lips'; Jeremiah answered, 'I do not know how to speak, for I am only a youth'; and Paul wrote to the Corinthians: 'I was with you in weakness and in much fear and trembling; and my speech and my message were not in plausible words of wisdom . . .'. Words like this remind us of the figure of the *'schlemihl'*, the man who always seems helpless yet does not go under but always gets up again. He is almost a symbol of the Jewish people. In his book *The Prophetic Faith* (p. 183) Buber writes that Yahweh increasingly becomes 'the God of the sufferers', and suffering increasingly becomes 'a door of approach to Him, as is already clear from the life of Jeremiah, where the way of martyrdom leads to an even purer and deeper fellowship with YHVH'. It is only in this way that we can grasp something of the secret of the Suffering Servant of God in Isaiah 53, of whom it is said that through his sufferings 'the will of the Lord shall prosper in his hand; he shall see . . . of the travail of his soul and be satisfied'. Throughout his life Jesus identified himself with this Servant, or at least took his life as a model. This was an essential element in the faith of the first Christians: that his utter acceptance of his helplessness, to the point of the cross – the sign of deepest humiliation – set in motion in our present reality the secret of the *shalom* of the new kingdom so that we will share in that secret, if we dare to go the same way. Dostoevsky wrote about *The Idiot*, and Paul speaks of the foolishness of the crucified Christ, but, he goes on, 'the foolishness of God is wiser than men, and the weakness of God is stronger than men' (I Cor. 1.23–25).

The secret of Jewish humour is again and again that suffering and helplessness are seen and accepted, but that a man rises above them, because in the depth and helplessness of suffering he recognizes, as it were, the divine and blessed secret, the *shalom*. Looking at Rembrandt's etchings, one could say that in the world of the scribes and Pharisees, with their power and standing among the people, Christ really was the Idiot, the Suffering Servant, the *'schlemihl'*. Yet in an amazing way he was a free man, much freer than the people's celebrated leaders, a man who, in his group of *vagantes*, knew how to realize something of the blessing of the *shalom*.

It is this aspect, I think, which the church has to introduce into the sub-culture of youth out of her tradition. In this way she can help young people to conquer the relapse into regression and to reach a true maturity through a profound 'commitment' to this secret. The church will have to prove in the process that Christ's blessing does not depend on his exalted humanity, but on his comprehension of the divine secret: that the only man who can find God and comprehend his secret is the one who is ready and able to accept his helplessness and his suffering for the cause as a way to authenticity and hence to God himself. God then becomes a 'power' which makes him free for love, humanity and gratitude.

I hope that church and clergy will be able to build 'communities' in the sub-culture of the young, communities of people who live from this secret and who want to try together to hold their ground in it. Perhaps we might also put it differently: if we lead our lives in time as a life in exodus, in the wilderness, then our progress, our pilgrimage, will – according to the texts of the Second Vatican Council – only lead to its goal if we can jointly give our personal and common life standard and quality. The forming of such 'communities' would make this possible.

In closing, let me come back briefly to some ideas which Hidding developed about the future of Christianity. Apart from the two structures which I have discussed in detail in connection with the relevant phases, he is concerned with the idea that in Christianity we have to do with a new structure, but that this structure is not yet sufficiently developed. In his opinion, therefore, Christianity still has its future before it. He believes that in this new structure the medium of God's revelation is no longer the image or the word; it is the *man* Jesus Christ. In his book *De evolutie van het godsdienstig bewustzijn* (The development of the religious consciousness) he writes:

> Jesus Christ, who in his person is God's revelation, represents the Father's kingdom in which love, peace, liberty, brotherhood, the forgiveness of sins and the healing of sickness are of pre-eminent importance. He lives from this reality and makes himself a sacrifice in order to save mankind. For self-denial, the sacrifice of oneself for the other, is the true confession and seal of the faith which rejects every power and every legal claim.

Hidding was not writing this with a view to the sub-culture of young people; his book was published long before there was any talk at all about a definite sub-culture. But his words can in my opinion be the guiding line for a Christian faith in the framework of the exodus experience of these years.

Finally, let us look at the question of how far this religious experience, which is only looming up in vague outline, can be linked with the

American 'process theology' developed by thinkers like Whitehead and Hartshorne. This is occasionally conjectured, but I have my doubts, the more so because I myself expect an illumination of the theology which is inherent in this experience to come from a religious deepening rather than from a rational process of thought. Moreover, in so far as I can hazard a judgment about process theology, I see it as a correction of the metaphysical elements in the picture of God belonging to the 'old' pattern, rather than a thinking through of these elements in the experience of God contained in a 'new' one. I have the impression that the deepest concerns of the younger generation do not come into play here: the dialectic of power and helplessness in God; the way in which freedom and love go together in man; the relationship between God and man in the breadth and depth of a spiritual experience.

17
Conclusion

In this book we have attempted to bring some kind of order into the sphere of religious manifestations with the help of modern psychological theories. In closing let me make one or two comments. First, because of the particular aspects under which, aided by these theories, we have viewed the wide field no very considerable insights have emerged. We have not done much more than to put out a few buoys. A book like Paul Pruyser's *Dynamic Psychology of Religion* is much more descriptive in what it has to say – even though it advocates a definite view on the basis of particular psychological theories – and is in this way far more complete. I have deliberately left unconsidered problems like conversion, which continually excites attention, or the meditation which has become of such topical interest today. I believe that we should try to discover how far they could be elucidated in the framework of the order I have suggested. Secondly, I have deliberately restricted myself. I see the system into which I have ordered the various factors as not much more than a working hypothesis which I am laying before my colleagues in this field for their consideration. I have the impression that the scientific investigation might for the moment derive the most profit from a closer examination of the hypothesis and from objections, conjectures and corrections from the other side.

At the same time I should like to go somewhat more closely into three problems which have probably occurred to the reader in reading the book. The first question is whether we can talk about an evolution in the field of religion – this being the deduction to be drawn from what I have said. My thesis is that there are particular aspects of religion which alter with the alteration of the cultural pattern. Religion, as we have seen, presents itself to the researcher in every society as a system of feelings, ideas and ways of behaviour; and this system is in its turn embedded in the cultural pattern of the society to which it belongs. We established that these cultural patterns have their foundation in patterns which were 'released' in the course of human development in the years of childhood. If we want to call the appearance of patterns which are released in the later phases of this development (in the years of the adolescent phase, for instance) an evolution, we can bring sound reasons in justification. It can be argued that the history of mankind is a progress with individual phases in which a mature pattern of individual and group life is increasingly achieved. To the extent to which religion is rooted in a cultural pattern, it takes part in this development.

But we can talk about evolution in another sense too. It seems that a development can be shown in every religion as well. We say that Hinduism, for example, shows a clear development in the direction of a spiritualization – we could even say, from primitiveness to maturity. In the orally based pattern, the 'spiritual' elements have a greater chance. It seems to me possible to show an evolution of this kind in Christianity which, as we saw, developed in the framework of the Oedipal pattern.

Finally, there is a development in personal life as well. In no culture is the child's religion the same as the religion of the adult person. Only we can discover here that the evolution often has to win its way through a tension full of contradictions. In personal life we are familiar with obviously regressive aspects of the religious development.

When we look more closely we discover that the regression seems to occur in the other two spheres as well. We saw that the present situation in the religious field especially cannot be understood without the influence of regressive factors. One can therefore only give a qualified answer to our question whether it is possible to talk about an evolution in the religious field.

What measure of scientific certainty can be ascribed to the theses developed in this book? In order to answer that question we must remember that this book was designed as an attempt to bring a little order into the confusing panorama of religious manifestations with which contemporary man is confronted – in the past but also in the present; in remote cultures but also in his own. With this aim we set up a working hypothesis and I have tried in this study to make it as acceptable as possible. The hypothesis was, that certain patterns are 'released' in the individual phases of the child's development (cultural factors, in the form of patterns of upbringing, also playing a role) and that in, or according to, these developmental patterns corresponding religious structures develop, or can do.

In the course of this investigation I have pointed out the different places where I am convinced that my hypothesis needs further examination. One of the most important problems in this connection is that there is uncertainty about the relationship of biological factors to the cultural ones in the various manifestations which we discovered in the different phases.

How far have I convinced professional theologians of the acceptability of my hypothesis? I already pointed to a particular problem at the beginning of the book. I said that among theologians there is – understandably – a resistance to a psychological study of religious phenomena, just as there was resistance to the historical treatment of religious questions. People fear a relativization and a degeneration of faith. I remarked here that I believe that this resistance will dwindle in the coming years, because it is highly valuable to be able to create order in the flight of appearances; but that an authentic faith has no need to be endangered by a psychological investigation.

Now that the result of the investigation is before us, I feel the need to reopen the question once more – no longer in general terms, but specifically, in the context of our investigation. I am concerned here with the problem which we dealt with when we were discussing the resistance to psychology: has the investigation endangered our faith, violating what we feel to be the truth, or drawing our attention away from God and towards man?

The following can be said here, I think.

First of all we must recognize that this enquiry does not concentrate on God; that is to say, it is not directed towards an illumination or strengthening of faith, but towards a number of human manifestations, namely the psychical aspects involved in the turning of human existence to God. But the mystery of the turning to God was the premise of all this, and this mystery was in no way infringed. For the believer himself – the man, that is to say, who is concerned with this mystery – it is probably difficult to accept an objective, scientific investigation of the human aspects of his relationship to God. Anyone who is happily in love is likely to be very unwilling to put up with an investigation of the factors that play a part in the relationship. But in a period at which there is so much confusion in the field of belief – and of love – it ought to be intelligible that a scientific investigation can have its particular function. At one time the psychology of religion was reproached with being a 'contemplation of one's own navel'. I hope that this will not be said about this book.

It is more difficult to react properly to the reproach of relativism. Is it true that an investigation like this one endangers faith, because it relativizes and thus attacks our concept of truth? If we term faith the attempt to live from a particular truth, then this presupposes that with faith a decision has been made in favour of a particular view of the truth. What am I demonstrating here? That it is a question of a many-faceted truth, not a single one. We discover that the truth from which people live manifests itself in various forms and presents itself in modern times in a bewildering multifariousness. We therefore cannot avoid dis-tinguishing between the form and the content of truth as a concept. For the believer himself a distinction of this kind is of course never relevant. He 'knows' only one truth, his own. But for the person who is trying to discover order in the confusion – a theologian, for example, who after all has a certain responsibility for the future of faith – it can be important if the differences in the forms of faith become clearer with the help of science – historical or psychological, and perhaps sociological as well; if science is able to show him the connection of the one mani-festation with the other. In this book my aim was to demonstrate that there is a connection with the developmental phases in human life. Some differences seem to me to become comprehensible in the process. A relation was discovered; they were relativized.

Have we now also landed in the cul de sac of relativism and is our faith endangered in the process? The question is a justifiable one. The believer wants to know how far his faith is *true*.

If I see it rightly, the psychologist (or historian) must answer as follows: For me your faith is true. I recognize it as such. Only, I discover that your faith is also bound to a particular period (and perhaps to particular people as well). I too have a belief which is also bound up with its period, and I am equally unable to escape from it, because I am also a child of my time. We cannot experience truth in any other way than in the forms of our own time. What happens in scholarship and science is nothing other than the circling round a mystery into which we can penetrate a little way, but which does not surrender its real heart to us. Our faith is therefore true in so far as it is directed towards this mystery. The fact that our faith is in part bound to a particular time or particular people is not an attack on the mystery. It at most means that we no longer have such a tense attitude towards the forms in which we come to know the mystery. We cannot escape from *our* forms – they belong to our truth; but we can face our own doubt and the doubts of other people more tolerantly if we are able to distinguish between content and form, as aspects that belong together and are yet different.

It is clear to me that in practice it is not easy for us to adopt this attitude. It demands from us that on the one hand we surrender to the mystery as it reveals itself to us, in childlike innocence, without thinking much about it; but that on the other we have to consider from time to time that not everyone is able to share our experience of the mystery in this particular form. But the train of thought is so logical that I am convinced that this attitude will gain ground more and more. Moreover, in a period of swift and decisive change, no one can avoid the problems existing here any longer. In addition, we can clearly see positive aspects about these changes as well. Above all, through them, within the changes in the cultural pattern, new light is shed on particular dark places in the tradition.

In my book *Gott in vaterloser Gesellschaft* I have already pointed out that present-day theology has discovered new aspects of the relationship between God and man. In this study my aim has been primarily to show, among other things, that the exodus experience of our time has opened the eyes of many people to the concept of suffering in human life, as well as to its meaning in the relationship between God and man. This has consequences for Christology as well. It can then be said that through the exodus experience, central themes of the Christian tradition are awakened to new life. I am thinking of the situation of man as a stranger in this world, which is coupled in modern theology in a paradoxical way with responsibility for life on earth, and expresses itself in mistrust of the 'sacral' nature of earthly structures.

Finally, we must ask how, in the present crisis of religious and church life, we can best develop a strategy for the future. I should like to say something about this, experimentally. A detailed treatment of the problem may be found in my book *Neue Wege kirchlichen Handelns. Planning of change.*

In my opinion we can start from the existence of two patterns; in practice the church generally belongs to the traditional one, whereas the new form shows itself in the sub-culture of our young people, as well as in certain religious and theological trends within the church itself. The second pattern has obviously not yet found its final form. The old and the new patterns stand in a particular relationship to one another. The new pattern, as we said on p. 293, represents a repressed part of the old one, with the result that the representatives of both patterns give the impression of being bound always to react negatively towards one another. Each experiences the other as a threat. I think it is essential for the representatives of the two patterns to arrive at positive communication with one another; above all, they must learn to see why they react so negatively to one another. Where this happens, a situation arises in which the two feel bound to one another, as in a common destiny and a common task.

Here the exodus model can perform good service. The church moves out into the wilderness too. Is it there as something from the past, which cannot detach itself from the order to which it belonged and which is now fading in our industrial society? Must it shrink more and more into a beautiful but saddening piece of folklore in a swiftly changing world? Or can it alter course and ask what the gospel could mean to men on their pilgrimage to a new society? Certain things might be said here. In the courses of 'clinical training' in which clergy learn to serve contemporary man through the gospel, we have discovered what demands are bound up with this: (*a*) to enter into the situation; (*b*) to enter together on the road out of the situation; (*c*) to let the gospel happen as the realization of the *shalom* on this common way. What, now, is the situation in which contemporary man finds himself? On the one hand he is freed from the old pattern, so that in many respects he is able to discover the world and life anew. I am thinking of sexuality, the physical, nature, etc. In all this men are discovering life as a feast; and in my opinion the church must be able to celebrate the feasts as well, and to make the discovery of the gospel into a festive event. On the other hand contemporary people seem to themselves positively helpless in the face of the huge demands with which the new situation is confronting them: the need to create a single world; the discovery of the poverty and backwardness of many parts of that world; environmental pollution; the aggression round us and in us; as well as society's swift and constant changes. In knowledge of its own helplessness and in awareness of this helplessness, the church must seek out man and help him to see his way and to believe in it. The church must help to found 'communities' – both temporary and permanent – in which people can learn to 'see' and understand themselves, to throw light on life for one another, and to take up their tasks together. In my opinion this is the way to realize the idea of being on the way together. In this great pilgrimage the church must know itself to be responsible, in the light of the gospel, for the quality of life, both individually and in society. Where people feel bound to one another like this, where they let the gospel become a happening in word and deed, we shall see the growth of the divine blessing which we mean by the ancient word *shalom*: a situation of freedom, peace, love, work and community. It is a reflection of the goal of our journey, of life in the new society.

What, then, is the specific character of the church in all this, and what is the task of the clergy? The church is the place where the future takes on visible form, in the proclamation, but above all in the feast of the new bond and relationship – in the Lord's Supper. The task of the priest or minister is to be the proclaimer, the organizer of the feast and the shepherd of the people, in the sense that he makes the community, its quality, and the participation of every individual member, his own personal responsibility.

There should be no speculations about this new church and its forms. They can only grow up in the course of our common experiments. We can only have Christ before our eyes and seek a way for ourselves.

Books Cited or Referred To

Publication is in London unless otherwise stated
ET = English translation

Anselm, *Cur Deus Homo*, quoted from *Anselm of Canterbury*, Vol. III, edited and translated by Jasper Hopkins and Herbert W. Richardson, SCM Press in preparation

Aquinas, Thomas, *Summa Theologiae*, Latin text and English translation, Blackfriars in conjunction with Eyre & Spottiswoode and McGraw-Hill, New York, 1964ff.

Augustine, *Confessions* (Library of Christian Classics VII), SCM Press and Westminster Press, Philadelphia, 1955

Basabe, Fernando M., *Japanese Youth Confronts Religion*, Tokyo, 1967

Beets, N., *Jeugd en welvaart*, Utrecht, 1968

Benedict, Ruth, *Patterns of Culture*, Routledge and Kegan Paul, 1935

Berg, J. H. van den, *De dingen*, Nijkerk, 1968

Bergson, Henri, 'Philosophical Intuition' (1911), *The Creative Mind*, ET, Philosophical Library, New York, 1946, pp. 126ff.

Bonhoeffer, Dietrich, *Letters and Papers from Prison*, ET, enlarged edition, SCM Press and Macmillan, New York, 1971

Brouwer, A. M., *Verzoening*, Neerbosch, 1947

Buber, Martin, *I and Thou*, T. & T. Clark and Scribner, New York, 1937

— *The Prophetic Faith*, ET Macmillan, New York, 1949; Harper Torchbooks, New York, 1960

Bühler, Charlotte, *Der menschliche Lebenslauf als psychologisches Problem* (1932), 2nd ed. revised, Göttingen, 1959

Buren, Paul M. van, *The Secular Meaning of the Gospel*, Macmillan, New York, and SCM Press, 1963

Calvin, John, *Institutes of the Christian Religion* (Library of Christian Classics XX–XXI), SCM Press and Westminster Press, Philadelphia, 1961

Cox, Harvey, *The Secular City*, Macmillan, New York, 1964; SCM Press, 1966

— *The Secular City Debate*, Macmillan, New York, 1966

— *The Feast of Fools*, Harvard University Press, Cambridge, Mass., 1969

Books cited or referred to

Deconchy, J.-P., *Structure génétique de l'idée de Dieu chez des catholiques français*, Editions Lumen Vitae, Brussels, 1967

Erikson, Erik H., *Childhood and Society* (1951), rev. ed., Penguin Books, 1965
— *Young Man Luther*, Norton, New York, 1958; Faber & Faber, 1959
— *Identity and the Life Cycle*, International Universities Press, New York, 1959
— *Insight and Responsibility*, Norton, New York, 1964; Faber & Faber, 1966
— *Identity. Youth and Crisis*, Norton, New York, and Faber & Faber, 1968
— *Gandhi's Truth. On the Origins of Militant Nonviolence*, Norton, New York, 1969; Faber & Faber, 1970
Erikson, Erik H. (ed.), *Youth: Change and Challenge*, Basic Books, New York, 1963
Evans, R. I., *Dialogue with Erik Erikson*, Harper, New York, 1967

Faber, H., *Over ziek zijn*, Assen, 1956
— *Problemen rond het ziekbed*, Assen, 1959
— *Pastoraal psychologische opstellen*, The Hague, 1961
— *Het Christelijk humanisme van Dr H. T. de Graaf*, Assen, 1963
— *Geloof en ongeloof in een industrieel tijdperk*, Assen, 1969, quoted from German trs., *Gott in vaterloser Gesellschaft*, Munich, 1972
— *Pastoral Care in the Modern Hospital*, ET SCM Press and Westminster Press, Philadelphia, 1971
— *Buigen of barsten, gedachten over 'planning of change'*, Meppel, 1970, quoted from German trs., *Neue Wege kirchlichen Handelns. 'Planning of Change'*, Gütersloh, 1972
Fortmann, Han M. M., *Werkelijkheid en waarde*, Hilversum, 1961
— *Als ziende de Onzienlijke*, 3 vols in 4, Hilversum, 1964
— *Hoogtijd*, Bilthoven, 1966
— *Hindoes en Boeddhisten*, Bilthoven, 1968
— *Oosterse Renaissance*, Bilthoven, 1970
— *Inleiding tot de cultuurpsychologie*, Vol. I, Bilthoven, 1971
Fournier, Alain, *Le grand Meaulnes*, Paris, 1913, ET Penguin Books, 1970
Freud, Anna, *Normality and Pathology in Childhood*, International Universities Press, New York, 1965; Hogarth Press, 1966
Freud, Sigmund, *Complete Psychological Works*, 23 vols, ET Hogarth Press and Macmillan, New York, 1953ff.
Freud, Sigmund, and Pfister, Oskar, see Meng
Fromm, Erich, *Psychoanalysis and Religion*, Yale University Press, New Haven, 1950; Gollancz, 1951
— *The Dogma of Christ*, Routledge & Kegan Paul and Holt, Rinehart & Winston, New York, 1963

Gehlen, Arnold, *Die Seele im technischen Zeitalter*, Rowohlt, 1957
Glock, C. Y., Ringer, B. B., and Babbie, E. R., *To Comfort and to Challenge*, University of California Press, 1967
Godin, A., and Hallez, M., *Images parentales et paternité divine*, Editions Lumen vitae, Brussels, 1964
Goethe, J. W. von, *Faust*, ET, Penguin Books, 1969

Graaf, H. T. de, *Om het eeuwig Goed*, Arnhem 1923,
Groen, J., et al., *Het acute myocardinfarct*, Haarlem, 1965
Groot, A. D. de, *Methodologie*, The Hague, 1961

Haas, G. C. de, *De onvoorziene generatie*, Amsterdam, 1966
— *Cultuur en cultuurbeleid*, Amsterdam, 1969
Hamilton, William, *The New Essence of Christianity*, Association Press, New York, and Longmans, 1966
Hartshorne, Charles, *Creative Synthesis and Philosophic Method*, SCM Press and Open Court Publishers, La Salle, Ill., 1970
Harlow, H. F., 'The Development of Affectional Patterns in Infant Monkeys' in *Determinants of Infant Behaviour* (Tavistock Study Group), Methuen, 1959
Hayes, Peter, *New Horizons in Psychiatry*, Penguin Books, 1964
Heidegger, Martin, *Being and Time*, ET SCM Press and Harper, New York, 1962
— *Vorträge und Aufsätze*, Pfullingen, 1954
Herzberg, Abel J., *Brieven aan mijn kleinzoon*, The Hague, 1964
Hessen, J., *Platonismus und Prophetismus*, Munich, 1939
Hidding, K. A. H., *De evolutie van het godsdienstig bewustzijn*, Utrecht and Antwerp, 1965
Hostie, R., SJ, *Analytische psychologie en godsdienst*, Utrecht, 1954
Huizinga, J., *Mensch en menigte in Amerika*, Haarlem, 1918
— *In de schaduwen van morgen*, Haarlem, 1935

Jaspers, Karl, *The Perennial Scope of Philosophy*, ET Philosophical Library, New York, 1949; Routledge & Kegan Paul, 1950
— *Philosophical Faith and Revelation*, ET Collins and Harper, New York, 1967
Jones, Ernest, *Essays in Applied Psychoanalysis*, 2 vols, 2nd ed. Hogarth Press and Clarke, Irwin, Toronto, 1951
— *Sigmund Freud, Life and Work*, 3 vols, Hogarth Press and Basic Books, New York, 1953–57
Jung, C. G., *Collected Works*, 17 vols, ET, Routledge & Kegan Paul and Pantheon Books, New York, 1953ff.
— *Memories, Dreams, Reflections*, ET (1963), Fontana Books, 1967

Kautsky, Karl, *Ursprung des Christentums*, Stuttgart, 1908
Klages, Ludwig, *Die Grundlagen der Charakterkunde*, Leipzig, 1910
— *Mensch und Erde*, Jena, 1926
Knight, James A., *For the Love of Money*, Lippincott, Philadelphia, 1968
Koran, The, quoted from *The Koran Interpreted*, trs. A. J. Arberry, Allen & Unwin and Macmillan, New York, 1955
Kraemer, H., *The Christian Message in a Non-Christian World*, Harper, New York, and Edinburgh House, 1938
Kristensen, W. Brede, *Het leven uit den dood*, Haarlem, 1926
— *The Meaning of Religion*, The Hague, 1960
Kuiper, P. C., *Nerosenleer*, Arnhem, 1966
— *Psychoanalyse. Actueel of verouderd?*, Deventer, 1972

Books cited or referred to

Lake, Frank, *Clinical Theology*, Darton, Longman & Todd, 1966
Lampl-De Groot, Jeanne, *The Development of the Mind*, Hogarth Press, 1966
Leary, Timothy, *The Psychedelic Experience: a Manual based on the Tibetan Book of the Dead*, University Books, New York, 1964
Leendertz, W., *Profielen van gedachten*, Haarlem, 1952
Leeuw, G. van der, *De primitieve mensch en de religie*, Groningen, 1937 (French trs., *L'homme primitif et la religion*, Paris, 1940)
Leeuwen, A. T. van, *Christianity in World History*, Edinburgh House, 1964
Levinas, E., *Totalité et infini*, The Hague, 1961
Linn, Louis, and Schwarz, Leo, *Psychiatry and Religious Experience*, Random House, New York, 1958
Luckmann, Thomas, *Das Problem der Religion in der modernen Gesellschaft*, Freiburg, 1963
Lynd, Helen M., *On Shame and the Search for Identity*, Harcourt Brace, New York, 1958

Malinowski, B., *Sex and Repression in Savage Societies*, Kegan Paul, 1927
Mead, Margaret, *Sex and Temperament in Three Primitive Societies*, Routledge, 1935
— *Culture and Commitment*, Bodley Head, 1970
Meng, H. and Freud, E. L. (eds), *Psychology and Faith: the Letters of Sigmund Freud and Oskar Pfister*, ET, Hogarth Press, 1963
Mitscherlich, Alexander, *Auf dem Weg zur vaterlosen Gesellschaft*, Munich, 1963; ET, *Society without the Father: a Contribution to Social Psychology*, Tavistock Publications, 1969

Neumann, Erich, *Depth Psychology and a New Ethic*, ET, Hodder & Stoughton, 1969; Harper Torchbooks, New York, 1973
— *Dieptepsychologie en de Ontwikkeling der Religie*, Arnhem, 1954
Niebuhr, Reinhold, *The Nature and Destiny of Man*, 2 vols, Nisbet and Scribner, New York, 1941–43
Nijk, A. J., *Secularisatie*, Rotterdam, 1968

Oosterhuis, Huub, *In het Voorbijgaan*, Utrecht, 1968
Otto, Rudolf, *The Idea of the Holy*, ET, Oxford University Press, 1923

Pedersen, J., *Israel. Its Life and Culture*, 4 vols. in 2, ET, Oxford University Press and Copenhagen, 1926–47
Perls, Frederick, et al., *Gestalt Therapy*, Messner, New York, and Pitman, 1951
Peursen, C. A. van, *Strategie van de cultuur*, Amsterdam and Brussels, 1970
— *Hij is het weer!: Beschouwingen over de betekenis van het woordje 'God'*, Kampen (1967)
Pfister, Oskar, *Die Frömmigkeit des Grafen L. von Zinzendorf*, Vienna, 1910
— *The Psychoanalytic Method*, ET, Kegan Paul, 1917
— *Christianity and Fear*, ET, Allen & Unwin, 1948
— see also Meng
Piers, G., and Singer, M. B., *Shame and Guilt*, C. C. Thomas, New York, 1953

Plokker, J. H., *Geschonden beeld*, The Hague and Paris, 1962
Pol, W. H. van de, *Het einde van het conventionele Christendom*, Roermond-Maaseik, 1966
Pruyser, Paul W., *A Dynamic Psychology of Religion*, Harper, New York, 1968

Radhakrishnan, S., *The Hindu View of Life*, Allen & Unwin, 1927
Rathenau, Walther, *Zur Kritik der Zeit*, Berlin, 1911
— *Zur Mechanik des Geistes*, Berlin, 1912
— *In Days to Come*, ET, Allen & Unwin, 1921
Reich, Charles A., *The Greening of America*, Random House, New York, 1970
(Cf. *The Con III Controversy*: The critics look at *The Greening of America*, compiled by P. Nobile, Pocket Books, New York, 1971)
Reik, Theodor, *Ritual. Psychoanalytical Studies*, ET (1931), International University Press, New York, 1958
Robbers, Herman, *De bruidstijd van Annie de Boog*, Amsterdam, 1901
Robinson, J. A. T., *Honest to God*, SCM Press and Westminster Press, Philadelphia, 1963
— and D. L. Edwards (eds), *The Honest to God Debate*, SCM Press and Westminster Press, Philadelphia, 1963
Roland Holst, A., *Over den dichter Leopold*, Maestricht, 1926
— *Een winter aan zee*, Maestricht, 1937
Roszak, Theodore, *The Making of a Counter Culture*, Faber & Faber, 1970
Rümke, H. C., *The Psychology of Unbelief. Character and Temperament in relation to Unbelief*, ET, Rockliff, 1952 (translation slightly altered)
— *De levenstijdperken van den man*, Amsterdam, 1938
— *Studies en voordrachten over psychiatrie*, Amsterdam, 1943

Schär, Hans, *Seelsorge und Psychotherapie*, Zurich, 1961
Scharfenberg, Joachim, *Sigmund Freud und seine Religionskritik als Herausforderung für den christlichen Glaube*, Göttingen, 1968
Schmölders, Günter, *Psychologie des Geldes*, Rowohlt, 1966
Sierksma, F., *De religieuze projectie*, Delft, 1957
Sölle, Dorothee, *Christ the Representative*, SCM Press and Fortress Press, Philadelphia, 1967
Snaith, Norman H., *The Distinctive Ideas of the Old Testament*, Epworth Press, 1944
Sperna Weiland, J., *Oriëntatie*, Baarn, 1966; ET, *New Ways in Theology*, Gil and Macmillan, Dublin, 1968
— *Voortgezette oriëntatie*, Baarn, 1971
— *Het einde van de religie*, Baarn, 1970
Spitz, R. A., *Vom Säugling zum Kleinkind (Naturgeschichte der Mutter-Kind-Beziehung im ersten Lebensjahr)*, Stuttgart, 1967
Spranger, Eduard, *Psychologie des Jugendalters*, Leipzig, 1925
Springer, J. L., *Waar, wat en wie is God?*, Wageningen, 1969
Storr, Anthony, *The Integrity of the Personality*, Penguin Books, 1963
Strijd, K., *Structuur en inhoud van Anselmus' Cur Deus Homo*, Assen, 1958
Sunden, Hjalmar, *Die Religion und die Rollen*, German trs., Berlin, 1966
Suzuki, D. T., *An Introduction to Zen Buddhism*, ET, Rider, 1969

Books cited or referred to

Tawney, R. H., *Religion and the Rise of Capitalism* (1926), Penguin Books, 1938
Tillich, Paul, *The Protestant Era*, ET, Nisbet and University of Chicago Press, 1951
— *The Shaking of the Foundations*, Scribner, New York, 1948; SCM Press, 1949
— *The Courage to Be*, ET (1952), Fontana Books, 1962
— *Systematic Theology*, 3 vols, Nisbet and University of Chicago Press, 1953–64
— *On the Boundary*, ET, Collins and Scribner, New York, 1967
Trüb, Hans, *Heilung aus der Begegnung*, Stuttgart, 1951

Vergote, A., *The Religious Man*, ET, Gill and Macmillan, Dublin, 1969
Verhoeven, C., *Rondom de leegte*, Utrecht, n.d.
Vervoort, C. E., *Gezin en schoolkeuze bij handarbeiders*, Dissertation, 1968 (not seen)
Vestdijk, S., *De toekomst der religie*, Arnhem, 1952
Vorster, D. A., *Nederlands mystiek. Protestant*, Amsterdam, 1958

Wach, Joachim, *Sociology of Religion*, University of Chicago Press and Routledge & Kegan Paul, 1944
Weber, Max, *The Protestant Ethic and the Spirit of Capitalism*, ET, Allen & Unwin, 1930
Weijel, J. A., *Medische Psychologie*, Utrecht, 1961
Winnicott, D. W., *Collected Papers*, Tavistock Publications and Basic Books, New York, 1958
Wit, J. de, *Problemen rond de moeder-kind-relatie*, Arnhem, 1963

Zilboorg, Gregory, *Freud and Religion: a Restatement of an Old Controversy*, Newman Press, Westminster, Maryland, 1958
— *Psychoanalysis and Religion*, Allen & Unwin, 1967

Index of Names

Index of Names

Index of Subjects

Achievement, 192, 194, 196, 298
Adolescent phase, 285ff.
Alienation, 121, 181, 182f., 228f., 306
Anal phase, 191ff.
Artists, 215ff.
Atonement, 272ff.
Autonomy, 194ff.

Baptists, 203, 205, 208
Basic trust, 75, 109, 118, 123, 148ff., passim
Belief, 73ff.
Bevindelijkheid, 261, 269, 273f.
Body, experience of the, 220

Calvinism, 87, 273f.
Capitalism, 202ff.
Caress, the, 164
Christianity, 269ff.
Christology, 312f.
Church, 323ff.
Church of England, 208, 274n.
Cleanliness training, 196
Clergy, role of, 22, 128ff.
Comfort – challenge, 310
Coming of age, 230
Compulsiveness, 192, 201, 234
Consciousness, extension of the, 305
Consciousness – unconsciousness, 10f.
Coronary thrombosis, 233ff.
Counter culture, 295
Craftsmen, 218
Crisis of religion, 171ff.
Cultural discontent, 297

Cultural factors, 154ff., 193, 243, 286, 289ff.
Cultural patterns, 125, 136
Culture and instinct, 14f.

Death, 168
Destiny, companions in, 301, 303
Discontent (with civilization), 297
Dispersion experience, 262ff., 309
Doubt, 193, 195
Dreams, 42f., 118f.
Drugs, 305f.

Emancipation, 158f., 162f., 165f.
Erogenous zones, 153, 244
Estrangement, *see* alienation
Exodus model, 311, 324

Fairy stories, 164, 288, 296
Faith – religion, 188
Father, 150, 257f. (*see also* Oedipal situation)
Fatherless society, 141f., 289f., 304f.
Father's house model, 311
Feminine identity and problems, 249ff.

Gestalt therapy, 302
God-is-dead theology, 290, 302
God's nearness, 261, 273
Groups, 305
Guilt, 13, 69, 245, 272f., 309

Helplessness, 309, 316
Hinduism, 169

Index of Subjects

Shalom, 161, 301, 316, 324
Shame, 193, 195, 197f.
'Shrunken' perception (Fortmann) 171ff.
Signs, 261, 280
Status, 196
Style, 311f, 315
Sub-culture of youth, 292ff.
Suffering, 62, 309
Superego, 10, 194, 201
Symbols, *see* Images

Technology, 221ff.
Technopolis, 227ff.

Totemism, 12f.
Tradition, 311
Transitional objects, *see* Intermediate or transitional objects
Trust, basic, *see* Basic trust

Uncleanness, 201
Unity, experience of, 162f. 167

Word, 248

Youth, modern, 236f., 292ff.

Zen Buddhism, 179ff.